The Heinkel He 219 Uhu

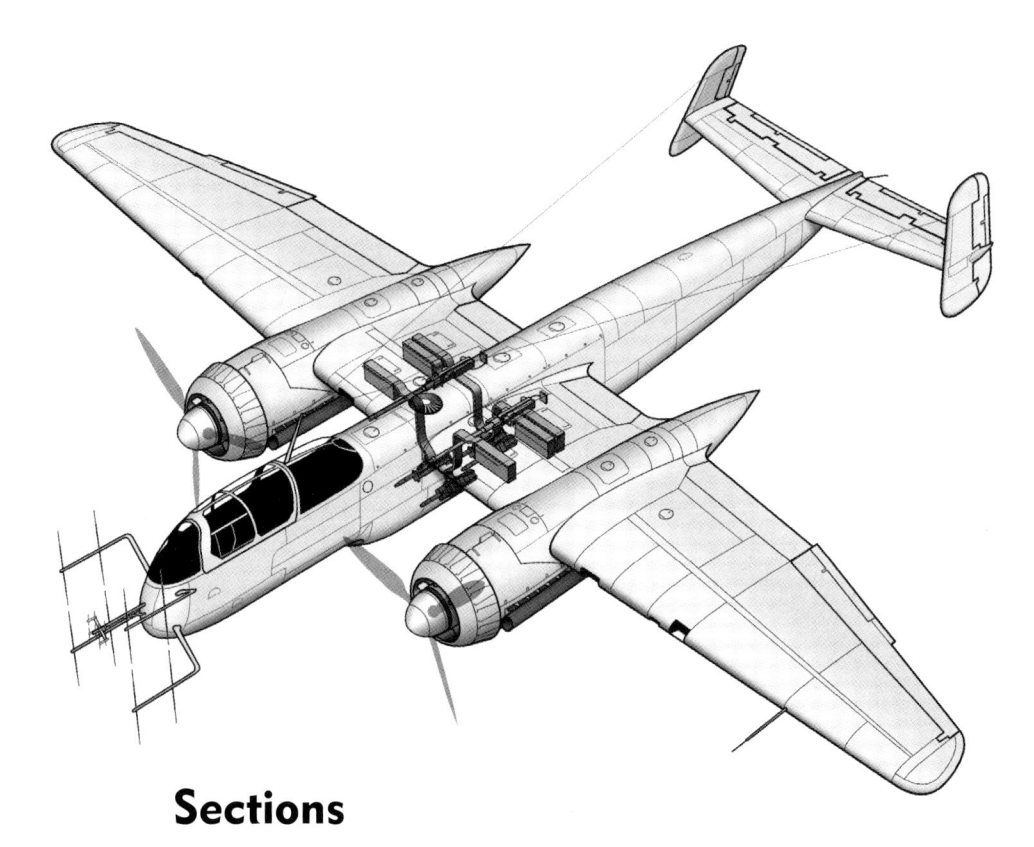

Sections

Introduction
A brief narrative history of the development and operational use of the He 219

1. Technical Description
Detailed coverage of the construction and equipment

2. Evolution – Prototype, Production and Projected Variants
3D-isometrics illustrating differences between variants

3. Camouflage & Markings
Colour side profiles, notes and photographs

4. Building the Uhu
Builds of the Dragon 1/72nd He 219A-2 by Libor Jekl and the Tamiya 1/48th He 219A-7 by Steve A. Evans

Appendices
I   He 219 Kit List
II He 219 Accessory & Mask List
III He 219 Decal List
IV Bibliography

He 219 Information

Airframe Album No.1 – Second Edition
The Heinkel He 219 'Uhu'
A Detailed Guide To The Luftwaffe's Ultimate Nightfighter
by Richard A. Franks

First published in 2012 & 2021
by Valiant Wings Publishing Ltd
Unit 3 Glenmore Business Park, Stanley Road, Bedford,
MK42 0XY, United Kingdom
+44 (0)1234 273434
valiant-wings@btconnect.com
www.valiant-wings.co.uk
valiantwingspublishing

© Richard A. Franks 2012 & 2021
© Richard J. Caruana – Colour Profiles, Side Profiles & Stencil Diagram
© Jacek Jackiewicz – Isometric Lineart
© Juraj Jankovic – Additional & Revised Isometric Lineart
© Jerry Boucher – Cover Art

The right of Richard A. Franks to be identified as the author of this work has been asserted in accordance with sections 77 and 78 of the Copyright Designs and Patents Act, 1988.

The 'Airframe Album' brand, along with the concept of the series, are the copyright of Richard A. Franks as defined by the Copyright Designs and Patents Act, 1988 and are used by Valiant Wings Publishing Ltd by agreement with the copyright holder.

All rights reserved. No part of this publication may be reproduced or transmitted in any form or by any means, electronic or mechanical, including photocopy, recording, or any other information storage and retrieval system, without permission in writing from the publishers.

ISBN 978-1-912932-18-4

Acknowledgments

The author would like to give a special word of thanks to Col. Scott Willey (USAF ret.) for his invaluable help with photographic access to the world's only surviving (complete) He 219. Special thanks must also go to Steve A. Evans & Libor Jekl for their excellent model builds and Jerry Boucher. Richard J, Caruana, Jacek Jackiewicz & Juraj Jankovic for their superb artwork.

We would also like to thank the following companies for their support of this title:
- Aires Hobby Models   www.aires.com
- CMK   www.cmkkits.com
- Eduard M.A.   www.eduard.com

Note

There are many different ways of writing aircraft designation, however for consistency throughout this title we have used one style, e.g. He 219 V1, He 219A-0 etc. We have used the original German term 'catapult' to describe the seat system used in the He 219, as the term 'ejection' is very much more modern and really relates to rocket-assisted ejection seats developed after WWII.

Cover

The cover artwork depicts a He 219A-0 of 3./NJG 3 in 1945. This artwork was specially commissioned for this title. © Jerry Boucher 2021

He 219A, G9+TK one of those surrendered at Westerland on the island of Sylt. Note the lack of tail or propellers and the fact that this aircraft had additional mottling added to the mid/lower fuselage sides (probably in dark green)

Note regarding images

In creating this title, we have sorted through just about every photo that we could find of the type. With less than 300 airframes built in total, of which the production variants were only in service during the last 12 months of WWII and combine this with the fact that a great deal of material was lost or destroyed in the latter stages of the war means that there are few images to choose from, many are of poor quality, have been copied many times or were only ever in official Allied reports (which were duplicated, not printed thus resulting in their quality being even poorer). On top of this only certain manuals survive and those that do are mainly for the A-0 series. As a result we have used the best images and diagrams we can find, but inevitably at times the quality of some of this material is not as good as we would have liked

He 219
Glossary

British forces captured a large number of intact He 219s at Grøve (modern day Karup) at the end of the war, a number of which are seen here all neatly lined up with their propellers removed to stop unauthorised flights (or engine running)

Aufklärer	Reconnaissance aircraft
Aufklaringsgruppe (AGr)	Reconnaissance Group
BFW	*Bayerische Flugzeugwerke* (Bf)
BMW	*Bayerische Motorenwerke* GmbH (Bavarian Motor Works)
BK	*Bordkanone* (on-board cannon)
DB	Daimler-Benz
Dipl. Ing.	*Diplom Ingeneur* (Master of Science)
DVS	*Deutsche Versuchsanstalt für Luftfahrt* (German Aviation Experimental Establishment)
Einsatzkommano	Operational detachment
Erprobungskommando	Test Detachment
E-Stelle	*Erprobungsstelle* (Test establishment)
Erprobungsgruppe (ErpG)	Test/Evaluation Group
ETC	*Elektrische Trägervorrichtung für cylinder bomben* (Electrically operated carriers for cylindrical bombs)
Fernaufklärungsgruppe	Long-range Reconnaissance Group
Flieger	Airman
Flugkapitän	Honorary title given to highly-regarded civil test pilots
Funkgerät (FuG)	Radio or radar equipment
Feldwebel (*Fw.*)	Sergeant (Sgt) (RAF)
General	Air Marshall (RAF) or Lieutenant General (USAAF)
Generalleutnant	Air Vice-Marshall (RAF) or Major General (USAAF)
Generalluftzeugmeister	Director-General of Luftwaffe Equipment
Generalmajor	Air Commodore (RAF) or Brigadier General (USAAF)
Gefreuter (*Gefr.*)	Aircraftman (RAF) or Technical Sergeant (USAAF)
Geschwader	Fighter Wing comprising three *Gruppen* and one Stab
GM-1	Nitrous Oxide injection system
Gruppe	Group
Hauptmann (*Hptm.*)	Flight Lieutenant (RAF) or Captain (USAAF)
IFF	Identification Friend or Foe
Jäger	Fighter
Jagdgeschwader (JG)	Fighter Wing
JUMO	Junkers Motorenbau
kg.	Kilogram (= 2.20462lb)
km/h	Kilometres per hour (= 0.621mph)
Kampfgeschwader (KG)	Bomber Wing
Kommano	Detachment
Kommanduer	Commanding Officer
Kommodore	Commander of a *Geschwader*
KW	Kilowatt (= 1.341hp)
Lt	Litre (= 0.22 Imperial Gallons)
Luftflotte	Air Fleet
m	Metre (3ft 3 3/8in)
Major	Squadron Leader (RAF) or Major (USAAF)
MG	*Machinengewehr* (machine-gun up to 20mm calibre)
MK	*Machinenkanone* (cannon over 20mm calibre)
MW50	Water Methanol injection system
Nachtjäger	Nightfighter
Nachtjagdgeschwader (NJG)	Night-fighter Wing
NII VVS	*Nauchno-Issledovatel'skij Institut Voyenno-vozdooshnykh Sily* (Russian Air Force Scientific Test Institute)
Oberfeldwebel (*Obfw.*)	Flight Sergeant (RAF)
Obergefreiter (*Obgefr.*)	Leading Aircraftman (RAF)
Oberleutnant (*Oblt*)	Flying Officer (RAF) or Lieutenant (USAAF)
Oberst	Group Captain (RAF), Colonel (USAAF)
Oberstleutnant (*Oberstlt.*)	Wing Commander (RAF)
OKL	*Oberkommando der Luftwaffe* (Luftwaffe High Command)
PS	*Pferdestarkes* (Metric Horsepower)
RAE	Royal Aircraft Establishment
Rb	*Reihenbildner* (aerial reconnaissance camera)
Revi (*Reflexvisier*)	Reflector gunsight
RLM	*Reichsluftfahrtministerium* (Reich Air Ministry)
rpg	Rounds per gun
rpm	Revolutions per minute
Rüstsatz	Field conversion pack
SC	*Sprengbombe-Cilindirsch* (Explosive bomb – cylindrical) GP bombs
SD	*Sprengbombe-Dickwandig* (Explosive bomb thick walls) fragmentation bomb
Slachtgruppe (Sch.G)	Close-support (ground-attack) group
Staffel	Equal to Squadron in RAF
Staffelkapitän	Commander of a squadron
Stammkenzeichen	Primary identification (code letters)
TsAGI	*Tsentral'niy Aero-Gidrodinamicheskiy Institut* (Central Aerodynamic and Hydrodynamic Research Institute VVS [Russian Air Force])
Technisches Amt	Technical Department of the RLM
Umrüst-Bausätze	Modification Construction Sets
Unteroffizier (*Uffz.*)	Corporal (RAF) & Sergeant (USAAF)
Versuchs or *Versuchsmuster*	Research or test aircraft (V-series)
Werknummer (W/Nr.)	Works (construction) number
Zerstörer	Heavy fighter (Destroyer)
Zerstörergeschwader (ZG)	Heavy fighter wing

Preface

The official requirement for an advanced night fighter was first issued by the *Reichsluftfahrtministerium* (RLM – Reich Air Ministry) in 1942. Robert Lusser however, undertook the initial design that ultimately led to the He 219 in 1940 as the P.1055. Lusser had only recently returned to Heinkel from Messerschmitt and he envisaged a type with a pressurised cockpit fitted with catapult [ejection] seats (the first planned for any combat aircraft), nose wheel undercarriage (a first for a Luftwaffe combat aircraft) and remote controlled barbette armament like that of the Ar 240 and Me 210/410. The powerplants were to be the 'coupled' DB610 units mounted mid-fuselage with the propeller shaft running forward through the two-seat cockpit and this was to give the type a top speed of 750km/h (465mph) and a range of 4,000km whilst carrying a 2,000kg bomb load. On the 11th January 1941 the RLM assigned the designation He 219 to the project and on the 12th February it was discussed in detail during a conference at Heinkel's Rostock-Marienehe facility, with representatives of the Technical Office (*Technisches Amt*) and Construction Inspectorate (*Bauaufsicht des Luftfahrtministerium*) of the RLM and the Luftwaffe test facility at Rechlin. Work on the new design was slow however because not only were Heinkel working on other projects, but the development of the projected engine type also ran into delays, with the exhaust-driven supercharged DB 613 still in its initial development stages, so the design had to be modified to offer alternative powerplants in the form of the DB 610 and DB 615. The potential problems with a suitable powerplant led to the initial design being revised from a mid-fuselage tandem to wing-mounted twin layout and also with a single DB 610 in the nose. Lusser also offered a new design, the P.1056, which was a dedicated night fighter armed with 20mm cannon.

The Need For A Nightfighter

By mid-1941 the war situation had changed markedly from when the initial Heinkel design had been submitted. Bomber Command had gone over to a night offensive, after disastrous daylight rates during the initial stages of WWII, so in reaction to this the *Kommandeur* of I./ZG 1, Wolfgang Falck created the Luftwaffe's first *Nachtjäger* (night fighter) unit with *NJG 1* in June 1940. As the Luftwaffe had always been conceived as an offensive force, there were no dedicated nightfighter types, the role being undertaken by types intended for use in the day such as the Do 17Z, Bf 110 and Ju 88. These types could initially easily deal with the relatively slow and poorly armed twin-engine types being used by Bomber Command at this point, such as the Hampden, Whitley and Wellington. However four-engine heavy bombers entered service with Bomber Command in the form of the Handley Page Halifax in November 1940 and the Short Stirling in early 1941. The commander of the Luftwaffe nightfighter force, *Generalmajor* Josef Kammhuber, was well aware of the new challenges the *Nachtjäger* would face in the coming months as a result of the introduction of these heavy bombers and had continually stressed to the Director-General of Luftwaffe Equipment (*Generalluftzugmeister*), *Generaloberst* Ernst Udet, the need for a dedicated aircraft type to fulfil the role. It was while Udet was visiting Heinkel's factory on the 17th July 1941, that he inspected a mock-up of their proposed new reconnaissance design (P.1055) and discussions turned to how the type might well be used as a nightfighter. Around this time a meeting between *Generalmajor* Josef Kammhuber and Adolf Hitler had resulted in Kammhuber being given special powers that effectively made him independent of the RLM or its *Technisches Amt* and in August *XII Fliegerkorps* was set up with Kammhuber becoming its commander and thus the first *General der Nachtjagd*. Well aware of Heinkel's design, he sent some of his most successful nightfighter pilots to visit Heinkel's factory at Rostock-Marienehe to view the work being undertaken there on a potential new nightfighter. From these meetings it became apparent that the

This image has been identified over the years as many variants, but it seems to show an early-series machine (V or A-0) as it has the arched frame in the rear canopy section for the rear-facing machine gun, which was deleted from all production machines

He 219
Introduction

This well-known image of the V1 in flight was actually heavily retouched by Heinkel at the time to show what looks like a day-fighter scheme applied to the type. This was probably due to Heinkel's desire to remind the RLM that the type (still not approved for production at this time), was potentially a multi-role type for both day and night operations

type would need the heaviest of armament, at least six 20mm cannon, so in mid-August 1941 Professor Heinkel sought permission from Udet to radically change their initial design to incorporate the necessary armament needed for the role. Once this was granted, the Heinkel design department, headed by Siegfried Günther and Karl Schwärzler, offered a new design (P.1060) that differed mainly in overall proportions, being smaller than the previous design, and being powered by two wing-mounted engines. Problems with engine types such as the DB 613 and DB 615 meant that the new design had to opt for the less powerful, but readily available DB 603. The new type was so different from the original project that Professor Heinkel requested a new type number for it, wanting 'He 250' if at all possible, but this was rejected, probably to stop awkward questions from higher up as well as from other aircraft manufacturers. The plans for the new nightfighter were submitted to the RLM on the 26th August 1941 and over the next few weeks the type underwent detailed scrutiny. Initially the RLM had requested a three-man crew, but after discussions with the General Staff it was decided in October 1941 that a two-man crew would be sufficient. In a conference at Rostock-Marienehe on the 24th October representatives of the RLM stated that due to the recent expansion of the offensive (Nazi Germany was at war with the Soviet Union by this stage), a dedicated nightfighter could not be considered and the type thus had to be multi-role, capable of being a destroyer (*Zerstörer*), high-altitude fighter and fast bomber. This was completely against the view of the recently promoted *Generalleutnant* Kammhuber, who felt that such multi-role capacity would dilute its effectiveness as a nightfighter.

With all this in mind, in January 1942 Heinkel submitted two proposals, the He 219A and the He 219B, the former being a DB 603G-powered nightfighter with *Zerstörer* capability, while the latter was a high-altitude fighter powered by two DB 614s with a 28.5m span wing; neither would come to fruition though, as both engine types never reached production. Armament options were also considered, with initially four 20mm MG 151/20s in the wing roots (this was later reduced to two) and some

form of rear-facing armament, probably via remotely-controlled FD 131Z barbettes, however Heinkel's He 177 had proved that these were not ready for service use, so a hand-held MG 131Z was proposed instead. Catapult seats were standard, situated in an armoured cockpit and the type used a tricycle undercarriage, something that the RLM had initially rejected, but by this date, this layout had proved to have some advantages. The type also had the option to carry radar, although Telefunken felt that their *Lichtenstein C-1* system would not be available until mid-1943. The situation that the nightfighter faced over Germany in 1942 had changed still further, with the Avro Lancaster being used in the very first Millennium (1,000 bomber) raid on Köln (Cologne) on the night of the 30th/31st May. This combined with the new bomber stream system, designed specifically to overwhelm the nightfighter force led Kummhuber to demand immediate production of the He 219, with a nightfighter unit of twenty to thirty of them to be ready by 1st May 1943.

In Doubt

In early 1942 GL/C, a branch of the RLM's *Technisches Amt*, felt that a production contract should be issued for the He 219, however at this stage there was still no official decision with regard production volume etc. On the 22nd January Kammhuber and Heinrich Beauvais, a Rechlin-based test pilot, inspected the He 219 nightfighter mock-up and decided that the overall layout was satisfactory. The creation of production drawings started shortly afterwards and by the end of March some 80% were complete. A final inspection of the mock-up was undertaken on the 21st April, then the technical drawings could be issued and production of the prototype could commence.

Daimler-Benz soon advised that their new G-version of the DB 603 would not be ready until mid-1943, so offered the standard A-series with revised ratios for the reduction gear (the DB 603C). Although the first four DB 603Cs were requested for delivery to Heinkel by the beginning of August 1942, Daimler-Benz responded that

The He 219 V1 taxies in at Rostock-Marienehe with the He 177 V15 in foreground complete with tail-mounted parachute for spinning trials; this type of parachute assembly was probably the same as later used by the He 219 V2 and V11

He 219
Introduction

that would not be possible before October 1942. This was all not to be though, as on the 27th May the RLM were informed by Daimler-Benz that serious crankshaft vibrations and other problems had led to the termination of the DB 603C series. Attention now turned to the DB 603B, with its standard 300mm drive shaft modified to 370mm, but this type also ran into problems and the RLM was forced to accept the DB 603A with the Junkers Jumo 213 as an alternative.

Even though the Heinkel factory was subjected to four heavy raids in late April 1942, it was only the final one on the night of the 26th/27th that caused major damage and even then the experimental shop, which housed the prototype He 219, escaped destruction. Forced with long repairs, it was decided to relocate some elements of the factory to Heidfeld air base, 20km south-east of Vienna; this new site would later be referred to as Schwechat (the name of the immediate local district). While work continued for the meantime on the He 219 V1 at Rostock, all later prototypes would be built at Schwechat.

The only image we have ever seen of the He 219 V2, showing its wreckage in Lobau forest on the 10th July 1943. Note the contract between fuselage cross, possibly indicating that this aircraft may have been dark green or grey, not black, overall?

The whole future of the He 219 was still not certain by this stage though, as Ernst Udet's suicide had resulted in his role being taken by *Generalfeldmarschall* Erhard Milch and in mid-June 1942 after a meeting about the type, he demanded a report be compiled on the precise technical requirements of a new-generation nightfighter, so that it could be checked to see how/if the He 219 met them. On the 25th June however, the RLM announced that the He 219 was earmarked for production at a rate of 200 per month, albeit that this was not a firm contract, more of a projection should the type actually go into production. Things changed once again on the 29th July 1942 when it was announced that He 219 production (should it start) would be at an accelerated rate and thus it was assigned Priority Level DE. Although this was felt by Heinkel to indicate the full support of the He 219 project, in a conference on the 18th August 1942 Milch stated that the Ju 188 should be considered for the nightfighter role, as the He 219 was far better suited to the multi-role configuration, further supported by the fact that the Ju 188 could be built with existing facilities, where the He 219 needed new ones; no final decision about the whole nightfighter question came from this conference though.

On the 1st September the RLM confirmed the contract for the production of four prototypes, even though

A close-up of the all-black He 219 V1 as it taxies in from a test flight, this image was taken before mid-1943, as four-blade propellers are fitted

they were also clearly leaning towards the Ju 188 in the nightfighter role even though the Ju 188 was heavier than the He 219, used 10% more materials and the prototype He 219 could be ready at least six months ahead of the prototype Ju 188 nightfighter. Production plan *Lieferplan 222/1* produced that month listed twelve prototype He 219s with 173 pre-production A-0 series airframes, as well as 117 production aircraft commencing from January 1944. Only the initial prototypes were a firm commitment though, the rest were all estimated projections as no contracts had been issued (and the figures were in error, later being reduced by fifty-six airframes). The new amended production plan was issued on the 16th November 1942, but on the 8th January 1943 Heinkel had to inform the RLM that the production levels could not be achieved due to a shortage in labour.

Prototypes

With all of the above going on, production of the first prototype He 219 (V1) continued at Rostock-Marienehe, while plans were put in place to make eleven more prototypes at Schwechat. As the V1 was nearing completion in September 1942 an inspection by Professor Heinkel cast serious doubt on the twin tail configuration and as a result work continued to produce a more conventional single vertical fin/rudder unit. This was ready at the end of September, but after structural tests of the twin tail layout confirmed its strength, the single tail unit was finally

Although the operational debut of the He 219 was pretty impressive, the end result was this wrecked airframe, as the He 219 V9 crash-landed at Venlo in the early hours of the 12th June 1943

The He 219 V5 photographed in the spring of 1943 Schwechat in overall black with four-blade propellers fitted

dropped from the He 219 design in early November.

The He 219 V1 flew for the first time on the 6th November 1942, from Rostock-Marienehe with Gotthold Peter at the controls. Work on the V2, V3 and V4 was underway at Schwechat, with the V2 first flying there on the 10th January 1943. *Generalfeldmarschall* Milch was still not in favour of the He 219 and his feud with Kammhuber in relation to the type was to plague it throughout the rest of its development and service career. By early March 1943 the RLM were discussing the urgent need for a new-generation nightfighter, but when *Reichsmarschall* Göring accused the German aircraft industry of failure on the 18th March the RLM admitted to how fast Heinkel had built the He 219, but then requested the type's termination, so that Heinkel could concentrate on their commitment to the He 177!

With the threat of cancellation hanging over it the He 219 V1 took part in a series of flights against a Ju 188 at Rechlin on the 25th and 26th March 1943 in which it demonstrated its superiority over the Ju 188. Within a few days of this the RLM issued a contract for the production of 120 He 219A-0 pre-production airframes at Schwechat, a massive amount for a such a series, but almost certainly due to the whole uncertainty of the He 219 production. The pre-production series has caused much confusion in published sources over the years, with many attributing them with *Versuchnummern*, this was never the case though and all A-0 series machines were identified by a numbering system from 1 to 106 (e.g. A-01, A-02 etc.) and were allocated a *Stammkennzeichen* (primary identification code) as follows:

- A-01 to A-10, W/Nrs.190051-190060, PK+QA to PK+QJ
- A-011 to A-025 W/Nrs.190061-190075, RL+AA to RL+AO
- A-026 to A-033 W/Nrs.190097-190104, RL+AP to RL+AW
- A-034 to A-059 W/Nrs.190105-190130, DV+DA to DV+DZ
- A-060 W/Nr.190131, GU+BA*
- A-061 to A-073 W/Nrs.190175-190187, GU+BB to GU+BN*
- A-074 to A-080 W/Nrs.190188-190194, BE+JA to BE+JG*
- A-081 to A-097 W/Nrs.190210-190226, BE+JH to BE+JX*
- A-098 to A-106 W/Nrs.190227-190235, unknown

Although some may later have been allocated a *Verbandskennizeichen* (unit identification code), the *Stammkennzeichen* remained on all documentation and was never allocated to another machine, even if the original was destroyed or scrapped.

These allocations are not confirmed by surviving documents, but are reasonably inferred from other confirmed period information

Oberst Viktor von Lossberg was appointed commissar in charge of the He 219 programme and had been one of the pilots involved in the fly-off between the He 219 V1 and Ju 188 at Rechlin. He was expected to provide solutions to the problems associated with the planned production of the He 219 and following his appointment production was decentralised. Even though production of the He 219 had been sanctioned by *Reichsmarschall* Göring, there was still no clear understanding of where the production was actually to take place. By late June 1943 the initial production batch of 150 airframes was envisaged to be 100 built at Mielec in Poland and 50 at Budzyn.

Service Entry

The first He 219s to reach a Luftwaffe unit were the V7, V8 and V9, which were sent to *I./NJG 1* at Venlo in May 1943; although the V8 left after a few days to undertake undercarriage trials at Rechlin. These were the first machines to feature the new lengthened and un-stepped fuselage off the production line. The official handover ceremony took place at Venlo on the 30th May. The V7 was retained in the training and familiarisation role by *I./NJG 1*, whist the V9 went on to make the operational debut of the type. On the night of the 11th/12th June 1943, *Major*

Werner Steib flew the V9 on a night sortie and claimed five RAF bombers. However, on making his landing approach he crashed and was lucky to escape without injury thanks to the entire nose section shearing off and sliding to a stop ahead of the rest of the crumpled airframe. During the next ten days three other V-series machines would claim twenty RAF aircraft, including the previously untouchable D.H. Mosquito. This made Kammhuber even more determined to have the type, so he continued to press for full production. A meeting on the 16th July 1943 envisaged that the type would enter full-scale production from January 1944, with a maximum monthly rate of fifty by March 1945, although this meeting also identified that the Ju 188 nightfighter would go into production in January 1945. This was followed by a meeting on the 26th July that highlighted the fact that Mielec and Budzyn could not meet the production figures required by the *Reichsmarschall* and on the 3rd August Milch ordered the He 219 into production at Rostock-Marienehe.

The first A-0 series airframes (W/Nrs.190051 and 190053) were delivered to *I./NJG 1* at Venlo on the 2nd September 1943 and each machine had the new FuG 220 *Lichtenstein* SN-2 radar in place of the FuG 202 *Lichtenstein* BC system that had been fitted to earlier machines, as FuG 202 had been effectively jammed with the use of *Window* by Bomber Command in late July. Initial calibration of the SN-2 system was undertake by Telefunken technicians at Diepensee, set on the southern edge of the Henschel factory at Schönefeld, however from December 1943 such calibration was routinely done at Schwechat.

Few images exist of certain prototype He 219s, these two, taken by British Intelligence, show the remains of the He 219 V11 at Schwechat, although going by the graffiti on the tail, there looks to be dates (30-5-53 and 1/3/53) that may mean this particular image was taken a lot later?

Schnellbomber

During the official handover ceremony at Venlo on the 30th May 1943, *Generalmajor* Dietrich Peltz the *Angriffsführer* (Commander of the Air War against England) was in attendance and discussions inevitably turned to the multi-role potential of the He 219 and thus its possible use as a fast bomber (*Schnellbomber*). During July 1943 trials were conducted to increase the type's range and although this could be extended to 3,350km, or 3,750km with a drop tank, the whole idea of using the He 219 as a bomber came to naught because at this stage even series production of the type was in serious doubt. Peltz maintained his interest in the type though and on the 13th May 1944 he test flew an example at Schwechat (most likely the V28). He found the type very good to fly, having good flying, take-off and landing characteristics, although it should be noted that the V28 was the first to be fitted with DB 603E engines, which had better high altitude performance than the standard DB 603A. Regardless of Peltz's continual interest in the type, he was unable to get the support of *Oberstleutnant* Siegfried Knemeyer, head of the *Entwicklungs-Abteilung* (Development Section of the RLM's Technical Department) and so the He 219 was never developed, nor used as a bomber.

The He 219 was also considered by the *Kriegsmarine* (Navy) in 1944 as a back-up to their U-Boats (how exactly is unknown), but again this came to nothing. The type was also considered as a training aircraft, with a six-page report on this being created in December 1944, but again it was rejected.

Termination?

The problem with labour shortages had a serious effect on He 219 production at Schwechat and an RLM inspection in October 1943 found the site to be poorly managed, with very poor work standards. The RLM concluded that Heinkel, in having moved production to Schwechat, had assumed that all was well, when in fact the management there were clearly not up to the task.

Having had to struggle to get production over the preference for the Ju 188 in the nightfighter role by both the RLM and *Generalfeldmarschall* Milch in November 1943 a new design from Junkers caught the attention of both parties as a potential replacement for the He 219. The high-altitude, multi-role Ju 388 had a pressurised cockpit

This is most likely the He 219 V17 (A-010) W/Nr.190060 PK+QJ seen in a hangar at Hörsching-Linz, Austria in the early summer of 1945, where it was captured by American forces (©USAAF)

and in late November 1943 it was suggested that He 219 production be terminated in favour of the Ju 388 in 1945, while the cancellation of the He 219 was also seen as being potentially beneficial to the new Dornier Do 335 programme. At a meeting on the 3rd December the RLM made a proposal that Heinkel should switch from making the He 219 to building Junkers and Dornier designs, albeit this was all envisaged for 1945/46 and thus never came into effect. On the 13th December the *General der Jagdflieger* called for development of a high-altitude He 219. Concerns were mounting at this time that the new Boeing B-29 Superfortress would be deployed over Europe and it was felt that the Ju 388 and Do 335 would not be available in time to counter it; fears that were unfounded, as the B-29 was never deployed in the European theatre of war.

Production Continues

With the He 219 to be built at Rostock-Marienehe, sub-assembles were to be built at Mielec and its supporting facility at Budzyn. Although initially only intended to make fuselages that were then shipped to Rostock-Marienehe, this was expanded in late 1943 when the sites were assigned the task of also making fuselages for the Schwechat facility. This production switch (Schwechat had originally made their own fuselages) did initially cause delays in airframe completion, but between the 15th February and 1st May 1944 they completed thirty-six fuselage for onward consignment (two fuselages at a time in a Me 321) to Schwechat.

As an interesting aside, around late December 1943 the name *Marder* (Marten, a small weasel-like carnivore) was proposed by the RLM for the He 219, Heinkel did not like the name and suggested *Hermes* (the Greek messenger of the Gods). The RLM wanted any such name limited to predatory animals or birds, so no agreement was reached at this point on a name for the He 219. The name *Uhu* (owl) is often given to the He 219 and although no official documents have ever been found confirming this, post-war interviews with personnel confirm that the name was sometimes used in conjunction with the type. As the name *Uhu* had already been allocated to the Focke-Wulf Fw 189, this is probably why it was never officially used; the name was also used for the FuG 135 guidance system.

About 40 He 219s were completed at Schwechat during 1943, eleven of which were prototypes and six (V2, V3, V11, V14, V17 & V28) were retained by Heinkel, while the rest were released to the Luftwaffe. At least eleven went to the test facilities at Rechlin, Lärz, Tarnewitz and Werneuchen and the remainder went into service with I./NJG 1 at Venlo.

Termination (Again) & Troubles

During the spring of 1944 the RLM once again made plans to stop He 219 production, using the claim that operational units did not want the type. Professor Heinkel immediately set up interviews with He 219 crews and on the 1st April 1944 sent these to *Generaldirektor* Karl Frydag, the head of the RLM's Committee for Aircraft Production. Regardless of the high praise the type got, on the 25th May 1945 *Reichsmarschall* Göring ordered a halt to He 219 production in favour of the Ju 388, with this to take effect as soon as the current production orders were fulfilled. This order did not stand for long though and was reversed by the *Reichsmarschall* on the 13th June

The situation for Heinkel had not improved in the later stages of 1943 and into 1944, the Italian surrender in September 1943 meant that Allied forces had a foothold in southern Europe, from where they could launch attacks into Austria. This meant that this previously 'safe' region was now under serious threat, including the Heinkel facility at Schwechat, which was targeted for attack first on the 17th March 1944, but heavy cloud obscured it. It was then attacked on the 23rd April and nearly 300 tons of bombs were dropped on the site, resulting in the deaths of 94 workers. The most serious attack came on the 26th June 1944, which also saw bombs dropped on the nearby Mauthausen concentration camp. The destruction of three flight hangars probably resulting in the loss

He 219
Introduction

Starting to look much more like a production aircraft, this is the He 219 V33 (A-013) W/Nr.190063 RL+AC fitted with FuG 220 and 218 radar, the early rear canopy glazing and short spinners

of at least five (W/Nrs.190225, 190227, 190230, 190231 and 190232) He 219s that were awaiting test flights, as there is no record of these machines after this date. The raid also resulted in the termination of A-0 production at the site, with only 106 of the planned 120 airframes being built. By July the Schwechat site was in turmoil, the He 177 production facility at Zwölfaxing had been damaged in a raid on the 8th July and was subsequently abandoned, with all remaining production capacity transferred to Schwechat. Mid-July the RLM instructed Schwechat to switch from A-2 to A-5 production, the problem was that the site was still recovering from the bombing of the 26th June and also production of the A-2 had only just begun there. In the end the directive was never initiated, as later events would overtake matters and He 162 production started there in the autumn of 1944 instead.

Production

The He 219A-2 started to come off the assembly lines at Rostock-Marienehe in late June 1944, having been preceded by a batch of fifteen A-0 pre-production airframes that were used to set up the assembly lines for series production. Production only went ahead for a short time though, as the factory was bombed on the 4th August 1944 by B-24s of the 8th Air Force. The bombers dropped incendiaries and delayed-action bombs, so this made clearing the site afterwards a slow and difficult process. Whilst the landing areas and dispersal bays were serviceable, two He 219s were damaged by incendiaries and two more by bomb splinters and the work areas received about 60% damage. On the 25th August over one hundred B-24s attacked the site again resulting in the destruction of two He 219s (W/Nrs.290017 and 290018) and damage to five others (W/Nrs.290010, 290011, 290015, 290016 and 290019, with 290016 receiving 60% damage and most likely being scrapped).

Production at Mielec ceased in August 1944 as Russian forces advanced westwards and threatened the plant. All machinery and equipment was moved to Gandersheim near Harz but it is not known if actual fuselage production moved as well. The facility at Barth, some 50km northeast of Rostock-Marienehe is known to have been used to support the main Heinkel factory and it is thought that fuselage production from August

Although a couple of He 219s were used for trials with a BMW 003 jet engine carried under the fuselage to boost short-term performance, no images survive other than this artist's impression (the codes are spurious)

1944 may well have been moved there. Sadly no official documents remain to support this, so the exact extent to which the Barth facility played in He 219 production remains a mystery.

The Schwechat site produced the A-2 variant from the summer of 1944, with the first five (W/Nrs.420319 to 420323) accepted by the Luftwaffe in September. By that stage though the site was involved in production of the He 162 Volksjäger, so He 219 production slowed to just ten machines during the last three months of 1944. The last five He 219s (W/Nrs.420371 to 420375) produced at the site were modified to be powered by Junkers Jumo 213E engines with water-methanol boost and these were designated as D-1s in official records and are believed to have been delivered to the Luftwaffe in March 1945.

Final Stages

Rostock-Marienehe switched from producing the A-2 variant to the new A-7 in November 1944. This version differed mainly from the previous one by having greater endurance thanks to additional fuel in the rear of each engine nacelle. Sadly the use of a greater amount of fuel came at a point when the Luftwaffe was starved of it and it is therefore unlikely the full potential of the increased endurance of the A-7 was ever fully realised in the last seven months of the war.

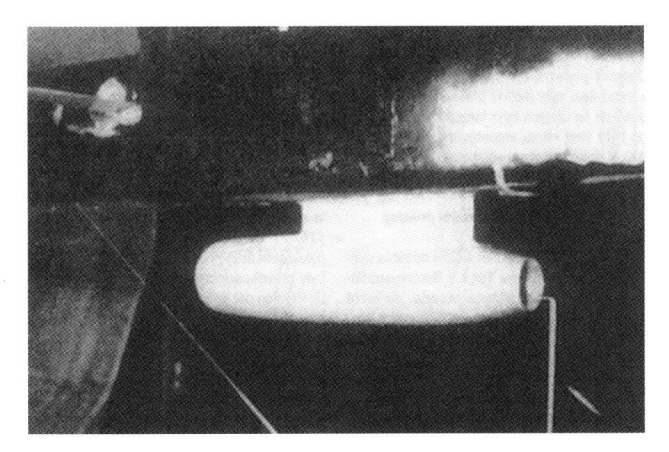

This shows the mock-up of the BMW 003 nacelle under the He 219 fuselage in the wind tunnel prior to actual flight tests of such an installation

Whilst production of the He 219 was to be at a rate of fifty per month in accordance with the *Lieferplan 227/I* of the 15th December 1944, on the 20th January 1945 however this was overturned, when the *Führer Emergency Programme* stated that piston-engine nightfighters were no longer to be built; although He 219 production was to continue until all current orders were complete. By the end of March 1945 production of the He 219 had come to a close, with all efforts now on the He 162.

Hütter Hü 211

Wolfgang Hütter, who specialised in glider construction, was asked by Heinkel to look into modification of the He 219 as a long-range, three-seat reconnaissance aircraft capable of evading the D.H. Mosquito. The new design borrowed much from the He 219, Ju 288 and Do 335, with just the wings and tail surfaces being completely new. Both of these were made of wood, to save weight, the wings having a 24.5m span and were of exceptionally high aspect ratio (15:1). The type was to be powered by two Junkers Jumo 222A/B-3 counter-rotating engines, which would give it a projected top speed of 715km/h at 7,300m, thus making it superior to the Do 335 (665km/h) or its projected *Zwilling* Do 635 (690km/h) version. Inspection of a mock-up took place at Ravensburg and Kirchheim/Teck in mid-December 1944, but the worsening situation for Nazi Germany meant that the project got no further. Some sources state that two prototypes were being built but were destroyed in an air raid in December 1944, while others claim that the project simply ground to a halt in January 1945 due to the lack of materials, manpower and continual problems with the Jumo 222.

Projects

A large number of developments of the He 219 were considered. The first was the B-series with its Jumo 222 engines, which it was hoped would allow the type to reach a top speed of 700km/h (435mph). The B-series also used a larger span of 22.06m to improve performance at altitude. Sadly the Jumo 222 never went into production and although it was planned for the long-span version to use the DB603 engine instead, only a few test airframes ever flew. The C-series was the next development, again using the Jumo 222 and long span, but with a revised (longer) fuselage of 17.15m that had a three-man cockpit from the Ju 388J and a powered turret in the tail. The series was intended for both the day bomber and nightfighter roles, but with the failure of the Jumo 222 engine, this series also came to naught. As already mentioned the D-series was a night fighter fitted with Jumo 213 engines, MW50 boost system and armament of 4x MG151/20 cannon in the ventral tray and 2x MK108 in a *Schrägemusik* installation. The last five He 219s (W/Nrs.420371 to 420375) produced at Schwechat were built to this configuration and it is believed they were delivered to the Luftwaffe in March 1945. The E-series was to be of mixed wood/metal construction and to feature a vastly increased span of 28.5m plus DB614 engines, however it never got any further than the drawing board. He 319 and He 419 development was also considered; see Section 2 of this title for more on these projects.

Although the He 219 seems to have achieved almost mythical status, it showed poor manoeuvrability due to high wing loading, which also resulted in a turn radius that was inferior to the Ju 88G, and it was never fast enough to be the 'Mosquito killer' it was often claimed to be. The type was also seriously underpowered, which in a two-engine aircraft was a very dangerous trait, as it made the loss of an engine on take-off or landing very serious indeed. Capt. Eric Brown summed up by saying that its "reputation was somewhat overrated", however that is probably true of many Luftwaffe types during the late-war period and even if the He 219 could not catch the Mosquito, it would certainly have wreaked havoc amongst the Allied bomber streams had the type had a totally uninterrupted production.

He 219
Introduction

Operational Service

Many claim this image shows a He 219A-5, but that sub-variant never actually went into production, so this is most likely an A-0 fitted with reduced armament and seen at Venlo in the summer of 1944 – to left might be *Fw.* Fritz Mabricht, so the one in the centre may be *Oblt* Josef Nabrich or Hptm Heinz Strüning

He 219A-0, W/Nr.190188, BE+JA flown by *Hptm.* Paul Förster (on the left) and *Fw.* Ernst Böhmer (on the right) and photographed at Venlo in May 1944 not long after this aircraft was delivered

He 219A-0, W/Nr.190116, DV+DL seen here having systems checks prior to delivery to *I./NJG 1* in April 1944

The only known image of a He 219 operational with *NJGr.10*, shows the He 219A-05, W/Nr.190055, PK+QF (some state PK+QE) at Rechlin-Lärz with mechanic Hermann Klauser standing on nose wheel. You can just make out the '05' under the 'F' on the nose cone

Forty-five He 219s were surrendered at Westerland, on the island of Sylt, although in this instance the entire tail assembly was removed as well as the propellers to stop unauthorised flights; the former resulting in some mix-ups when certain airframes were returned to airworthiness for testing

He 219
Introduction

He 219A, W/Nr.290068 probably on a delivery flight to Wrlzow in late September 1944 in the black underside scheme seen on two specific production batches

Another view of the remains of W/Nr.290004 G9+DH at Paderborn, which was the subject of an extensive study by American intelligence *(©USAAF)*

As Allied troops moved forward that came across more and more wrecked He 219s, this shows the remains of W/Nr.290004 G9+DH found at Paderborn by US forces in May 1945. The aircraft had been damaged in a forced landing and is most likely to have been blown-up to stop it falling into Allied hands *(©USAAF)*

Quite a few relatively intact airframes were discovered, this shows W/Nr.190176 found at Lechfeld by US forces at the end of the war *(©USAAF)*

W/Nr.211116, G9+VL seen here as found by Allied troops in May 1945 was destroyed in an air raid on Münster-Handorf in late March 1945 with the wreck being blown up by the retreating Germans *(©USAAF)*

below: W/Nr.310112 was surrendered at Grøve (some state Westerland, but the retention of the tail and the layout of the other aircraft looks like Grøve), this machine lacks any squadron codes, so was probably used in a non-operational role

He 219
Introduction

The Survivor

On the 16th June 1945 a team of officers and men of the USAAF Intelligence Service, under the command of Col. Harold E. Watson, were instructed to obtain three Heinkel He 219s captured by the RAF at Grøve, Denmark as part of Operation LUSTY (LUftwaffe Secret TechnoloY). These machines had previously been operated by *NJG 1* (*Nachtjagdgeschwader* 1 – Night Fighter Squadron 1) at the base. It is thought that another three machines captured at Westerland on the island of Sylt were also allocated to the American team, but to date no trace of these has ever been found. The Grøve airframes were made airworthy by 'Watson's Whizzers', as Col. Watson's team was known, and flown to Cherbourg, France. From here the aircraft were sprayed with a preservative coating for a long sea journey and loaded onto HMS Reaper as part of Project Sea Horse. The three He 219s were as follows:

- He 219A-0, W/Nr.210903, had been operated by II./NJG 1 at Deelan, The Netherlands by the 6th *Staffel* (as G9+LP). Transferred to I./NJG 1 at Venlo around the 11th July 1944. When surrendered to the RAF in May 1945 it was marked as SP+CR indicating that it was used in a non-operational role (e.g. training). Allocated the number 'USA 8' by the RAF prior to its collection and was Loading Position No.15 on HMS Reaper
- He 219A-2, W/Nr.290060, when surrendered to the RAF it carried the code CS+QC, denoting that it was also used in a non-operational (e.g. training) role. It was allocated the number 'USA 9' by the RAF and was collected by Col. Watson on the 26th June 1945, where it was flown by Capt. Fred McIntosh to Cherbourg for loading onto HMS Reaper
- He 219A-2, W/Nr.290202, when surrendered it was marked as GI+KQ, once again indicating that it was in a non-operational role. It was marked as 'USA 10' by the RAF and after being passed to Col. Watson it was flown to Cherbourg on the 27th June 1945 by Heinz Braun to be loaded on HMS Reaper

HMS Reaper arrived at Newark, where all the aircraft were transferred ashore and reassembled at Ford Field.

He 219s amongst other captured equipment on board HMS Reaper prior to sailing to American from France

A He 219 on the rear of the deck of HMS Reaper at Cherbourg prior to sailing for America

He 219s amongst other captured Luftwaffe types after arriving in the USA and being unloaded on barges at Newark Army Air Field

He 219A-2, W/Nr.290060 marked as 'USA 9' (later FE-613) seen at Freeman Field

He 219A-0, W/Nr.210903 as FE-612 seen at Freeman Field in reapplied Luftwaffe markings

Each machine was allocated an 'FE' code, standing for 'Foreign Equipment', as follows:
- He 219A-0, W/Nr.210903 = FE-612
- He 219A-5, W/Nr.290060 = FE-613
- He 219A-2, W/Nr.290202 = FE-614

The 'FE' code system was later replaced by 'T2', indicating the Office of Air Force Intelligence, although only W/Nr.210903 seems to have actually had the 'FE' element replaced by 'T2', the other two retained their FE-number

Once ready all three aircraft were flown to Freeman Field, Indiana during August 1945.

The history of FE-612 and FE-613 are quite short, as FE-612 was initially intended for storage and preservation, but its place was taken by FE-614 and it therefore got allocated to the Display Branch of the USAF and after display as a static exhibit at various air shows it ended up in storage at Freeman Field by 17th May 1946 and was finally scrapped there in 1950. FE-613 was held as a spare source for FE-614 and by 1st August 1946 it was in storage at Freeman Field. Nothing is known of it from this date, so it is presumed to have been scrapped on site.

FE-614 fared better as initially it was slated for restoration to airworthy status, and this was claimed to

This shows He 219A-2, W/Nr.290202 marked as 'T2-614', the only image of a captured He 219 in American we have even seen with the 'T2' codes applied

He 219A-2, W/Nr.290202, FE-614/T2-614 seen in storage with other ex-Luftwaffe aircraft at No.803 (Special) Depot, Park Ridge, Illinois in the late 1940s

He 219
Introduction

be "90% complete" by August 1946. However, changes in USAF policy and a lack of interest in propeller-driven aircraft due to the dawn of the jet age, resulted in it never returning to airworthiness and instead it was allocated for preservation. On the 17th September 1946 the airframe was moved from Freeman Field to No.803 Special Depot at Orchard Place Airport, Park Ridge, Illinois, near the present O'Hare International Airport. It was stored in a vacant US Government factory there that had previously been used by the Dodge Automobile Company to build Douglas C-54s. Ownership of FE-614 transferred to the Smithsonian Institute's National Air Museum on January 3rd 1949 and with the need for the facility at Park Ridge, FE-614 along with 82 other aircraft was crated and shipped to the Smithsonian Institute's Paul E. Garber Preservation, Restoration and Storage Facility at Silver Hill in early 1955.

W/Nr.290202 remained in deep storage at the Garber Facility for the next 45 years and it was not until the beginning of the 21st century that the fuselage was moved into the Restoration Facility at Silver Hill. On completion of the restoration and with the opening of the Steven F. Udvar-Hazy Center by Dulles Airport in 2011, the fuselage was moved in and placed on a special cradle for display. With the planned eventual closure of the Paul E. Garber Facility there was an inevitable delay in the remaining restoration work, as all the airframes there had to be moved to the new storage buildings at Dulles. The engine nacelles were completed and put on display with the fuselage, then in July 2014 the wings were completed at the Paul E. Garber Facility, but it took until 2019 for them to be reunited with the fuselage, seeing the airframe back on its undercarriage for the first time in over fifty years. With complete renovation work on the downtown NASM museum site in Washington D.C. it will be a few more years before the airframe can be fully kitted out (work to produce a replica of the radar antenna is in hand, as the originals were lost before the airframe ever came into the care of NASM), but at least you now have a fairly complete He 219 on display.

Not quite the last survivor…

In October 2011 divers located the remains of a He 219 laying in about 3 metres of water, 100 metres from the shore, north of Hirtshals, Denmark. In co-operation with the *Danmarks Flyvehistoriske Selskab* the remains were raised from Tannis Bay on the 23rd April 2012. Although in numerous pieces, and with one engine and the tail still unaccounted for, the airframe will undergo conservation with the hope of eventually incorporating it into a static exhibit to be displayed at the *Forvars-og Garnisonsmuseum* (Defence and Garrison Museum), Aalborg, Denmark.

He 219A-2, W/Nr.290202 in storage, most likely outside at Park Ridge, Illinois once the aircraft there had been allocated to the Air Museum of the Smithsonian Institute (later to become NASM), but after they had been removed from indoors storage so the Park Ridge site could be re-activated for C-54 production *(via J.M. Gradidge†)*

And, what might have been...

The RAF obtained numerous He 219s at the end of the war, captured at Grøve (modern-day Karup) or Westerland on the island of Sylt, but only six are shown as having been allocated Air Ministry (AirMin or AM) codes and earmarked for further flying, they are as follows.

- He 219A-2, W/Nr.290126, D5+BL of 3./NJG 1 (*although probably never used operationally by them*), surrendered to the RAF at Grøve, Denmark, allocated AirMin 20, flown to Schleswig 1st August 1945, ferried to RAE Farnborough 3rd August and was test flown there on the 7th August, flown to No.6 MU RAF Brize Norton by Lt Cdr Eric Brown on the 21st August 1945, scrapped at No.6 MU and struck off charge 14th August 1947
- He 219A-7, W/Nr.310109, unit and codes unknown*, surrendered to the RAF at Grøve, Denmark, allocated AirMin 21, flown to Schleswig 7th August 1945, ferried to RAE Farnborough 11th August 1945, Lt Cdr Eric Brown states he flew this to Abingdon on the 30th August 1945 and on to Brize Norton on the 31st. Declared surplus to requirements November 1947 and transported to No.34 MU, Sleap 23rd January 1948 where it was scrapped
- He 219A-7, W/Nr.310189, D5+CL of I./NJG3, surrendered to the RAF at Grøve, Denmark, allocated AirMin 22, ferried from Schleswig to RAE Farnborough 27th August 1945, displayed statically during the German Aircraft Exhibit at Farnborough 29/10/45

Thirty-one of the forty-five He 219s surrendered at Westerland on the island of Sylt

The only image we have ever seen of AirMin 21, He 219A-7, W/Nr.310109

He 219A-2, W/Nr.290126, D5+BL as surrendered at Grøve

He 219A-2, W/Nr.290126, D5+BL at Grøve, but now in British markings; this was taken on orthochromatic film, so the colours are not how the human eye sees them

He 219A-2, W.Nr.290126, D5+BL seen at RAE Farnborough

He 219
Introduction

He 219A-7, W/Nr.310189 probably seen at Farnborough not long after arriving there

He 219A-7, W/Nr.310189, D5+CL as AirMin 22 at Farnborough during the 29th October to 9th November 1945 exhibition of captured German technology

He 219A-7, W/Nr.310189, AirMin 22 during the exhibition of captured German technology in October/November 1945

He 219A-7, W/Nr.310189, AirMin 22 in the scrap compound at Farnborough, the '100' marked on it most likely relates to a lot number in a disposal list, so the airframe could be sold as scrap

He 219
Introduction

The only image we have ever seen of AirMin 43

He 219A-7, W/Nr.310106 as AirMin 44 with German crew climbing into cockpit, so probably prior to being ferried from its point of capture to the UK in 1945

An odd one this, as this image of He 219A-7, W/Nr.310106, AirMin 44 states it shows the airframe at Ford, however later images claim to show it at Tangmere, but it has the FuG 218 radar dipoles and the bulge in the canopy for the FuG 350 Naxos are both visible, whilst neither of these are visible in this 'earlier' shot?

He 219A-7, W/Nr.310106, AirMin 44, this image claims to show the aircraft at Tangmere and the FuG 218 dipoles and FuG 350 Naxos bulge above the canopy are clearly visible

to 9/11/45, noted in the scrapyard at Farnborough on the 15th December 1946 and presumed scrapped there by early 1947
- He 219A, W/Nr.310200, D5+DL of I./NJG3, surrendered to the RAF at Grøve, Denmark, allocated AirMin 23 – this aircraft crashed whilst being flown by an RAF pilot at Grøve on the 21st July 1945
- He 219A-7, W/Nr., unit and codes unknown/unrecorded, surrendered to the RAF at Westerland on the island of Sylt, allocated AirMin 43, this aircraft was at RAE Farnborough at some stage, as the only known image looks like it was taken there going by all the other British types in the background, subsequent use unknown, scrapped at No.6 MU, Brize Norton in August 1947 – *To make He 219s unairworthy after the surrender, RAF technicians removed the fin/rudders and propellers, so this may explain why two W/Nrs (310215 and 319114) are quoted in some sources, as this may have had fins from two different machines fitted to return it to airworthiness. W/Nr.310215 is visible on the port vertical fin of the only known image of this machine*
- He 219A-7, W/Nr.310106, unit and codes not recorded, surrendered to the RAF at Westerland on the island of Sylt, allocated AirMin 44, to RAF Ford, a satellite airfield for the Central Fighter Establishment at Tangmere on the 24th June 1945 (*aircraft had FuG 218 Neptun radar in place of the more usual FuG 220 and had the passive FuG 350 Naxos system in the upper canopy*), transferred to the Night Fighter Development Wing at Tangmere on the 27th July 1945, flown from Tangmere to No.6 MU, Brize Norton 19th October 1945 by Lt Cdr Eric Brown (although he states he flew it from Tangmere to Farnborough on that day) and was struck off charge (scrapped) there on the 14th August 1947

* – *Some sources state this was G9+VN, however all machines at Grøve (modern-day Karup) were assigned to NJG 3 with the code G5+xx*

The Czech Connection

The history of the He 219 in Czechoslovakia is short, as two examples were captured by Russian forces at the end of the war. These were overhauled at the Letov aircraft factory in the early 1950s with a view to returning them to airworthiness. Once the first machine was test flown it transferred to the Aviation Research Institute (VZLU) at Prague and was apparently used in catapult seat trials. It was later handed over to the Czechoslovakian Air Force and designated the LB-79 (LB = *Lehka Bombardovaci* – light bomber), although the type was never used in the bombing role. Both machines were apparently scrapped in late 1952 and to date their original *Werknummer* and thus sub-variant remain unknown.

Technical Description

What follows is an extensive selection of images and diagrams that will help you understand the physical nature of the Heinkel He 219 series.

There is only one complete He 219 left in the world today, He 219A-2, W/Nr.290202, and it is owned by the Smithsonian Institute's National Air & Museum and displayed at the Steven F. Udvar-Hazy Center by Dulles Airport *(©S. Willey)*

This coverage is broken down as follows, in line with the original Flugzeug-Handbuch (D(Luft)T219), with additional images from the Ersatzteilliste (Parts List).

Group 1 – Fuselage
1 – Cockpit Interior
2 – Canopy
3 – Nose Section
4 – Main & Aft Fuselage

Group 2 – Undercarriage
1 – Nose
2 – Main

Group 3 – Tail
1 – Tailplanes
2 – Vertical Fins & Rudders

Group 4 – Fuel, Oil, Oxygen & De-icing Systems

Group 5 – Wings

Group 6 – Engines & Nacelles

Group 7 – Weapons
1 – Armament
2 – Sighting

Group 8 – Electrical Equipment
1 – Radio
2 – Radar
3 – Misc Electrical

Group 9 – Miscellaneous
1 – Access Panels
2 – Covers etc.

Please note that throughout this section where translations for the original German text is offered, these are not always literal, as they would not make sense, so we have often offered a translation that will (we hope) make sense to an English speaking audience.

Group 1 – Side 1
Fuselage
Cockpit Interior

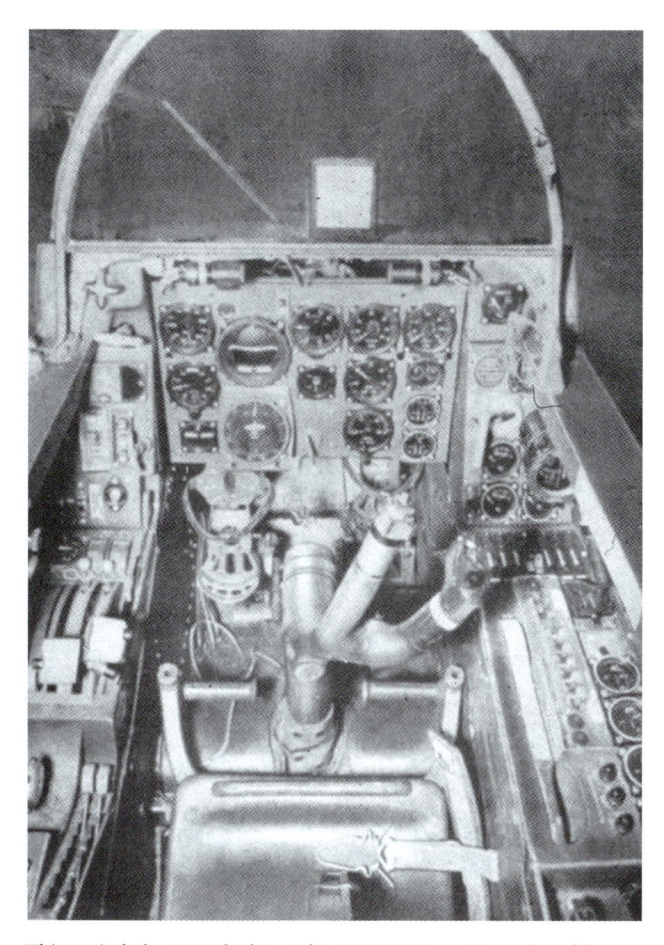

This period photograph shows the main instrument panel, rudder pedals, side consoles and control column in a pre-production He 219A-0

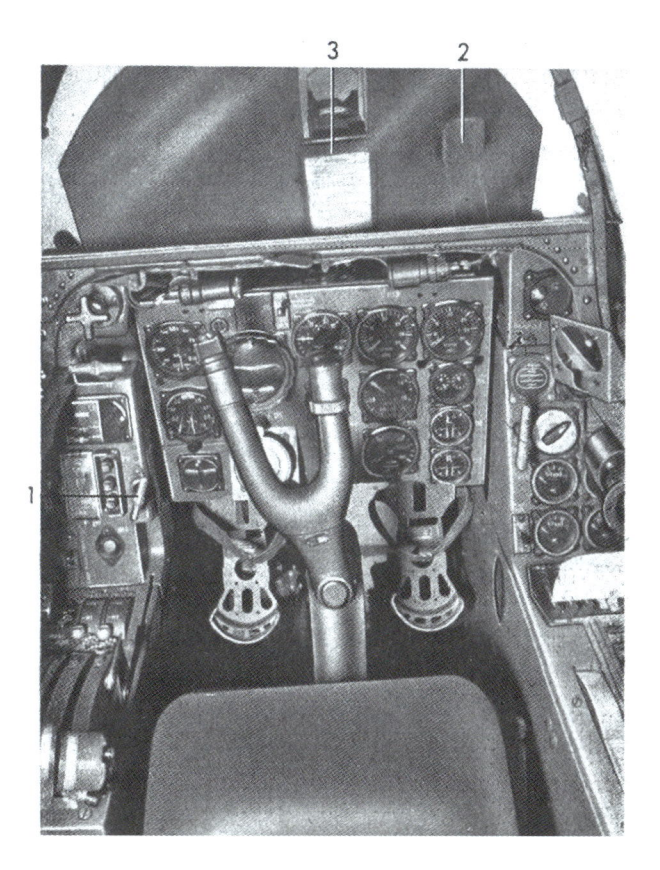

This is an overall view of the front cockpit area in the A-2 with the National Air & Space Museum (©*NASM*)

This is another period photograph, which although showing the armoured panel, also gives a clearer overall view of the main instrument panel, control column etc.
1. Handle for armoured plate (release)
2. Rubber buffer
3. Cover (actually an instruction/warning placard)

Note: Through this title we have used the original German term 'catapult' to describe the seat system used in the He 219, as the term 'ejection' is very much more modern and really relates to rocket-assisted ejection seats developed after WWII.

Group 1 – Side 2
Fuselage
Cockpit Interior

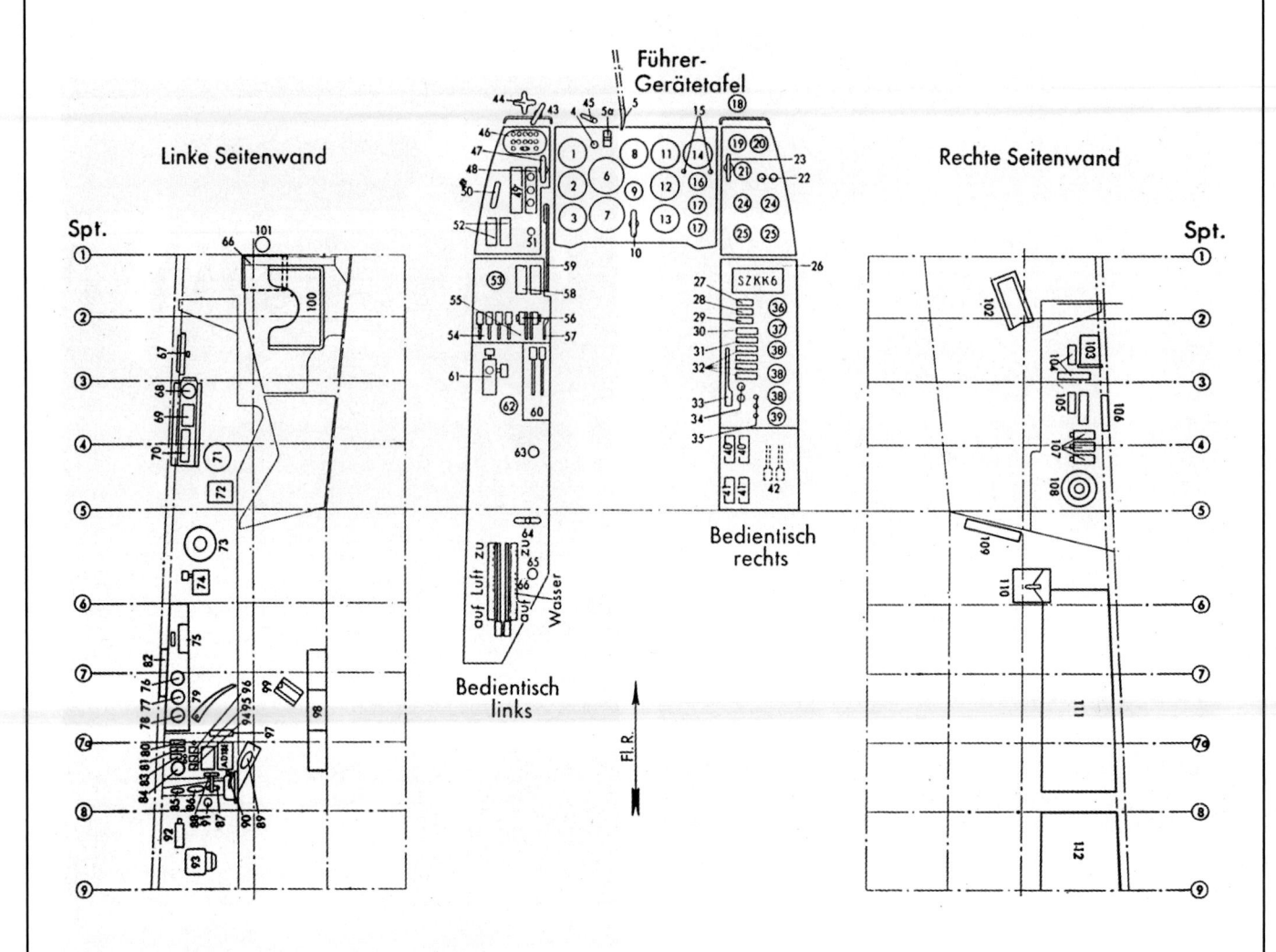

These diagrams show the main instrument panel and side console for the A-0 series, but also apply to the production A-2 and A-7 series

1. Airspeed indicator
2. Fine coarse altimeter
2. Emergency turn/bank indicator
4. Indicator for pitot tube
5. Windshield wipers
5a. Emergency switch for course control (FuBl 2)
6. Artificial horizon
8. Variometer
9. F307
10. Emergency pull for windscreen washer
11. RPM indicator
12. Dual boost gauge
13. Fu Ng 101 (radio altimeter)
14. RPM indicator
15. Indicator for propeller brake
16. Dual position indicator for propellers
17. Double pressure gauge
18. Clock
19. Oxygen gauge
20. Oxygen pressure gauge
22. Coolant level warning
23. Canopy (emergency) release
24. Coolant level warning
25. Lubricant temperature gauge
26. Ammunition counter
27. Toggle switch for landing lights
28. Toggle switch for identification lights
29. Toggle switch for UV lighting
30. Pitot tube heater
31. Main switch for course control (FuBl 2)
32. Fuel tank pumps
33. Catapult (ejection) seat lever
34. Selector knobs (radio)
35. Fuel level warning lamps
36. Gyro control switch
37. Blank
38. Fuel gauge
39. Compressed air pressure gauge
40. Starter switch
41. Starting aid
42. Emergency fuel drain
43. Landing gear T-lever
44. Nose wheel emergency release valve
45. Windscreen washer lever
46. 12-lamp device (undercarriage/flap position)
47. Armoured cover
48. Landing flap T-switch
49. Landing gear switch
50. Flap emergency release valve
51. Mains emergency switch
52. Automatic propeller switch
53. Flap indicator
54. Propeller switch lever
55. Propeller pitch control
56. Throttle with thumb switch (propeller adjustment)
57. Locking lever
58. Ignition switch
59. Rudder locking lever
60. Emergency pull for radiator flap
61. Trim adjustment
62. Double oil pressure gauge
63. Accumulator gauge
64. Rubber dinghy emergency release
65. Access ladder release
66. Oxygen regulation
67. Ventilation flap
68. Blank
69. Junction box for intercommunication
70. Control unit for FuG 17 (FT)
71. Detonating cord for destruction charge
72. Connection for heated clothing
75. Destruction switch for FT (radio/radar) devices
76. Outside air temperature gauge
77. Oxygen pressure gauge
78. Oxygen flow gauge
79. Catapult (ejection) seat lever
80. Selector switch for FuG 10 and FuG 16
81. Altimeter toggle switch
82. Operator plate for de-icing system
83. Toggle switch for UV lighting
84. Compressed air pressure gauge
85. Voltage ammeter
86. Altimeter
87. Blank
88. Canopy (emergency) release
89. Airspeed indicator
90. FuG 10 button
91. Release for trailing antenna
92. Ballast
93. Resistance unit
94. Toggle switch for propeller de-icing
95. Switch for de-icing (heating) in area
96. Toggle switch for tail unit de-icing
97. Hand lamp
98. Cartridge flare box
99. Holder for flare gun
100. Map pocket
101. Intercom outboard connection
102. Deviation table
103. Emergency compass
104. UV lights
105. Device light
106. Operating plate for seat catapult system
107. Ballasts for UV lamps
108. Oxygen regulator for pilot
109. Electrical distributor
110. First aid kit
111. Main switchboard
112. Space for FT (radio/radar) distributors

Group 1 – Side 7
Fuselage
Cockpit Interior

Quick look at the rear bulkhead, as most of this area is filled with radio and radar equipment, so is covered in detail elsewhere in this section. Please note that all the silver-coloured boxes are American in origin and thus not original (©S. Willey)

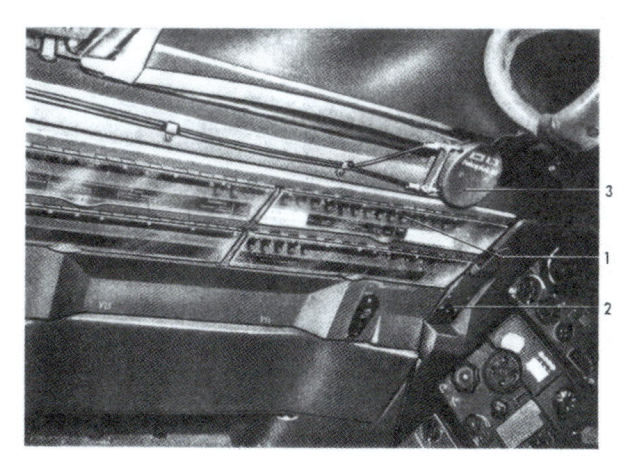

The starboard sidewall of the rear cockpit area is pretty devoid of equipment save for the various electric switches (©S. Willey)

This diagram from the Flight Handbook shows the starboard rear sidewall with all its original equipment in situ

The port sidewall of the rear cockpit area is even cleaner than that of the starboard, about all there is here is this little area of instruments and switches in the bottom rear corner (©S. Willey)

This period photo gives an overall view of the port sidewall area in the rear cockpit as it would have appeared in service

Here is an overall shot of the port rear cockpit sidewall area in the NASM example after renovation. The large red lever operates the catapult seat and canopy jettison. Note the stitching along the canopy sill, this is the sealing strip that goes around the entire canopy edge (©S. Willey)

Group 1 – Side 8
Fuselage
30 | Canopy

An overall shot of the starboard side of the canopy on the NASM example (©S. Willey)

Whilst NASM's He 219 was being put on its wheel in 2019, the front windscreen was removed, allowing a good view of how the main canopy's front frame fits over that armoured windscreen inside (©S. Willey)

This period photo shows the opening (jettisonable) section of the canopy, viewed from the starboard rear – this is an early (A-0) series version, as it has a sliding ventilation panel on both sides, later production variants only had this on the port side

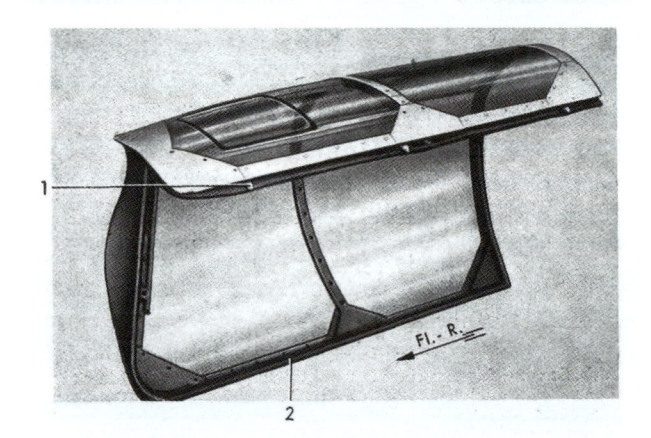

This shows the guide pins (1) and the rubber seal (2) on the edge of the main canopy – this is a later (production) version with the single sliding panel on the port side

This photo from the manual shows the canopy in the fully open position. The keyed items are as follows: 1 Halteseile (Tethers); 2 Führungsrohre (Guide Tubes); 3 Stützstrebe (Support Strut)

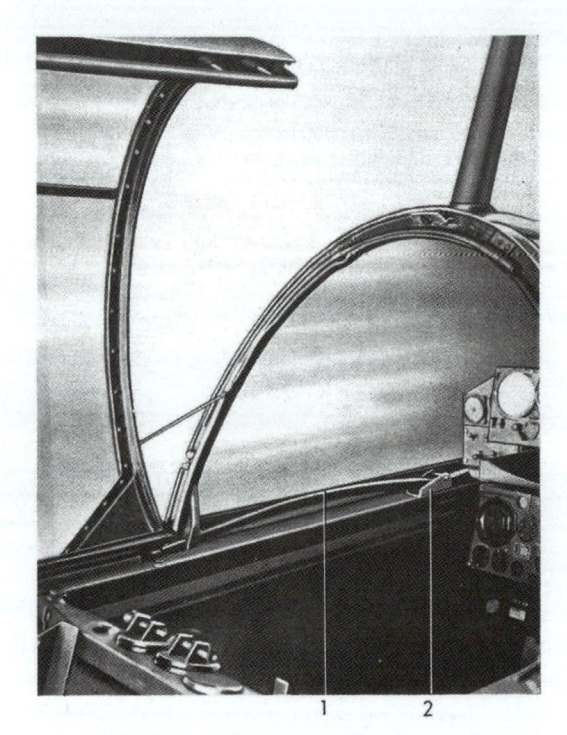

Here is a closer look at the tension spring (1), situated on the starboard side of the rear cockpit sill, for the hinged canopy section – '2' is the securing bracket

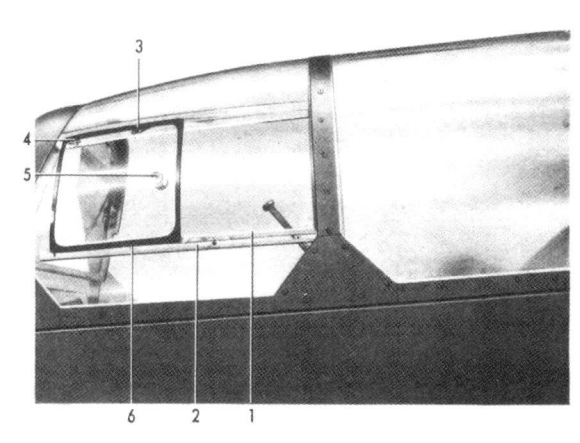

Group 1 – Side 9
Fuselage
Canopy

This photo from the manual shows the sliding panel in the port forward section of the main canopy. The keyed items are as follows: 1. Gleitschienen (Slides); 2. Plexiglasleisten (Perspex strips); 3. Blattfedern (Leaf spring); 4. Anschlag (Stop); 5, Griffknopf (Handle Knob); 6. Linsenschrauben (Glass Screws)

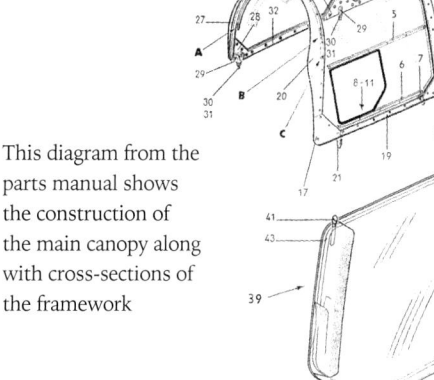

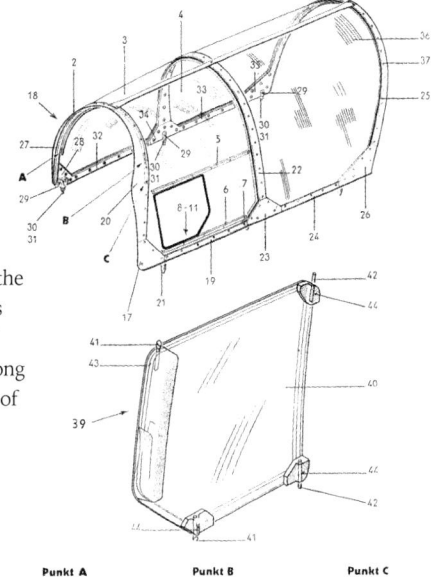

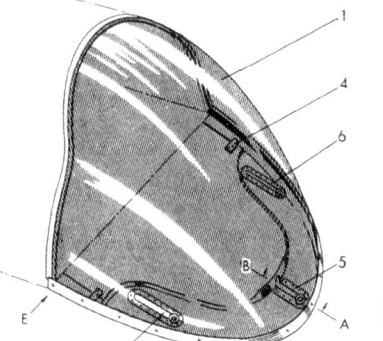

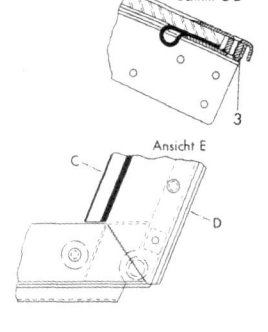

This diagram from the parts manual shows the construction of the main canopy along with cross-sections of the framework

This diagram from the parts manual shows the construction of the windscreen glazing and framework. The keyed items are as follows: 1. Verglasung (Glazing); 2. Randprofil (Edge Profile); 3. Randleiste mit Gummi (Edge with rubber); 4. Halter (Holder); 5. Vordere Lasche (Front Flap); 6. Seitliche Laschen (Lateral Tabs); 7. Befestigungsschrauben (Mounting Screws)

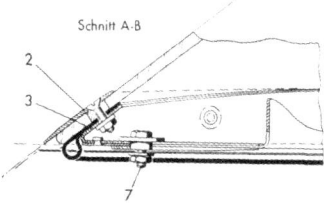

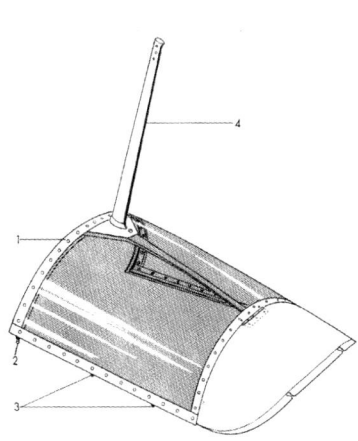

This diagram from the parts manual shows the construction of the rear glazing and framework. The keyed items are as follows: 1. Metallrahmen (Metal Frame); 2. Verschlußstücke (Closure): 3. Führungsstifte (Guide Pins): 4. Antennenmast (Antenna Mast)

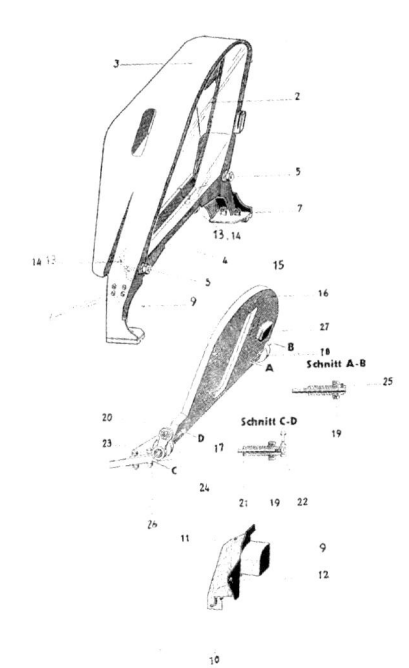

This parts manual diagram shows the construction of the forward canopy framework containing the armoured glass, as well as the separate 'blast shield' armour plate

This period image shows the armoured windscreen in more detail
1. Armoured windscreen
2. Sheet metal frame
3. Mounting holes for windscreen
4. Windshield wiper

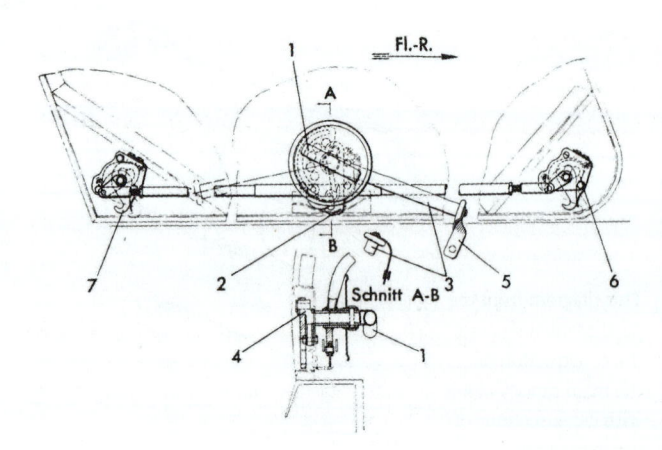

Group 1 – Side 10
Fuselage
Canopy

This diagram shows the operation of the canopy release wheel fitted to the port mid-canopy sill interior. The keyed items are as follows:
1. Handgriff (Handle); 2 Haken mit Anschlag (Hooks with stopper); 3. Doppelhebel mit Segment (Segment with double lever); 4. Kurbelwelle (Crankshaft); 5. Lederschlaufe mit Druckknopf (Leather strap with push button); 6. Vorderes Schloß (Front lock); 7. Hinteres Schloß (Rear lock)

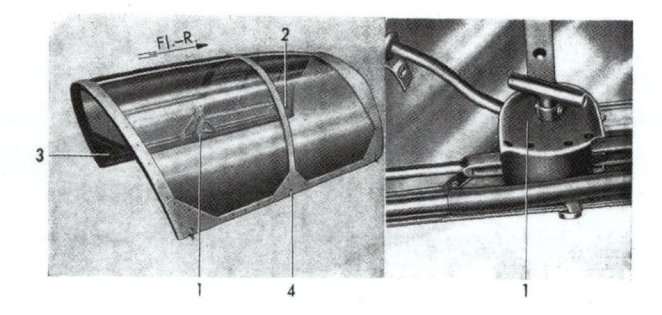

This is canopy release lever in NASM's example. the sliding (ventilation) panel forward of this in the canopy means that in an emergency this lever could be reached from outside plus groundcrew could open the canopy from outside as well (©S. Willey)

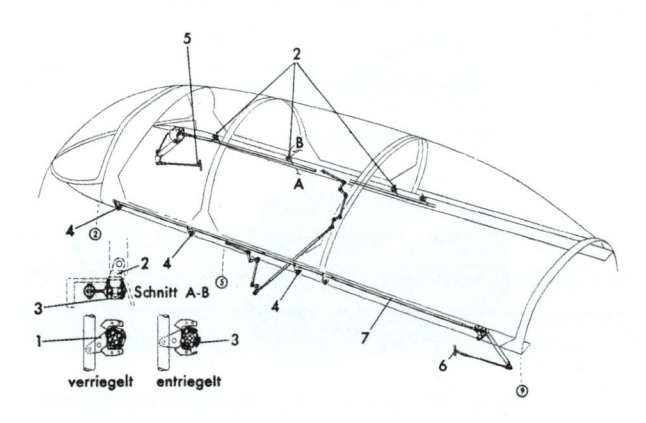

Oddly, in the manual, the style of the canopy release lever is quite different. This is from the A-0 manual, although the canopy style is the later one with the single ventilation panel in the port side, so at some stage in late A-0 or early A-2 production, this system was revised/simplified to that seen in NASM's A-2
1. Middle lock
2. Front lock
3. Rear lock
4. Hinge eyes

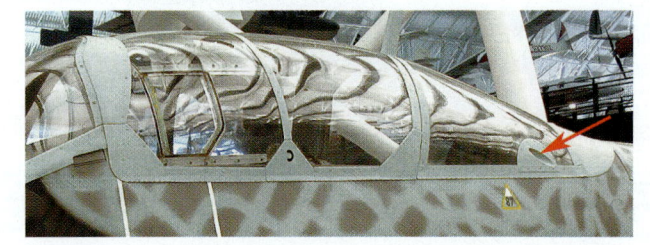

Here is an overall diagram of the canopy release system
1. Lever
2. Hinge eyes
3. Closures
4. Hook
5. Operation T-handle for the pilot
6. Operation T-handle for the observer

This shot of the port side of the canopy of the NASM example shows the sliding panel that is only on this side, plus (arrowed) the flare port (©S. Willey)

This shot just shows the difference in the canopy shape etc. on the early prototype machines. Note the 'hump' to the rear of the canopy and the arc-shaped framework you can see inside, this was for the planned rearward-facing machine-gun, but this was deleted early on in development

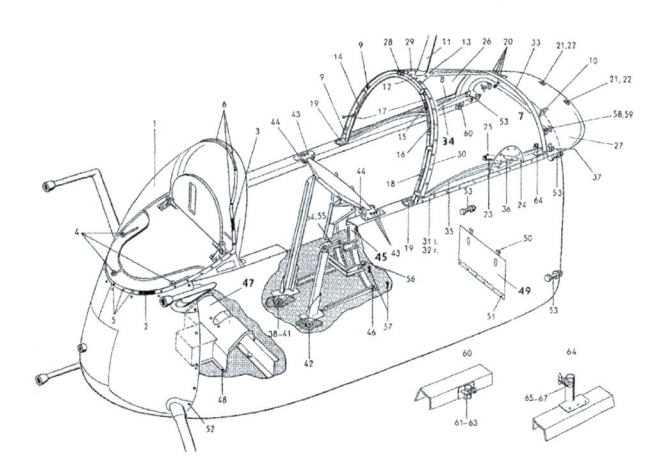

Group 1 – Side 11
Fuselage
Nose Section

This diagram from the parts manual shows the construction of the nose section with all the fixings and latches in that area. Items 24 & 25 are the flare port

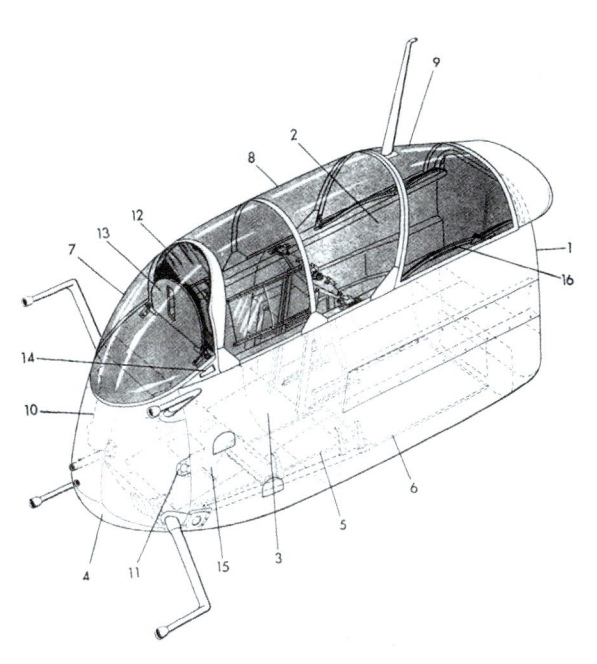

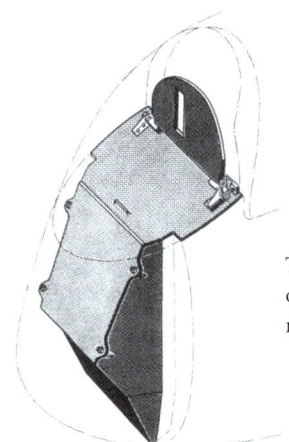

This diagram shows the shape of the armour plate box in the nose area

This diagram is a general overview of the cockpit/forward nose area. The keyed items are as follows:

1. Kanzelseitenwand, links (Cockpit sidewall, left)
2. Kanzelseitenwand, rechts (Cockpit sidewall, right)
3. Fußboden (Floor)
4. Kanzelspitze (Nose cone)
5. Bugradklappe, vorn (Nose wheel door, front)
6. Bugradklappe, hinten (Nose wheel door, rear)
7. Glashaube, vorn (Glass cover, front)
8. Einstiegklappe (Access hatch)
9. Glashaube, hinten (Glass cover, rear)
10. Bugpanzerung (Armour plate)
11. Halterung für Außenbordanschluß (Outboard bracket for connecting [e.g. jacking point])
12. Panzerscheibe (Armour disc)
13. Klappbare Panzerblende (Folding armour plate)
14. Griffklappe (Handle flap)
15. Abdeckblech für Steuerung (Cover plate for control)
16. Abwurffeder für Glashaube (Spring discharge for glass cover [i.e. canopy release springs])

Here is a more detailed image of the armoured nose section

1. Upper panel (covered)
2. Front plate, upper
3. Front plate, lower
4. Side panel
5. Connection plate
6. Fastening screws for nose cone
7. Cover plate

Whilst being put up on its wheels, NASM's A-2 had the nose cone and windscreen removed, allowing you to see the armoured section in more detail (©S. Willey)

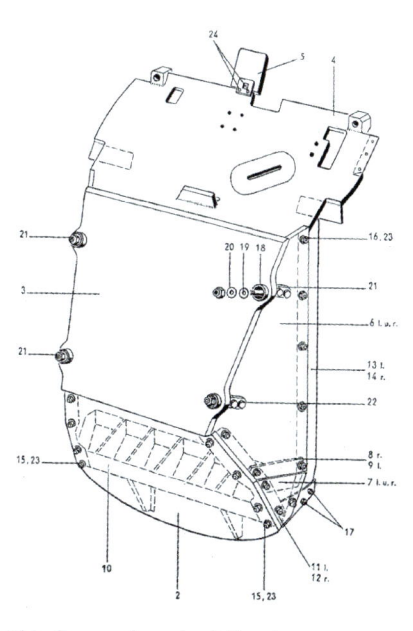

This diagram from the A-7-series parts manual allows you to see each element of the armoured nose in detail

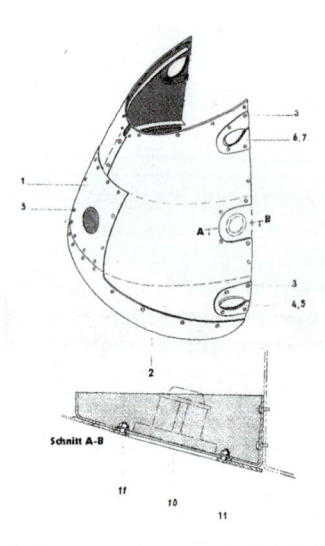

Fuselage
Nose Section
Group 1 – Side 12

This diagram shows the construction of the nose cone, as well as external electric socket mounting point (marked 'Schnitt A-B')

This photo of the fuselage in deep storage before any renovation work started, does highlight the jacking pick-up point, as well as the cold air intake
(©S. Willey)

This head-on shot of the now-restored fuselage does show just how slender the He 219 was. The yellow object is most likely a de-icer spray nozzle, although it is not shown in any period parts manual diagrams?
(©S. Willey)

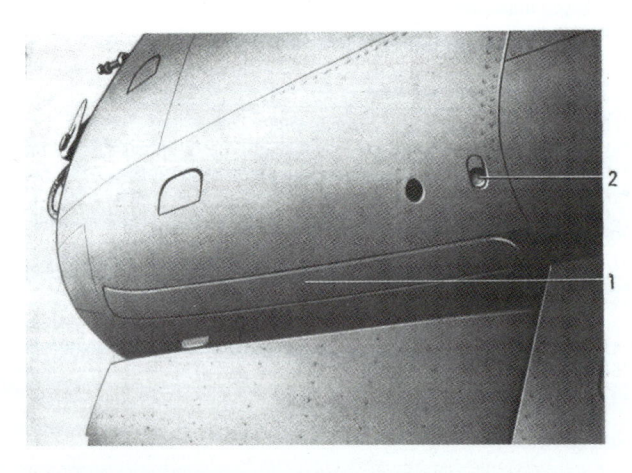

This period image shows the access ladder installed in the port side of the forward fuselage. The keyed items are as follows: 1. Einstiegsleiter (Ladder); 2. Drücker (Handle)

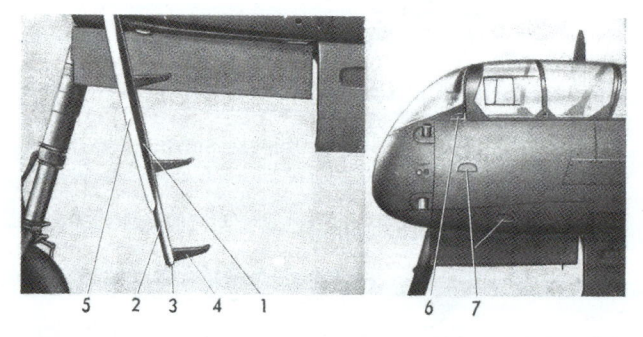

These two images from the A-0 flight manual shows the access ladder and hand/footsteps in detail

1. Ladder, upper part
2. Extension strut
3. Locking pin
4. Rungs
5. Outer cover
6. Hand-hold (flap)
7. Climbing steps (flap)

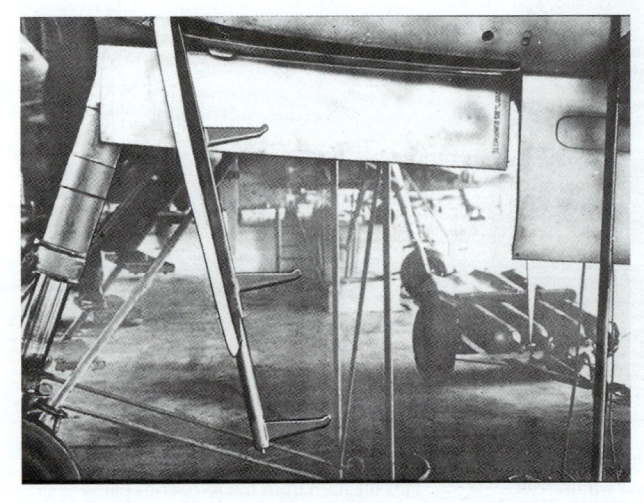

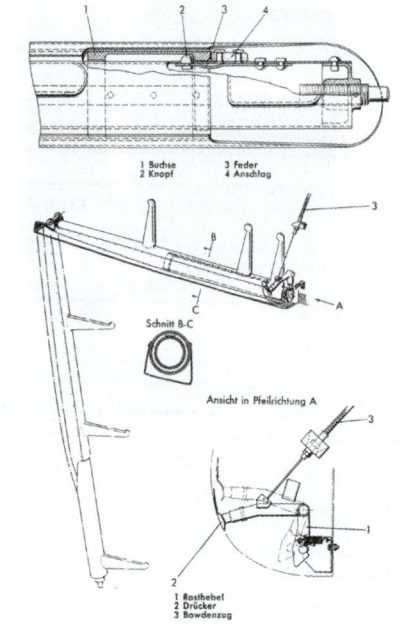

This period diagram shows the construction of the access ladder in the port side of the forward fuselage. The keyed items are as follows: 1. Rasthebel (Locking lever); 2. Drücker (Handle); 3. Bowdenzug (Bowden {cable})

This period image show the ladder extended and comes from a series of images of the A-0 series, but still applied to all variants

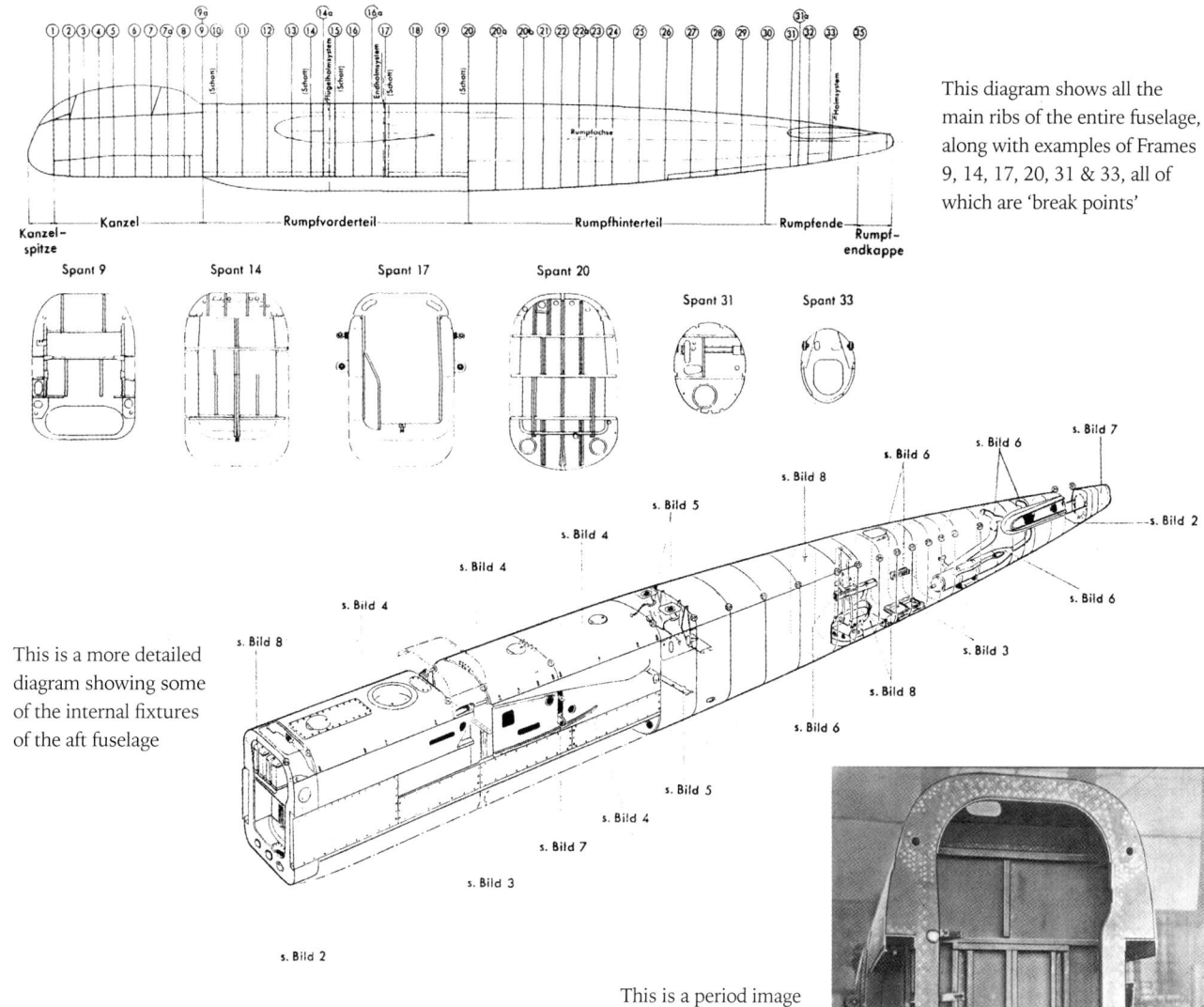

Group 1 – Side 13
Fuselage
Main & Aft

This diagram shows all the main ribs of the entire fuselage, along with examples of Frames 9, 14, 17, 20, 31 & 33, all of which are 'break points'

This is a more detailed diagram showing some of the internal fixtures of the aft fuselage

This is a period image of Frame 9, the break point between the mid-fuselage and nose section

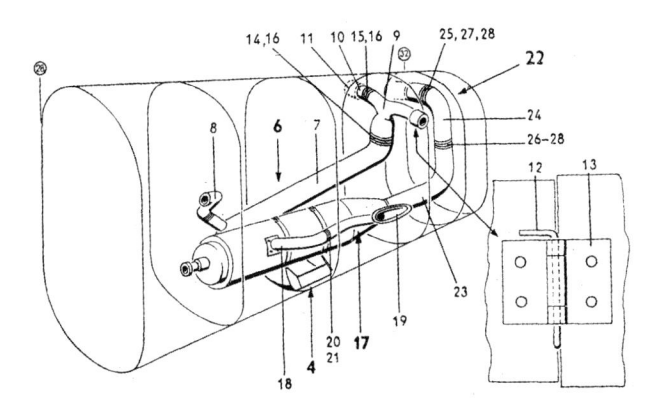

This diagram shows the BLO 30/U fuselage heating and tailplane de-icing unit in the rear fuselage

This is a detailed period image of the BLO 30/U heater unit

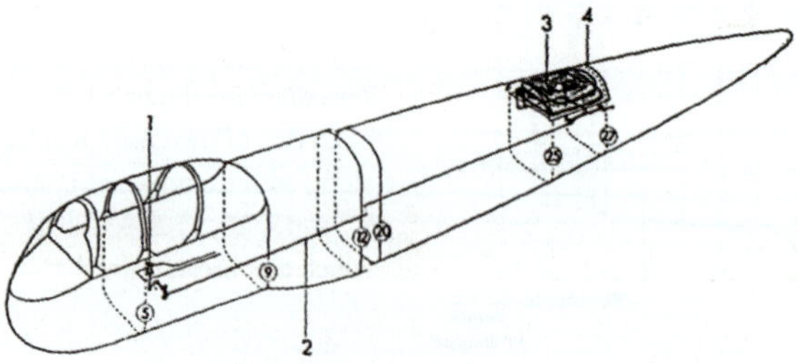

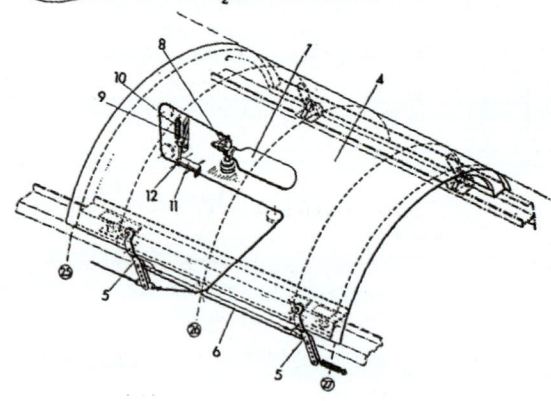

Group 1 – Side 14
Fuselage
Main & Aft

This diagram shows the placement between frames 25 and 27 of the rescue dinghy

1. Handle
2. Cable
3. Compartment with dinghy
4. Lid
5. Locking latch
6. Connecting rod
7. Carbon dioxide bottle
8. Opening lever
9. Cutting blade
10. Mainspring
11. Locking plate
12. Cams

A quick look at the wing root area, this is the port side, forward section and you can see the hole straight through the fuselage for the wing spar box *(©S. Willey)*

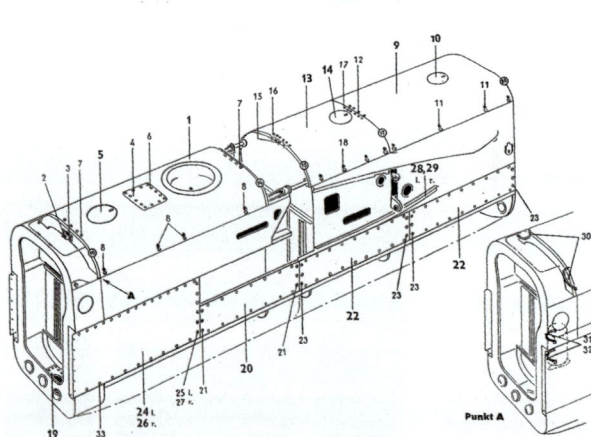

This diagram from the parts manual shows the mid-section between frames 9 and 20

This shot shows the rear section of the port wing root area, with the aft spar pick-up attachment prominent *(©S. Willey)*

In each fuselage side there is a cable duct, this period image shows the one on the port side

1. Pipelines
2. Control rods for elevation and rudder control
3. Control rods for elevator, rudder and trim tab
4. Engine linkages and cables

Here is the cable duct in the starboard fuselage side

1. Aileron control rods
2. Pressure-tight feed-throughs

Fuselage
Main & Aft

Group 1 – Side 15

Here is the whole wing root area on the starboard side viewed from the back *(©S. Willey)*

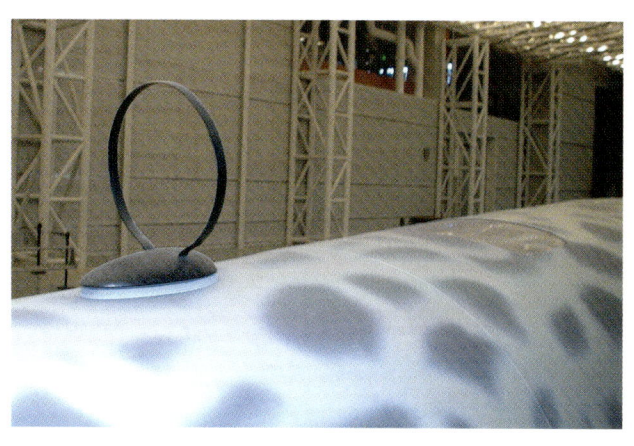

Here is the DF loop on the rear dorsal spine. The clear panel forward of it is for the jump seat in the rear fuselage – this was not fitted to all He 219As *(©S. Willey)*

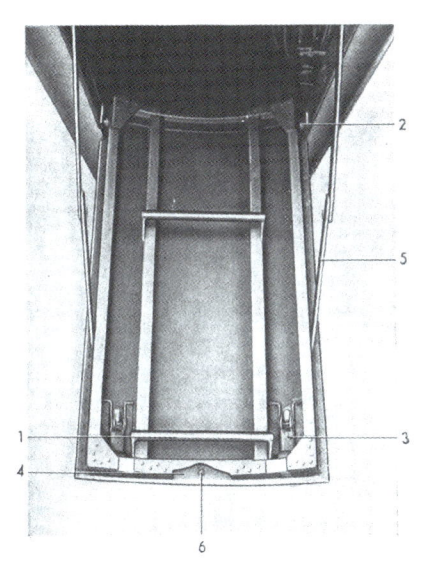

This is the access hatch in the underside of the fuselage on NASM's A-2
1. Ladder steps
2. Bearing fittings with bearing bolts
3. Latches
4. Flap fitting
5. Holding rods
6. Bolt

Directly below the DF loop in the fuselage underside is this access hatch *(©S. Willey)*

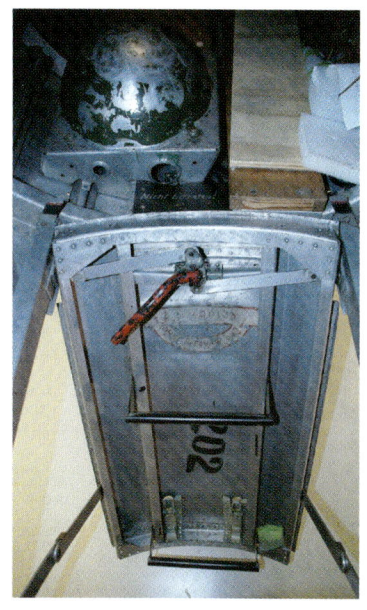

This is the interior of the hatch *(©S. Willey)*

From the hatch, if you turn round and look back you will see the BLO 30/U heater unit and its pipework *(©S. Willey)*

This is the main body of the BLO 30/U heater *(©S. Willey)*

Group 1 – Side 16
Fuselage
Main & Aft

If you turn around and look forward from the hatch, this is what you see. The units to the right are navigational and electrical equipment, the compressed air bottles either side further forward are the charging units for the Schräge Musik installation, as are the boxes on the far bulkhead (they are ammo bins, plus you can make out the ammo chutes in the middle and on either side), but in this machine the guns themselves are not fitted *(©S. Willey)*

Here is a look at the electrical boxes on the starboard side – you can see one clearly marked as 'FuG 220' *(©S. Willey)*

Here is the simple 'jump seat' just forward of the ventral hatch
1. Base
2. Panel to which the waist belt is fastened
3. Waist belt
4. Seat board
5. Back strap

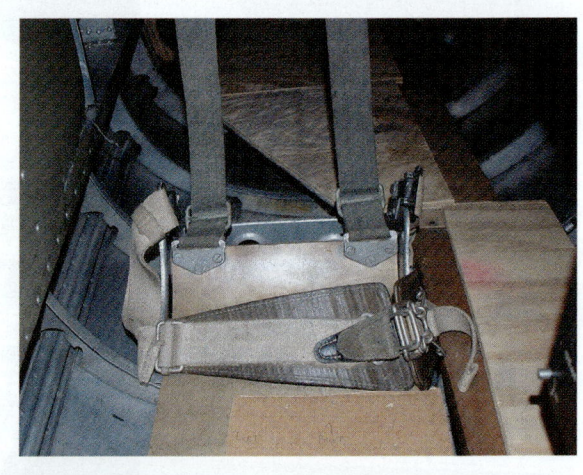

This is the simple 'jump seat' in NASM's example *(©S. Willey)*

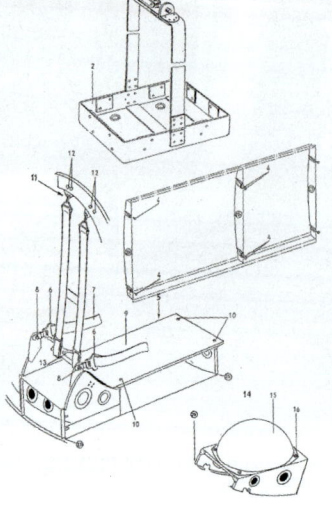

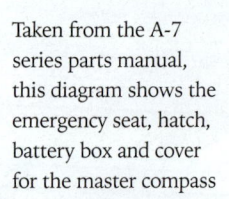

Taken from the A-7 series parts manual, this diagram shows the emergency seat, hatch, battery box and cover for the master compass

If you look straight up and forward from the ventral hatch you can see the clear panel in the dorsal spine (not a standard fitment, but you can just make it out in some period images), plus the mounts for the jump seat shoulder straps *(©S. Willey)*

Group 1 – Side 17
Fuselage
Main & Aft

Although not shown on any post-war cutaways of the type, the NASM machine has this large bowl just forward of the escape hatch, it should cover a repeater compass, hence the 'keep off' (Nicht Betreten!) marking (©S. Willey)

This montaged image shows you the area on the starboard fuselage side, directly alongside and slightly forward of the ventral access hatch (©S. Willey)

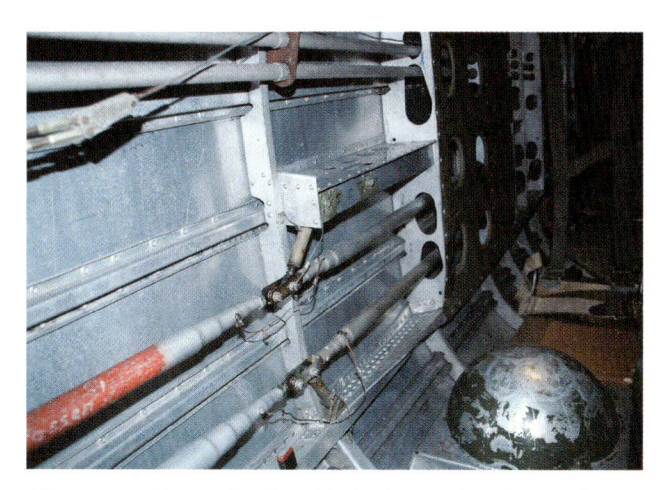

All you get on the port fuselage side, in the same location, are these control rod runs (©S. Willey)

The control rods continue to run further aft on the port fuselage side (©S. Willey)

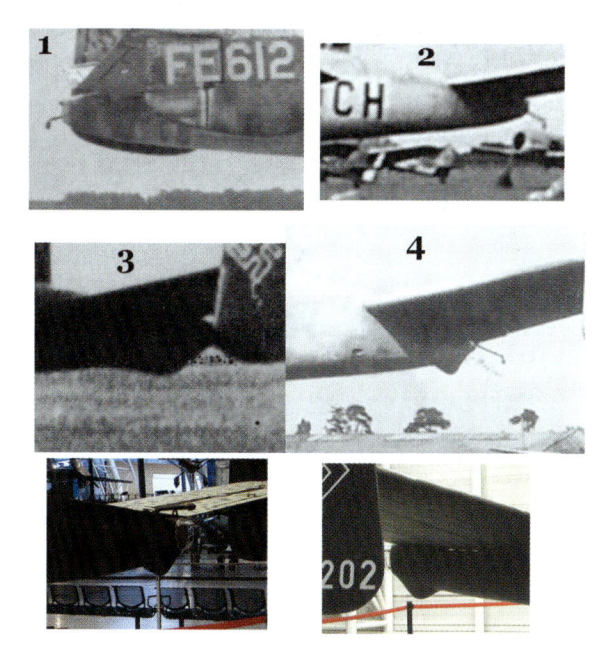

One thing to note about the He 219A is with regard the underside of the rear fuselage, as some machines have the bulge of the bumper unit in this location, while others do not and there seems no rhyme or reason to this. Our montaged images consist of photo 1 He 219A-0, W/Nr.210903 and photo 2 He 219A-2, W/Nr.290070, neither of which have the tail bumper, while photo 3 is the He 219 V1, and photo 4 is He 219A-7, W/Nr.310189 both with the bulge. If you are now thinking that the A-0 and A-2 lacked the bulge, while the prototypes and A-7 had it, think again as the bottom row shows NASM's He 219A-2, W/Nr. 290202, which has the bulge- confusing or what!

Group 2 – Side 1
Undercarriage 1
40 | Nose Wheel

A period image from the A-0 series manual that shows the front (1) and rear (2) nose wheel doors

Here is an overall view of the nose leg, wheel and doors of the A-2 preserved by NASM
(©S. Willey)

This period photo shows the forward (narrow) nose wheel undercarriage door, viewed from the front

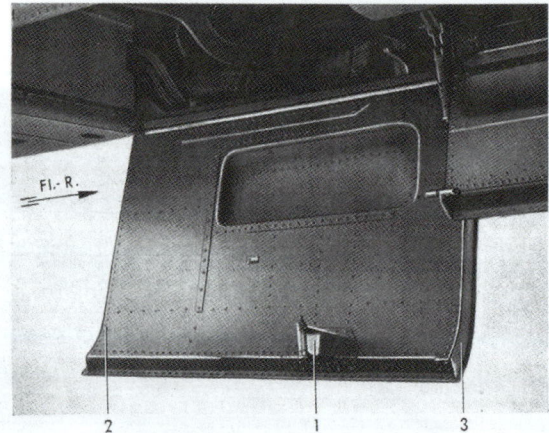

This is the larger, rear nose wheel door
1. Locking bracket
2. Front edge
3. Rear edge

This diagram from the A-7 series parts manual shows the two nose wheel doors in detail

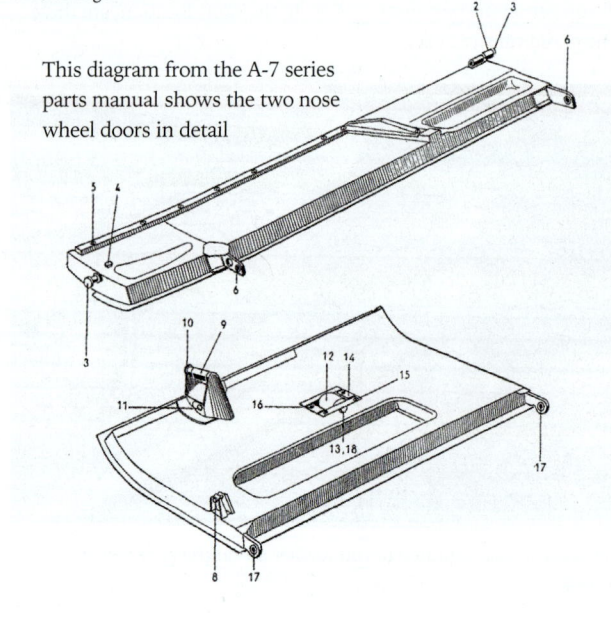

This shows the rear nose wheel door's attachment and operating system
1. Strut
2. Wire rope (closure)
3. Wire rope tensioner
4. Attachment of the closure strut (the wire on the cam visible in the middle of this strut, is operated by the wire that also closes the front door)

Group 2 – Side 2
Undercarriage
Nose Wheel

The front nose wheel door is closed via a wire and pulley system, as seen in this diagram, with the lower one showing how the 'up' lock is linked via a switch to the indicator unit (2) in the instrument panel in the cockpit

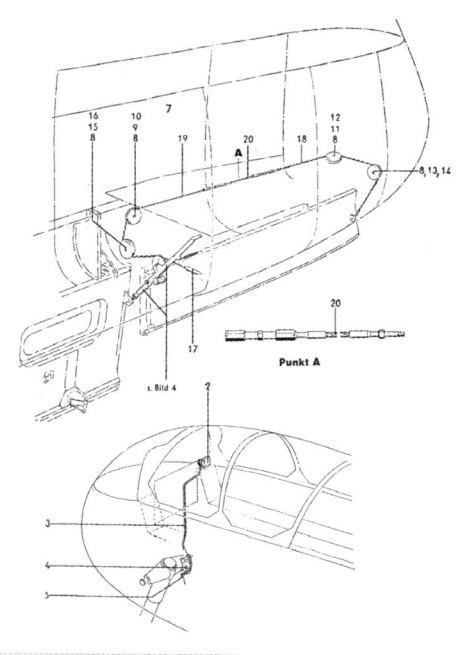

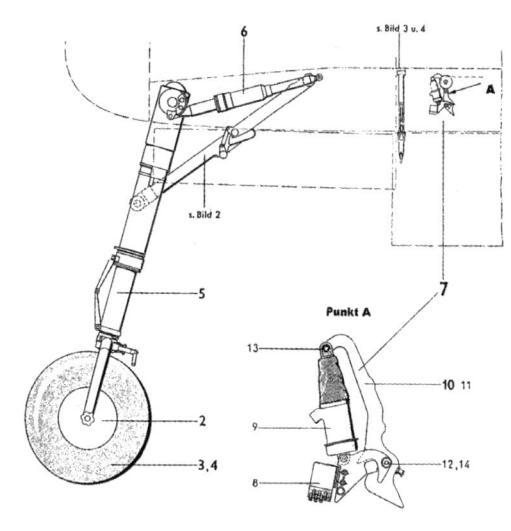

The item marked as 'Punkt A' is the lock for the nose wheel strut, which links with the unit that projects above the wheel on the yoke. This also shows the cylinder (6) that retracts the nose oleo.

Here is a period image showing the 'up lock' seen in the previous diagram as 'Punkt A'
1. Lower locking hook
2. Upper locking hook
3. Locking cylinder
4. Signal switch
5. Emergency release wire

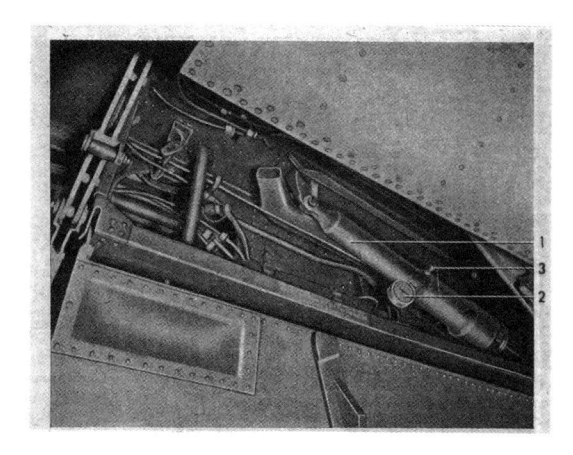

The shows the pneumatic cylinder fitted in the front section of the bay roof, that is used to extend the nose wheel in an emergency
1. Lifting cylinder
2. Pressure gauge
3. Compressed air filling valve

This period photograph shows the nose oleo and wheel, viewed from the starboard side. Going by the radar antenna masts and the black overall scheme, this is probably one of the initial prototypes (V1 through V4) as the V5 & V6 had different radar supports

This shot of the nose oleo and wheel was probably taken at the same time as the well-known 'assembly stage' images, so this is an early A-0 series machine. Note the two black maker's plates mid-oleo

AA01/12/41 — Valiant Wings Publishing — Issued: July 2021

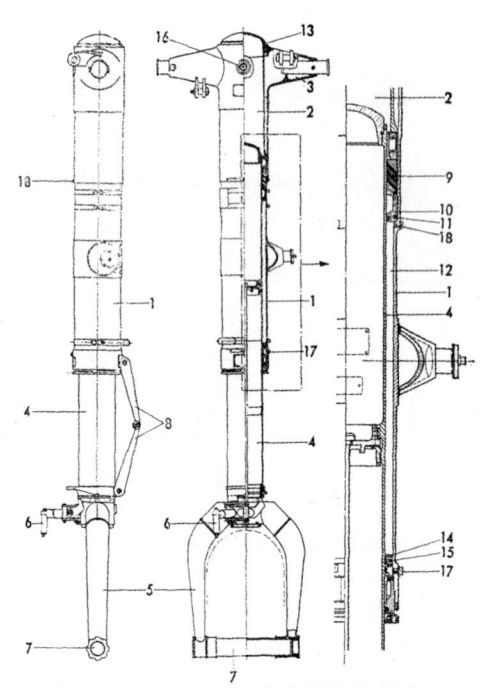

Group 2 – Side 3
Undercarriage 1
Nose Wheel

This diagrams shows the construction of the nose wheel oleo strut

1. Cylinder
2. Space for compressed air
3. Crossmember
4. Piston rod
5. Wheel fork
6. Lug for locking unit in wheel well roof
7. Wheel axle
8. Compression linkage
9. Packing (seal)
10. Lower pressure ring
11. Oval cuff ring
12. Expansion compartment
13. Screw ring
14. Throttle (feed) ring
15. Piston ring
16. Filling valve for compressed air
17. Filling valve for oil
18. Vent screw

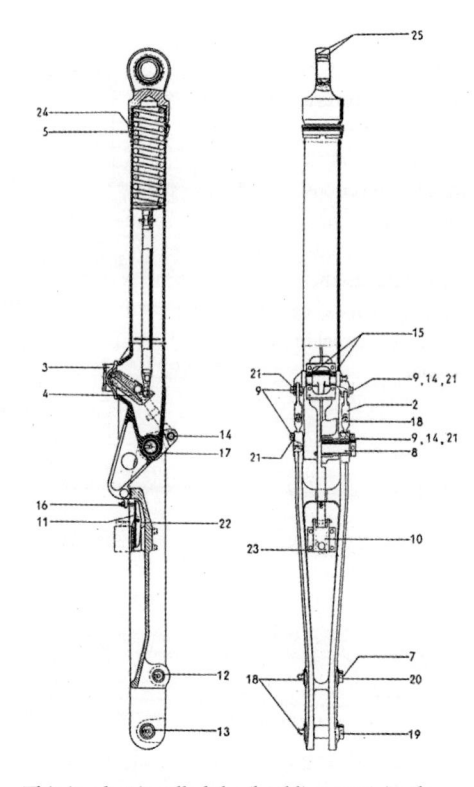

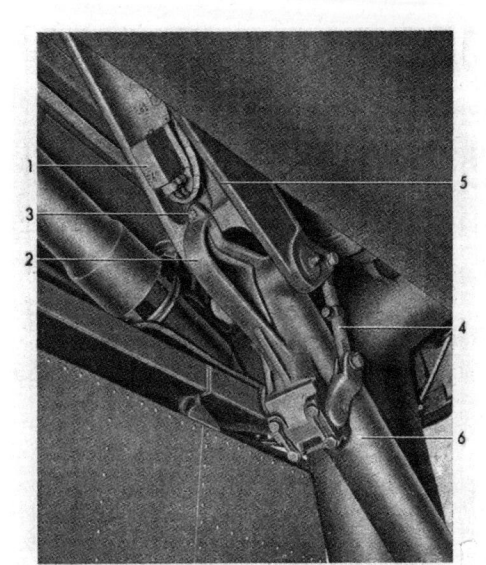

At the top of the 'buckling strut' you have various linkage and controls

1. Signal switch
2. Actuating lever for signal switch
3. Adjustment screw
4. Buckling strut lever rod
5. Upper buckling strut
6. Lower buckling strut

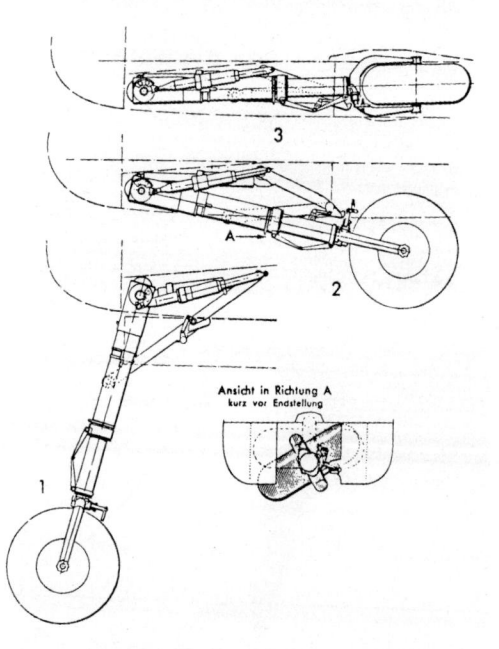

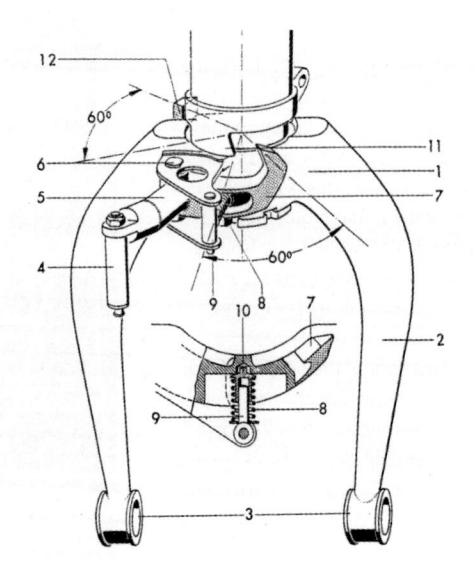

This is what is called the 'buckling arm', its the linkage arm that hinges as the oleo leg retracts backwards

This diagram from the Flight Handbook shows the construction and movement limitations to the nose wheel yoke. The keyed items are as follows: 1. Gabelkopf (Clevis); 2, Gabelrohr (Fork tube); 3. Achslager (Axle position); 4. Führungsrolle (Towing pick-up); 5. Hebel (Lever); 6. Gelenkbolzen (Hinge Pin); 7. Rasthaken (Latching hooks); 8. Feder (Spring); 9. Bolzen (Bolt); 10 Federteller (Spring Plate); 11. Anschlag an der Kolbenstange (Stop on the piston rod); 12. Anschlagstück (Stop piece)

This period diagram shows the retraction method for the nose oleo on the He 219. The keyed items are as follows: Bugfahrwerk ausgefahred (Nose gear extended); Bugfahrwerk halb eingefahred (Führungsrolle trifft auf Führung im Rumpf) (Nose gear retracted half [Guide roller hits guide in the fuselage]); Bugfahrwerk eingefahren (Nose gear retracted). Ansicht in Richtung A, kurz vor Endstellung (View in direction A, just before final position)

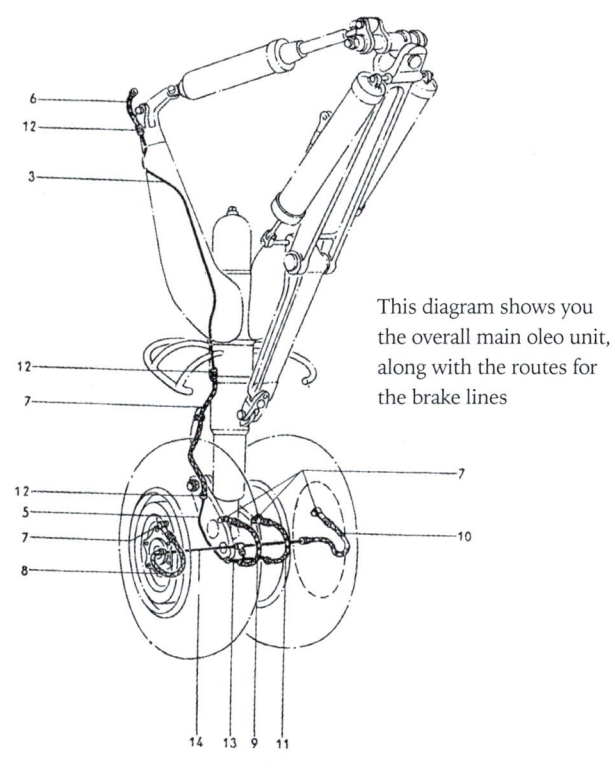

Group 2 – Side 4
Undercarriage
Main

This diagram shows you the overall main oleo unit, along with the routes for the brake lines

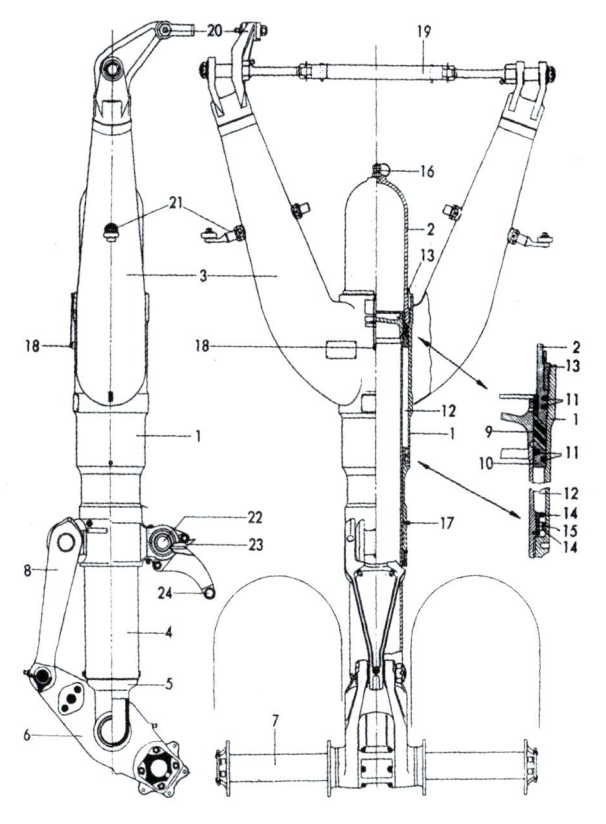

This diagram shows the construction of the main oleo leg.

1. Zylinder (Cylinder); 2. Lufttopf (Air pot); 3. Arm; 4. Kolbenstange (Piston rod); 5. Achskreuzstück (Axle piece); 6. Schwinge (Swing arm); 7. Radachse (Wheel axle); 8. Lenker (Link); 9 Packung (Gasket); 10. Oberer Druckring (upper thrust ring); 11. Ovalringmanschette (Oval collar); 12. Fettraum (Oil chamber); 13. Schraubring (Threaded ring); 14. Drosselring (Restrictor ring); 15. Kolbenring (Piston ring); 16. Füllventil für Preßluft (Charging valve for compressed air); 17 Füllventil für fett (Filler valve for grease {grease nipple}); 18. Entlüftungsschraube (Bleed screw); 19 Zugstange (Tie rod); 20. Anschluß für Einfahrzylinder (Connector for control linkage); 21. Rollenhalter (Roller holder); 22. Anschluß für Knickstrebe (Connecting rod for articulating); 23. Seilführungsrille (cable guide groove); 24. Rastbolzen (Locking bolt)

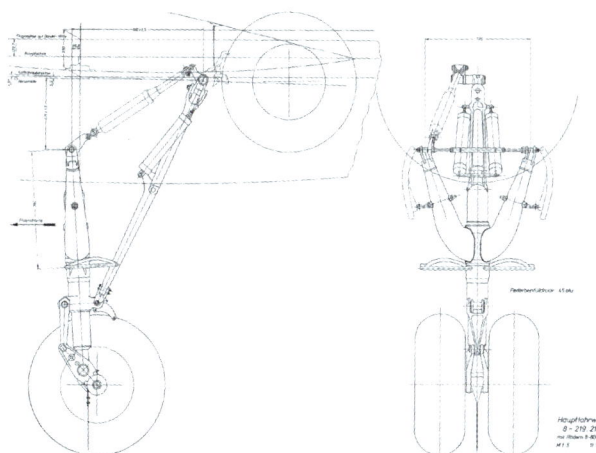

This period diagram shows all the geometry of the main undercarriage unit

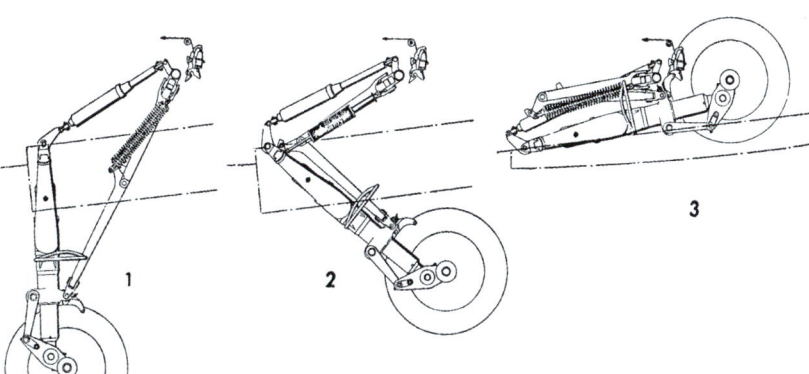

This diagram shows the retraction procedure for the main undercarriage leg. . The keyed items are as follows: Fahrwerk ausgefahred (Landing gear extended); Fahrwerk beim Einfahren (Landing gear during retraction); Fahrwerk eingefahren (Landing gear retracted)

Here is the main body of the oleo unit during restoration (©S. Willey)

Group 2 – Side 5
Undercarriage 1
44 | Main

This period image shows the axles with the wheels removed, as well as the brake pipework

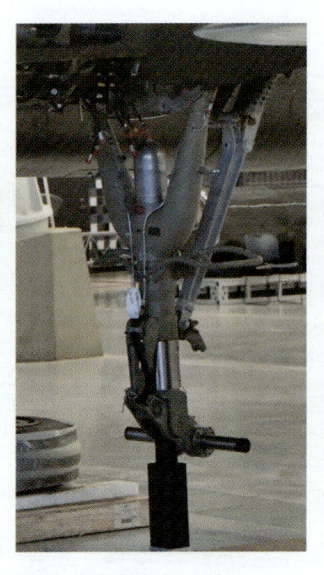

Whilst NASM's example was being put back on its wheels in 2019, this afforded a good overall view of the main oleo struts, retraction 'buckle' arm, wheel guards etc. (©S. Willey)

Here is the completely restored main oleo of the NASM He 219 viewed from the front (©S. Willey)

This is the rear of the restored main oleo unit (©S. Willey)

This period image shows the whole main oleo leg with the wheels etc. all in situ; note the route of the brake lines down the front of the strut and the tabs on the top of each leg that align with the corresponding tabs on each undercarriage door to keep the latter in position when open

This period image shows a main oleo installed in the nacelle, but with the doors removed, so you can see the linkage and springs in the back

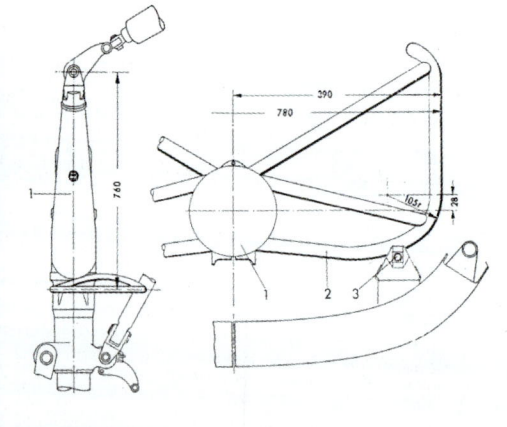

The He 219 only had partial mudguards, which were made up of a framework as seen here. The keyed items are as follows: 1. Luftfederbein (Air shock); 2. Führungsbügel (Guide brackets); 3. Gleitrolle an Fahrwerkklappe (Sliding roller to the suspension damper).

This montaged shot shows the original main wheel on the left, and the restored one on the right. The stencils around the rim read – *'Rad nicht teilen bevor Reifen luftleer!'* ('Wheel must be deflated prior to dismantling'), *'Rad ausgewuchtet'* ('Wheel balanced') and *'Reifendruck 4.2 atü'* ('Tyre pressure of 4.2 atmospheres' = approx. 61.7psi)

Undercarriage

Main

Group 2 – Side 6 — 45

This image and diagram shows the spring units in the back of the main undercarriage unit

1. Sleeve
2. Connection head
3. Threaded sleeve
4. Compression spring
5. Plate washer
6. Compression bar
7. Tie rod head
8. Clamping bush
9. Upper part of 'buckling' strut
10. Retraction cylinder

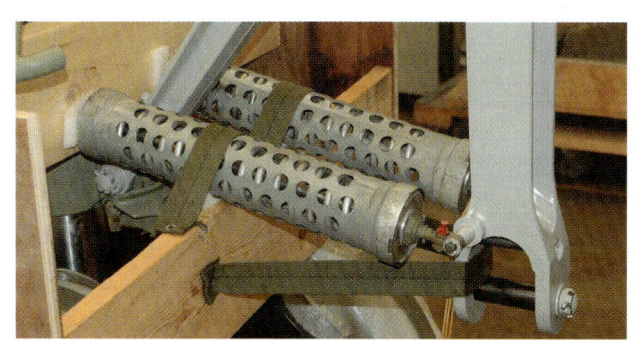

Here is a close-up of the spring units in the back of the main oleo leg (©S. Willey)

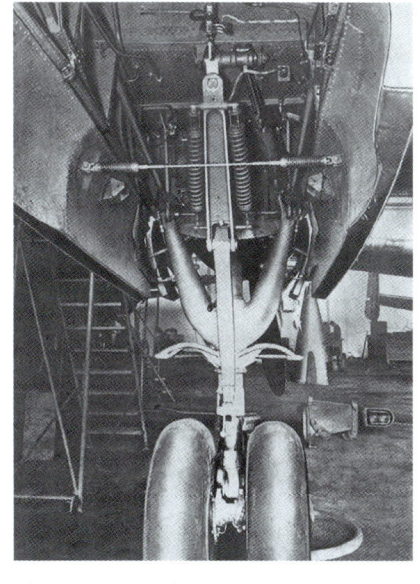

This is a period image of the spring units behind each main undercarriage leg

This overall period image shows the main strut, springs, retraction jack and linkage for each of the main doors, the bar between these two latter items is what the oleo strikes to pull the doors closed (the springs on each end giving the unit enough 'give' to bend around the leg once the doors fully close)

This overall period image of the starboard main undercarriage bay and leg of He 219A-2, W/Nr.290004, G9+DH found wrecked at Paderborn by US forces in May 1945 does afford quite a lot of information about undercarriage bay roof etc. not normally visible in most images

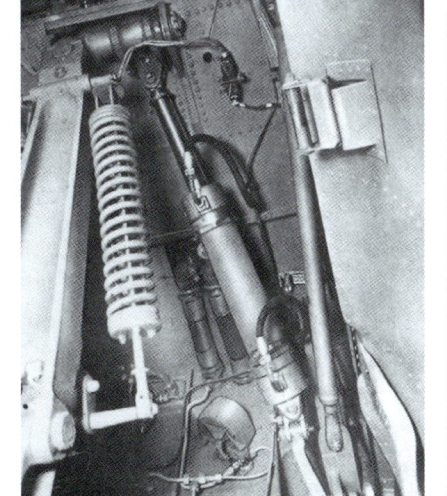

This is a closer look at the cylinder that retracts the main leg and is situated outboard in both bays

If you want to know what stops the He 219, these are the brake shoes and hydraulic cams from the main wheels (©S. Willey)

Group 2 – Side 7
Undercarriage
Main

An odd angle, this shot nonetheless shows the whole nacelle interior of the port wing during restoration. The front half is for the engine, only the rear bit (which is the middle once the aft nacelle is added) relates to the undercarriage. The arrowed area will be seen in the next image (©S. Willey)

This is the area arrowed in the previous photo, it is the front bulkhead of the main u/c bay in the port wing after restoration (©S. Willey)

Here is a period image of the outer side of the main undercarriage bay, note the cylinder seen in the previous image to orientate yourself

This is a closer look at the outer corner of the port u/c bay front bulkhead. The tank is marked 'Einspritz-Behälter Intava-Einspritz' (Fuel injection tank – has fuel injection) and the arrowed item we will see in more detail in the next image (©S. Willey)

Here is the cover arrowed in the previous image, the label reads 'Nachdem Einspritzen Sicherungs deckel umlegen' (After injecting, secure cover by folding over) (©S. Willey)

Further back on the outer edge of the u/c bay is one of these oil filtration units (©S. Willey)

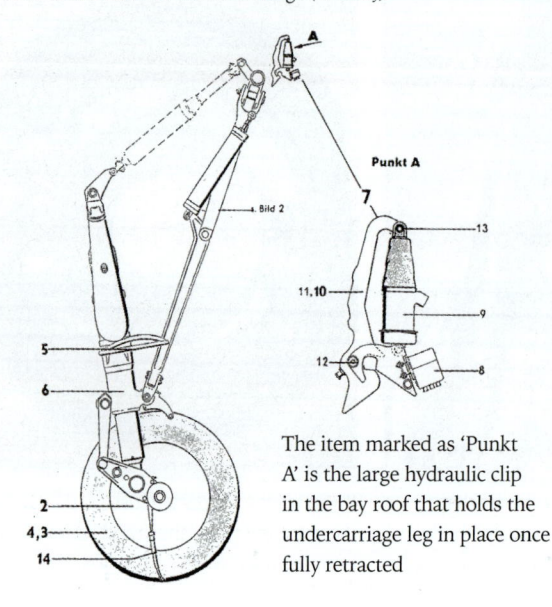

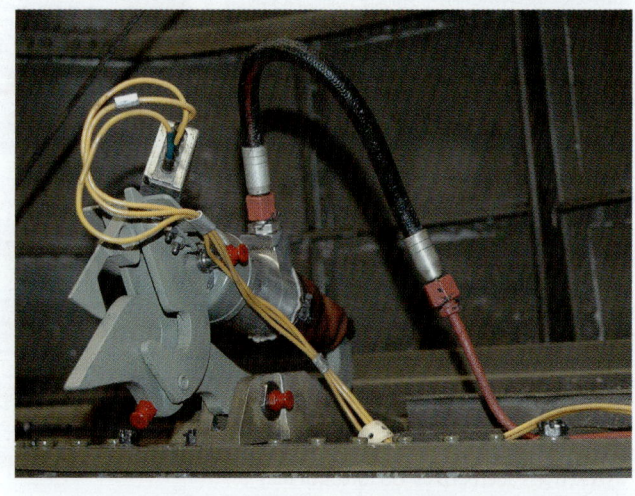

The item marked as 'Punkt A' is the large hydraulic clip in the bay roof that holds the undercarriage leg in place once fully retracted

Here is a close look at the hydraulic 'up lock', the wiring relates to the switch that operates the indicator in the cockpit to tell the pilot if the wheels are up or down (©S. Willey)

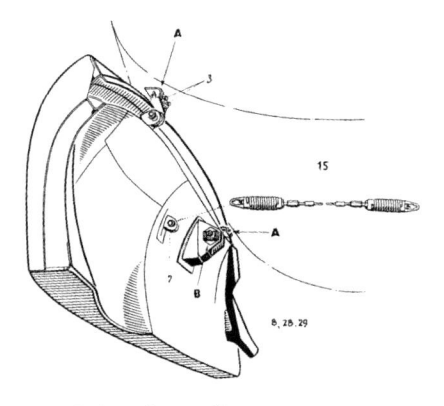

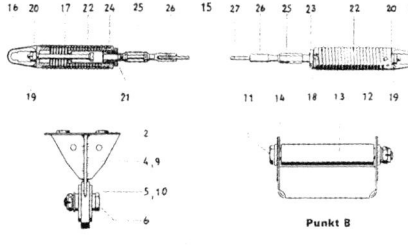

Group 2 – Side 8
Undercarriage 1
Main 47

This diagram from the parts manual shows the construction of the left main u/c door, along with the hinges and wire that closes them

While this shows the construction of the right main u/c door, along with the hinges and wire that closes them

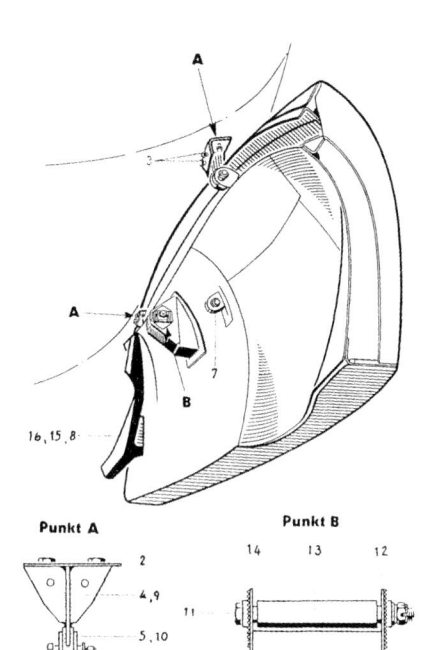

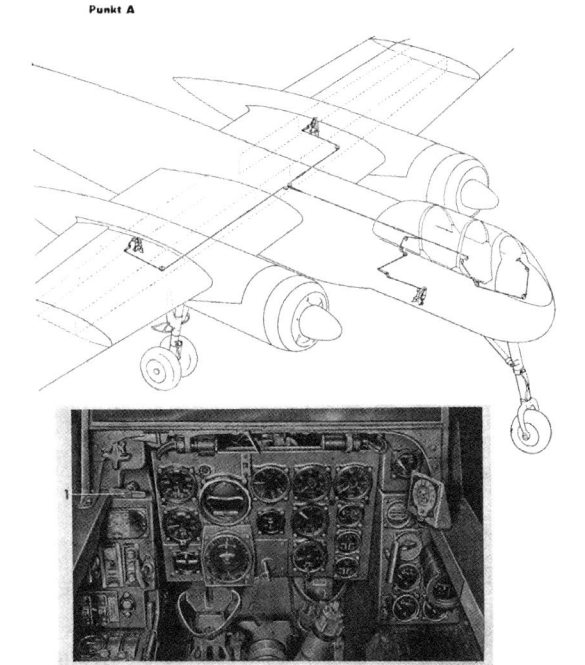

This shows all the various controls and instruments relating to the undercarriage in the cockpit
1. Landing gear switch
2. Emergency (release) handle
3. Compressed air valve for emergency extension of the nose gear
4. Mechanical display device for position of the nose gear

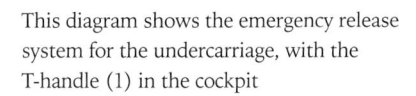

This diagram shows the emergency release system for the undercarriage, with the T-handle (1) in the cockpit

The position of the undercarriage is shown via this twelve-light unit that is mounted above the landing gear switch (1) in the previous image, on the port side of the instrument panel; note that similar lights for the position of the landing flaps can be seen on the righthand side of the unit
1. Signal lamp for the starboard undercarriage
2. Signal lamp for the port undercarriage
3. Signal lamp for the nose oleo

If you wonder where all the hydraulic power comes from, this is the accumulator and it is situated in the fuselage, between frame 9 and the first fuel cell – this is a view from the top looking down

AA01/12/47 Valiant Wings Publishing Issued: July 2021

Group 3 – Side 1
Tail
Tailplanes

This shows all the linkage for the elevators and trim tabs

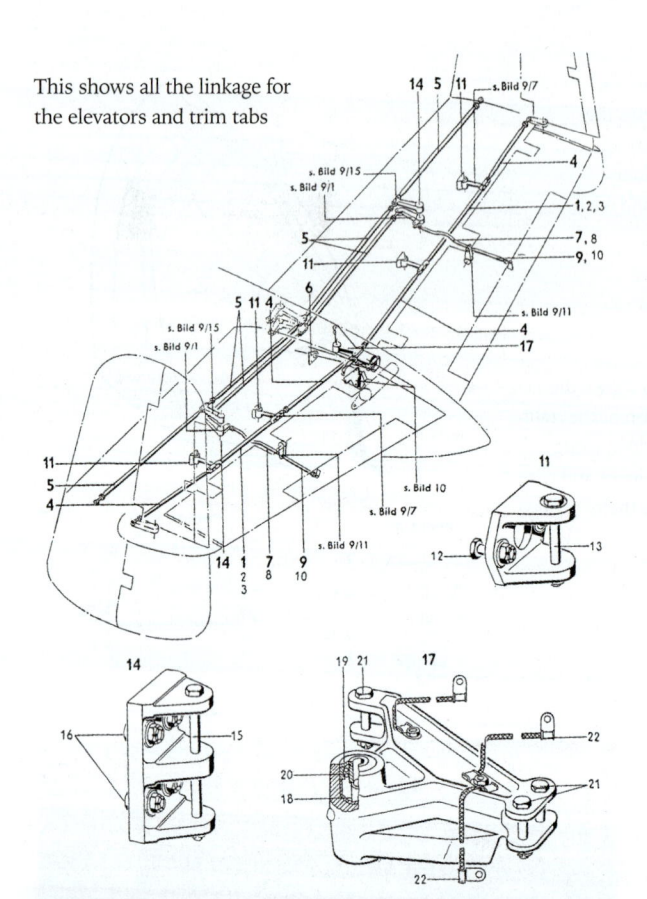

Nice overall shot of the tail of the He 219. The tube at the top of the tail light is for a rear-facing radar mast, which is not fitted any more on this machine (©S. Willey)

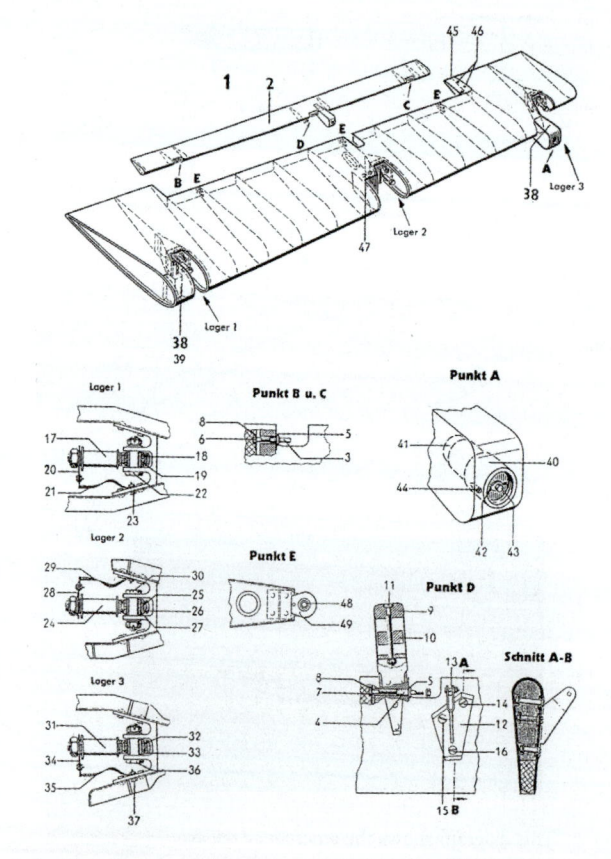

This is the linkage under the port tailplane trim tab, and the braided wire you can see attached is an earthing wire to reduce static (©S. Willey)

A detailed diagram of the elevator and trim tab, with some areas offered in even more detail

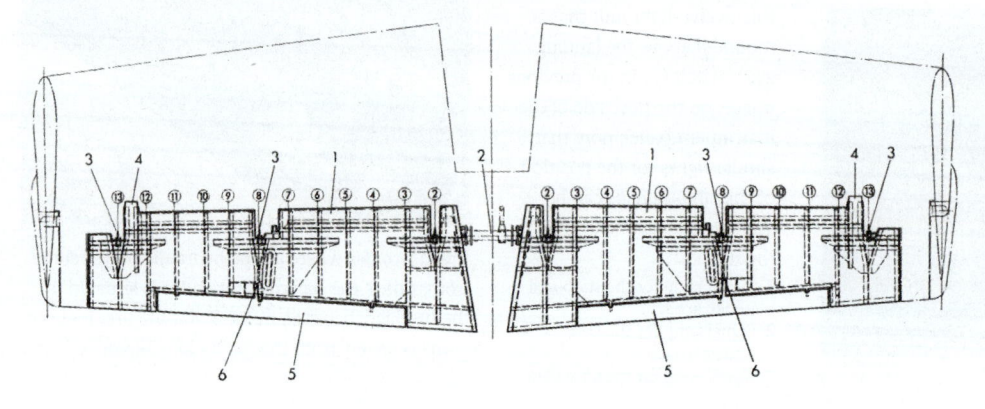

This diagram shows the structure inside each elevator

1. Elevator
2. Coupling shaft
3. Rudder bearing
4. Balance weight
5. Trim tabs
6. Balance weight of the trim tab

Group 3 – Side 2
Tail
Tailplanes

49

This is a useful shot, not just because it shows details of the tailplanes before fitment, but because it shows where the lifting eyelet fits into the upper surface. This is usually just a hole in the tailplane skin and the eyelet is stowed elsewhere in the airframe
(©S. Willey)

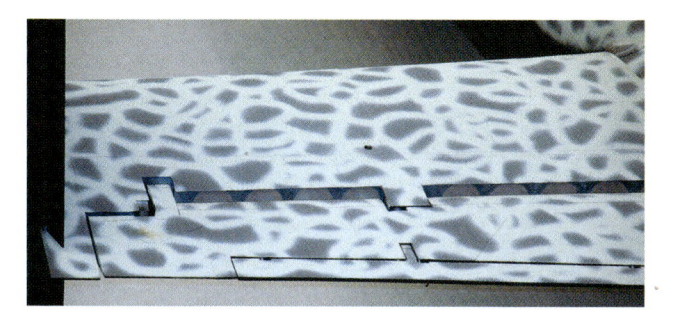

Here you can see the tailplanes once installed, the hole for the lifting eyelet is now very visible. The scallop shapes inside the hinge line are the round holes of the ribs closed over with clear doped linen, as this was how the aircraft was originally (©S. Willey)

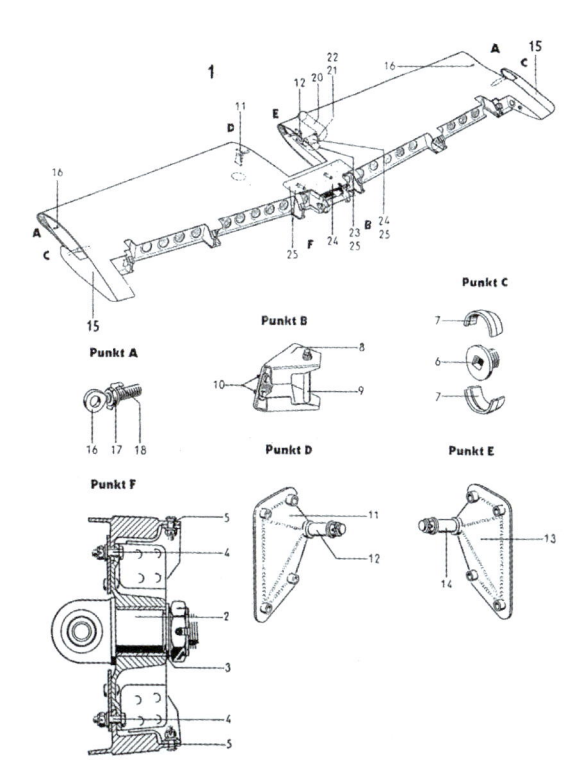

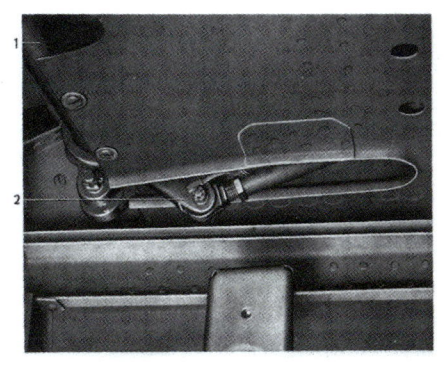

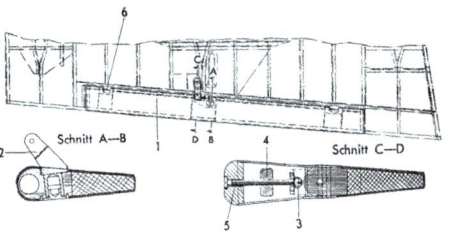

This period image and diagram show the linkage for the elevator (upper) and its trim tab (lower)

Upper Image
1. Elevator torque shaft
2. Drive lever of the torque shaft
Lower Diagram
1. Elevator trim tab
2. Connection horn
3. Castle nut
4. Adjustable balance weight
5. Spindle screw
6. Hinges

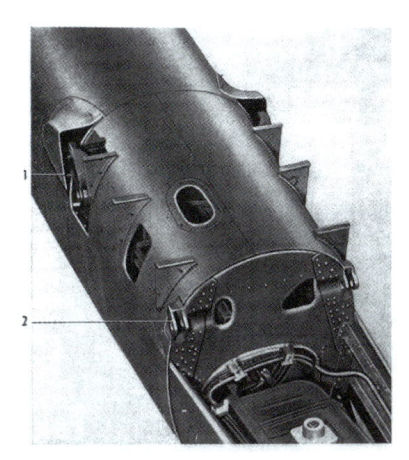

This period image shows how the tailplane attaches to the rear fuselage with the front connection to the fin adjustment shaft (1) and the rear connection to hull bulkhead 33 (2)

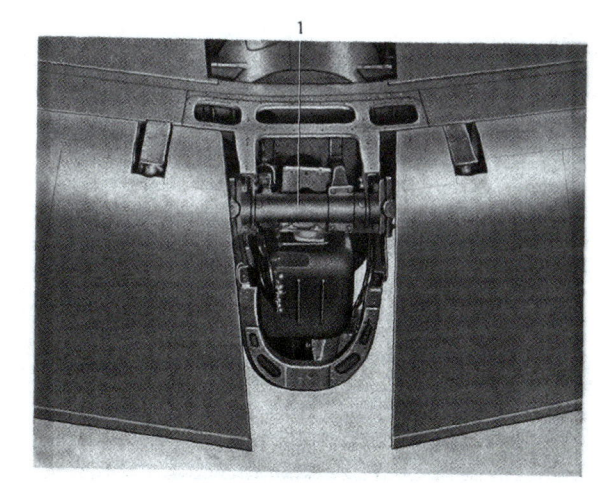

This diagram shows the tailplane unit, with the holes in the hinge area that were covered over with doped linen in the previous image

Once in place the elevators are linked via this torque tube (1)

AA01/13/49 Valiant Wings Publishing Issued: July 2021

Group 3 – Side 3	
Tail	**1**
50	Tailplanes

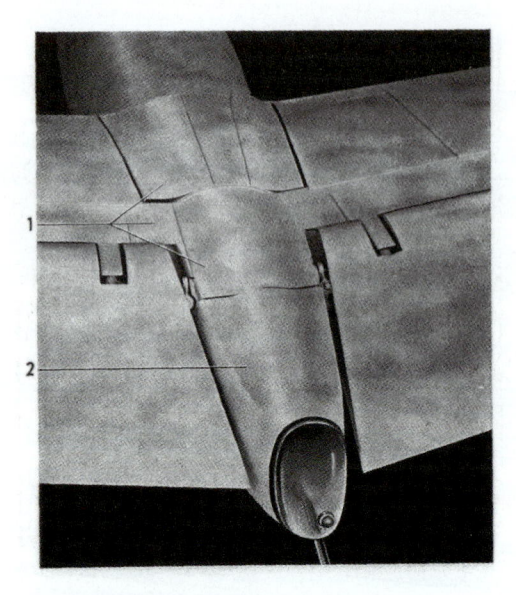

This period images shows the separate panels (1) used to cover over the tailplane join with the fuselage and the fuselage end cap (2)

Although a bit fuzzy, this image does show you all the fillets at the tailplane junction with the fuselage. The extreme tip of the fuselage is all black, as that is how it was when the paint was stripped during restoration *(©S. Willey)*

Viewed directly from the back you can see how much dihedral there is in the tailplanes *(©S. Willey)*

This diagram shows the tail cone area in detail
1. Bracket for tailing aerial unit
2. Connection fitting for tailing aerial reel
3. Front cap (metal)
4. End cap (clear)

This is a close-up of the clear cover in the extreme tip of the fuselage. This is not a light cover, it is the tail cone, the navigation light is the small silver unit with the lens at the top of the cone. The hole in it is for the trailing aerial lead that was carried here when no rearward-facing radar was installed *(©S. Willey)*

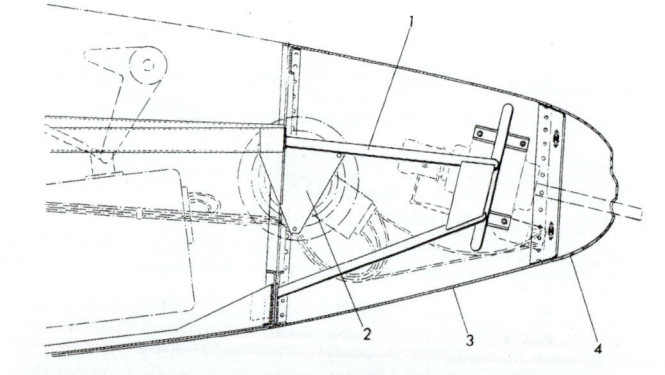

In the leading edge of the starboard tailplane only is this air intake *(©S. Willey)*

Group 3 – Side 4
Tail
Fins/Rudders

Note: See the section on Controls & Control Surfaces for the elevators

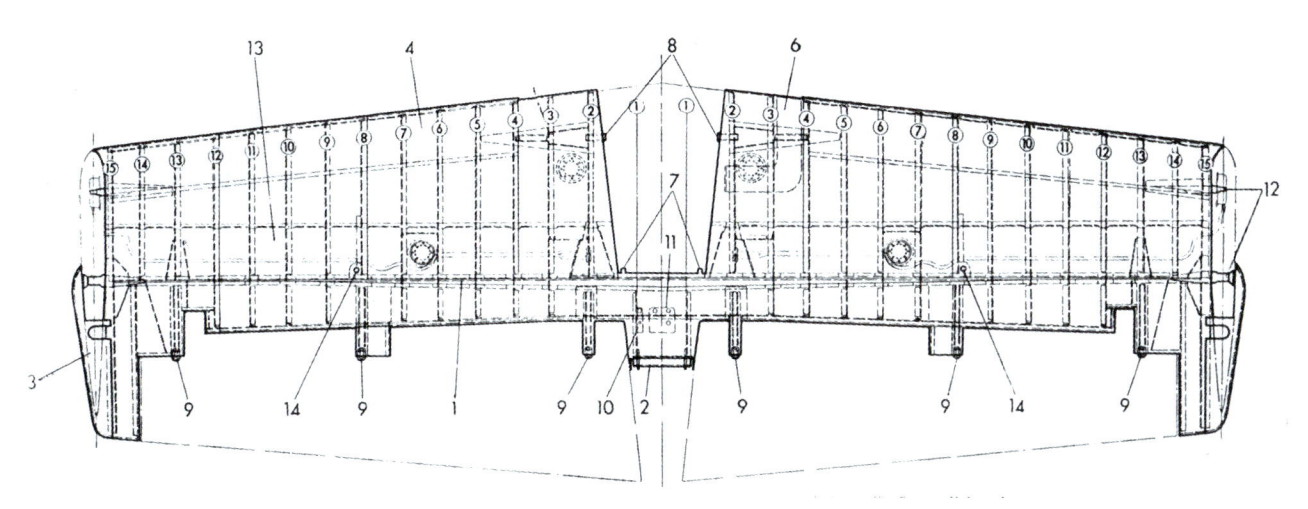

This diagram from the parts manual shows the construction of the tailplanes

1. Hauptholm (Main spar)
2. Kupplungswelle (Coupling shaft)
3. Endkappe (End cap)
4. Enteiserröhre (De-icer {skinning})
6. Ansaugkanal (Intake)
7. Hinterer Anschluß (Rear connection)
8. Vorderer Anschluß (Front connection)
9. Beschlag für Ruderlager (Fittings for control surface bearings)
10. Anschlußplatte für Feststellriegel (Höhenruderfeststellung) (Support plate for locking bar (Elevator setting)
11. Anschlußplatte für Feststellriegel (Seitenruderfeststellung) (Support plate for locking bar (rudder setting))
12. Anschlußbeschläge für die Seitenflosse (Connecting fittings for the vertical stabilisers)
13. Abnehmbare Beplankungsplatte auf der Unterseite (Detachable panelling underneath)
14. Heißbeschlag (Lifting eyelet fitting)

A period photo of the tail including the the vertical fins and rudders

Bit of a weird shot I know, but with the whole tail unit off the fuselage you get a nice overall shot of the unit. Note that the trim tab linkage is not handed, so on the starboard side it is above, whilst on the port it is below *(©S. Willey)*

An overall shot of the starboard fin and rudder on NASM's A-2, although the chord of the lower rudder section looking greater, is purely an optical illusion caused by you seeing the trailing edge of the elevator *(©S. Willey)*

Here is the tail unit secured back to the fuselage when it was being put back on its wheels in 2019 *(©S. Willey)*

Tail
Fins/Rudders
Group 3 – Side 5

A closer look at the port fin and rudder allows you to see all the various cut-outs in the rudder for the hinges and to clear the elevators, plus you can just make out the holes inside the structure that are covered with clear doped linen, just like on the tailplanes (©S. Willey)

This is a useful shot of the inner face of the starboard fin and rudder unit, as it proves once again that the rudders are not handed because the trim tab linkage is on the inside on this starboard unit, but in the previous shot of the port unit you will see it is on the outside (©S. Willey)

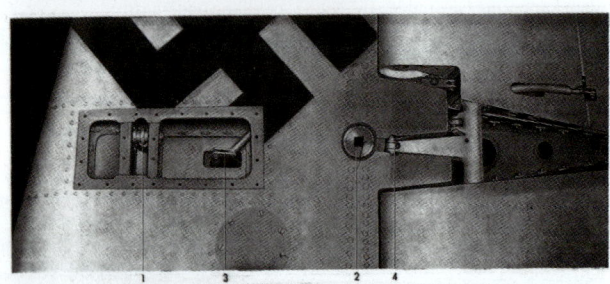

This period image from the maintenance manual shows the access panel on the fin/rudder. The keyed items are as follows: 1. Vorderer Anschluß (Front connector); 2. Hinterer Anschluß (Rear connector); 3. Anschluß des Seitentrimmgestäges (Connector for the trim tab control rod); 4. Anschluß des Seitenrudergestäges (Connector for the rudder control rod)

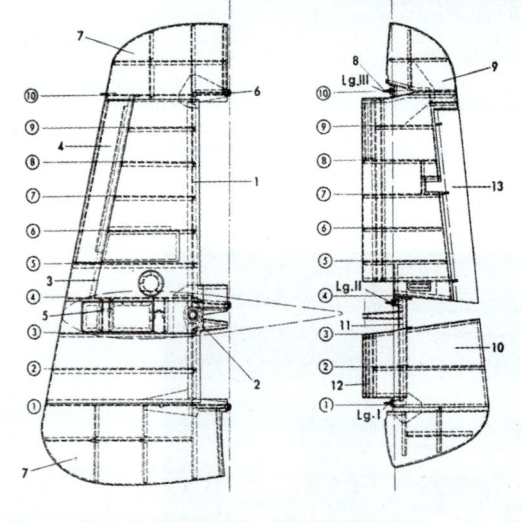

This diagram from the parts manual shows the construction of the vertical fin and rudder

1. Hauptholm (Main spar)
2. Hinterer Anschluß (Rear connection)
3. Vorderholm (Front spar)
4. Nasenröhre (Leading-edge box section)
5. Vorderer Anschluß (Front connection)
6. Beschlag für die Ruderlager (Fittings for the rudder bearings)
7. Endkappe (End cap)
8. Ruderlager (Rudder bearings)
9. Oberteil (Upper part)
10. Unterteil (Lower part)
11. Stahlrohr mit Antriebshebel (Steel tubing with actuating lever)
12. Ausgleichsgewichte (Counterweights)
13. Trimmruder (Trim tab)

This is a more detailed diagram (from the A-7 parts manual) of a vertical fin

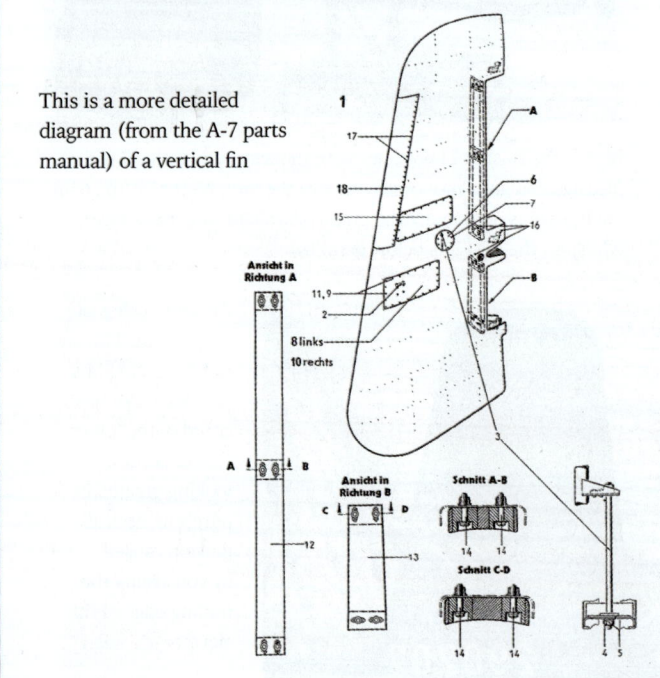

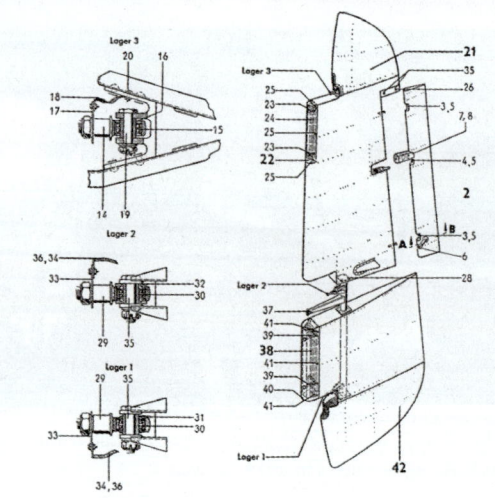

This is a more detailed diagram (from the A-7 parts manual) of a rudder

Group 4 – Side 1
Systems
Fuel

1

53

This diagram shows the fuel system with the interconnecting, feed and overflow pipes

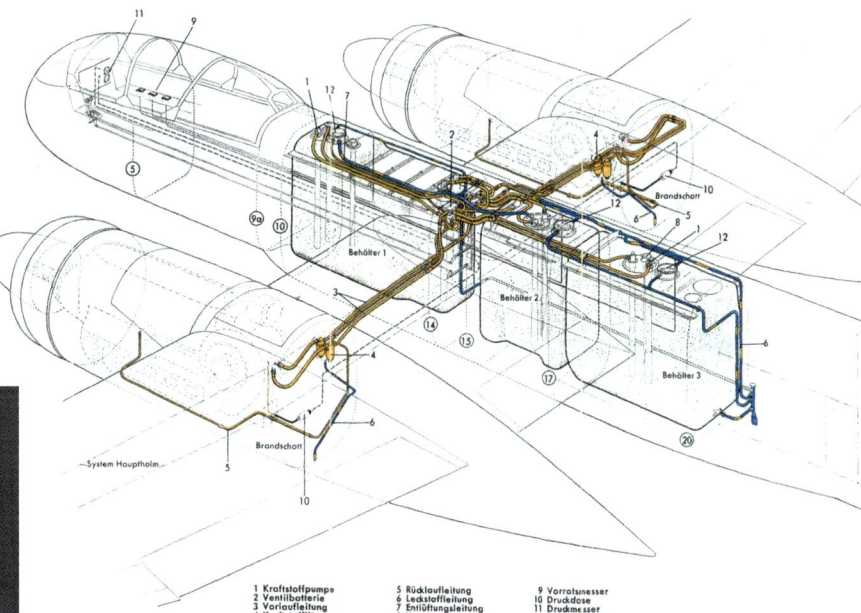

1 Kraftstoffpumpe
2 Ventilbatterie
3 Vorlaufleitung
4 Kraftstoffilter
5 Rücklaufleitung
6 Leckstoffleitung
7 Entlüftungsleitung
8 Vorratsgeber
9 Vorratsmesser
10 Druckdose
11 Druckmesser
12 Kraftstoffeinfüllköpfe

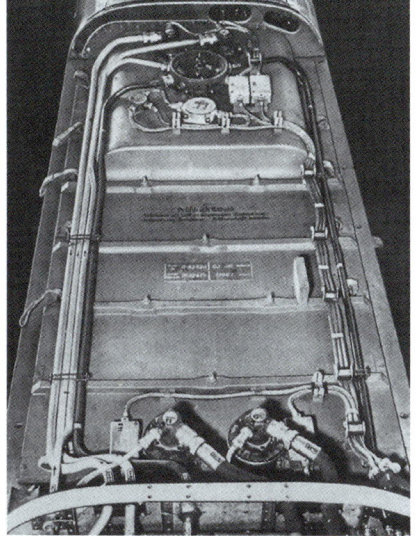

This period photograph shows the forward fuselage fuel cell (marked as 'Behälter 1' in the previous diagram), looking forward

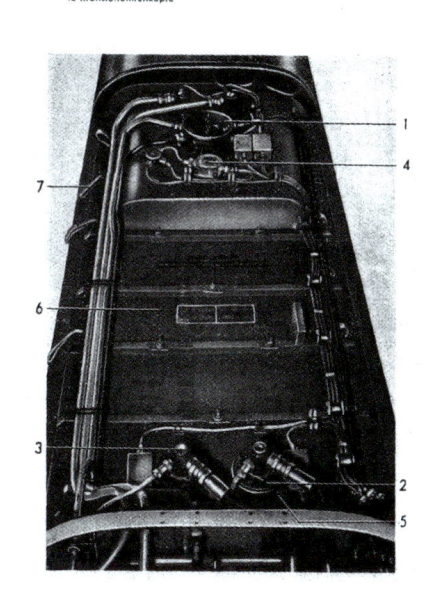

Although not the best quality, this shows the forward fuselage fuel cell with a few details noted
1. Main fuel tank head
2. Sub fuel tank heads
3. Reservoir pump
4. Contents (level) indicator unit
5. Intermediate flange
6. Container support structure
7. Leather straps

This period photo shows the middle fuselage fuel cell (front of the aircraft is at the bottom of the image)

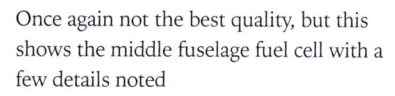

Once again not the best quality, but this shows the middle fuselage fuel cell with a few details noted

1. Main fuel tank head
2. Fuel filler point
3. Reservoir pumps
4. Contents (level) indicator unit
5. Filling point flange
6. Container support structure
7. Leather straps

Here you can see the middle tank on NASM's A-2 whilst it was uncovered during assembly in 2019
(©S. Willey)

AA01/14/53

Valiant Wings Publishing

Issued: July 2021

Group 4 – Side 2
Systems
Fuel/Oil

At Frame 14, between the front and middle tanks you have this bank of fuel valves (1)

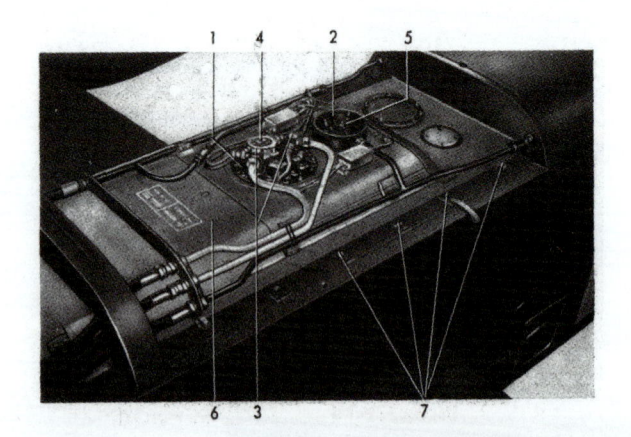

Not a great image, but this photo from the manual shows the aft fuselage fuel cell

1. Main fuel tank head
2. Fuel filler point
3. Fuel tank pump
4. Contents (level) indicator unit
5. Filler point flange
6. Container support frame
7. Leather strap

The fuel gauges (1) are located on the starboard side console in the cockpit along with the fuel level warning lamps (2)

The filters for the fuel system are located in the rear of the starboard undercarriage bay

1. Protective box   2. Filters   3. Leak lines

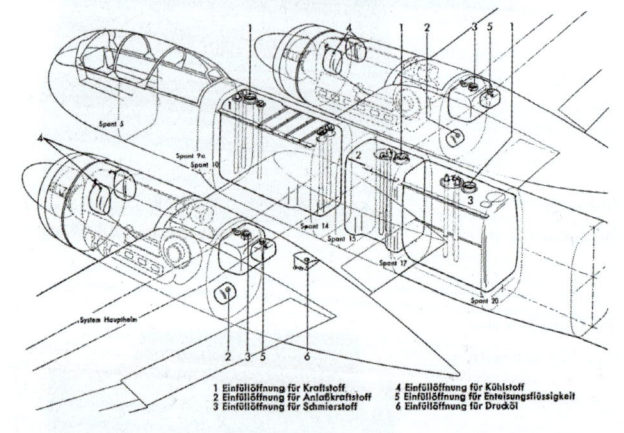

This diagram shows the location of the oil tanks (2) as well as the fuel (1), coolant (3) and drain fuel (4) tanks

Here is a look at the bay containing the oil tank in NASM's example during restoration, the access panel behind it is for the propeller de-icer tank (©S. Willey)

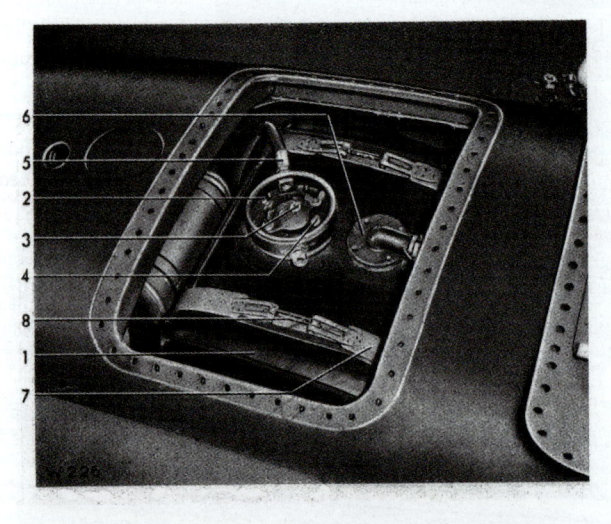

This is a more detailed look at what is visible of the oil tank once the access cover is removed

1. Oil tank
2. Filling point
3. Filling flange
4. Dipstick
5. Leak drainage line
6. Vent head
7. Retaining strap
8. Turnbuckle tensioner

Group 4 – Side 3
Systems
Oxygen/De-Icing

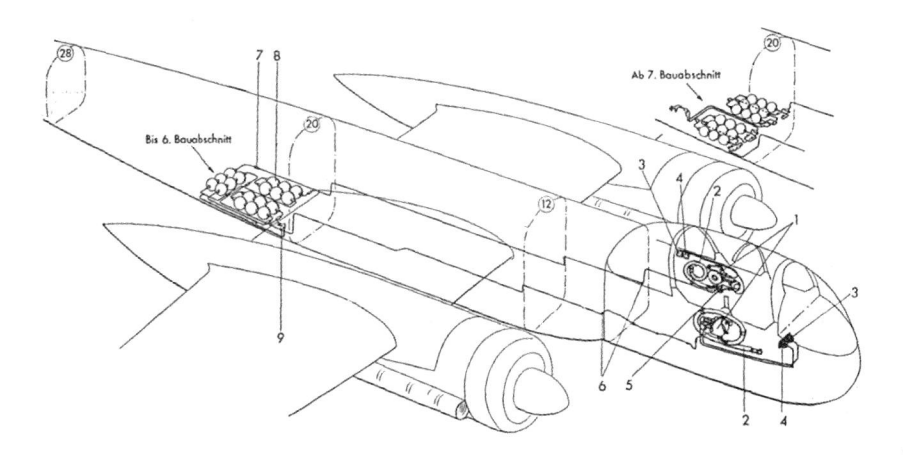

This gives an overview of the oxygen system

1. Oxygen (breathing) unit
2. Breathing tube
3. Oxygen pressure meter
4. Oxygen flow monitor
5. Globe valve
6. Screw coupling
7. Check valve
8. Spherical oxygen bottles
9. Outboard connection/charger point

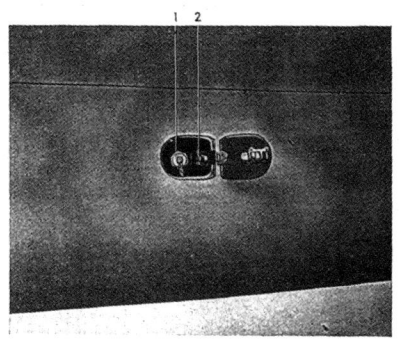

Mentioned in the previous illustration as item 9, this is the oxygen charger point situated on the starboard fuselage side, just aft of the wing trailing edge

This image from the A-0 series flight manual shows the oxygen unit on the starboard sidewall in the pilot's cockpit and is applicable to all variants (there is an identical unit on the port side of the rear cockpit for the observer)

Not a great quality images, but this shot from the manual gives you an idea what the spherical oxygen bottles in the rear fuselage and (for the A-2 and A-7) in the port wheel well, look like

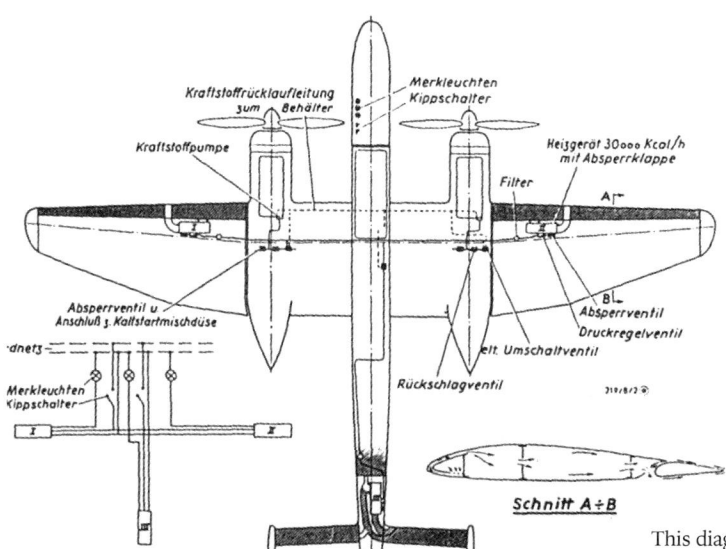

Here is a period image of one of the heater units in the leading edge of the wing

This diagram shows the tailplane and wing leading edge de-icing system for the He 219, feed by heater units in each wing (see Group 5 for more detail) and rear fuselage (see Group 1 for more details)

Group 5 – Side 1
Wings
1

56 | Wings

This shows the wing's construction

1. Main spar
2. End spar
3. Nose spar, inside and outside
4. Nose ribs
5. End rib
6. Nacelle
7. End of the nacelle
8. Wing tip
9. Cover in lower panelling
10. Landing gear door
11. Connection of the main spar
12. Bearing fittings
13. Split aileron
14. Split landing flap, inside
15. Split landing flap, outside
16. De-icing heater unit

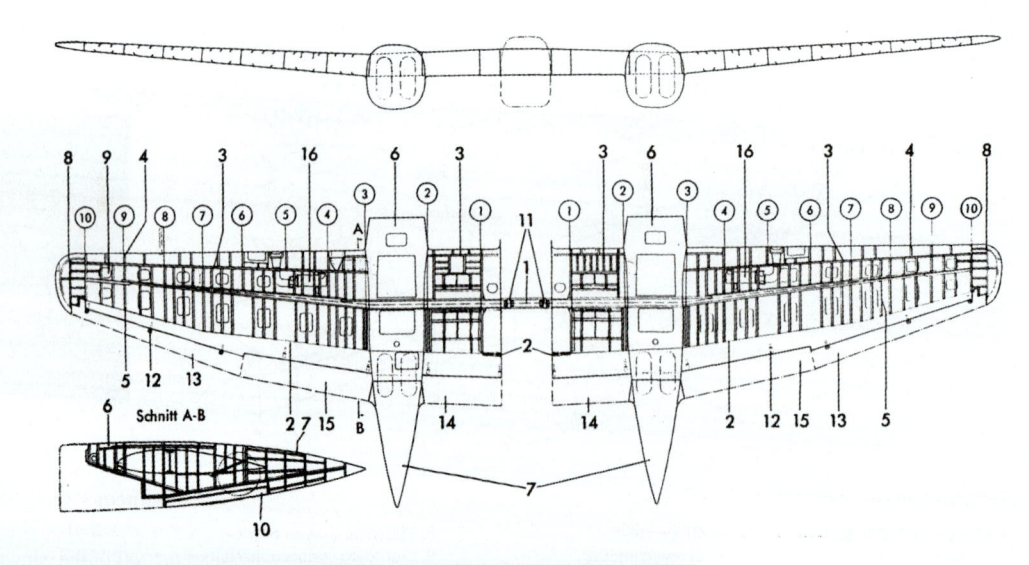

This is the wing of NASM's example, being rolled out on completion of its restoration in July 2014 (©NASM)

The main spar is a single piece that thus travels through the fuselage (©S. Willey)

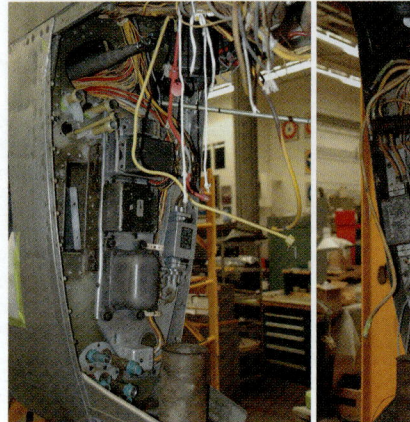

This period image shows how the main spar connects to the fuselage

1. Main spar
2. Shackle
3. Fuselage bulkhead 14a
4. Fuselage bulkhead 15
5. Bolt

This montage image shows the area at the front of the wing root of the port (right) and starboard (left) sides (©S. Willey)

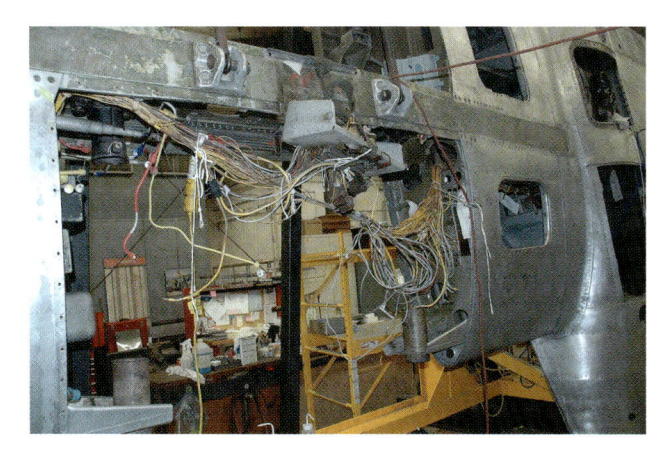

Group 5 – Side 2	
Wings	**1**
Wings	57

This closer view of the wing mid-section shows the spar, as well as the various electrical cables in this area and (at top) the tie-rods (©S. Willey)

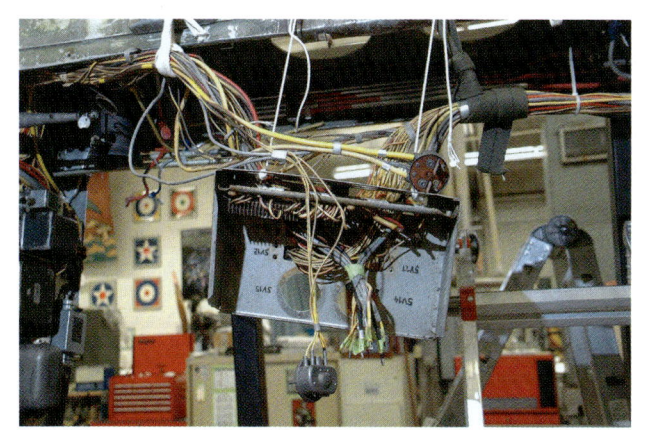

This is a close-up of the mass of wires seen in the mid-span area (©S. Willey)

This is the upper front section of the engine nacelle in the starboard wing (©S. Willey)

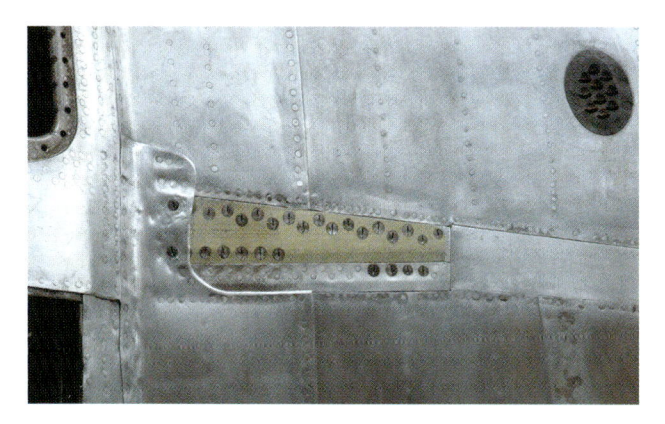

This section of the spar is exposed just outboard of the engine nacelle. This is steel, not aluminium like the surrounding areas (©S. Willey)

This shot of the starboard wing, shown earlier in renovation, and you can see the oil tank is removed exposing the de-icer tank behind it (©S. Willey)

This montage images shows the oil tank removed from the wing – upper surface on the left and lower on the right (©S. Willey)

This shot taken from the back of the port wing prior to the start of restoration, shows all the access panels open – the smallest one nearest the camera is the de-icer tank, the next one is the oil tank and the large one is for the engine. You can also see where the lifting eyelets go (©S. Willey)

Group 5 – Side 3
Wings

This is a shot of the port wing trailing edge, with all the paint stripped during restoration, which allows you to see the structure usually covered by the control surfaces
(©S. Willey)

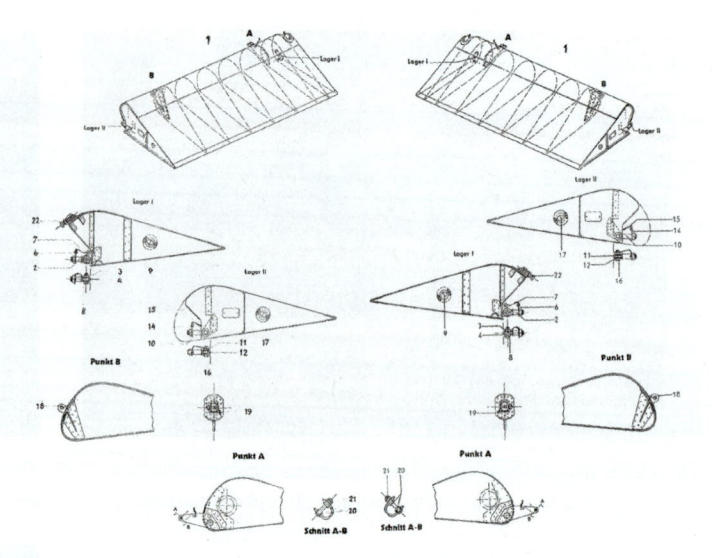

The inner and middle trailing edge of each wing contain landing flaps, this shows the inboard sections of the port (on the left) and starboard (on the right) units

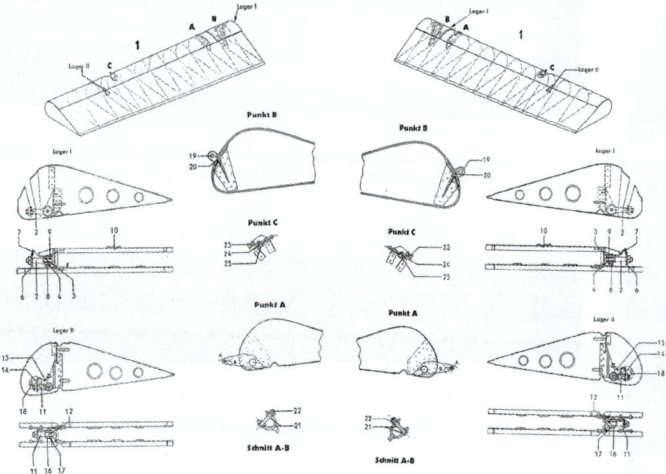

While this shows the outboard sections of the port (on the left) and starboard (on the right) units

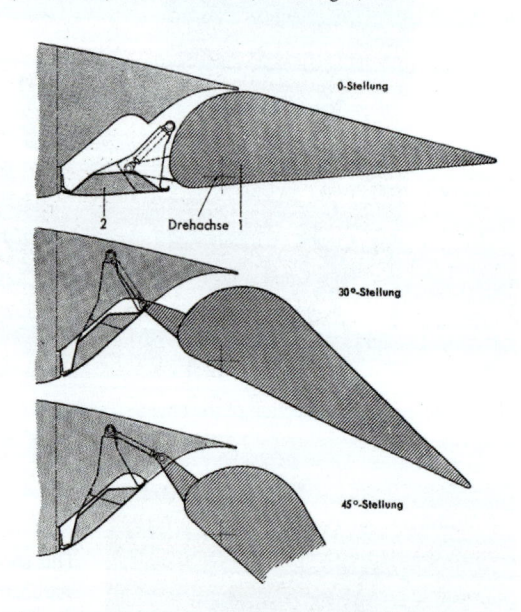

This shows the movement of each landing flap, along with how the landing flap (1) draws in the cover to fill the resulting gap (2)

This image shows the connection of the rear spar, but it also allows you to see (hanging down) the cover that fills the gap left as the landing flaps are lowered [seen as '2' in diagram above right]

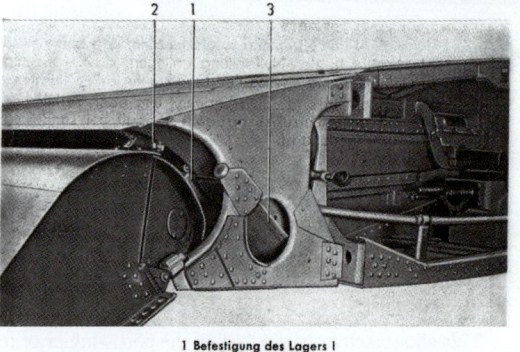

With the wing off, this is the view at the root end, again showing that cover for the gap left by the flap as it lowers (3)

1 Befestigung des Lagers I (achsial beweglich)
2 Einstellbarer Anschlag
3 Spaltabdeckklappe

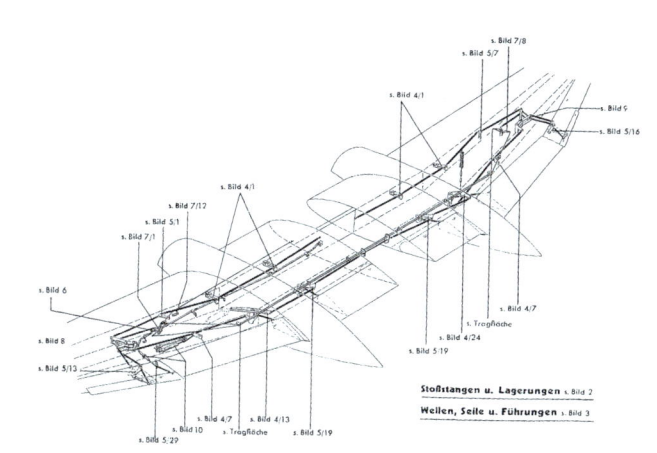

Group 5 – Side 4
Wings

59

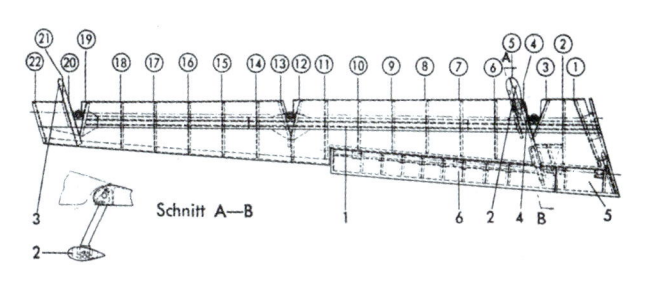

This shows the construction of the aileron

1. Spar (shaped profile)
2. Inner counterweight
3. External counterweight
4. Hinge
5. Trim tabs (left only)
6. Relief tab on the left (right has the same size as trim tabs 5 and 6 together)

Here you can see all the linkage for the two sections of landing flap and each aileron of each wing

This shot shows the aileron from the starboard wing during stripping and renovation – the sanding down process also confirms the camouflage application, as it is the RLM 76 that has been removed, leaving the dark RLM 75 patches, confirming that RLM 76 was applied OVER the RLM 75 (©S. Willey)

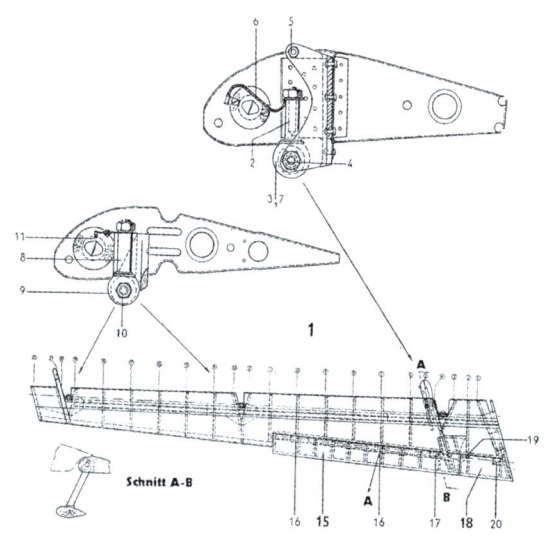

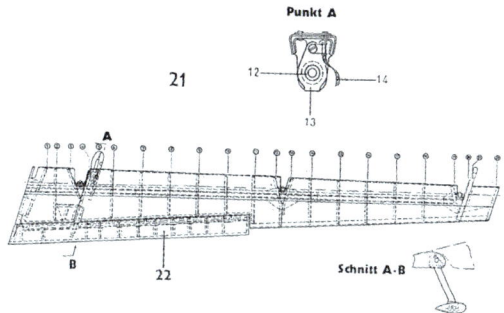

This shows both ailerons along with cross-sections to show how they pick-up the hinges on the wing

This is the balance weight mounted on the underside of the aileron (©S. Willey)

Here you can see the underside of the aileron from the port wing during renovation – the balance weight is visible and in this instance the trim tab has been removed and you can see all the mounting bearings (©S. Willey)

Group 5 – Side 5
Wings

60 | Wings

The ailerons are long on the He 219, so there is another counterweight built in at the tip, as can be seen here. You can also see how the unit was mounted via the bracket and linkage visible (©S. Willey)

The control surfaces are mounted via this type of bracket – this is the trim tab on the starboard aileron. The trim tab has a channel into which the lug on the main aileron slips, then a bolt goes through to be wire-locked in place. There is a small bearing in the lug (©S. Willey)

This shows the trim tab and relief tab linkage as well as the counterweight on the aileron

1. Trim tab drive rod
2. Covering caps of the main aileron drive
3. Trim rudder (left only)
4. Relief tab
5. Inner counterweight of the aileron

This shot of the outer section of the starboard wing on NASM's example does allow you to see all the hinges for the aileron, as well as the cut-out towards the top for the external counterweight (1) seen in the previous diagram (©S. Willey)

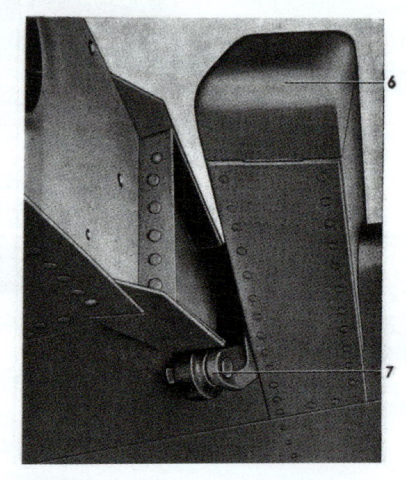

This period images shows the aileron counterweight built in at the tip (see top left-hand image)
1. External counterweight
2. Third (outermost) aileron bearing

This montage image shows the bulkhead in the port wing, with the inner (at left) and outer (at right) faces

Viewed from the underside, this shot shows the forward (engine) bay as well as the aft (undercarriage) bay in the port wing. The arrowed area is shown in detail in the next image (©S. Willey)

This close-up of the area highlighted in the previous image, shows all the oil filtration units in this area. The pulley and wire unit is for the control surfaces (©S. Willey)

	Group 5 – Side 6	1
	Wings	
	Wings	61

This is the upper surface of the starboard wing, just outboard of the engine nacelle. The grille is to allow heat from the heater unit to disperse (©S. Willey)

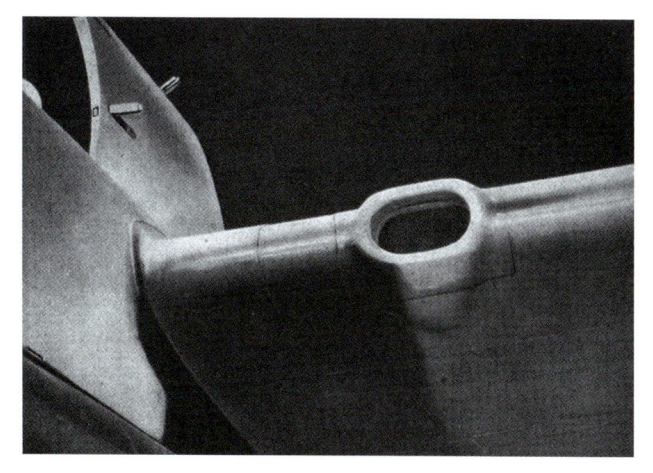

The leading edge of the wing has three intakes, this shows the inner one in its early style, as seen here in an image of the A-0 series

Later, the A-2 and A-7 series adopted this shaped inner intake, seen here on G9+CL (possibly) found at Nindlach at the end of the war

Outboard of the engine nacelle there are two intakes, the inner one (1) is for the engine supercharger, while the outer one (2) is for the de-icer heater (©S. Willey)

The inner (1) intake was originally smaller than the 'sharksmouth' one seen on NASM's A-2, as seen here (arrowed) on the He 219 V33 (A-013) W/Nr.190063 RL+AC in early 1944

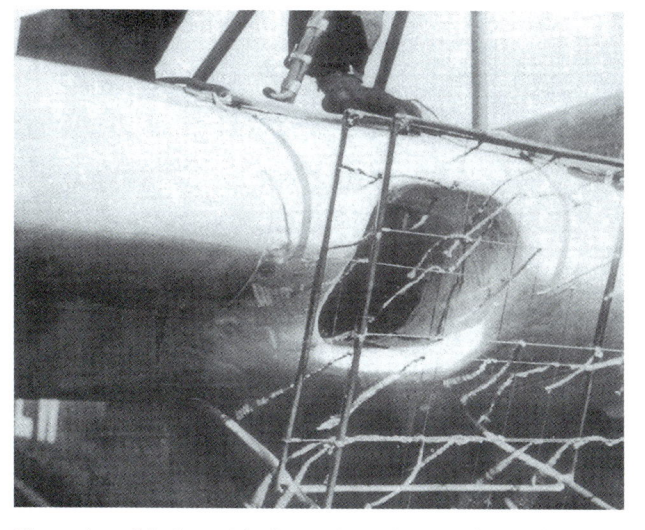

The testing of the larger 'sharksmouth' intake took place early on in development, with this style of unit seen being tested by the V1 probably in late 1943 or early 1944

The heater intake was not always present, or could be covered up, as seen here on G9+CL (possibly) found at Nindlach at the end of the war

Wings

Group 5 – Side 7

Now looking at the wing underside, this is the outer section of the port wing (©S. Willey)

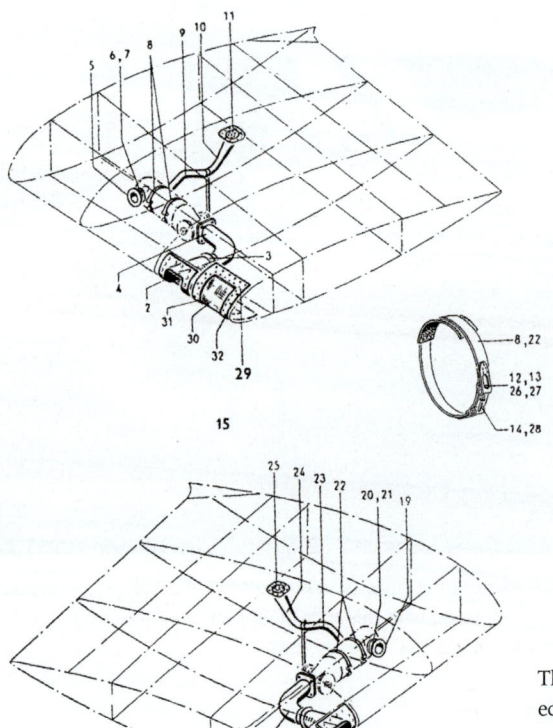

This is the wing underside for the starboard side – the blue tape highlighted the position/size/style of the original underwing cross (©S. Willey)

This is the wing heater unit in the leading edge of the starboard wing, there is another one in the port unit (©S. Willey)

This is the intake for the wing heater in the wing leading edge of both wings, this is the starboard one (©S. Willey)

This is a close-up of the heater unit in the port wing (©S. Willey)

This diagram shows the installation of the heater in the wing leading edge, as well as the pipe leading from it to the grille in the upper wing surface

Group 5 – Side 8	**1**
Wings	
Wings	63

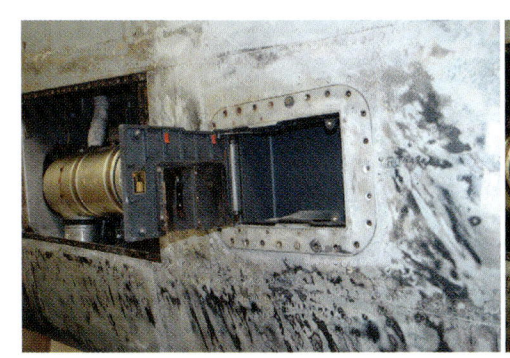

This montage shows the bay inboard of the heater unit in the port wing *(©S. Willey)*

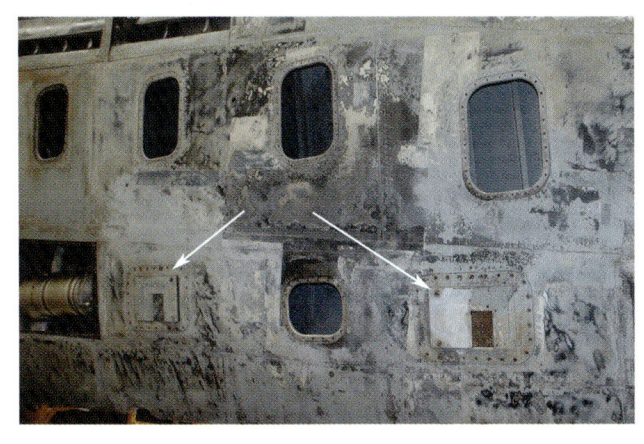

In this image you can see the bay shown in the previous image arrowed on the left and a similar bay on the right – these are bays for the radio altimeter units *(©S. Willey)*

This shot shows that under the access panel at the wing trailing edge, just outboard of the nacelle, is this actuator, which must be for the flaps *(©S. Willey)*

This montage shot shows the interior of the bay highlighted in the previous couple of images *(©S. Willey)*

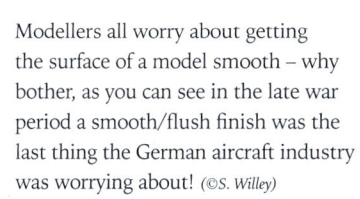

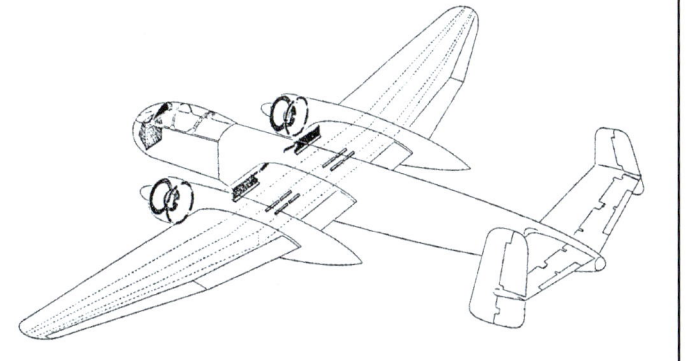

Modellers all worry about getting the surface of a model smooth – why bother, as you can see in the late war period a smooth/flush finish was the last thing the German aircraft industry was worrying about! *(©S. Willey)*

This wartime diagram shows the armour plate fitted to the engine cowls, as well as the cockpit and ahead of the wing-mounted ammo bays

Group 6 – Side 1
Engines

Engines

This period photo shows the port side of the DB603A engine

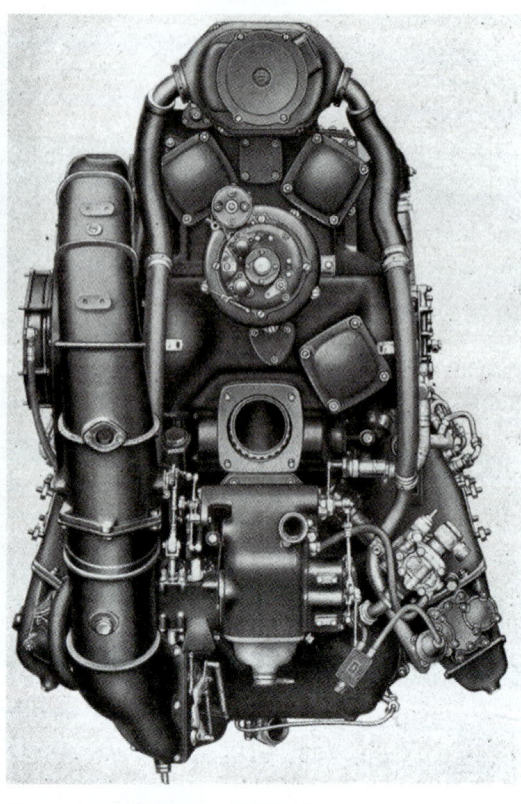

This is the DB603A viewed from the rear

This is the DB603A viewed from the front

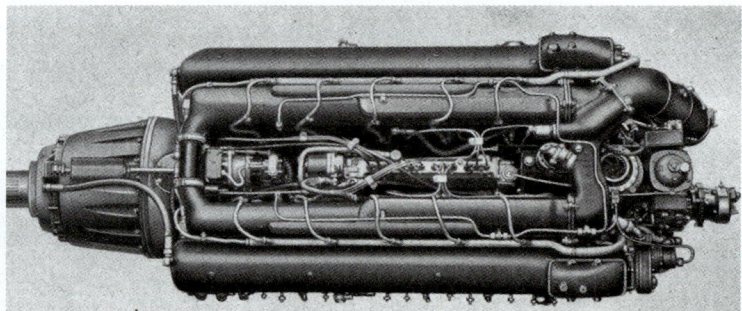

This is the DB603A viewed from directly on top

This view, taken of the DB603A on show at Berlin-Gatow Museum, shows the reduction gear housing and prop shaft (©P. Skulski)

This view of the Berlin-Gatow DB603A shows the supercharger housing on the port side (©P. Skulski)

Group 6 – Side 2
Engines

In this view you can see the engine bearer pick-up points as well as the individual exhaust outlets (©P. Skulski)

From this angle you can see the upside-down nature of the DB603, as well as all the ancillary items on the rear of the main casings. There is no motor-cannon option for this engine (©P. Skulski)

Here is the DB603 of the NASM He 219, stripped down during renovation (©S. Willey)

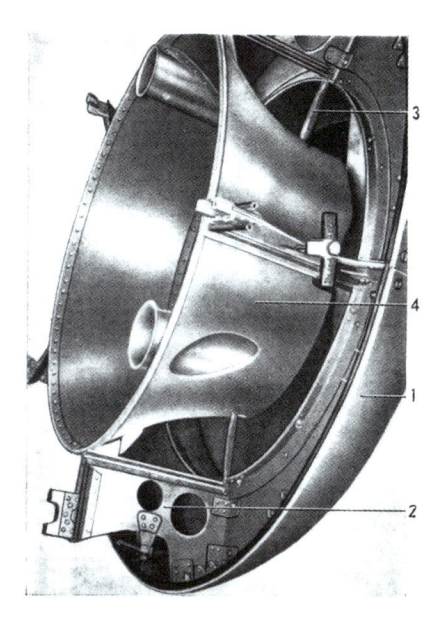

This period image shows the front baffle plate for each engine, part of which you could see attached to the engine in the previous image

1. Front frame arch
2. Separation frame/support
3. Support struts
4. Baffle

This is the back of the engine in the NASM He 219, showing all the ancillary equipment in this area (©S. Willey)

Here is NASM's He 219 engine now with the front cowl ring/gills fitted, plus the exhaust stacks and surrounds (©S. Willey)

Group 6 – Side 3	**1**
Engines	
66	Cowling

Here is the front cowl ring and gills fitted to the engine unit *(©S. Willey)*

This period images show the various elements of the front cowling
1. Front frame
2. Intermediate flaps
3. Drive flaps
4. Support struts
5. Oil radiators
6. Baffle
7. Coolant radiators
8. Ventilation duct

This view into the front of the cowl shows the annular radiator unit within as well as the linkage for the cowl gills built in behind the spinner backplate *(©S. Willey)*

This is a close-up of how the cowl gills overlap *(©S. Willey)*

This period images gives a little more information on what is visible under the cowl flaps

1. Frame
2. Cooler
3. Rubber seal
4. Flap drive
5. Main flaps (driven)
6. Intermediate flaps (moved by main flaps, no drive linkage)

This shot shows how the cowl gill linkage is fitted *(©S. Willey)*

Group 6 – Side 4
Engines
Cowling

These period images from the flight handbook show the access panels that hinge open aft of the cowl gills

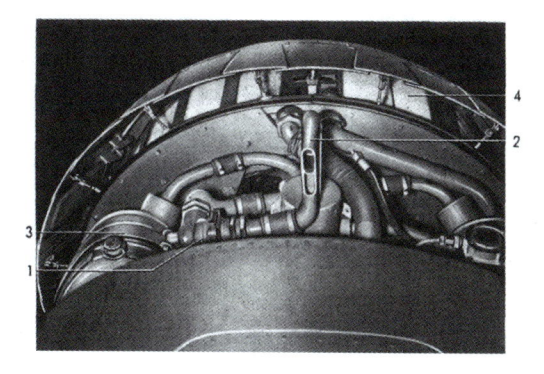

The little bulge seen above the cowls in the previous image is more clearly seen here (2)
1. Pressure equalization valve
2. Vent outlet for coolant tank
3. Coolant storage tank
4. Coolant radiator

The coolant tank vent was simplified from the A-0 series version seen in the previous image, this shows the basic pipes used instead and is seen here on NASM's A-2 (©S. Willey)

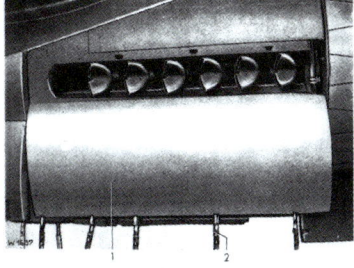

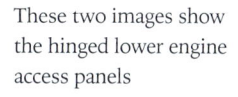

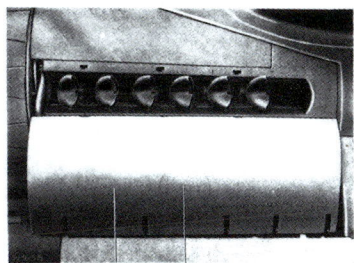

These two images show the hinged lower engine access panels
(Upper)
1. Access panel
2. Tensioner and manual closure (latch)
(Lower)
1. Access panel
2. Access (round) cover

This is an overview of the engine cowlings
1. Radiator support
2. Exhaust duct with Fla-V (flame damper) system
3. Upper engine access panel
4. Lower engine access panel
5. Front part of the nacelle

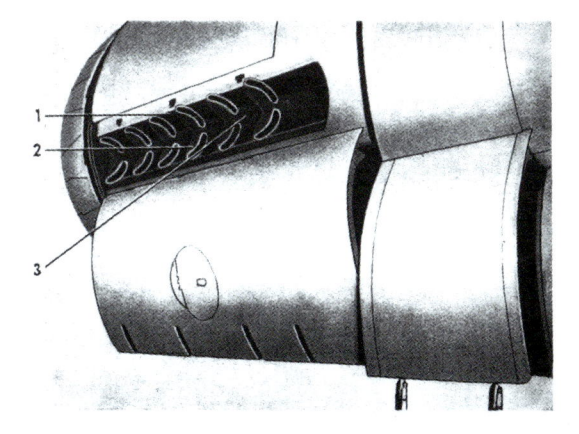

Here is a detailed look at the exhausts without flame dampers fitted, although it also allows you to see how the front and rear lower panels hinge open

The exhausts look a little different on the A-2 preserved by NASM though, so obviously between the A-0 and A-2 production these were revised (©S. Willey)

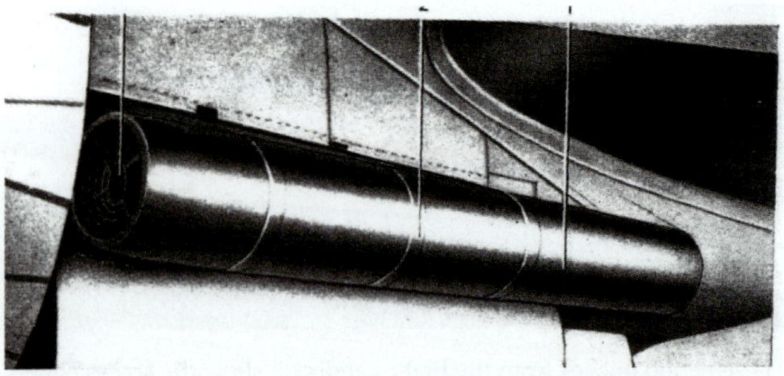

Group 6 – Side 5
Engines
Nacelles

Viewed from the back, you can see how the revised exhausts of NASM's A-2 had the front four stacks separate, but the rear two are joined together *(©S. Willey)*

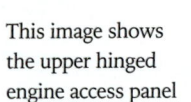

While here you have the exhausts with flame dampers fitted

This image shows the upper hinged engine access panel
1. Interior trim
2. Door bearing (hinge)
3. Tether

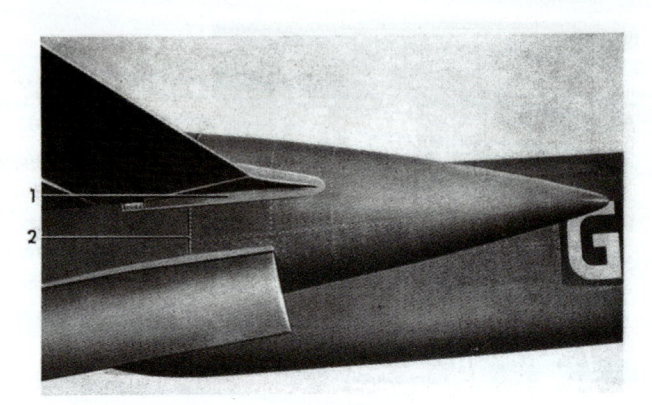

This period image, shows the long nacelles used for most A-0 and all production variants (albeit seen here fitted for the first time on the V1)
1. Fairing panel
2. Forward edge/joint of the end cap

This is the aft nacelle, which contains a 300lt fuel cell *(©S. Willey)*

This is the filler point for the fuel cell in the rear of the nacelle *(©S. Willey)*

This period image from the A-0 manual shows the forward section of the engine nacelle and is applicable to all variants
1. Connection for the engine (bearing)
2. Double bulkhead
3. Support strut
4. Longitudinal struts, two-part
5. Bottom flap
6. Main spar, firewall removed
7. Armoured plate over the main spar
8. Fire bulkhead

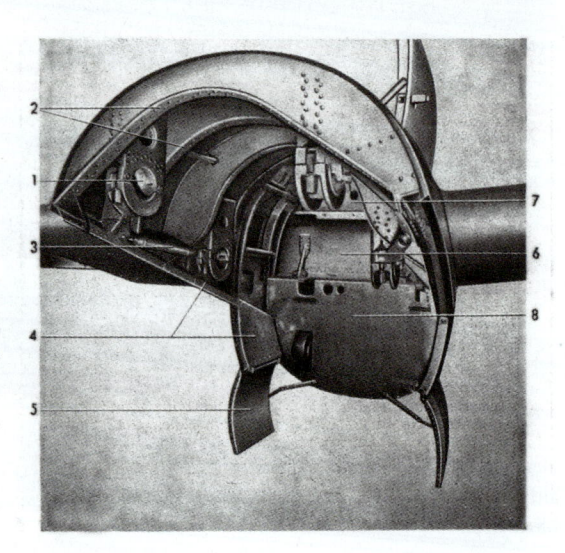

This is the bulkhead on the aft nacelle unit, looking backwards *(©S. Willey)*

Group 6 – Side 6	**1**
Engines	
Nacelles	69

This is how the engine is suspended from the wing – this is the port side *(©S. Willey)*

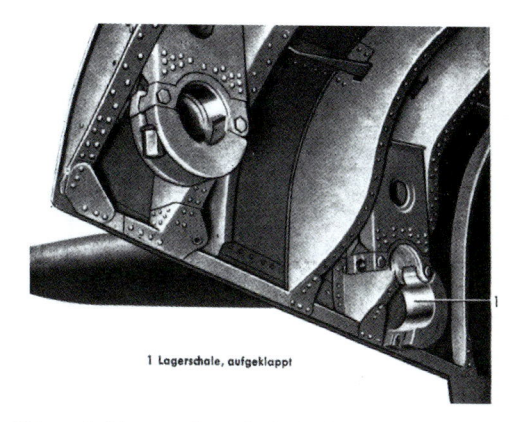

1 Lagerschale, aufgeklappt

This period images shows both the front and rear engine pickups, with the back one shown with the bearing shell open (1)

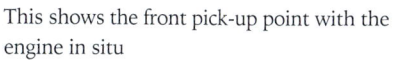

1 Behälter
2 Anlaßpumpe
3 Verschlußschraube
4 Ablaßverschraubung

This shows the front pick-up point with the engine in situ
1. Bearing shell
2. Rubberised bearings
3. Flange

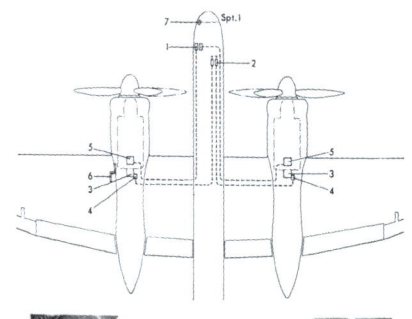

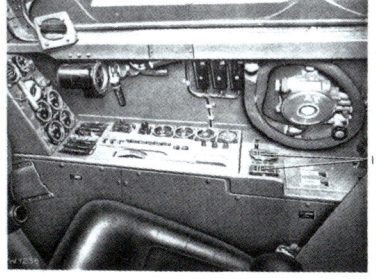

This diagram shows the engine starter system's installation, while the image shows the controls on the starboard side console in the pilot's cockpit

1. Ignition switch
2. Starter switch
3. Inertia starter
4. Dome magnet
5. Twin pull magnet
6. Starting crank
7. Outboard electrical connection socket

This is the engine starter fuel system on the forward bulkhead inside each undercarriage bay
1. Starter fuel container
2. Starter pump
3. Screw filler cap
4. Drain screw connection

Here are the restored engines and rear nacelles laid out for display *(©S. Willey)*

The engine and aft nacelle pods after restoration *(©S. Willey)*

Group 6 – Side 7
Engines

It was intended for the He 219 to use the Jumo 213E engine, so the following couple of images show such a unit (from a Ta 152) that is on display in the USA *(©G. Papadimitriou)*

This is the Jumo 213E viewed from above and behind *(©G. Papadimitriou)*

This is the Jumo 213E viewed from directly ahead, the annual radiator unit inside the cowl ring is evident *(©G. Papadimitriou)*

Had the engine ever reached production, various He 219 variants and developments would have used the massive Jumo 222 *(©G. Papadimitriou)*

Viewed from the front you can see that the Jumo 222 is basically three V-engines joined around a common crankshaft *(©G. Papadimitriou)*

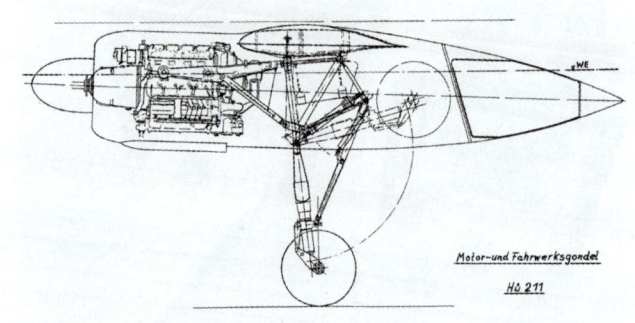

Had it ever gone into production the Hütter Hü 211 would have used a Jumo 222, as shown in this diagram of the proposed nacelle layout

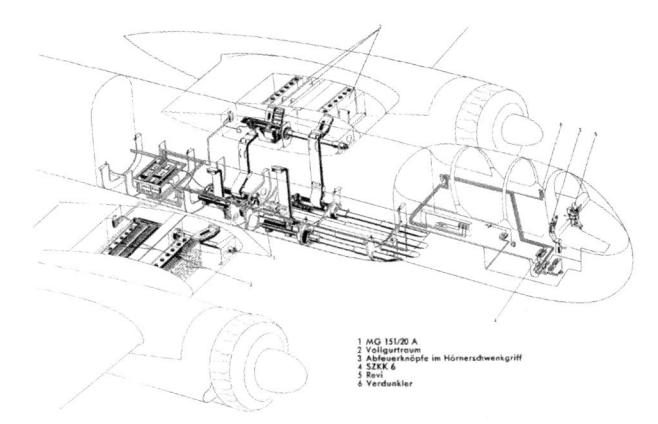

Group 7 – Side 1	
Weapons	**1**
Armament	71

This flight manual diagram shows the armament fitted to the He 219A-series with the M1 Rüstatze. The keyed items are as follows: 1. MG151/20A; 2. Vollgurtraum (Ammunition bays); Abfeuerknöpfe im Hörnerschwenkgriff (Firing button in the horns of the control column); 4. SZKK6; 5. Revi (Gunsight); 6. Verdunkler (Dimmer unit)

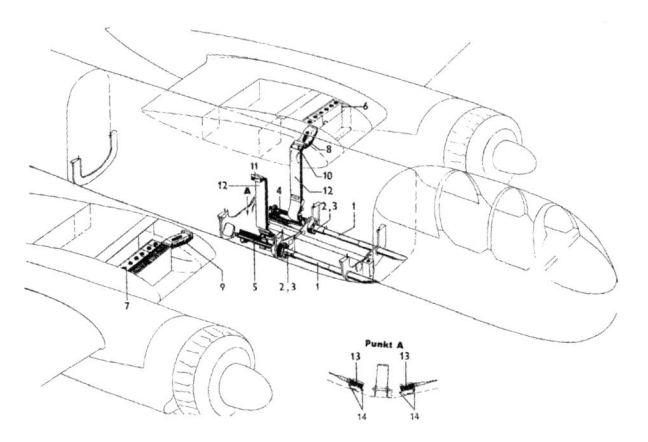

This diagram shows the fitment of just a pair of MG151/20 cannon in the ventral tray

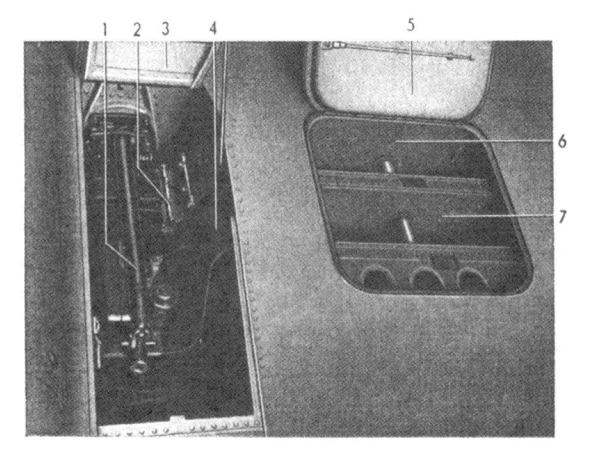

This period photo from the flight manual shows the wing root gun bays on the starboard side. The keyed items are as follows: 1. MG151/20 (Cannon); 2. Bedienungsklappe am Zuführhals (Control flap on the ammunition feed); 3. Bedienungsklappe fur Flügelwaffe (Wing cover for servicing weapon); 4. Zuführkanal fur hintere Rumpfwaffe (Feeder channel for rear ammunition bay); 5. Deckel für Vollgurtkasten (Cover for ammunition bays); 6. Vollgurtkasten für Flügelwaffe (Ammunition belt box for wing weapon); 7. Vollgurtkasten fur hintere Rumpfwaffe (Ammunition belt box for rear fuselage weapon)

This period image shows the wing root gun bays. Item 1 is the MG151/20 cannon, 2 are the access panels, 3 the feed chutes for the wing guns and 4 the feed chutes for the rear fuselage guns

This diagram shows the wing root cannon along with the mounting cradle and retaining strap

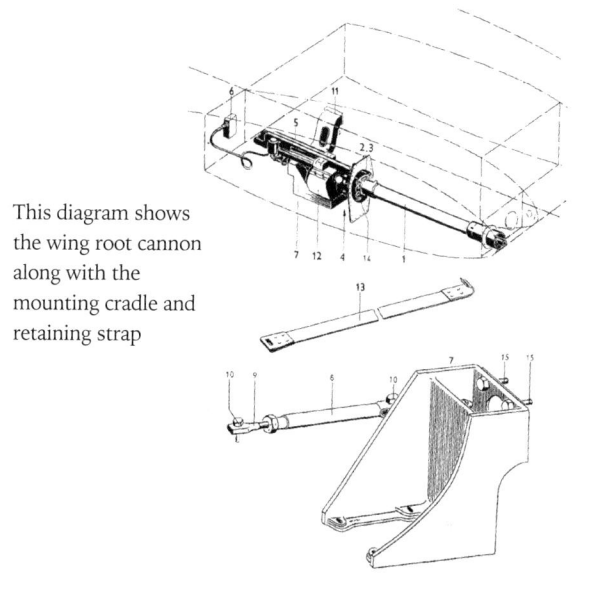

Here is a period image of the wing root cannon blast tube
1. Front carriage bearing
2. Blast tune sliding part
3. Blast tube port in the nose spar
4. Lock button

Group 7 – Side 2
Weapons
Armament

Another period photo of the port wing root gun, this shows the access cover (1), the cocking lever (2), the pneumatic cable (3), the EDSK-B 1 switching/firing unit (4) and button for the locking trunnion (5)

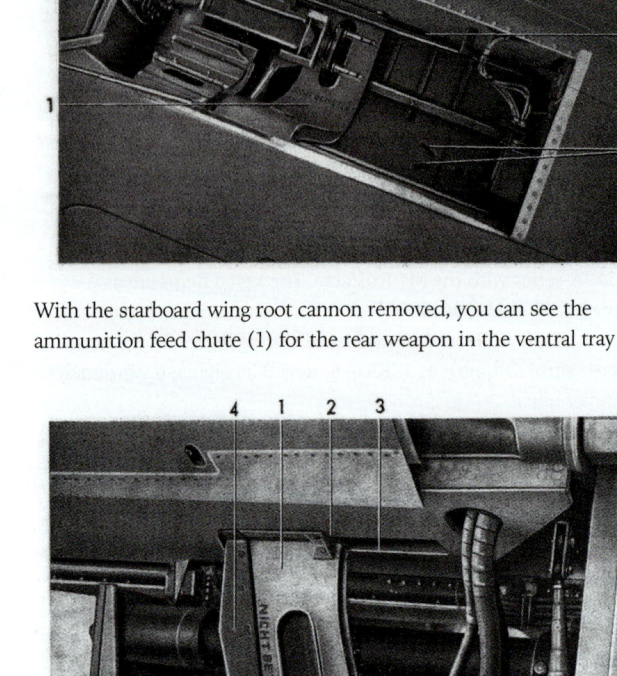

This image of the front of the starboard wing root shows the ammunition feed chute (1) for the front weapon in the ventral tray with an armoured plate (4) at the front

With the starboard wing root cannon removed, you can see the ammunition feed chute (1) for the rear weapon in the ventral tray

With the wing of the NASM example separated from the fuselage you get to see the wing root bay and associated equipment in detail – this is the port wing unit (©S. Willey)

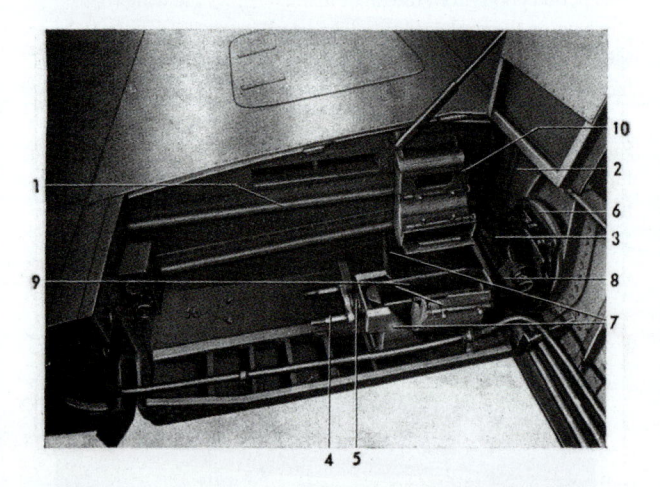

Here is the same area in a period image from the manual
1. Wing rib 1
2. Main wing spar
3. Front gun mount
4. Rear carriage bearing guide pin
5. Rear carriage bearing adjustment device
6. Connection fitting on the main spar
7. Bearing block with strut
8. Ventilation channel (for cartridges and belt links)
9. Ammunition belt feed with flaps

Group 7 – Side 3	**1**
Weapons	
Armament	73

Here are the wing root bays prior to restoration, but with the access panels still fixed and in the open position *(©S. Willey)*

This view from further back on the NASM example shows the wing root cannon bay in the starboard wing *(©S. Willey)*

This period diagram from the manual shows all the access panels and removable panels in the inner wing area. These include the access covers for the wing root guns (3)

1 Nasenverkleidungsblech
2 Verkleidungsblech des Holmkanals
3 Schnellverschlußklappe für das MG
4 Verkleidungsblech der seitl. Verteilertafel bzw. des Leitungsschachtes
5 Hintere Verkleidung
6 Innere Landeklappe
7 Gondelende

Here you have the gun ports in the ventral tray of the NASM example – this machine only had 2x MG151/20 fitted in this location *(©S. Willey)*

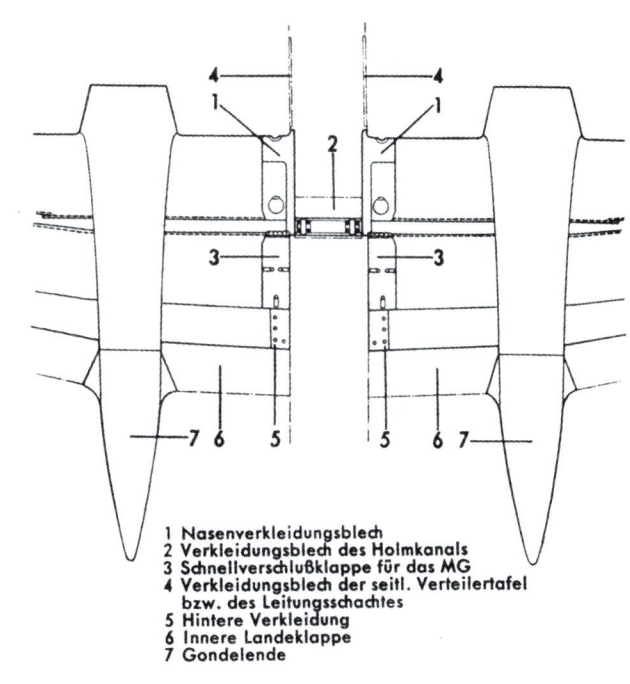

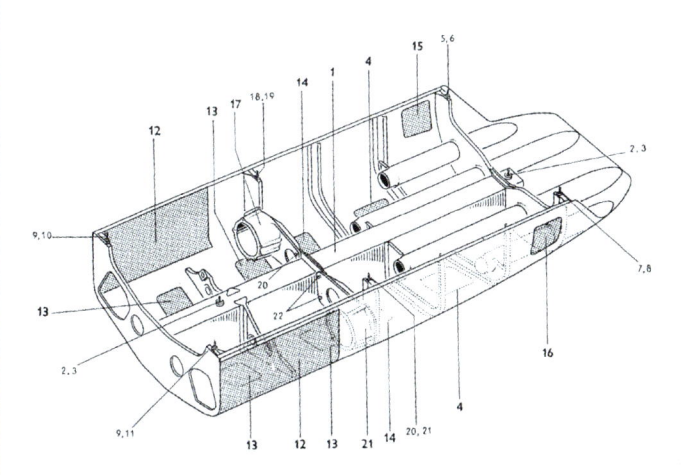

This diagram from the manual shows the construction of the forward half of the ventral tray

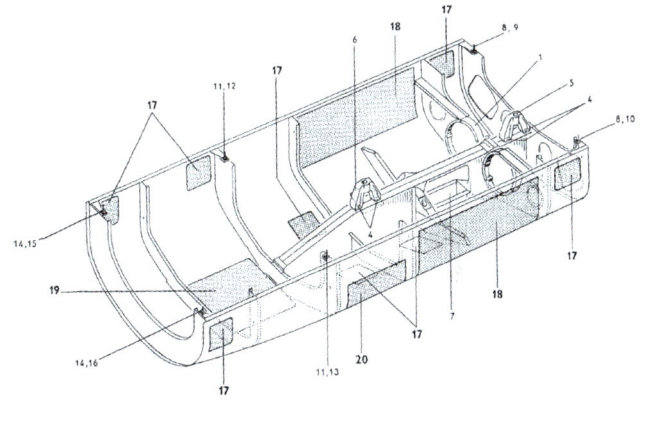

This diagram shows the aft section of the ventral tray – the dark areas are all access panels

AA01/17/73 — Valiant Wings Publishing — Issued: July 2021

Weapons
Armament
Group 7 – Side 4 — 1

The starboard rear weapons bay without the MG 151/20 installed
1. Ammunition feed chute
2. Empty belt channel
3. Vent duct
4. Ammunition feed chute (chute part IV)
5. Attachment point of the weapon tray

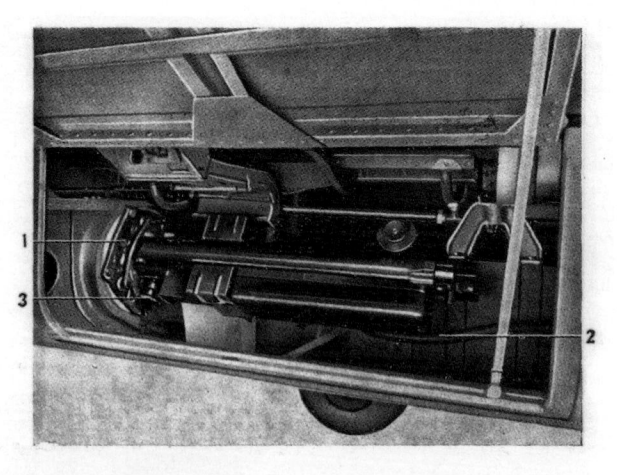

Here is the starboard rear weapons bay with the MG 151/20 in situ
1. Lever for barrel clamp
2. Electrical weapon connection cable
3. Button of the trunnion lock

The starboard front weapons bay without the MG 151/20 installed
1. Bearing flange for the rear carriage bracket
2. Ammunition feed chute (chute part IV)
3. Sleeve channel
4. Empty belt channel
5. Vent duct
6. Electrical socket for EDSK-B 1 switching/firing unit
7. Rear mounting

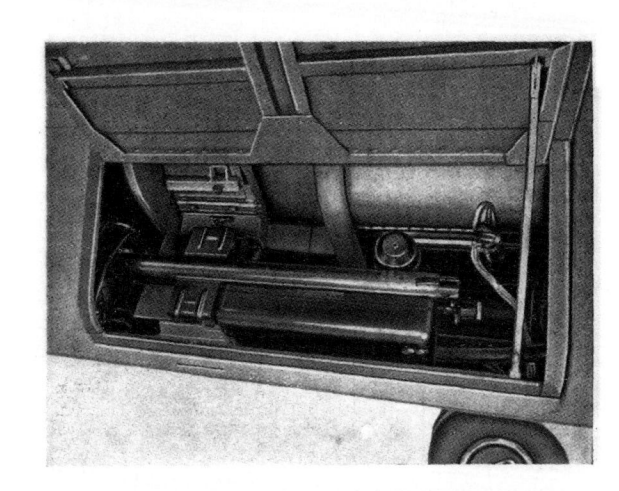

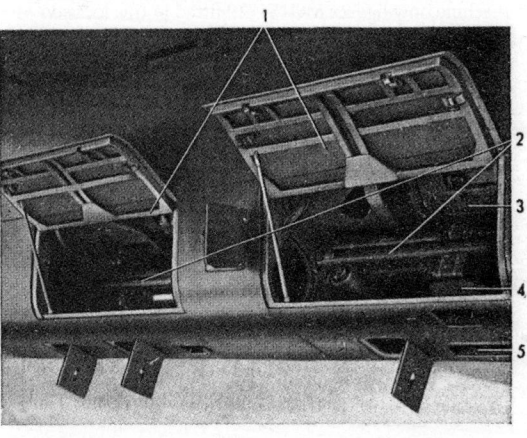

Here is the starboard front weapons bay with the MG 151/20 in situ

Here are both access doors open for the weapons on the starboard side, plus the smaller doors on the side and underneath
1. Access doors for ventral weapons
2. MG 151/20 cannon
3. Control flap on the ammunition feed channel
4. Empty belt ejection chute
5. Case ejection port

This diagram from the service manual shows some of the other access panels on the port side of the ventral tray. These include the access port for mounting the gun boring/synchronising equipment (3) and the two main doors to access the guns themselves (4). Items 1 and 2 are just the 'front' and 'rear' of the ventral tray and all the other access panels are just inspection hatches for the weapons, ammunition feeds and other equipment in the ventral tray

Group 7 – Side 5
Weapons
Armament

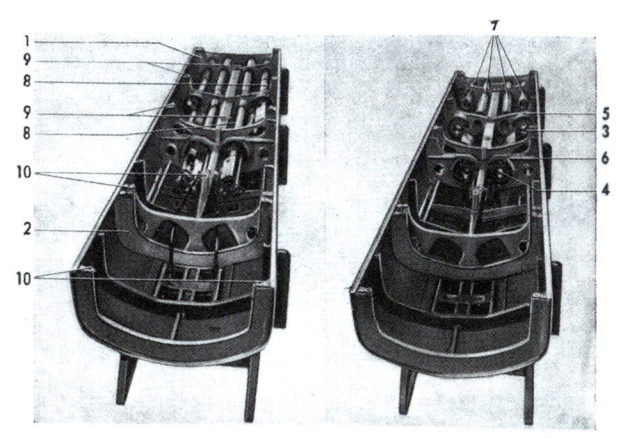

These two period images show the ventral tray with (left) or without (right) the weapons fitted
1. Front gun tray
2. Rear gun tray
3. Carriages (mounts) for front weapons
4. Carriages (mounts) for rear weapons
5. Weapons storage in the front hull
6. Weapons storage in the rear tray
7. Blast tubes
8. Attachment points of the front weapons tray
9. Attachment points of the rear weapons tray

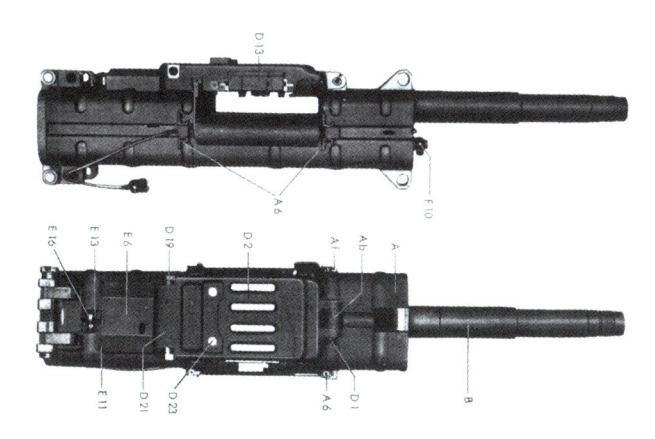

The MK108 30mm cannon

The small size of this 30mm cannon is evident, as is the rather odd colour, not your usual 'gunmetal' shade and probably a combination of the metal used and preservatives applied *(©P. Skulski)*

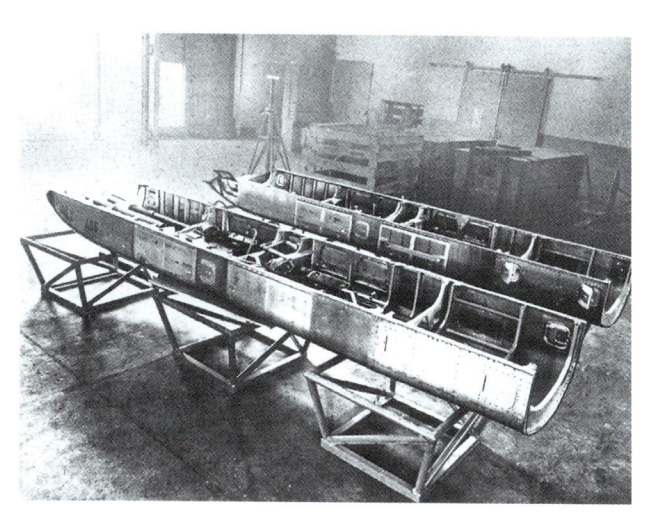

This period images shows two weapons trays, the one nearest being clearing marked as 'A06' denoting that it was intended for the sixth pre-production airframe

Now this image shows the installation of the MK108 in the forward (outer) positions in the ventral tray. This was not a well used installation, as the weapons when fired could result in the tray detaching!

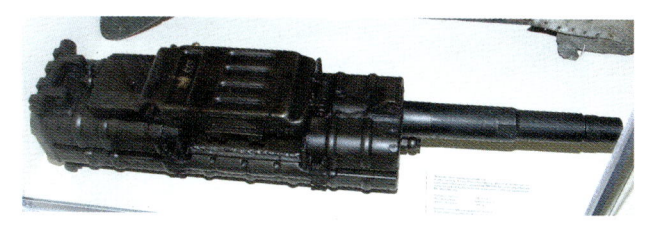

This view of an MK108 preserved in Germany shows the overall compactness of the design *(©P. Skulski)*

In this view of the right side of the MK108 you can see how production was simplified with many parts made from pressings *(©P. Skulski)*

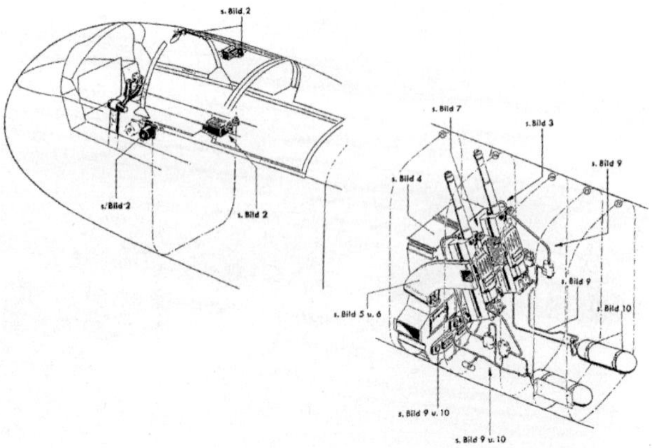

Group 7 – Side 6
Weapons
Armament

This diagram shows the *Schrägemusik* installation in the aft fuselage of the He 219, along with its associated sighting equipment in the cockpit, which we will cover in more detail in the next section

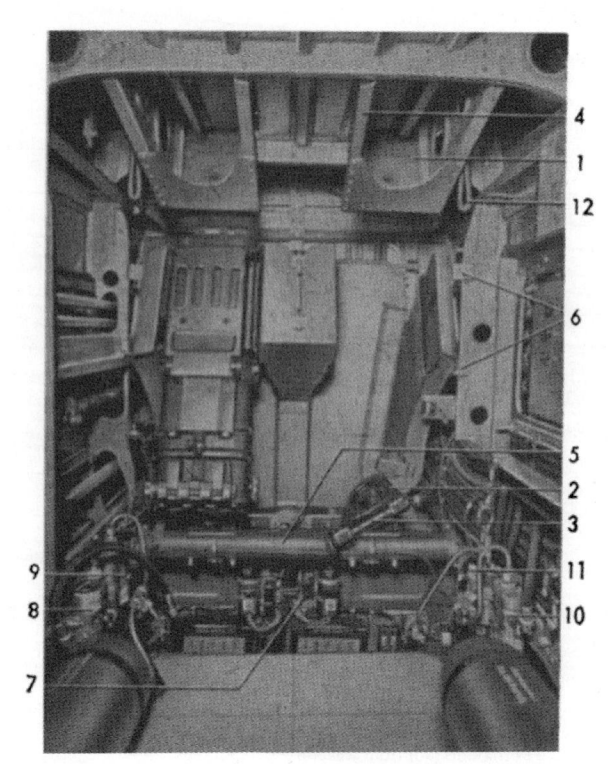

This shows the *Schrägemusik* installation with the starboard cannon removed – you are looking towards the front of the aircraft

1. Fastening screws for the upper weapon bracket
2. Adjusting bearing St.L. 103/108
3. Adjusting bearing St.L. 103/108 worm shaft
4. Upper weapon mounting
5. Lower weapon mounting
6. Angle plates for feed chutes
7. Device panel for electrical equipment
8. EPD 101 A for firing left weapon
9. EPD 101 A for cocking left weapon
10. EPD 101 A for firing right weapon
11. EPD 101 A for cocking the right weapon
12. Loops for gun lid holder

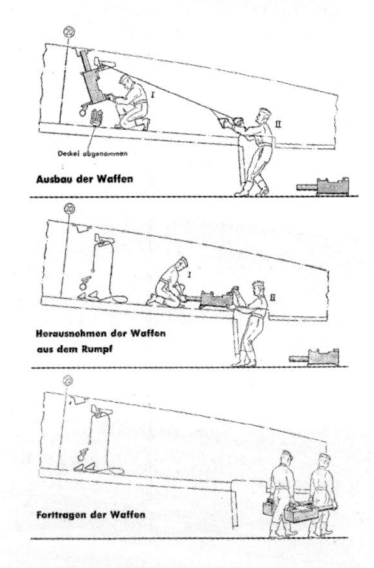

These diagrams show the three stages for removing the *Schrägemusik* MK 108s

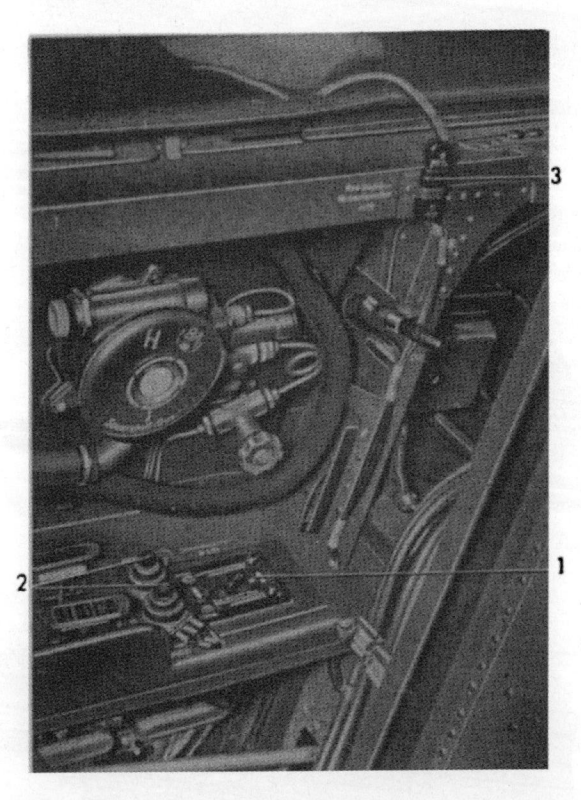

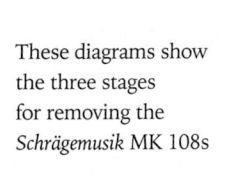

This shows some of the controls relating to the *Schrägemusik* located in the rear starboard sidewall of the pilot's cockpit
1. SZKK-2 control unit with safety switch
2. Push button switch for weapons cocking
3. Revi gunsight plug-in connection for inclined armament

This shows the dimmer switches for the gunsight of the *Schrägemusik* (1) and fixed forward-firing (2) armament, on the upper port sidewall of the the pilot's cockpit

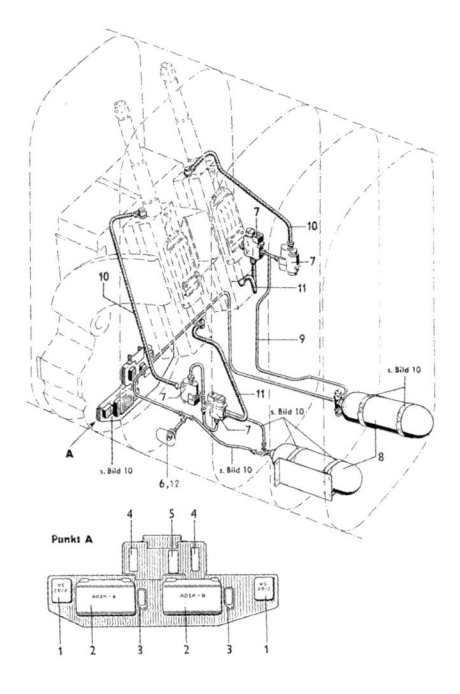

Group 7 – Side 7
Weapons
Armament

This shows the compressed air bottles associated with charging the the cannon in the *Schrägemusik* installation

Here is a more detailed image of the compressed air supply for the right *Schrägemusik* cannon (the left side is similar)
1. Compressed air flap with Dräger DHAG/5 valve
2. EPD 101A for cocking weapon
3. EPD 101A for firing weapon
4. Hose assembly for firing weapon
5. Hose line for cocking weapon

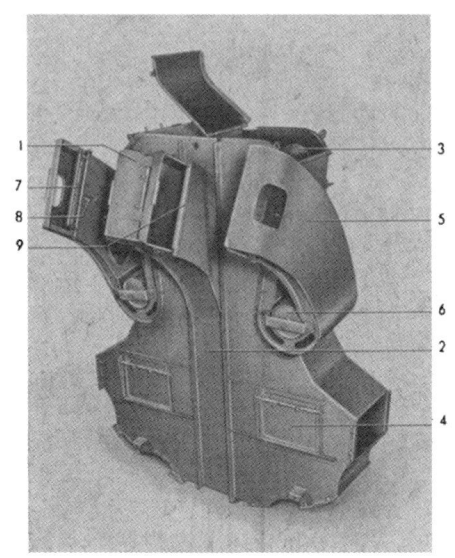

This is the ammunition bin for both of the MK 108s in the *Schrägemusik* installation, seen fitted with both feed and discharge chutes

1. Upper discharge chute with cover
2. Downward discharge duct, with cover plate
3. Deflection roller in the ammunition container
4. Flaps in the ammunition container
5. Feed channel
6. Feed channel deflection roller
7. Feed duct baffle
8. Feed channel belt lock
9. Belt separator

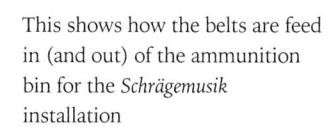

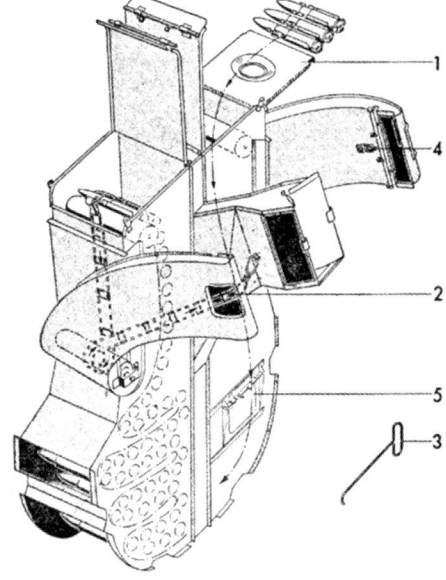

This shows how the belts are feed in (and out) of the ammunition bin for the *Schrägemusik* installation

1. Guard
2. Belt retractor channel
3. Belt retractor tool
4. Belt lock
5. Access/viewing flap

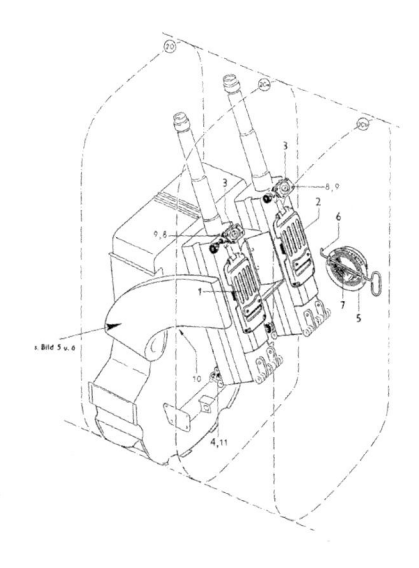

This is an overall view of the Mk 108 cannon in the *Schrägemusik* installation

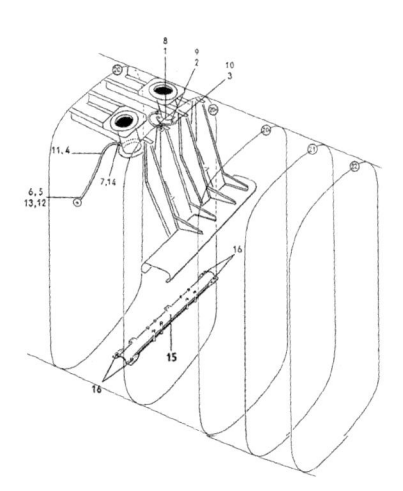

While this shows the *Schrägemusik* ports in the upper decking and the mounting frames without the weapons or ammunition bin fitted

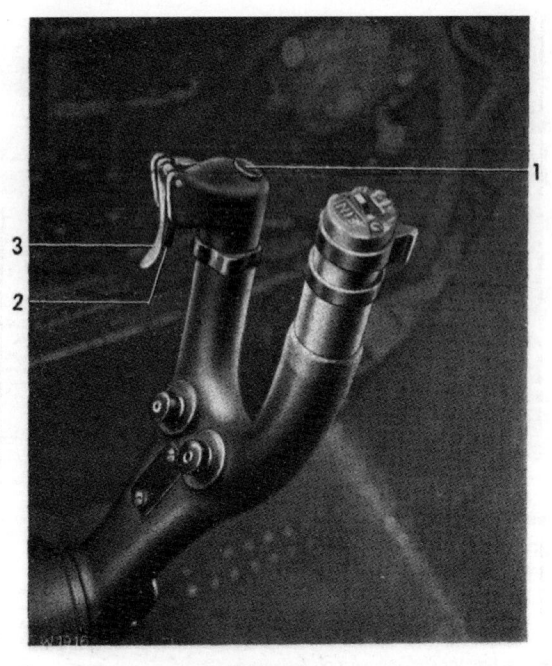

Group 7 – Side 8
Weapons
Armament

1 Abfeuerknopf für Rumpfwaffen
2 Abfeuerknopf für Flügelwaffen (unter Schießhebel)
3 Schießhebel für Flügelwaffen

This shows the various weapons related controls on the HSG 559 control column
1. Firing button for ventral weapons
2. Firing button for wing weapons (under the trigger)
3. Firing trigger for wing weapons

1 SZKK 6   2 Sicherungsschalter

In the front cockpit, on the front of the starboard side console are the SZKK 6 control unit (1) for the cannon (left and right) and the safety switch (2) to activate the firing circuit for all weapons

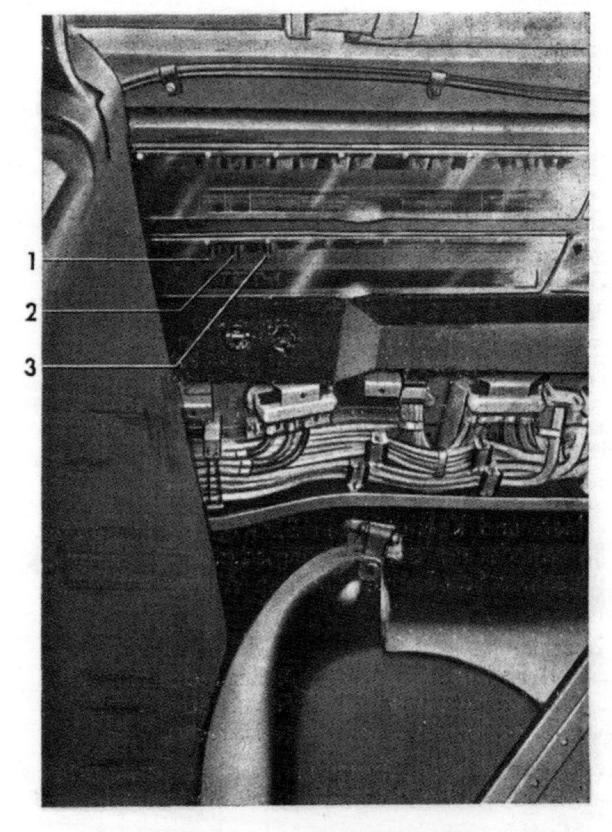

In the rear cockpit, on the starboard side distribution panel are the auto switches for the wing (1), or ventral (2) weapons, as well as the Revi gunsight (3)

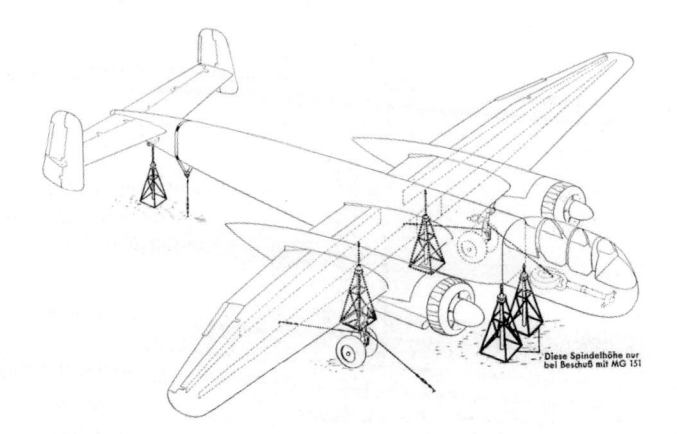

1 Selbstschalter P 3 für Flügelwaffen
2 Selbstschalter P 4 für Rumpfwaffen
3 Selbstschalter P 5 für Revi

This diagram shows how the aircraft was jacked for gun alignment and harmonisation – the note states that the front two jacks are to be used when firing the ventral cannon

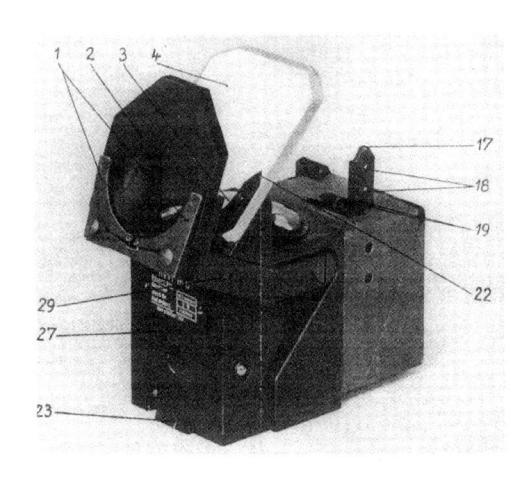

Group 7 – Side 9
Weapons
Sighting

These two views show a Revi 16B gunsight from the front and rear

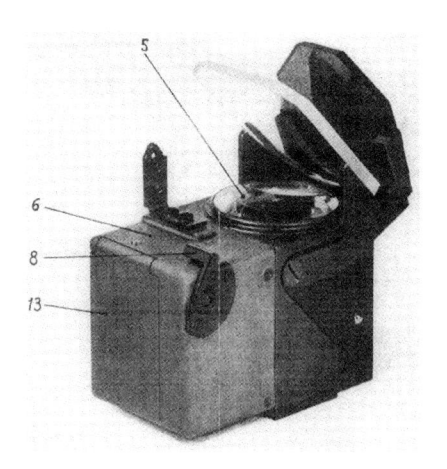

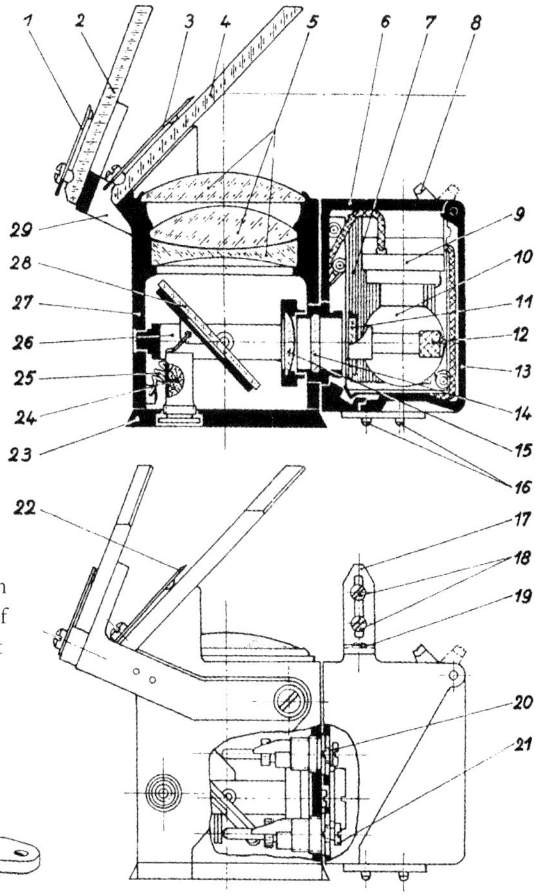

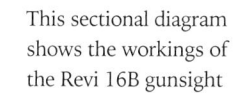

This sectional diagram shows the workings of the Revi 16B gunsight

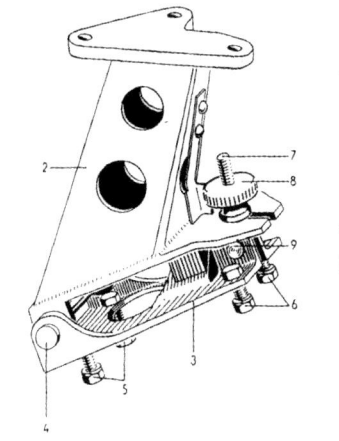

This is the mounting unit for the Revi 16B gunsight

This diagram for the flight manual shows the armoured glass (1) and the Revi gunsight. Item 4 is the windscreen wiper!

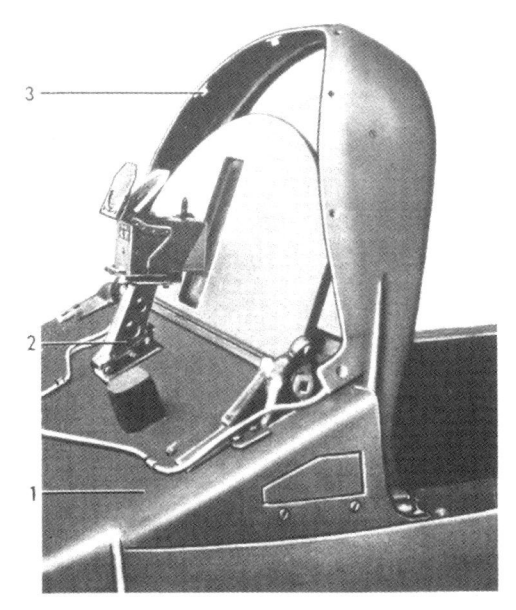

Here is the period photo from the manual showing the Revi gunsight (2) and the surround for the armoured glass with its attachment points for the windscreen (3)

Group 7 – Side 10
Weapons
80 | Sighting

Here is a diagram from the flight manual showing the Revi 16B gunsight
Gunsight (1), the mounting block (2), the swivel adjustment bolt (3), the base plate (4) the lever for the sun glare filter (5) and the operating rod for the night filter (6)

On the port side console in the front cockpit is the dimmer switch (1) the Revi gunsight

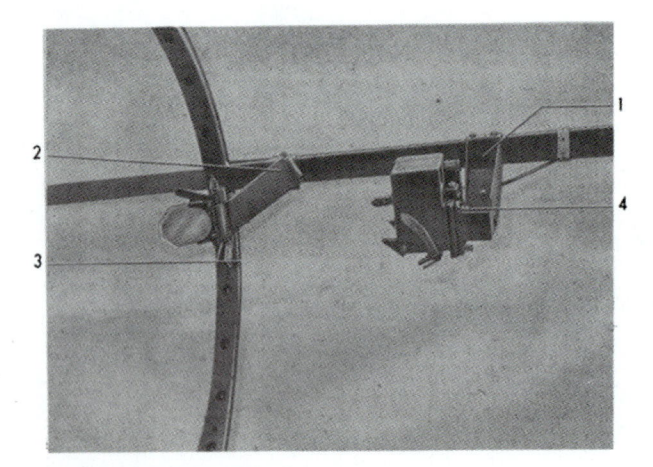

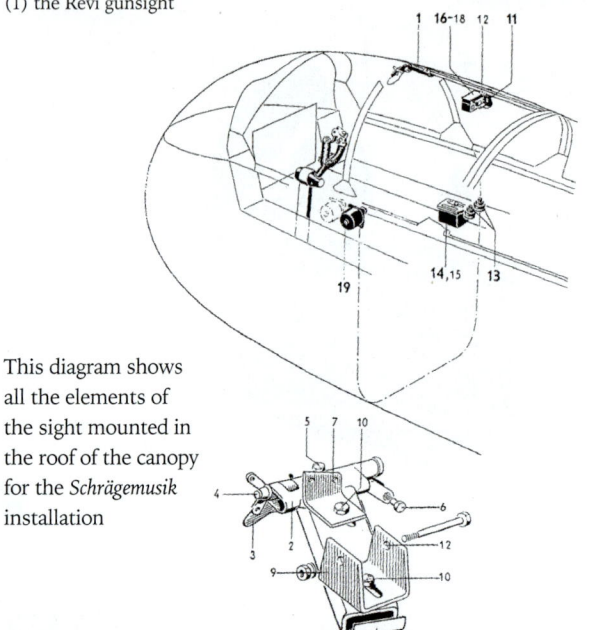

This diagram shows all the elements of the sight mounted in the roof of the canopy for the *Schrägemusik* installation

This period image shows the Revi 16N gunsight installation in the canopy roof
1. Bracket for Revi gunsight body
2. Bracket for lens
3. Adjusting screw for height adjustment
4. Adjustment screw for Revi gunsight body

This montaged image shows the complete *Schrägemusik* gunsight installation, with the sighting glass arrowed and the sight projector body further back (©S. Willey)

This montaged image shows the projector body for the sight mounted in the canopy top
(©S. Willey)

AA01/17/80 — Valiant Wings Publishing — Issued: July 2021

Group 8 – Side 1
Electrical
Radio

This period photo from the flight manual shows the radio equipment in the back of the He 219. Missing from the top row are the FuG 212 (1) and the FuG 220 (2) radar display units

3. Homing Indicator AFN 2
4. Remote Operating Device FBG 2 [for Receiver Control E BL 3 F]
5. FuG 10P Receiver E 10a K
6. Remotely operated device FBG 213 [for FuG 220)]
7. Switch Box SchK 213 [for FuG 220)
8. Switch Box Schk 17a (8)
9. FuG 10 Homing-receiver EZ 6 [Long]
10. FuG 16ZE (later machines used the FuG 16ZY)
11. Remote control unit FBG 3 [for FuG 10P]
12. FuG 10P Transmitter S 10K
13. Radio Compass PTK/p 2
14. FuG 10P Transmitter S 10L
15. Junction Box ADb 11/16 ZE
16. Bowden cable for FuG 220 [Remote control hand switch HU 220 for dipoles]

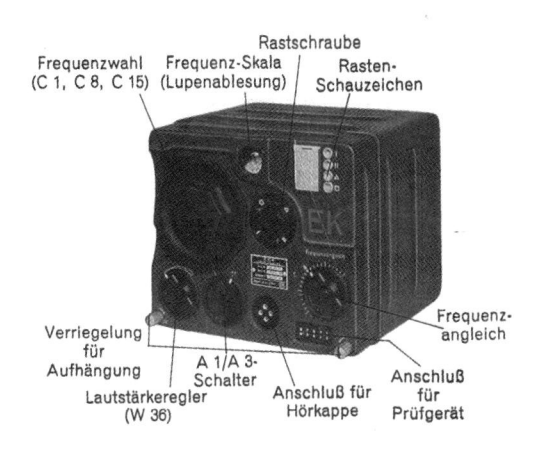

From the previous overall image, here is the FuG 10P Receiver E 10a K (5)

This is the remote control unit FBG 3 for the FuG 10P (11)

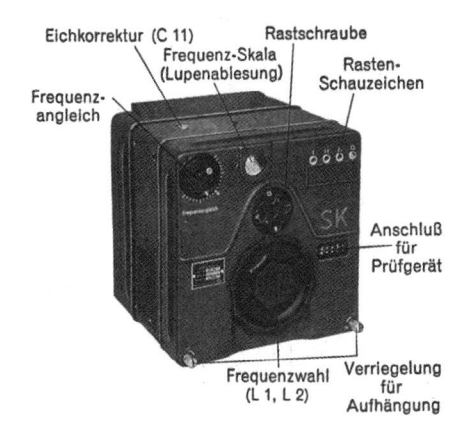

This is the FuG 10P Transmitter S 10K (12)

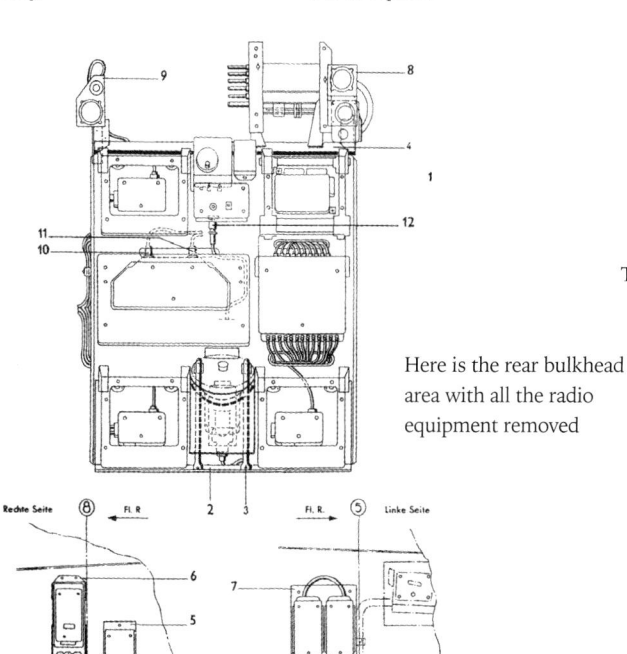

Here is the rear bulkhead area with all the radio equipment removed

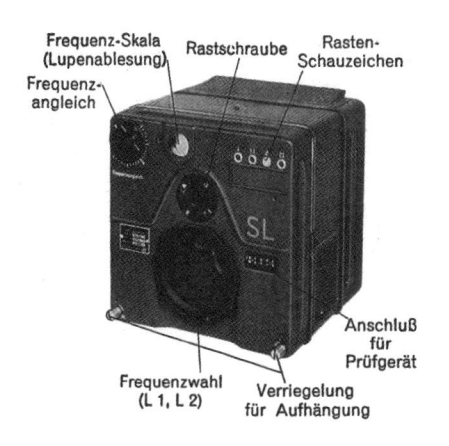

This is the FuG 10P Transmitter S 10L (14)

Group 8 – Side 2
Electrical
Radio

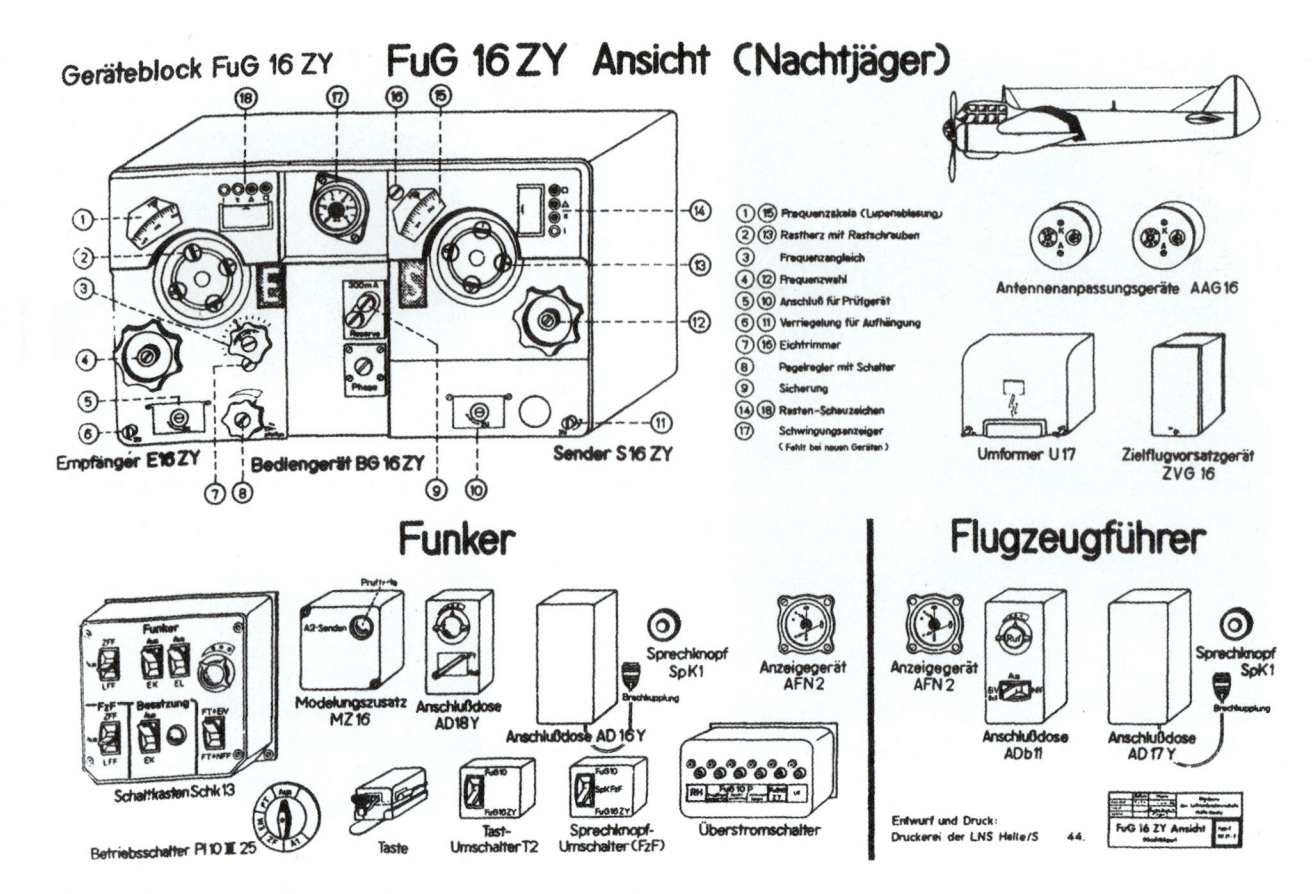

Here is the diagram relating to the fitment of the FuG 16ZY in nightfighters

The listed items are as follows: Geräteblock FuG 16ZY (Device Block FuG 16ZY [basically means 'Unit FuG 16ZY']); FuG 16ZY Ansicht (Nachtjäger) (FuG 16ZY View Nightfighter)); Empfänger E16ZY (Receiver E16ZY); Bediengerät BG 16ZY (Control Device BG 16ZY); Sender S 16ZY (Transmitter S 16ZY); Frequenzskala (Lupenablesung) (Frequency Scale (Readout Magnifier)); Rastherz mit Rastschrauben (Turning head with locking screws); Frequenzabgleich (Frequency Adjustment); Anschluß für Prüfgerät (Connectors for testing); Verriegelung für Aufhängung (Locks for suspension [e.g. securing pins]); Eichtrimmer (Calibration trimmer); Pegelregler mit Schalter (Lever control with switch); Sicherung (Fuse); Rasten-Scheuzeichen (Warning marks); Schwingungsanzeiger (Fehlt bei neuen Geräten) (Indicator oscillation) (Missing on new equipment)); Antennenanpassungsgeräte AAG 16 (Antenna adjustment device AAG 16); Umformer U17 (Converter U17); Zielflugvorsatzgerät ZVG 16 (Homing supplementary unit ZVG 16); Flugzeugführer (Pilot [i.e. at pilot's station/position]); Anzeigegerät AFN 2 (Display unit AFN 2); Anschlußdose ADb 11 (Junction box ADb 11); Anschlußdose AD 17Y (Junction box AD 17Y); Sprechknopf SpK 1 (Intercom button SpK 1); Funker (Radio operator [e.g. at radio operator's station/position]); Schaltkasten Schk 13 (Switchbox Schk 13); Modelungszusatz MZ 16 (Additional averaging device MZ 16); Anschlußdose AD 18Y (Junction box AD 18Y); Anschlußdose AD 16Y (Junction box AD 16Y); Sprechknopf SpK 1 (Intercom buttom SpK 1); Anzeigegerät AFN 2 (Display unit AFN 2); Überstromschalter (Over current switch [e.g. fuses/trips]); Sprechknopf-Umschalter (FzF) (Intercom button switch (FzF)); Tast-Umschalter T2 (Task switcher T2 [e.g. switch between FuG 16ZY and FuG 10]); Taste (Key [e.g. Morse Key]); Betriebsschalter PI 10 II 25 (Power switch PI 10 II 25)

As you can see, very little remains of the radio equipment in the back of the NASM example, as most was removed and replaced with American equipment for the planned test flying. The only two remaining items are the Switch Box Schk 17a (nearest) and the Switch Box SchK 213 for the FuG 220 (farthest with red winder) (©S. Willey)

This close-up shot of the two remaining original German units in the NASM machine show the SchK 213 unit nearest the camera – item 7 from the first image in this section (©S, Willey)

Group 8 – Side 3
Electrical

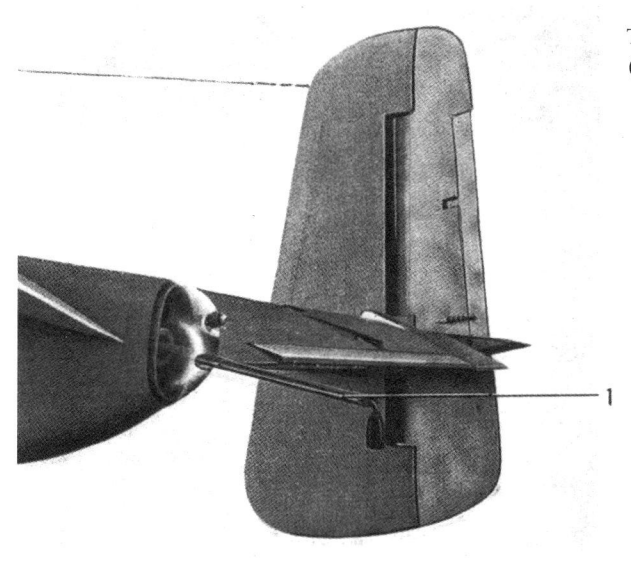

Radio

83

The FuG X radio used a trailing aerial that project through this tube (1) in the clear cap at the rear of the fuselage

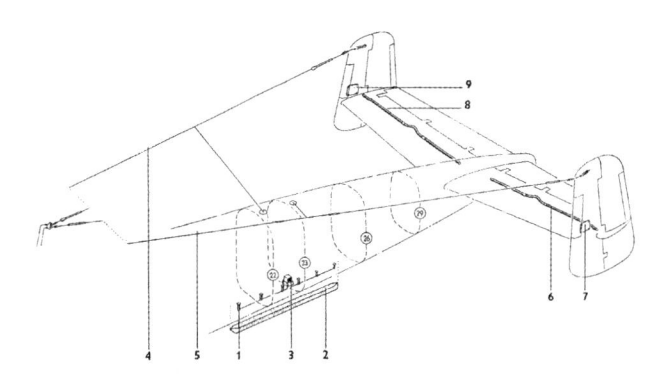

This period diagram shows the aerial leads from the rear canopy antenna, plus the ventral antenna

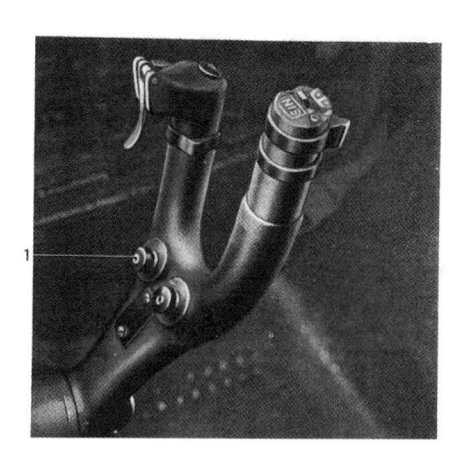

In the cockpit the intercom talk button (1) was situated on the front of the HSG 559 control yoke

Radio related items on the port sidewall of the pilot's cockpit include the 1. Control Unit BG 25 (1) for the FuG 25 and the junction box for the ADb 11 intercom system

This shows the radio related items on the port side of the observer's cockpit
1. Head rest of the radio operator's seat
2. Selector switch 'FuG 10-Fug 16'
3. 'Measure distance' toggle switch
4. Explosion (destruction) switch for FuG 25A
5. Electrical control unit for shearing device of the trailing aerial
6. Frame control switch RSS 6
7. Junction box for AD 18E
8. FuG 10P button T2

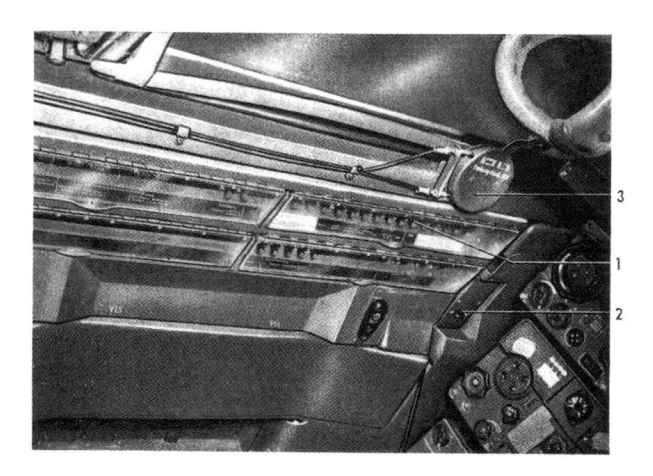

Whilst on the starboard side of the observer's cockpit are the following:
1. Self-switch for all devices connected to the on-board network
2. FuG 10P switching device: Telephony (F32)
3. Bowden cable as shown in Fig. 2/16

Group 8 – Side 4
Electrical
Radar

This diagram from the flight manual shows the FuG 212 (left) and FuG 220 (right) radars

The only radar unit left in the NASM He 219 is the FuG 220 unit – this is the unit prior to renovation (©S. Willey)

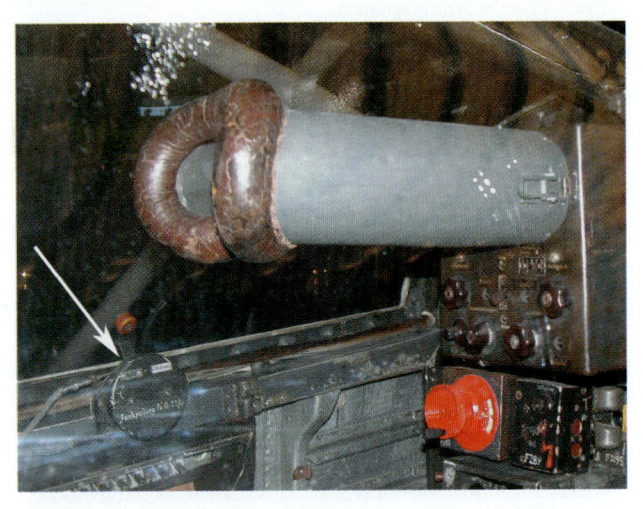

Here is the FuG 220 unit, complete with the glare guard/eye piece fitted – the unit was not restored, it was just preserved in line with NASM's policy. The arrowed item is the control unit for the FuG 220 dipoles (©S. Willey)

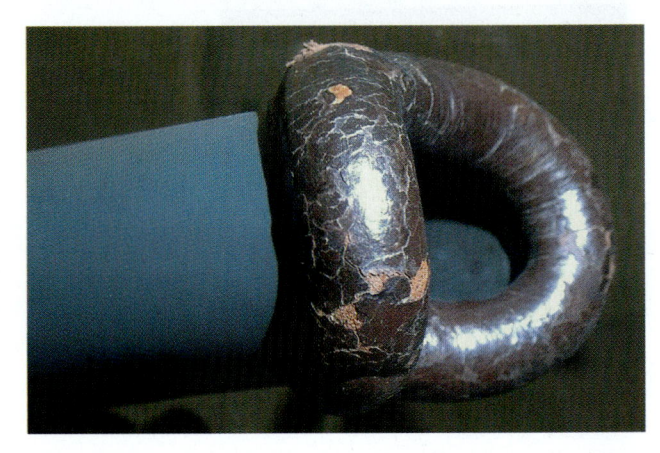

This close-up of the glare guard/eye piece shows that it has a padded leather surround (©S. Willey)

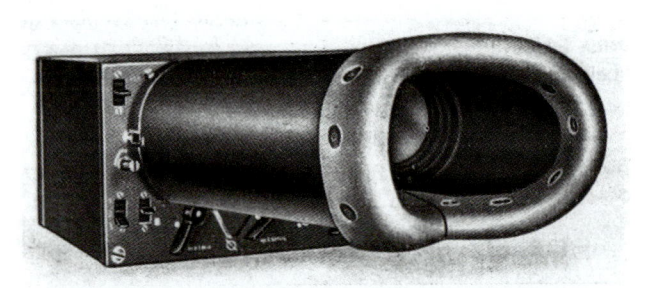

This photo from the flight manual shows the FuG 212 unit with its glare guard/eye piece in place. The FuG 212 had three screens, while the FuG 220 only had two, hence the wider guard on the FuG 212

This wartime photograph show the nose area of the He 219

1. Beplankung (Plating)
2. Abnehmbarer Mittelstreifen (Removable centre strip)
3. Verkleidungsbleche (Cladding panels)
4. Halterung für Lichtensteinantenne (Antenna mount for Lichtenstein)
5. Außenbordanschluß (Outboard connection)
6. Öffnung für Kaltluftzuleitung (Opening for cold air supply)

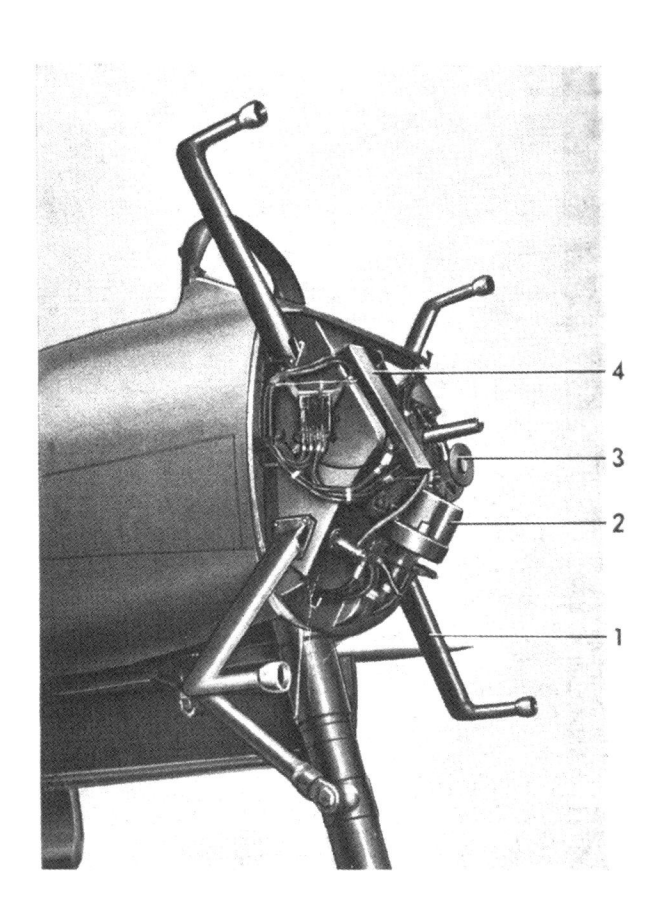

Group 8 – Side 5
Electrical
Radar

85

This photo shows a He 219 captured by US servicemen at Bindach in early 1945 – note that the SN-2 antlers are vertical *(©USAAF)*

This photo from the flight manual shows the nose cone removed from the He 219. The keyed items are as follows: 1. Halterungen für SN-2-Antenne (Brackets for SN-2 antenna); 2. Drehverteiler (Rotary distributors); 3. Rohr fur Kaltluftzuleitung (Cold air feed pipe); 4. Kabelabgleichkasten (Cable alignment box)

This shot of a He 219 captured by the RAF at Grøve (modern day Kastrup) in 1945 shows the SN-2d antlers are at 45° *(©RAF Official)*

This wartime image, although not that clear, does show the FuG 220 antenna, as well as, in the middle, the antenna for the FuG 212

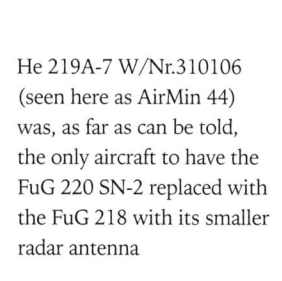

He 219A-7 W/Nr.310106 (seen here as AirMin 44) was, as far as can be told, the only aircraft to have the FuG 220 SN-2 replaced with the FuG 218 with its smaller radar antenna

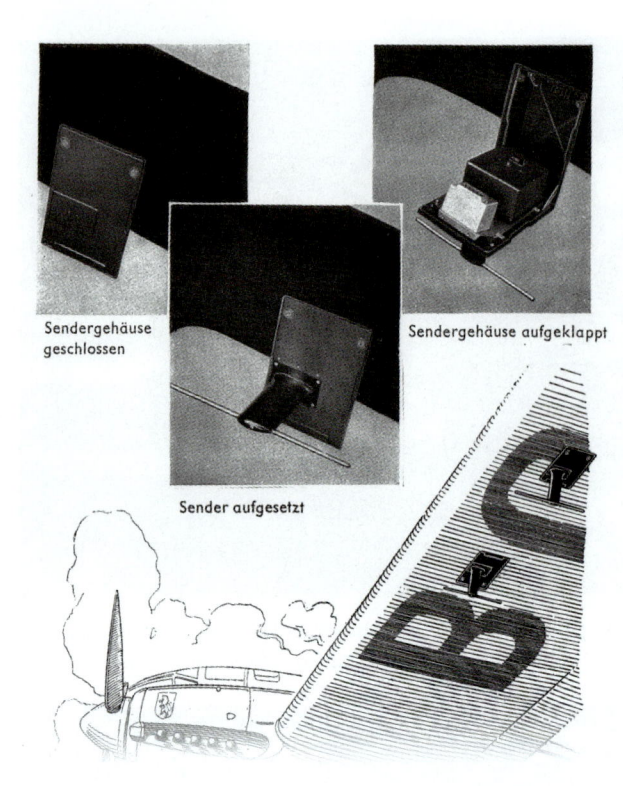

Group 8 – Side 6
Electrical
Miscellaneous

This wartime diagram shows the FuG 101 radio altimeter, in this instance fitted to a He 111, but it is the same as used by the He 219

Bild 8: Sedergehäuse (Figure 8: Transmitter housing)
Bild 9: Sendergehäuse aufgeklappt (Figure 9. Transmitter housing open)
Bild 10: Sender aufgesetzt (Figure 10. Transmitter in position)

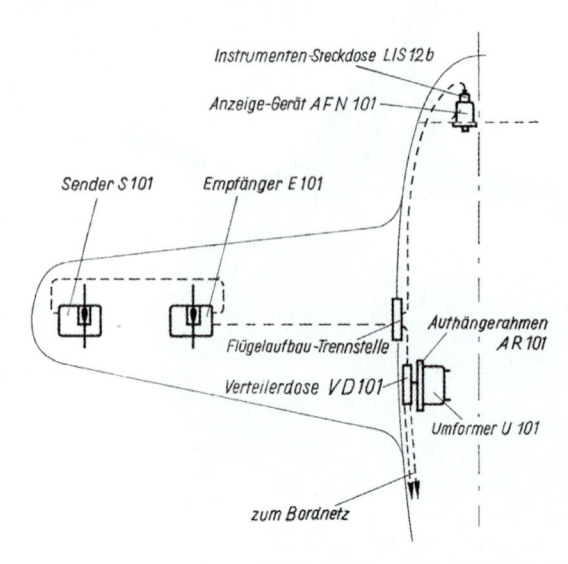

This diagram shows you the overall installation of the FuG 101 radio altimeter

Instrumenten-Steckdose LIS 12b – Instrument socket LIS 12b
Anzeige-Gerät AFN 101 – Display device AFN 101
Sender S101 – Transmitter S101
Empfänger E101 – Receiver E101
Flüglaufbau-Trennstelle – Wing superstructure separation point
Verteilerdose VD101 – Distribution box VD101
Aufhängerahmen AR 101 – Suspension frame AR 101
Umformer U101 – Transformer U101
zum Bordnetz – to the on-board network

Bezeichnung	Baumuster	Anforder-zeichen	Gewicht etwa
Sender	S 101	Ln 28 332	2,7 kg
Empfänger	E 101	Ln 28 333	2,9 kg
Umformer	U 101	Ln 28 331	4,3 kg

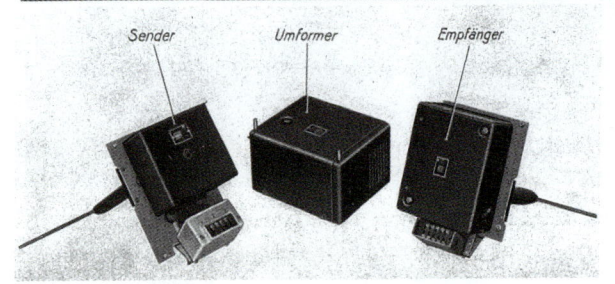

Here are the three main elements of the FuG 101 radio altimeter
Sender – Transmitter
Umformer – Transformer
Empfänger – Receiver

Here is one of the FuG 101 antenna with the stem still painted
(©S. Willey)

Here is the other FuG 101 antenna with the outer paint removed
(©S. Willey)

This is a close-up of the material used for the main stem on the FuG 101 antenna – it looks like an early plastic (©S. Willey)

Group 8 – Side 7
Electrical

Miscellaneous | 87

This is what is underneath the FuG 101 antenna – the item marked S101A is the sender (transmitter) unit (©S. Willey)

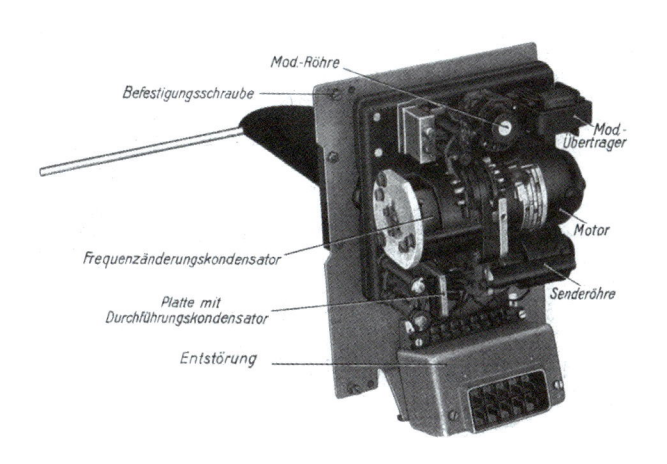

This is the interior of the Sender S101

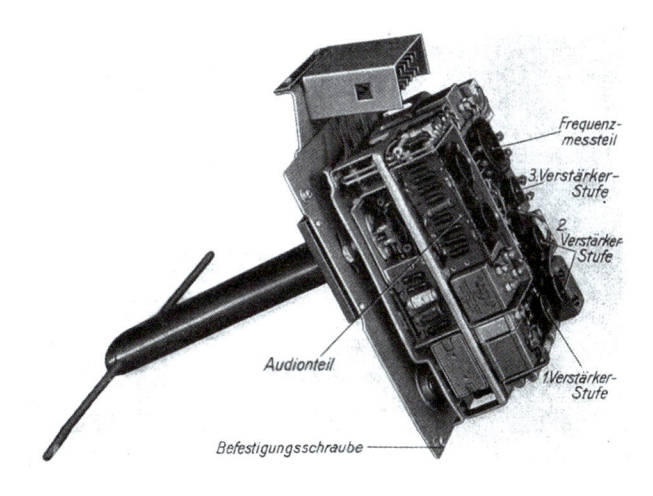

This is the interior of the Receiver E101

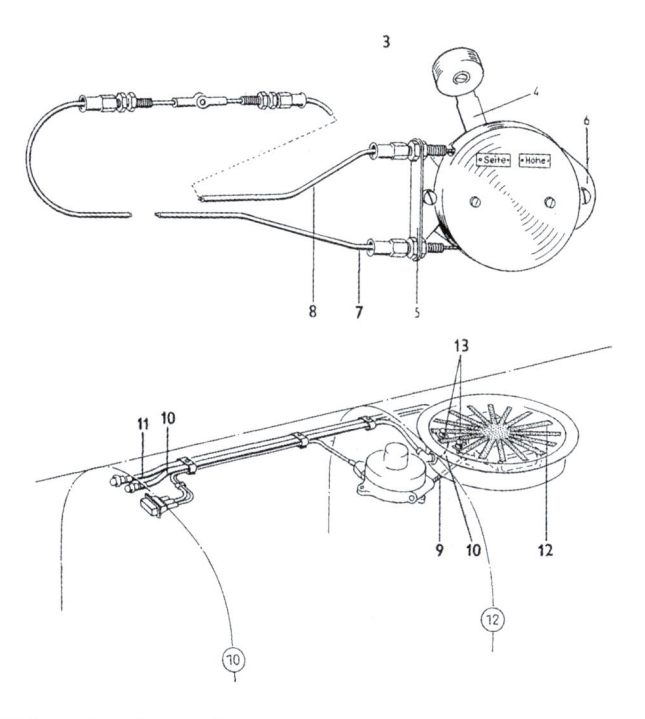

This wartime diagram shows the DF loop (Peilgerät E26) that is on the dorsal spine of the He 219 along with its control unit situated on the starboard canopy sill in the observer's cockpit

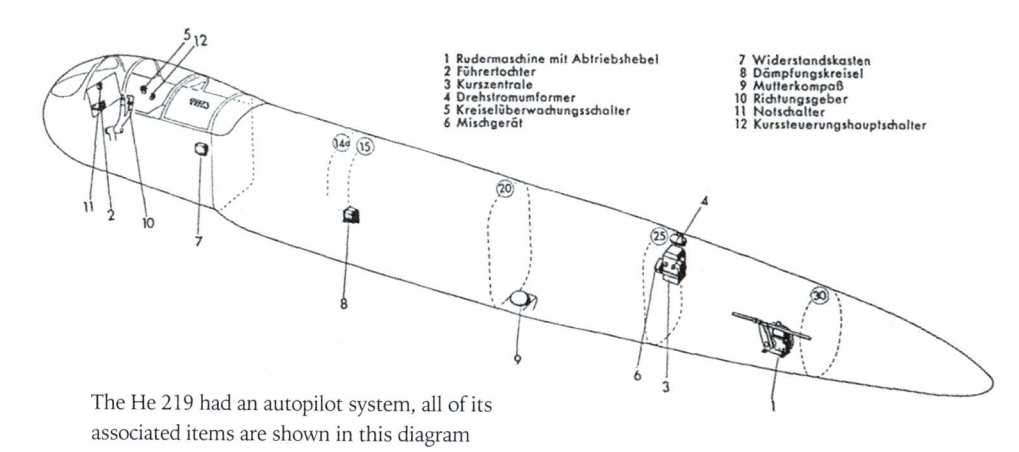

1 Rudermaschine mit Abtriebshebel
2 Führertochter
3 Kurszentrale
4 Drehstromumformer
5 Kreiselüberwachungsschalter
6 Mischgerät
7 Widerstandskasten
8 Dämpfungskreisel
9 Mutterkompaß
10 Richtungsgeber
11 Notschalter
12 Kurssteuerungshauptschalter

1. Rudder control unit with output lever
2. Master compass
3. Course control unit
4. Power converter
5. Gyro monitoring switch
6. Mixer unit
7. Resistance box
8. Damping gyro
9. Mother compass
10. Direction indicator
11. Emergency switch
12. Heading main switch

The He 219 had an autopilot system, all of its associated items are shown in this diagram

AA01/18/87 | Valiant Wings Publishing | Issued: July 2021

Group 8 – Side 8
Electrical
Miscellaneous

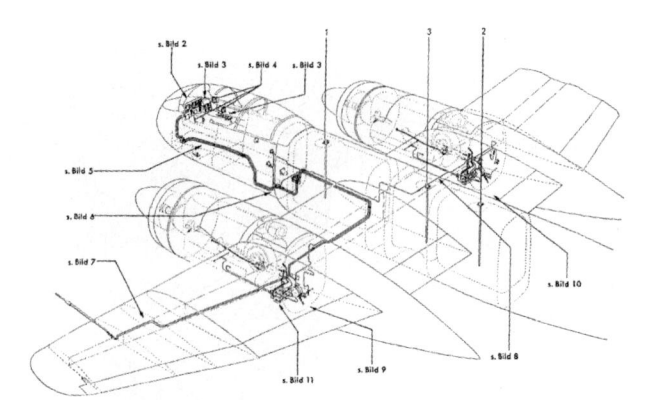

This diagram show the wiring for the pitot (Marked 's. Bild 7' [see Figure 7]), the temperature and oil pressure systems for each engine and the fuselage fuel cell contents gauges (Marked: '1', '2' and '3')

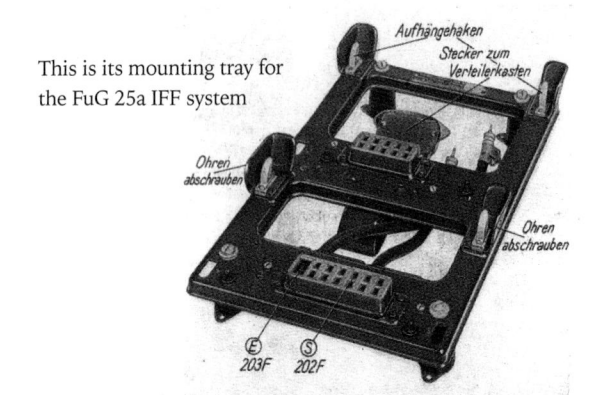

This is its mounting tray for the FuG 25a IFF system

In the main instrument panel are the following radio navigational related items
1. Homing device (display for radio navigation) AFN 2
2. Radio altimeter (display for radio navigation) AFN 101
3. Rotary switch (course activation [autopilot])

Here are all of the associated units for the FuG 25a, most of which are attached to the mounting tray on the starboard side mid-fuselage

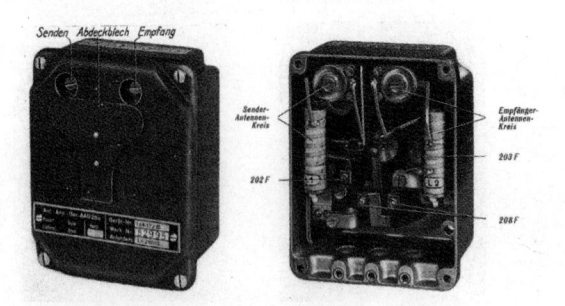

Antenna matching device

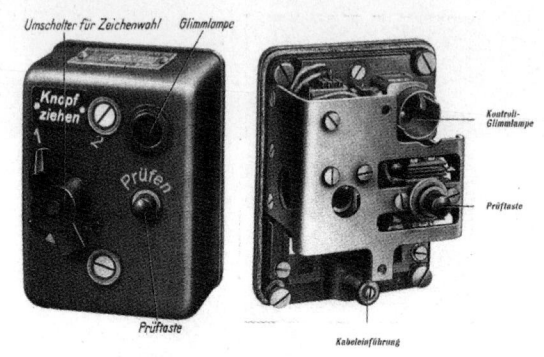

Control unit

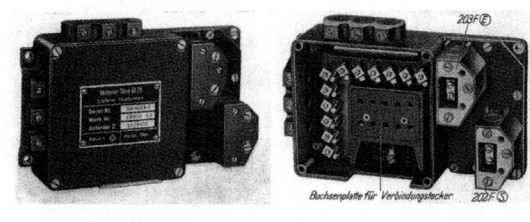

Junction Box

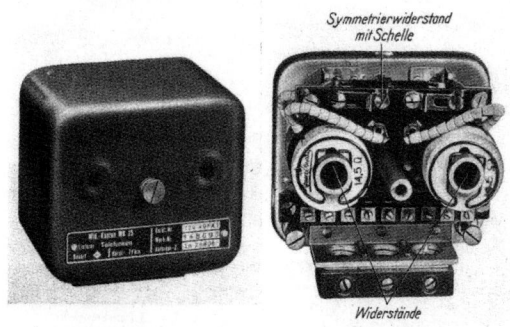

Resistance box

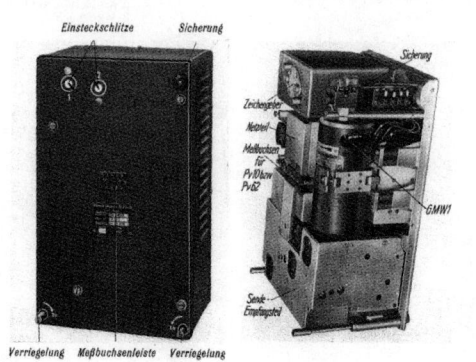

Transceiver unit

Group 9 – Side 1
Miscellaneous
Panels

Note: oddly neither of these diagrams ever came with a list of what each panel was for?

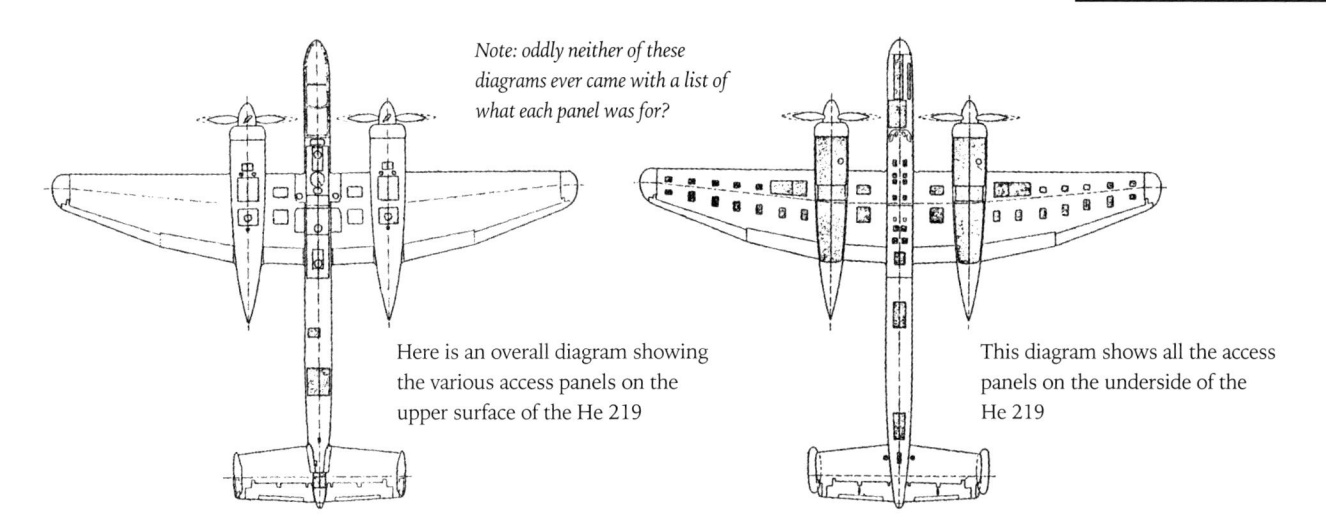

Here is an overall diagram showing the various access panels on the upper surface of the He 219

This diagram shows all the access panels on the underside of the He 219

This diagram shows the panels in the upper surface of the wings

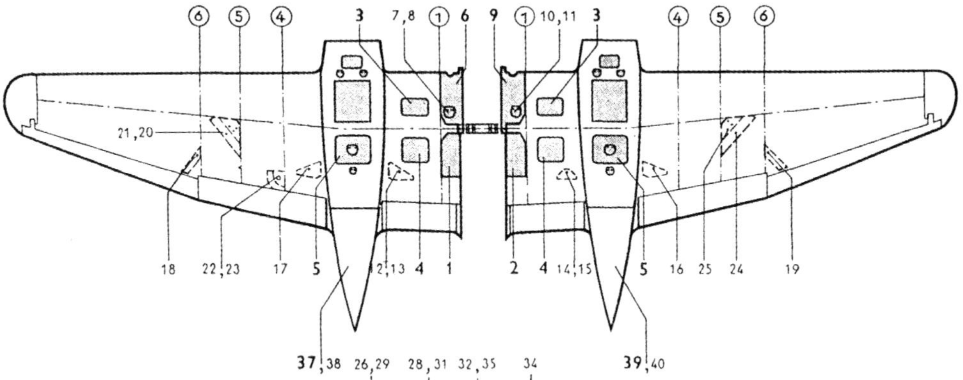

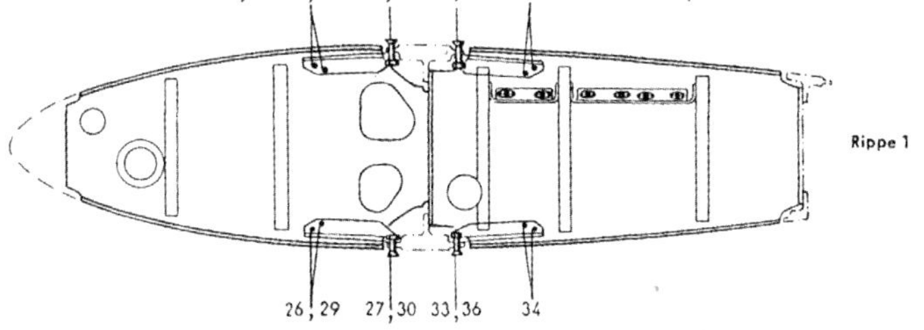

1. MG 151 cover, left
2. MG 151 cover, right
3. Ammunition cover, front
4. Ammunition cover, butt
5. Access panel for oil tank
6. Left duct flap
7. Handhole cover (for 6)
8. Countersunk screws (for 6)
9. Right flap
10. Handhole cover (for 9)
11. Countersunk screws (for 9)
12. Hexagon bolts (for the bearing for the flap drive lever inside, left)
13. Hexagon bolts (for the bearing for the flap drive lever inside, left)
14. Hexagon bolts (for the bearing for the flap drive lever inside, right)
15. Hexagon bolts (for the bearing for the flap drive lever inside, right)
16. Bolt for flap drive lever outside, right
17. Bolt for flap drive lever outside, left
18. Hexagon bolt for aileron drive lever, left
19. Hexagon bolt for aileron drive lever, right
20. Hexagon bolts (for the control cable, left)
21. Hexagon bolts (for the control cable, left)
22. Spherical bearings (for the landing flap cylinders)
23. Hexagon bolts (for the landing flap cylinders)

24. Hexagon bolts (for the control cable, right)
25. Hexagon bolts (for the control cable, right)
26. Hexagon bolts (Leading edge rib 1, left)
27. Countersunk screws (Leading edge rib 1, left)
28. Countersunk screws (Leading edge rib 1, left)
29. Hexagon bolts (Leading edge rib 1, right)
30. Countersunk screws (Leading edge rib 1, right)
31. Countersunk screws (Leading edge rib 1, right)
32. Countersunk screws (Spar cap rib 1, left)
33. Countersunk screws (Spar cap rib 1, left)
34. Hexagon bolts (Spar cap rib 1, left)
35. Countersunk screws (Spar cap rib 1, right)
36. Countersunk screws (Spar cap rib 1, right)
37. End of the engine nacelle, left
38. Hex bolts (for 37)
39. End of the engine nacelle, right
40. Hex bolts (for 39)

This diagram shows the panels in the under surface of the wings

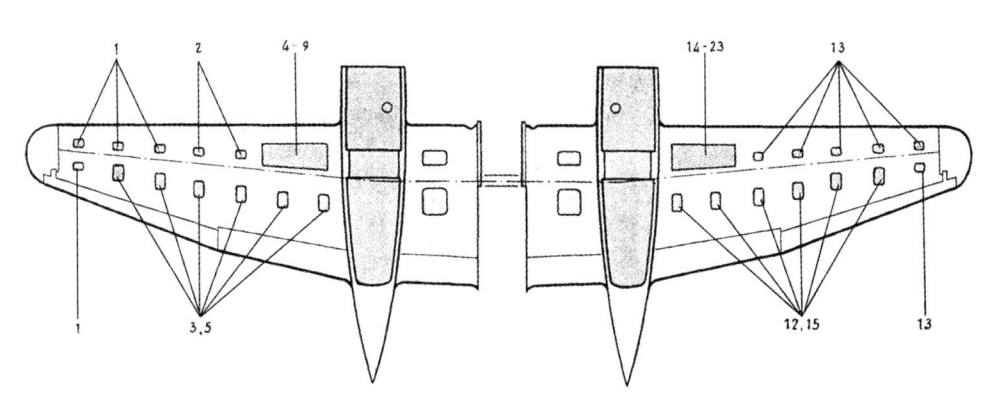

1. Access panel (wing interior, right)
2. Access panel (wing interior, right)
3. Access panel (wing interior, right)
4. Access panel/cover over de-icing heater unit, right
5. Countersunk screws (for 3 & 4)
6. Countersunk screws (for 4)
7. Countersunk screws (for 4)
8. Countersunk screws (for 4)
9. Countersunk screws (for 4)
12. Access panel (wing interior, left)
13. Access panel (wing interior, left)
14. Access panel/cover over de-icing heater unit, left

15. Countersunk screws (for 12 & 14)
16. Countersunk screws (for 14)
17. Countersunk screws (for 14)
18. Countersunk screws (for 14)
19. Countersunk screws (for 14)
20. Countersunk screws (for 14)
21. Block of wood (for 14)
22. Countersunk screws
23. Countersunk screw (for 14)

Group 9 – Side 2
Miscellaneous
Panels/Covers

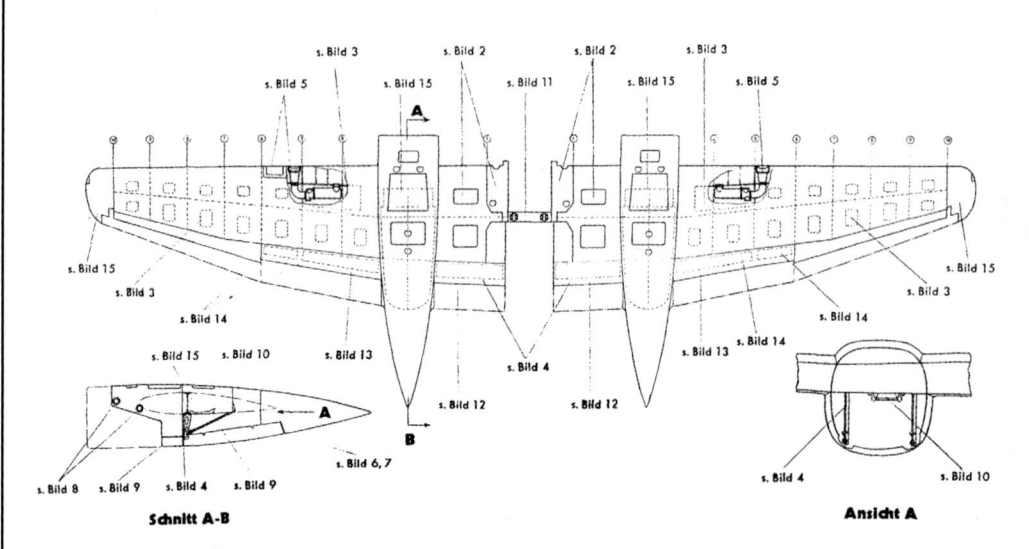

This diagram also shows the access panels in the upper wing surfaces and nacelles, but it also shows (as dotted lines) all the panels on the underside as well. Nearly all of those under the outer wing panels are inspection panels, although the FuG 101 antenna is fitted in two of them under the starboard side

Note: oddly none of these three diagrams ever came with a list of what each panel was for?

This diagram shows all the access panels on the right and left sides of the fuselage

1. Fuel cells
2. Rescue dinghy
3. Access hatch
4. Cannon access doors
5. Electrical wiring and control rod access

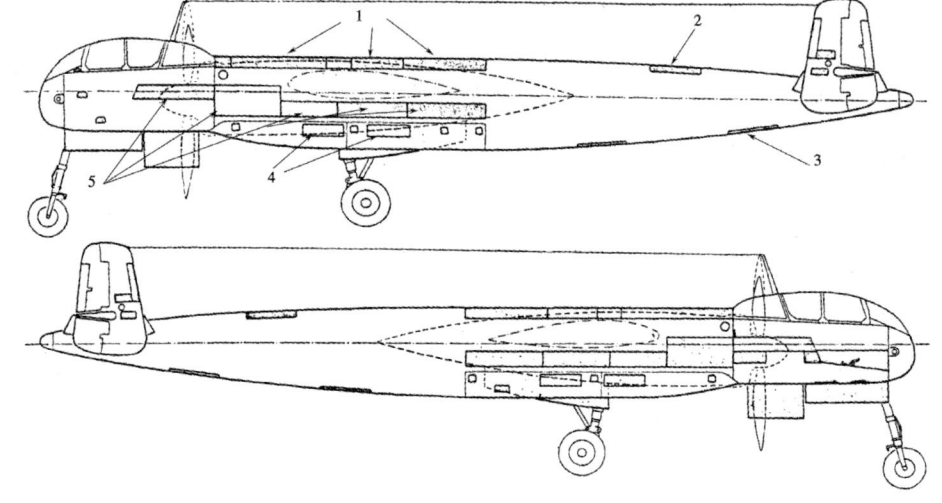

This diagram shows the correct manner (with a tow bar and rope to the upper part of the oleo) to tow the He 219

This diagram show the protective covers for the wheels, engines and canopy

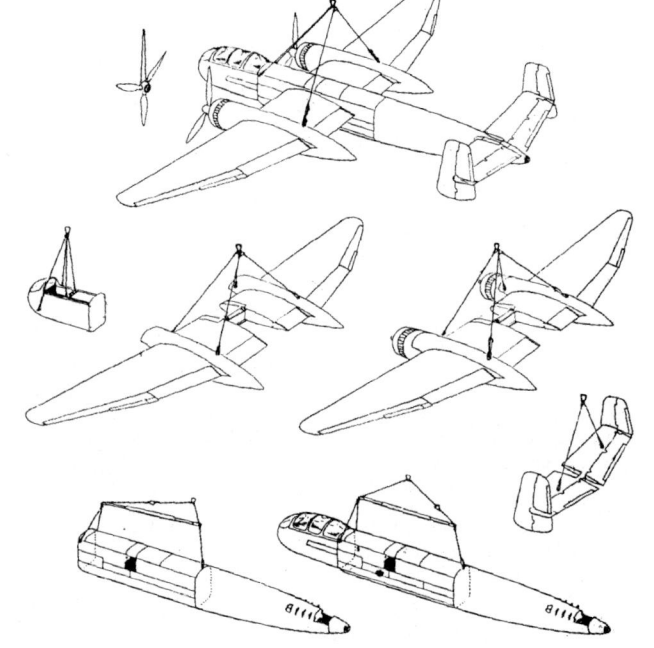

This diagram shows the positions of the lifting eyelets to allow sub-assembles or the whole airframe to be lifted

AA01/19/90   Valiant Wings Publishing   Issued: July 2021

Evolution
Prototype, Production and Projected Variants

With so many versions of the Heinkel He 219 series as potential modelling subjects we thought it would be useful to show you the differences between each variant to assist you in making them.

Most published titles on the He 219 since the war have based the details of the various sub-variants on an unattributed document called *'Entwicklung der He 219 Baureihen;* (Development of the He 219 Series). Sadly this work is seriously flawed with many inaccuracies and these errors have often been duplicated in others works. We have therefore fully updated this section, so that it reflects the current thinking with regard the He 219's prototype, production and projected variants. Any that are included for which no period photographic or documentary evidence exists, are marked as such and should be taken as subjective.

All artwork © Jacek Jackiewicz, Additions and revisions © Juraj Jankovic

Prototypes

He 219 V1 – Initial form
W/Nr.219001
Stammkenzeichen: VG+LW

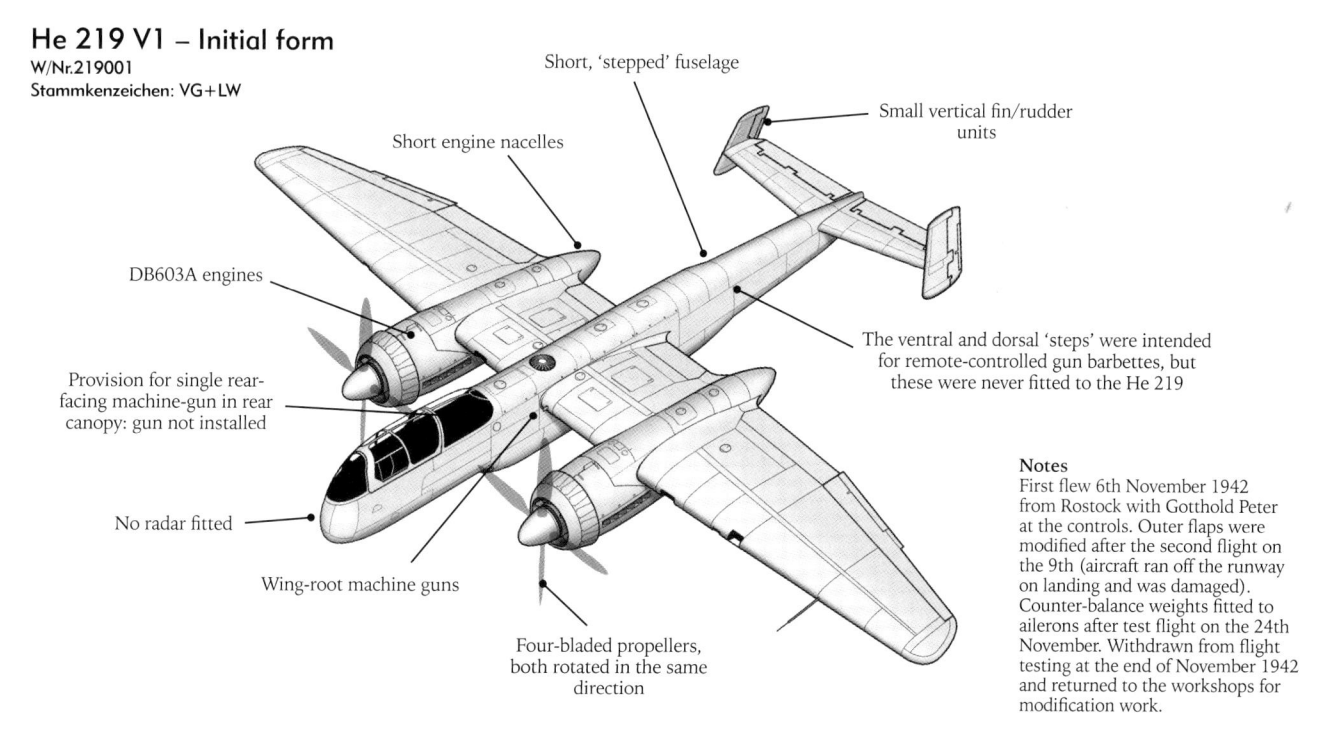

Labels on diagram:
- Short, 'stepped' fuselage
- Small vertical fin/rudder units
- Short engine nacelles
- DB603A engines
- The ventral and dorsal 'steps' were intended for remote-controlled gun barbettes, but these were never fitted to the He 219
- Provision for single rear-facing machine-gun in rear canopy: gun not installed
- No radar fitted
- Wing-root machine guns
- Four-bladed propellers, both rotated in the same direction

Notes
First flew 6th November 1942 from Rostock with Gotthold Peter at the controls. Outer flaps were modified after the second flight on the 9th (aircraft ran off the runway on landing and was damaged). Counter-balance weights fitted to ailerons after test flight on the 24th November. Withdrawn from flight testing at the end of November 1942 and returned to the workshops for modification work.

Although retouched, this image shows the V1 with the initial four-blade propellers fitted

This shows the V1 with four-blade propellers about to start a take-off run for a test flight

He 219 Evolution 2
Prototypes

He 219 V1 – Revised Form
W/Nr.219001
Stammkenzeichen: VG+LW
All modifications undertaken in December 1942/early 1943

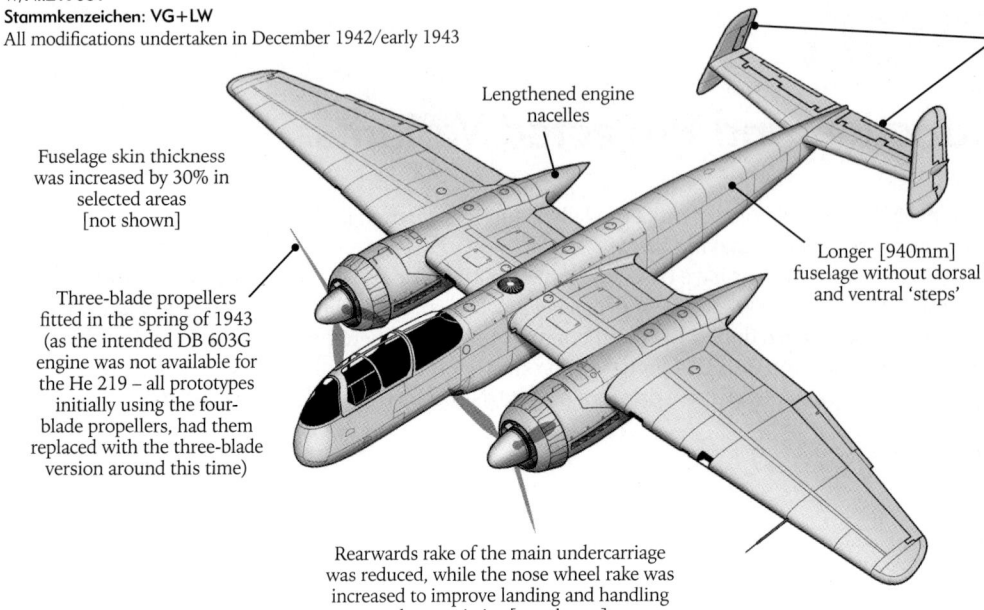

Fuselage skin thickness was increased by 30% in selected areas [not shown]

Three-blade propellers fitted in the spring of 1943 (as the intended DB 603G engine was not available for the He 219 – all prototypes initially using the four-blade propellers, had them replaced with the three-blade version around this time)

Lengthened engine nacelles

Substantially larger tail finlets and horizontal tail surfaces (the later fitted with trim tabs – this was standard from now on with the He 219 prototype and production machines)

Longer [940mm] fuselage without dorsal and ventral 'steps'

Rearwards rake of the main undercarriage was reduced, while the nose wheel rake was increased to improve landing and handling characteristics [not shown]

Notes
Modifications undertaken during November/December 1942 and the modified airframe was flown to *E-Stelle* Rechlin on the 17th December 1942 (probably with just the modifications made to the fuselage) and again on the 10th January 1943 (now with the tail modifications as well), returning to Rostock-Marienhe afterwards. Final modifications were completed in late January 1943, with the aircraft being test flown on the 30th. Used for general handling trials, stall and landing tests.

This shows the V1 in revised form with three-blade propellers fitted

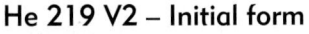

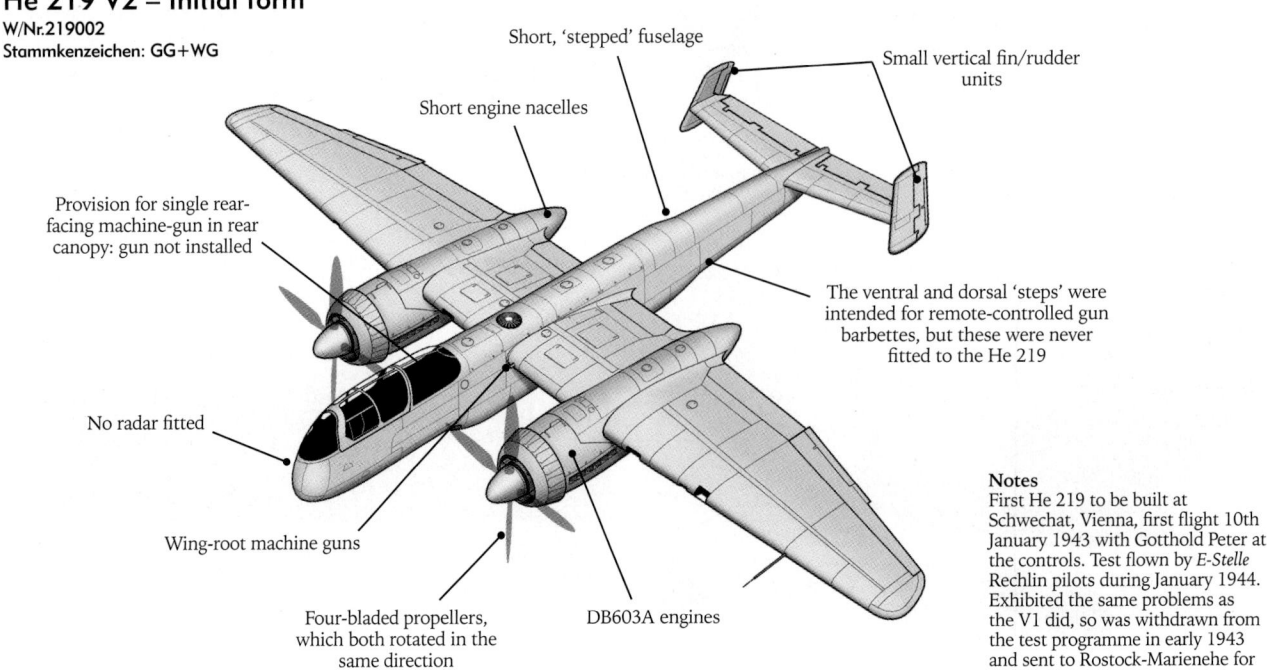

He 219 V2 – Initial form
W/Nr.219002
Stammkenzeichen: GG+WG

Short, 'stepped' fuselage

Small vertical fin/rudder units

Short engine nacelles

Provision for single rear-facing machine-gun in rear canopy: gun not installed

The ventral and dorsal 'steps' were intended for remote-controlled gun barbettes, but these were never fitted to the He 219

No radar fitted

Wing-root machine guns

Four-bladed propellers, which both rotated in the same direction

DB603A engines

Notes
First He 219 to be built at Schwechat, Vienna, first flight 10th January 1943 with Gotthold Peter at the controls. Test flown by *E-Stelle* Rechlin pilots during January 1944. Exhibited the same problems as the V1 did, so was withdrawn from the test programme in early 1943 and sent to Rostock-Marienehe for modification.

He 219
Evolution
Prototypes
2
93

He 219 V2 – Revised form
W/Nr.219002
Stammkenzeichen: GG+WG
Same as He 219 V2 – Initial Form except:

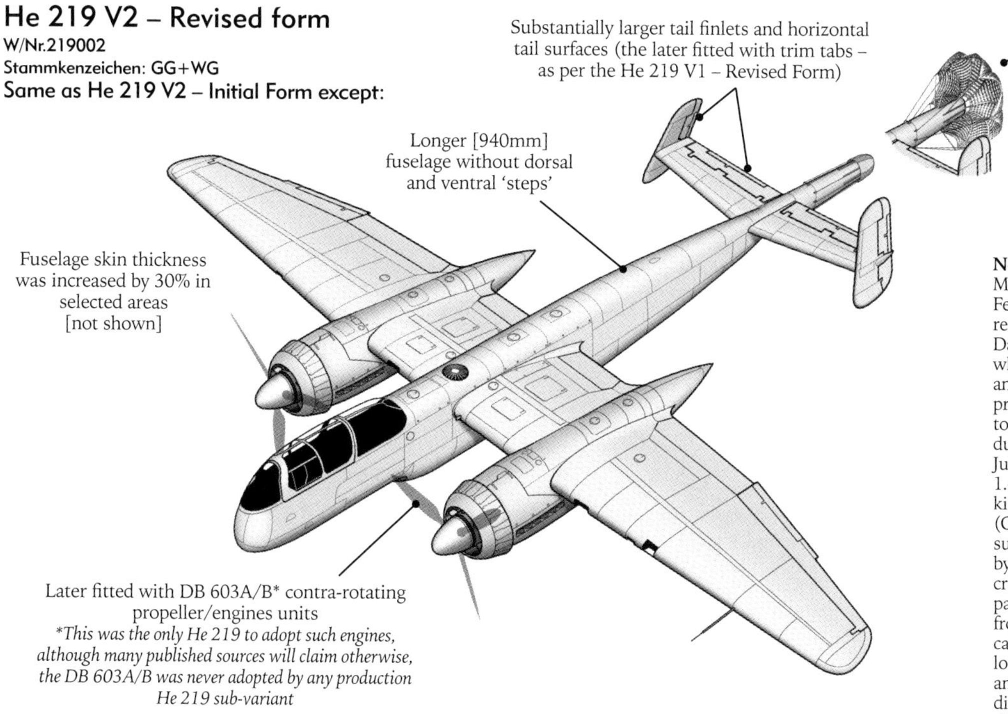

Fuselage skin thickness was increased by 30% in selected areas [not shown]

Substantially larger tail finlets and horizontal tail surfaces (the later fitted with trim tabs – as per the He 219 V1 – Revised Form)

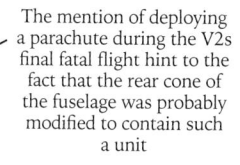

Longer [940mm] fuselage without dorsal and ventral 'steps'

The mention of deploying a parachute during the V2s final fatal flight hint to the fact that the rear cone of the fuselage was probably modified to contain such a unit

Later fitted with DB 603A/B* contra-rotating propeller/engines units
*This was the only He 219 to adopt such engines, although many published sources will claim otherwise, the DB 603A/B was never adopted by any production He 219 sub-variant

Notes
Modifications completed by the 8th February 1943, with the aircraft returning to test flying on the 9th. Damaged on the 16th February when the hinged canopy broke free and struck the spinning starboard propeller. Repaired and returned to flight testing on the 18th. Lost during diving trials on the 10th July 1943, crashing in Lobau forest 1.4km southwest of Muuhlleiten, killing Heinkel test pilot Könitzer (Consten, the flight engineer survived, the first airman to be saved by using an catapult seat system); crash caused by pilot deploying parachute when unable to recover from a dive (700km/h+), the forces caused an outside loop, the pilot losing consciousness and the tail and brake parachute broke away; the dive testing role was taken over by the V11.

He 219 V3
W/Nr.219003
Stammkenzeichen: unknown

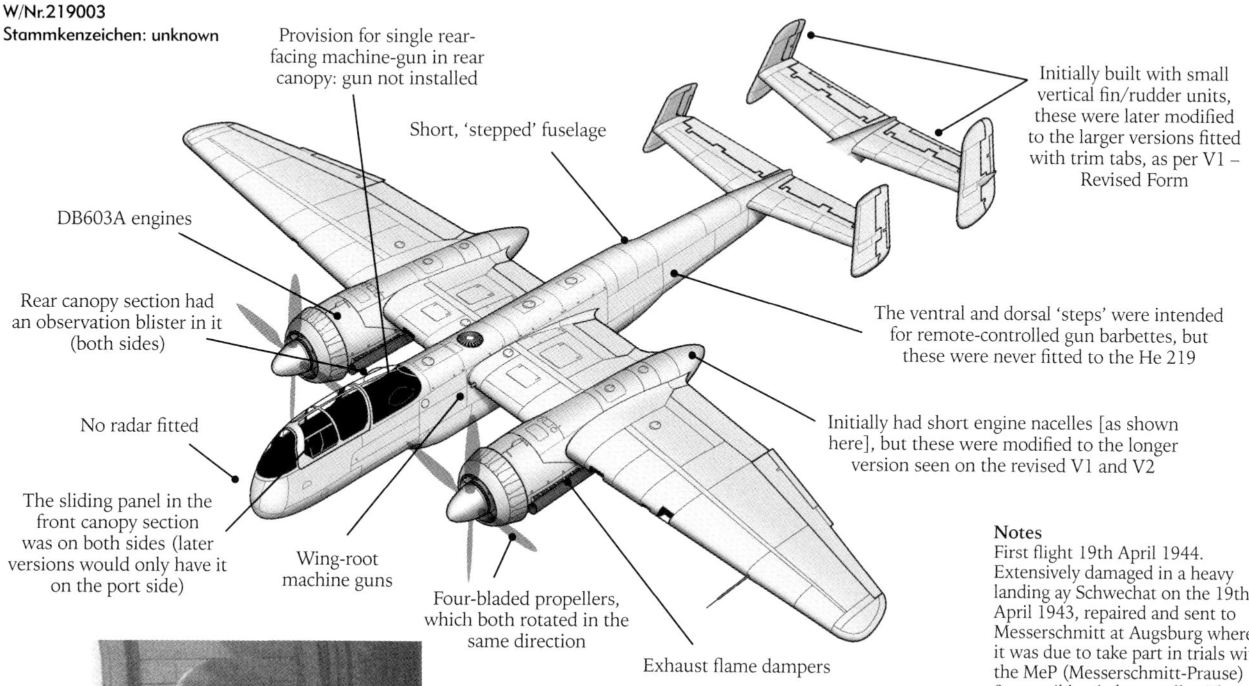

Provision for single rear-facing machine-gun in rear canopy: gun not installed

Short, 'stepped' fuselage

Initially built with small vertical fin/rudder units, these were later modified to the larger versions fitted with trim tabs, as per V1 – Revised Form

DB603A engines

Rear canopy section had an observation blister in it (both sides)

No radar fitted

The sliding panel in the front canopy section was on both sides (later versions would only have it on the port side)

Wing-root machine guns

Four-bladed propellers, which both rotated in the same direction

Exhaust flame dampers

The ventral and dorsal 'steps' were intended for remote-controlled gun barbettes, but these were never fitted to the He 219

Initially had short engine nacelles [as shown here], but these were modified to the longer version seen on the revised V1 and V2

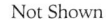

Not Shown
• Fitted with cockpit heating
• Undertook wing and tail de-icing system trials
• Used for autopilot and compass system trials

Notes
First flight 19th April 1944. Extensively damaged in a heavy landing ay Schwechat on the 19th April 1943, repaired and sent to Messerschmitt at Augsburg where it was due to take part in trials with the MeP (Messerschmitt-Prause) 8 reversible-pitch propeller. The aircraft waited a considerable time for these to be available, so it is not known if it ever actually took part in such trials (two other He 219s were later used for MeP (Messerschmitt-Prause) 8 reversible propeller trials). Tail section found by British forces at the Schwechat factory in Austria at the end of the war.

This image, taken from a British Intelligence report (hence it being so grainy), shows the tail of the V3 found at Schwechat in May 1945. Mottling can be just made out on the original but the fact that the swastika and 'V3' have contrast, means that the overall colour by this stage could not have been black, so was it RLM 75 with RLM 02 blotches (or the other way around)?

Valiant Wings Publishing

Issued: July 2021

He 219 Evolution	**2**
Prototypes	

Although blurred, this is the only image of the V3 we have ever seen, it does confirm the fitment of the four-blade propellers, the blister either side of the rear canopy and sliding panel in each side of the forward canopy

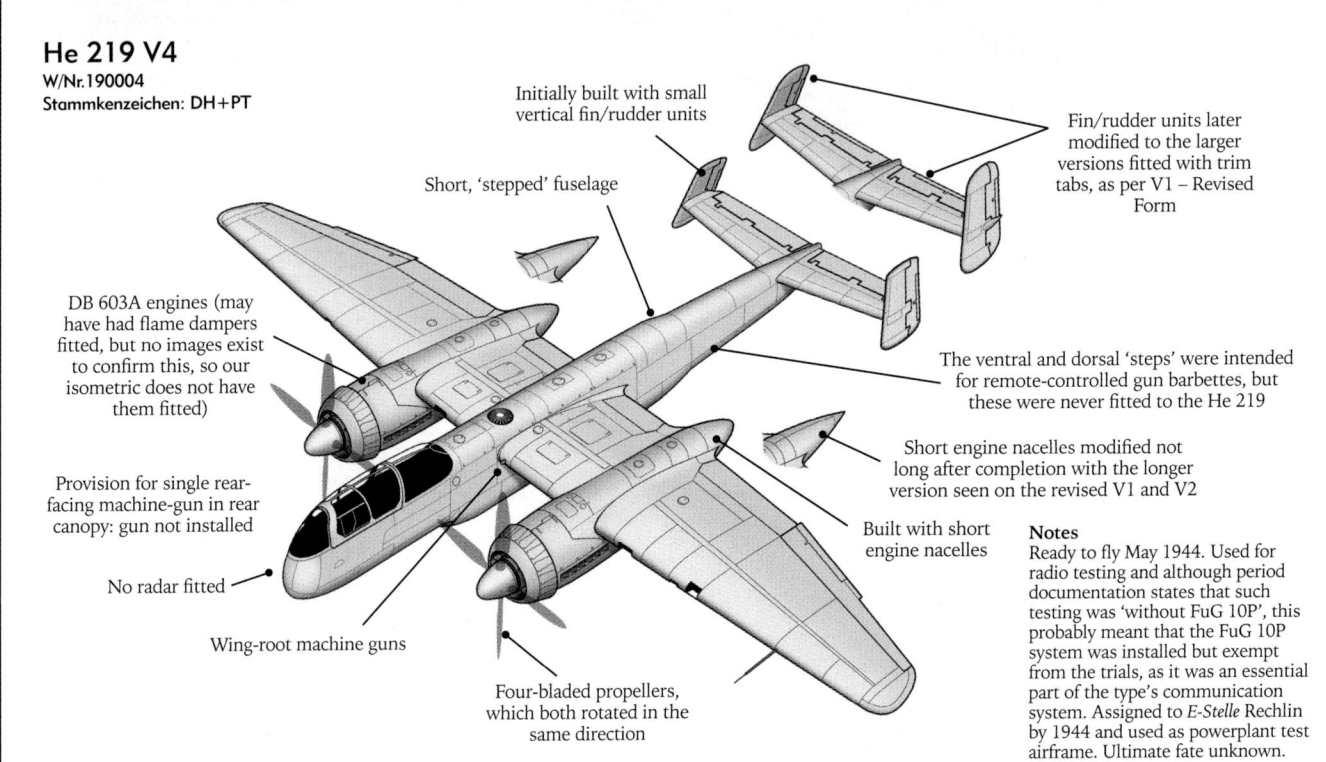

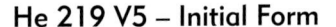

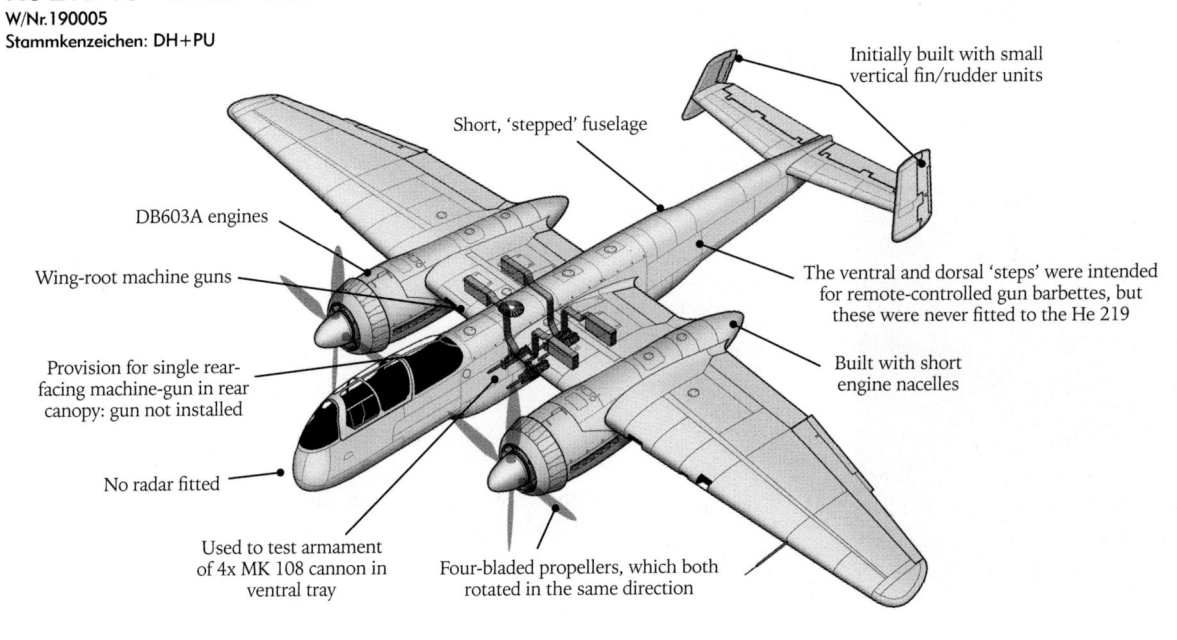

He 219 V4
W/Nr.190004
Stammkenzeichen: DH+PT

- Initially built with small vertical fin/rudder units
- Fin/rudder units later modified to the larger versions fitted with trim tabs, as per V1 – Revised Form
- Short, 'stepped' fuselage
- DB 603A engines (may have had flame dampers fitted, but no images exist to confirm this, so our isometric does not have them fitted)
- The ventral and dorsal 'steps' were intended for remote-controlled gun barbettes, but these were never fitted to the He 219
- Short engine nacelles modified not long after completion with the longer version seen on the revised V1 and V2
- Provision for single rear-facing machine-gun in rear canopy: gun not installed
- Built with short engine nacelles
- No radar fitted
- Wing-root machine guns
- Four-bladed propellers, which both rotated in the same direction

Notes
Ready to fly May 1944. Used for radio testing and although period documentation states that such testing was 'without FuG 10P', this probably meant that the FuG 10P system was installed but exempt from the trials, as it was an essential part of the type's communication system. Assigned to *E-Stelle* Rechlin by 1944 and used as powerplant test airframe. Ultimate fate unknown.

He 219 V5 – Initial Form
W/Nr.190005
Stammkenzeichen: DH+PU

- Initially built with small vertical fin/rudder units
- Short, 'stepped' fuselage
- DB603A engines
- Wing-root machine guns
- The ventral and dorsal 'steps' were intended for remote-controlled gun barbettes, but these were never fitted to the He 219
- Provision for single rear-facing machine-gun in rear canopy: gun not installed
- Built with short engine nacelles
- No radar fitted
- Used to test armament of 4x MK 108 cannon in ventral tray
- Four-bladed propellers, which both rotated in the same direction

AA01/20/94 — Valiant Wings Publishing — Issued: July 2021

He 219 V5 – Revised Form
W/Nr.190005
Stammkenzeichen: DH+PU
Same as He 218 V5 – Initial Form except:

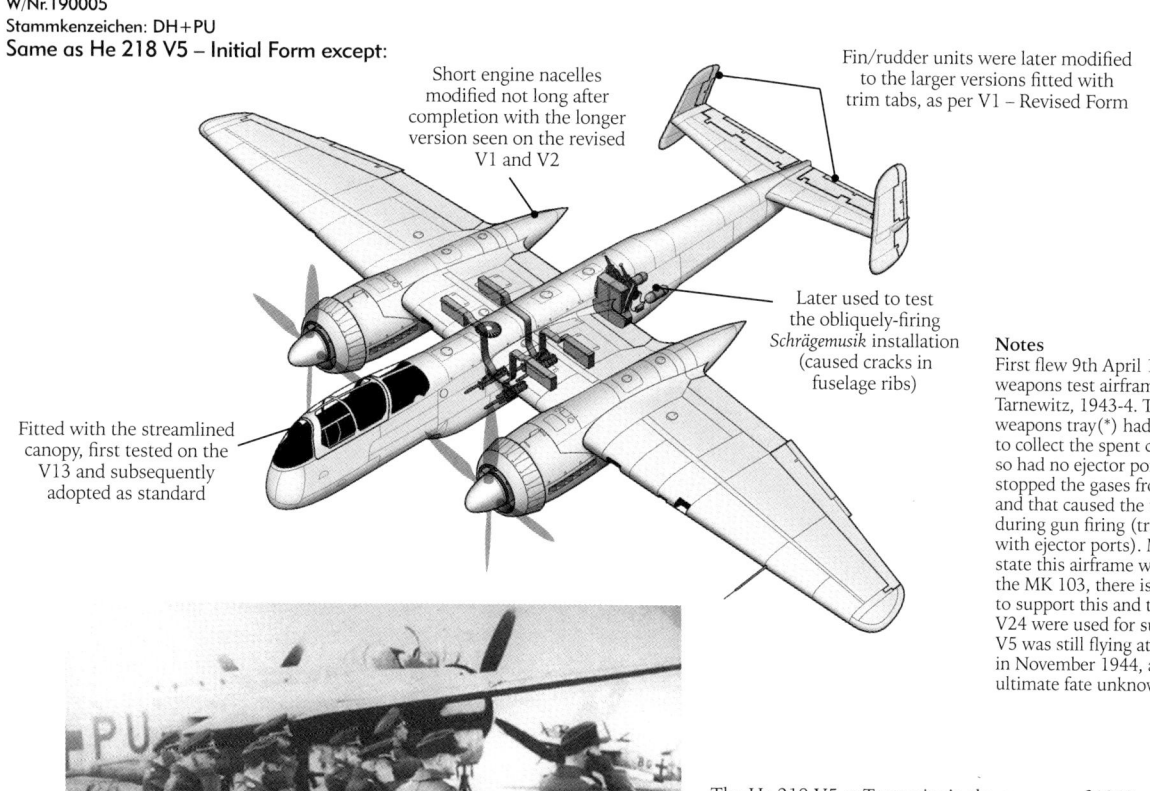

Short engine nacelles modified not long after completion with the longer version seen on the revised V1 and V2

Fin/rudder units were later modified to the larger versions fitted with trim tabs, as per V1 – Revised Form

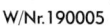

Later used to test the obliquely-firing *Schrägemusik* installation (caused cracks in fuselage ribs)

Fitted with the streamlined canopy, first tested on the V13 and subsequently adopted as standard

Notes
First flew 9th April 1943, used as weapons test airframe at *E-Stelle* Tarnewitz, 1943-4. The ventral weapons tray(*) had been designed to collect the spent cartridge cases, so had no ejector ports, this in turn stopped the gases from escaping and that caused the tray to bulge during gun firing (tray later modified with ejector ports). Many sources state this airframe was used to test the MK 103, there is no evidence to support this and the V18 and V24 were used for such trials. The V5 was still flying at Ludwigslust in November 1944, although its ultimate fate unknown.

The He 219 V5 at Tarnewitz in the summer of 1943 during weapons firing display, by this stage the aircraft was most likely in the 'standard' RLM75/RLM 76 scheme (although some claim it was plain RLM 76 oevrall)

He 219 V6
W/Nr.190006
Stammkenzeichen: DH+PV

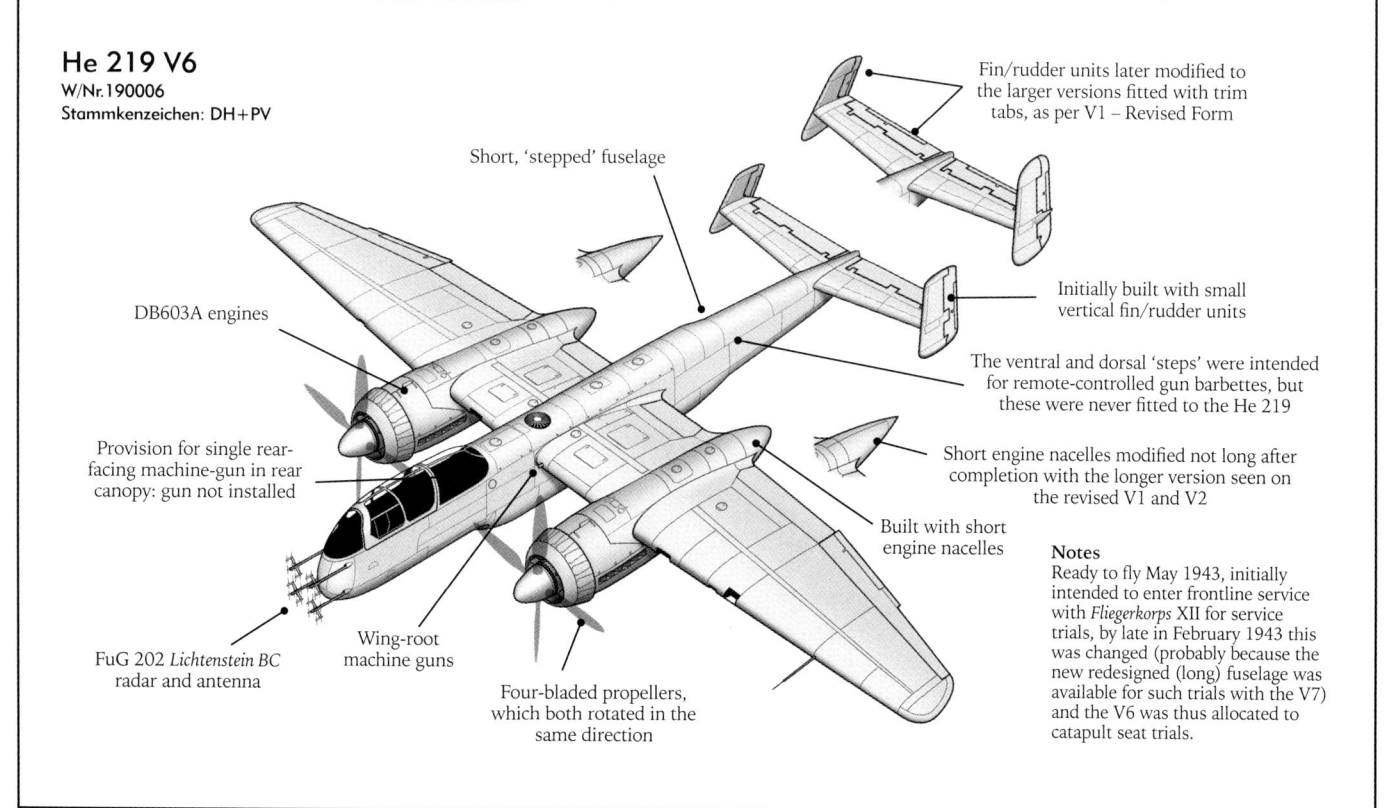

Short, 'stepped' fuselage

Fin/rudder units later modified to the larger versions fitted with trim tabs, as per V1 – Revised Form

DB603A engines

Initially built with small vertical fin/rudder units

The ventral and dorsal 'steps' were intended for remote-controlled gun barbettes, but these were never fitted to the He 219

Provision for single rear-facing machine-gun in rear canopy: gun not installed

Short engine nacelles modified not long after completion with the longer version seen on the revised V1 and V2

Built with short engine nacelles

FuG 202 *Lichtenstein BC* radar and antenna

Wing-root machine guns

Four-bladed propellers, which both rotated in the same direction

Notes
Ready to fly May 1943, initially intended to enter frontline service with *Fliegerkorps* XII for service trials, by late in February 1943 this was changed (probably because the new redesigned (long) fuselage was available for such trials with the V7) and the V6 was thus allocated to catapult seat trials.

He 219 Evolution 2
Prototypes

He 219 V6 – Catapult Seat Trials
Same as He 219 V6 except:

Delivered to *E-Stelle* Rechlin in 1943 for catapult seat trials and modified as follows:

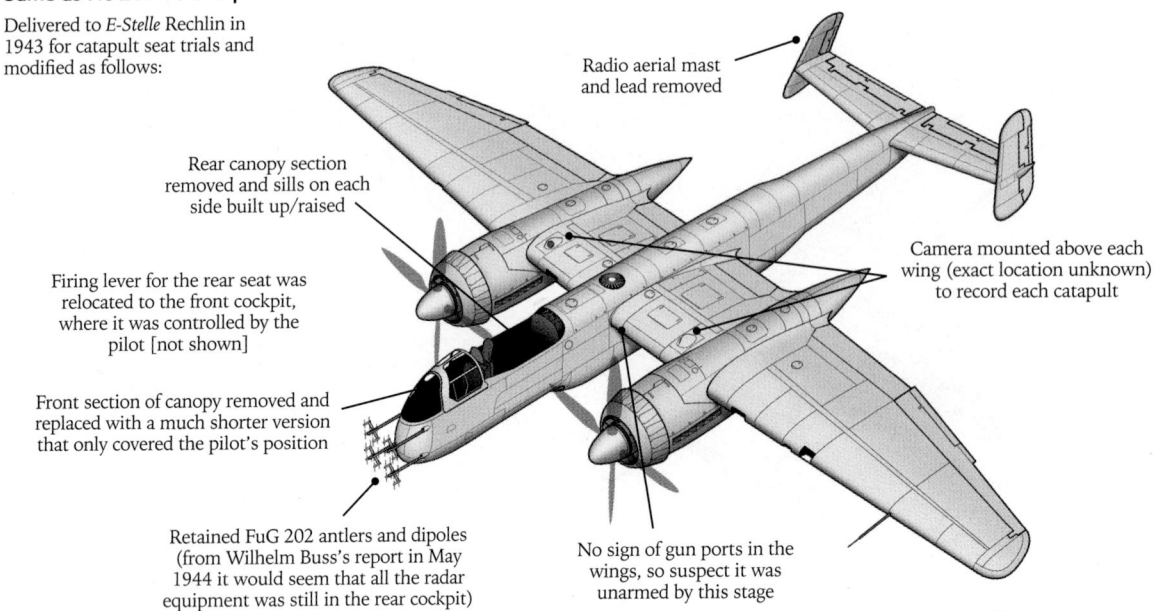

- Rear canopy section removed and sills on each side built up/raised
- Firing lever for the rear seat was relocated to the front cockpit, where it was controlled by the pilot [not shown]
- Front section of canopy removed and replaced with a much shorter version that only covered the pilot's position
- Retained FuG 202 antlers and dipoles (from Wilhelm Buss's report in May 1944 it would seem that all the radar equipment was still in the rear cockpit)
- Radio aerial mast and lead removed
- Camera mounted above each wing (exact location unknown) to record each catapult
- No sign of gun ports in the wings, so suspect it was unarmed by this stage

Notes
Delivered to *E-Stelle* Rechlin in 1943 for catapult seat trials. The seat was fired by compressed air at approx. 1050psi, not an explosive charge as Heinkel would later adopt with the He 162.

Not the best quality, but the only image we have ever seen of the V6, this shows it at *E-Stelle* Rechlin for catapult seat trials, note Ju 87 in background, which was probably also used for catapult trials as well, because there are in-flight firing sequence images of such trials from the type

He 219 V7
W/Nr.190007
Stammkenzeichen: DH+PW
Verbandskennzeichen: G9+DB

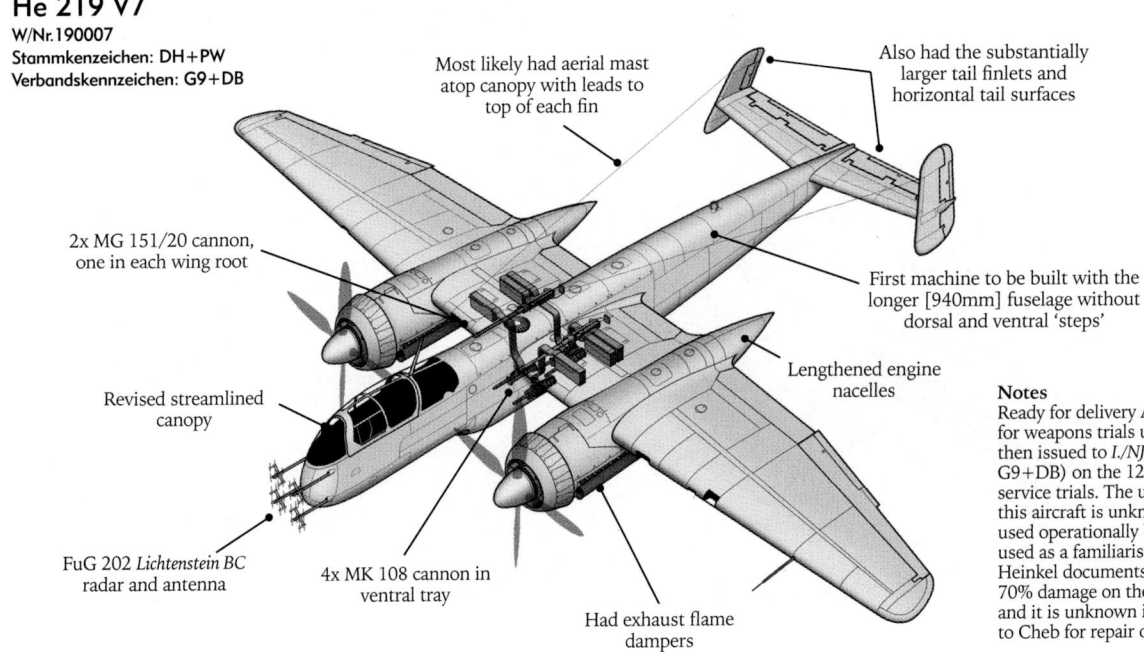

- Most likely had aerial mast atop canopy with leads to top of each fin
- Also had the substantially larger tail finlets and horizontal tail surfaces
- 2x MG 151/20 cannon, one in each wing root
- First machine to be built with the longer [940mm] fuselage without dorsal and ventral 'steps'
- Revised streamlined canopy
- Lengthened engine nacelles
- FuG 202 *Lichtenstein BC* radar and antenna
- 4x MK 108 cannon in ventral tray
- Had exhaust flame dampers

Notes
Ready for delivery April 1943, used for weapons trials until May 1943, then issued to I./NJG1 at Venlo (as G9+DB) on the 12th May 1943 for service trials. The ultimate fate of this aircraft is unknown (it was not used operationally by I./NJG 1, it was used as a familiarisation airframe), Heinkel documents state it received 70% damage on the 19th April 1944, and it is unknown if it was thus sent to Cheb for repair or scrapped?

He 219 Evolution
Prototypes

He 219 V8
W/Nr.190008
Stammkenzeichen: DH+PX
Verbandskennzeichen: G9+EB

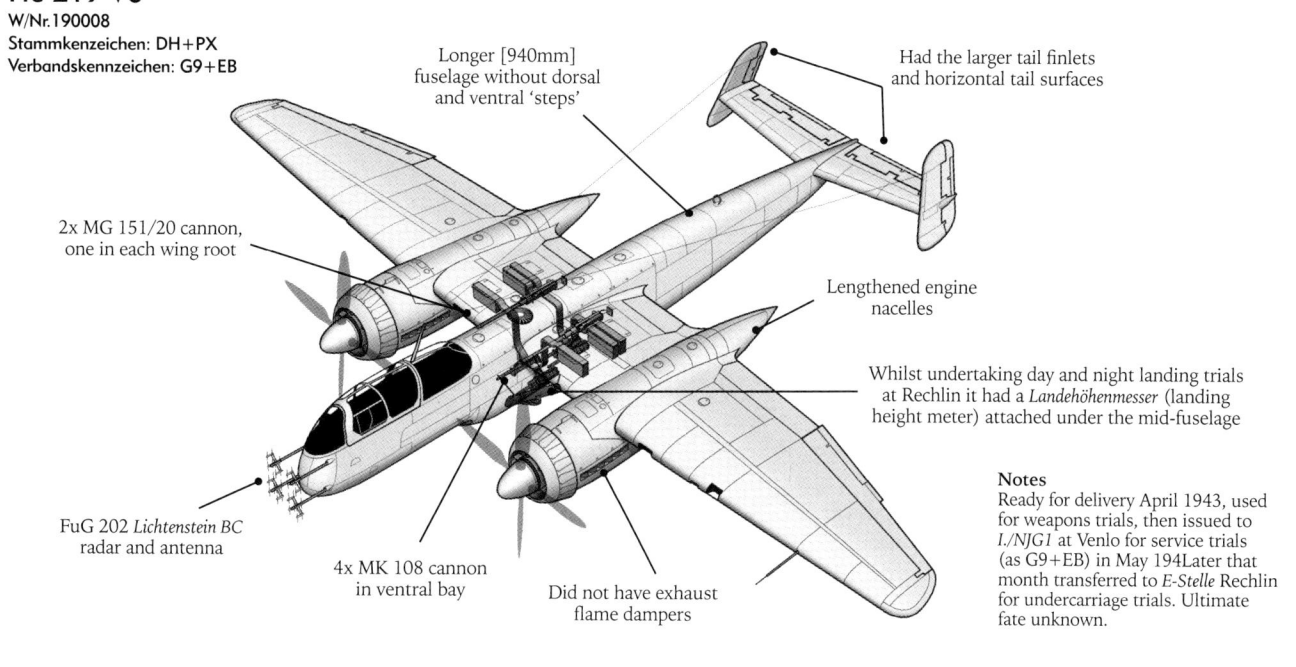

- Longer [940mm] fuselage without dorsal and ventral 'steps'
- Had the larger tail finlets and horizontal tail surfaces
- 2x MG 151/20 cannon, one in each wing root
- Lengthened engine nacelles
- Whilst undertaking day and night landing trials at Rechlin it had a *Landehöhenmesser* (landing height meter) attached under the mid-fuselage
- FuG 202 *Lichtenstein BC* radar and antenna
- 4x MK 108 cannon in ventral bay
- Did not have exhaust flame dampers

Notes
Ready for delivery April 1943, used for weapons trials, then issued to *I./NJG1* at Venlo for service trials (as G9+EB) in May 194Later that month transferred to *E-Stelle* Rechlin for undercarriage trials. Ultimate fate unknown.

He 219 V9
W/Nr.190009
Stammkenzeichen: DH+PY
Verbandskennzeichen: G9+FB

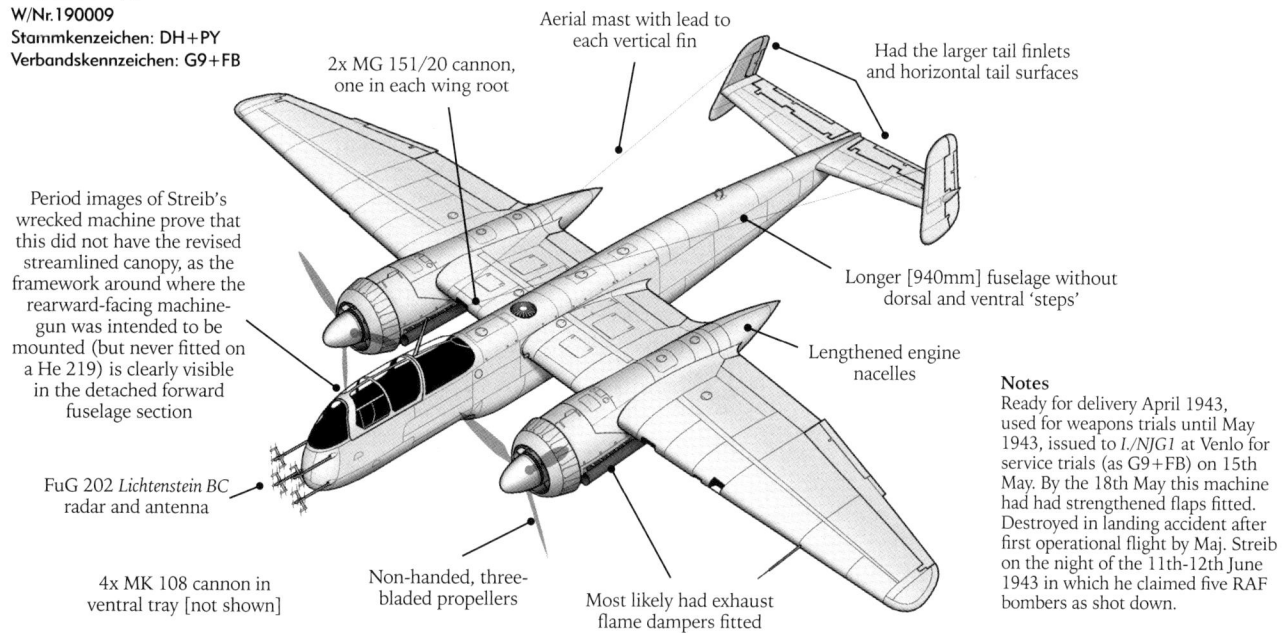

- Aerial mast with lead to each vertical fin
- 2x MG 151/20 cannon, one in each wing root
- Had the larger tail finlets and horizontal tail surfaces
- Period images of Streib's wrecked machine prove that this did not have the revised streamlined canopy, as the framework around where the rearward-facing machine-gun was intended to be mounted (but never fitted on a He 219) is clearly visible in the detached forward fuselage section
- Longer [940mm] fuselage without dorsal and ventral 'steps'
- Lengthened engine nacelles
- FuG 202 *Lichtenstein BC* radar and antenna
- 4x MK 108 cannon in ventral tray [not shown]
- Non-handed, three-bladed propellers
- Most likely had exhaust flame dampers fitted

Notes
Ready for delivery April 1943, used for weapons trials until May 1943, issued to *I./NJG1* at Venlo for service trials (as G9+FB) on 15th May. By the 18th May this machine had had strengthened flaps fitted. Destroyed in landing accident after first operational flight by Maj. Streib on the night of the 11th-12th June 1943 in which he claimed five RAF bombers as shot down.

He 219 V10
W/Nr.190010
Stammkenzeichen: DH+PZ
Verbandskennzeichen: G9+FB
Same as V9 (above)

Notes
Ready for delivery May 1943, was initially delivered to NJG1 at Venlo for service trials (as G9+FB, taking this identification from the V9, lost on the 1th-12th June) in early July 1943. Sustained 20% damage at Venlo on the 15th August 1943, when it had to make a belly landing. Repaired and returned to service three weeks later, but lost in combat on the 5th/6th September 1943; the first operational loss of a He 219.

The wreckage of the V9 after its first operational sortie flown by Maj. Streib and following its crash-landing at Venlo in the early hours of the 12th June 1943

He 219
Evolution 2
Prototypes

He 219 V11
W/Nr.190011
Stammkenzeichen VO+BC

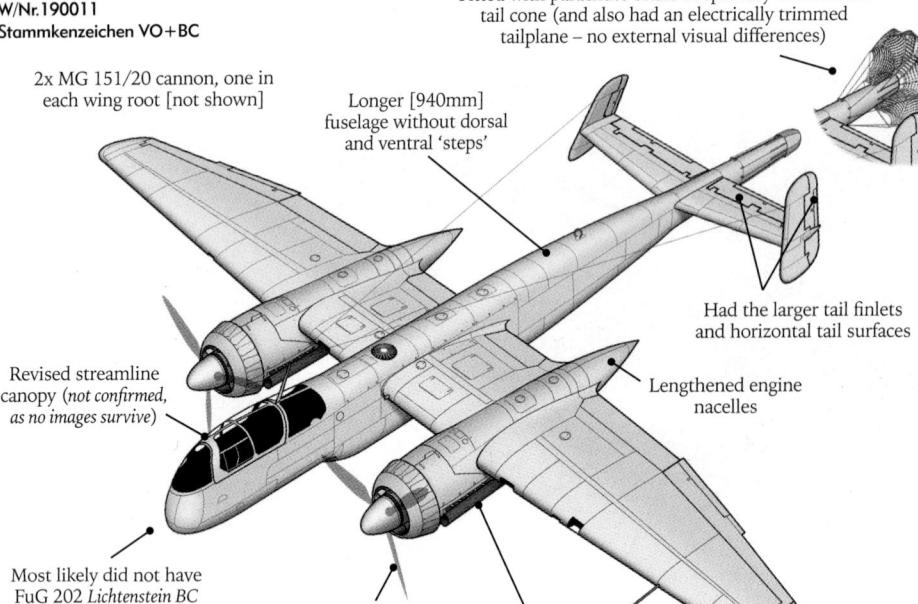

- 2x MG 151/20 cannon, one in each wing root [not shown]
- Fitted with parachute brake in specially constructed tail cone (and also had an electrically trimmed tailplane – no external visual differences)
- Longer [940mm] fuselage without dorsal and ventral 'steps'
- Had the larger tail finlets and horizontal tail surfaces
- Lengthened engine nacelles
- Revised streamline canopy (*not confirmed, as no images survive*)
- Most likely did not have FuG 202 *Lichtenstein BC* radar and antenna
- Non-handed, three-bladed propellers
- 4x MK 108 cannon in ventral tray [not shown]
- Probably exhaust flame dampers (not confirmed)

Notes
Initially marked for service trials with *Fliegerkorps* XII, but instead of being ferried to *NJG 1* at Venlo it was sent to *E-Stelle* Rechlin on the 5th July 1943. Many published sources will quote other details for this W/Nr., but study of a British Field Intelligence report from August 1945 confirms that this W/Nr. was the V11 and it had most likely taken over diving trials after the loss of the V2 in July 1943 (the catapult seat system was modified to operate automatically ('Dead Man's Handle') if the crew became incapacitated). It was engaged in further trials from March to July 1944, after which it to be returned to Heinkel for further modification (returning the automatic catapult seat system back to its original form most likely). By 2nd January 1945 the V11s trial programme had been closed down and it was intended to send the airframe to Cheb to be scrapped, however it was found by British forces in 1945 with the fuselage on a stand near a railway siding at Schwechat*, the wings, nacelles and burnt-out engines elsewhere on the airfield and the vertical fin/rudders at an undisclosed location on site.

He 219 V12
W/Nr.190012
Stammkenzeichen unknown
Verbandskennzeichen: G9+FK
Same as He 219 V9 (page 97)

Notes
Originally this was earmarked to be the test airframe for remotely-controlled barbettes, however by the end of February 1943 this layout had been abandoned for the He 219. It was therefore issued to the *Stab* flight of I./NJG1 at Venlo for service trials. First operational sortie undertaken on the 30th/31st August, but damaged by return fire. Repaired, it returned to operations on the 5th/6th September. In November 1943 it went to Rechlin for rectification work, then was allocated to 2./NJG 1 as G9+FK. It was destroyed in an air raid on Venlo airfield on the 25th February 1944.

The fuselage of the He 219 V11, W/Nr.190011, VO+BC found on a trailer at Schwechat at the end of the war. Note the revised extreme tip of tail where the recovery parachute was housed

He 219 V13*
W/Nr.190052
Stammkenzeichen PK+QB
Same as He 219 V9 except:

This was the He 219A-02

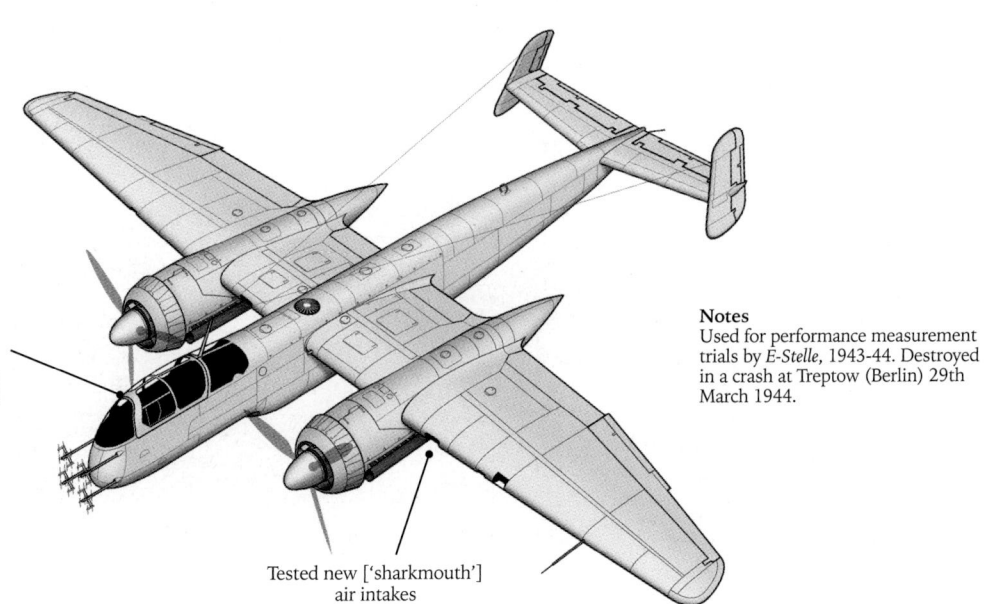

- First aircraft to test the new streamlined canopy that would be adopted as standard and retrofitted to many early production and V-series airframes
- Tested new ['sharkmouth'] air intakes

Notes
Used for performance measurement trials by *E-Stelle*, 1943-44. Destroyed in a crash at Treptow (Berlin) 29th March 1944.

He 219
Evolution
Prototypes

99

Again, not good quality, this image shows the He 219 V8, W/Nr.190008, DH+PX at Rechlin on the 3rd September 1943 during an exhibit of captured Allied aircraft types; it is fitted with the Landehöhenmesser under the fuselage probably relating to radio altimeter trials

He 219 V14*
W/Nr.190058
Stammkenzeichen PK+QH
This was the He 219A-08

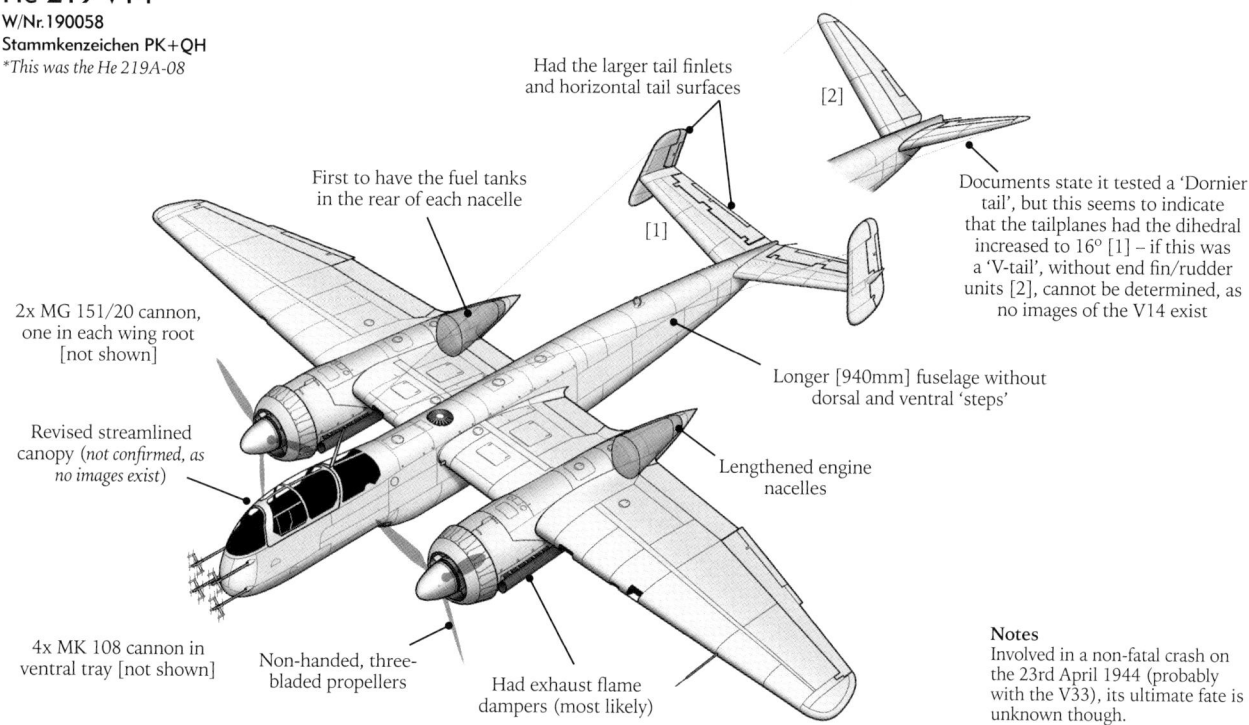

Had the larger tail finlets and horizontal tail surfaces

First to have the fuel tanks in the rear of each nacelle

[1]

[2]

Documents state it tested a 'Dornier tail', but this seems to indicate that the tailplanes had the dihedral increased to 16° [1] – if this was a 'V-tail', without end fin/rudder units [2], cannot be determined, as no images of the V14 exist

2x MG 151/20 cannon, one in each wing root [not shown]

Revised streamlined canopy (*not confirmed, as no images exist*)

Longer [940mm] fuselage without dorsal and ventral 'steps'

Lengthened engine nacelles

4x MK 108 cannon in ventral tray [not shown]

Non-handed, three-bladed propellers

Had exhaust flame dampers (most likely)

Notes
Involved in a non-fatal crash on the 23rd April 1944 (probably with the V33), its ultimate fate is unknown though.

He 219 V15*
W/Nr.190064
Stammkenzeichen RL+AD
This was the He 219A-014

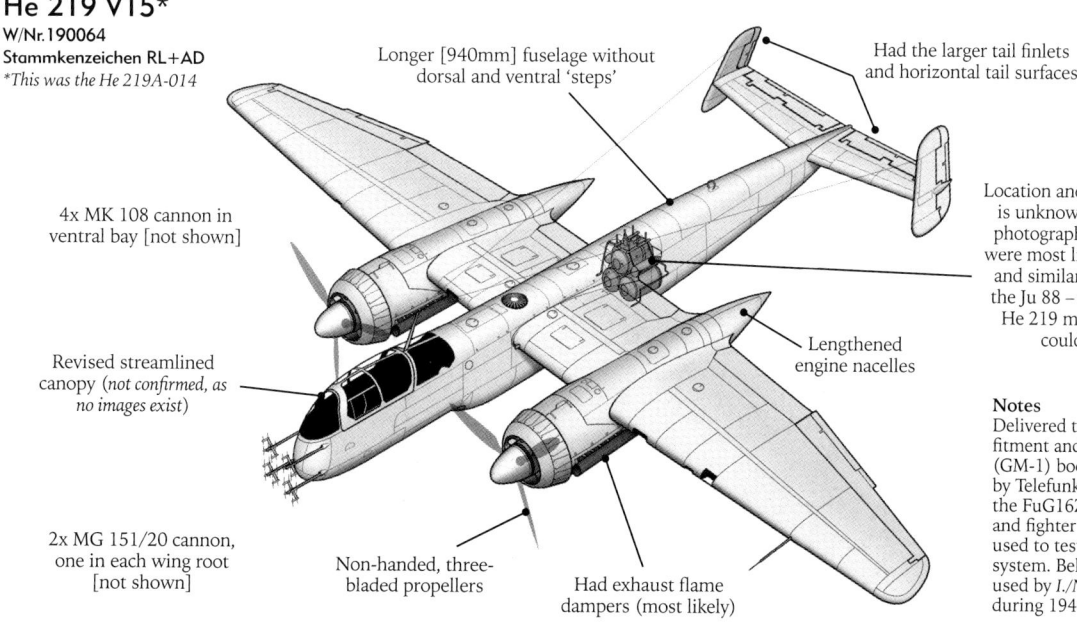

Longer [940mm] fuselage without dorsal and ventral 'steps'

Had the larger tail finlets and horizontal tail surfaces

4x MK 108 cannon in ventral bay [not shown]

Location and size of the GM-1 tanks is unknown, as no documents or photographs exist of the V15, but were most likely in the rear fuselage and similar to the system used by the Ju 88 – fitment of GM-1 in any He 219 meant that *Schrägemusik* could not be installed

Revised streamlined canopy (*not confirmed, as no images exist*)

Lengthened engine nacelles

2x MG 151/20 cannon, one in each wing root [not shown]

Non-handed, three-bladed propellers

Had exhaust flame dampers (most likely)

Notes
Delivered to *E-Stelle* Rechlin for fitment and tests of a nitrous oxide (GM-1) boost system. Also used by Telefunken AG for trials with the FuG16ZY as a VHF voice radio and fighter control system. Also used to test the FuG 135 guidance system. Believed to have been used by I./NJG 1 as a '*Moskitojäger*' during 1944.

He 219 Evolution 2
Prototypes

He 219 V16*
W/Nr.190193
Stammkenzeichen BE+JF
This was the He 219A-079

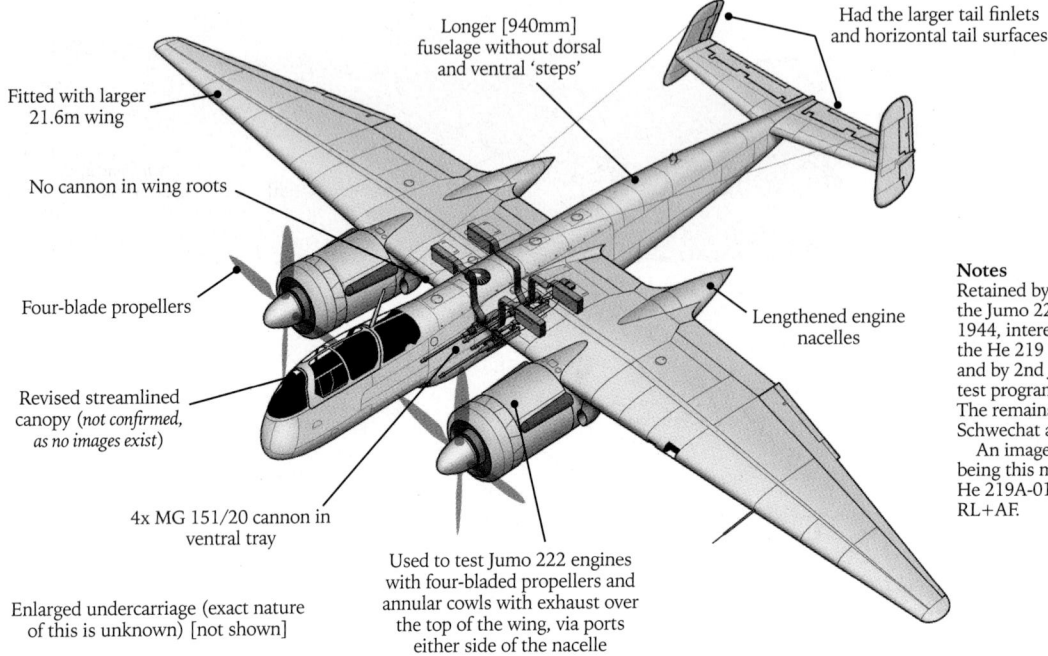

- Fitted with larger 21.6m wing
- No cannon in wing roots
- Four-blade propellers
- Revised streamlined canopy (*not confirmed, as no images exist*)
- 4x MG 151/20 cannon in ventral tray
- Enlarged undercarriage (exact nature of this is unknown) [not shown]
- Longer [940mm] fuselage without dorsal and ventral 'steps'
- Had the larger tail finlets and horizontal tail surfaces
- Lengthened engine nacelles
- Used to test Jumo 222 engines with four-bladed propellers and annular cowls with exhaust over the top of the wing, via ports either side of the nacelle

Notes
Retained by Heinkel for trials with the Jumo 22First flew 23rd July 1944, interest in the engine type for the He 219 had waned by late 1944 and by 2nd January 1945 the V16's test programme was shut down. The remains were found by Allies at Schwechat at the end of the war.

An image often attributed as being this machine is in fact the He 219A-016, W/Nr.190066, RL+AF.

He 219 V17*
W/Nr.190060
Stammkenzeichen PK+QJ
This was the He 219A-010 (BMW 003 test airframe) after rebuild

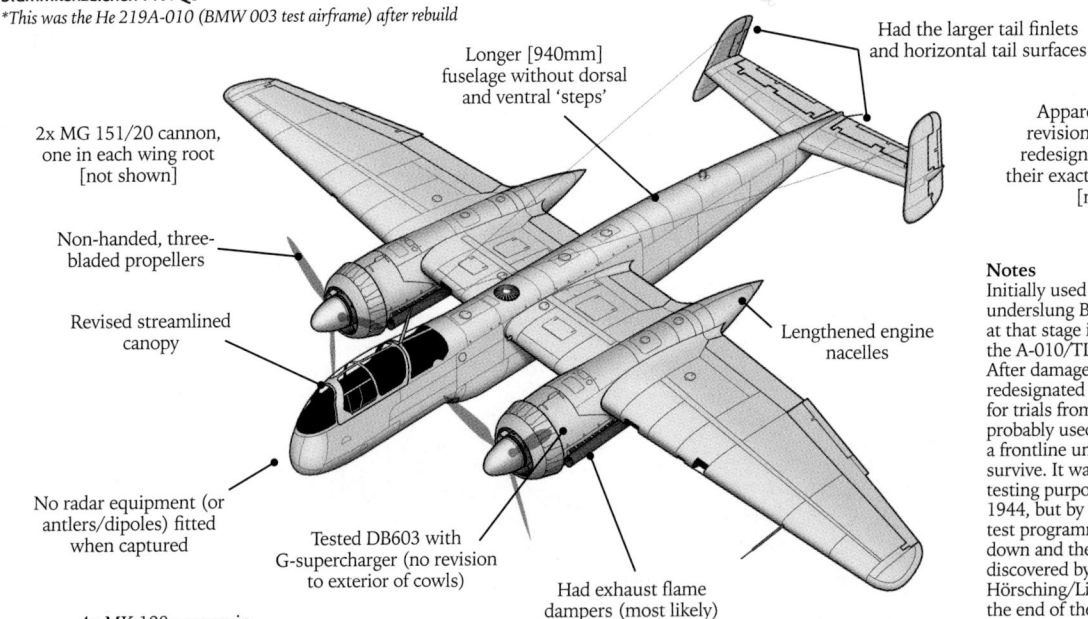

- 2x MG 151/20 cannon, one in each wing root [not shown]
- Non-handed, three-bladed propellers
- Revised streamlined canopy
- No radar equipment (or antlers/dipoles) fitted when captured
- 4x MK 108 cannon in ventral tray [not shown]
- Tested DB603 with G-supercharger (no revision to exterior of cowls)
- Had exhaust flame dampers (most likely)
- Longer [940mm] fuselage without dorsal and ventral 'steps'
- Had the larger tail finlets and horizontal tail surfaces
- Apparently the engine revisions also resulted in redesigned air intakes, but their exact nature is unknown [not shown]
- Lengthened engine nacelles

Notes
Initially used for trials with an underslung BMW 003, although at that stage it was designed the A-010/TL (see elsewhere). After damage and rebuilt, it was redesignated the V17 and used for trials from early 1944. It was probably used as a *Moskitojäger* with a frontline unit, but no records survive. It was intended for special testing purposes at Ainring in late 1944, but by 2nd January 1945 its test programme had been closed down and the complete airframe was discovered by American troops at Hörsching/Linz airfield in Austria at the end of the war.

The He 219 V17 (A-010), W/Nr.190060, PK+QJ was captured at Hörsching-Linz, Austria by American forces and is seen here in the scrap compound there in the summer of 1945

He 219
Evolution
Prototypes

He 219 V18*
W/Nr.190071
Stammkenzeichen RL+AK
This was the He 219A-021

- 2x MG 151/20 cannon, one in each wing root [not shown]
- Non-handed, three-bladed propellers
- Revised streamlined canopy
- Radar system fitted unconfirmed, so shown here with FuG 202 Lichtenstein BC radar and antenna
- Oblique-firing Schrägemusik installation in rear fuselage
- Lengthened engine nacelles
- Initially fitted with 6x MK 108 30mm cannon in ventral tray (February 1944) [not shown], but by August/September 1944 it had 4x MG 151/20 cannon in the ventral tray
- Had the larger tail finlets and horizontal tail surfaces
- Longer [940mm] fuselage without dorsal and ventral 'steps'
- Fuel tanks in the rear of each nacelle
- Had exhaust flame dampers (most likely)

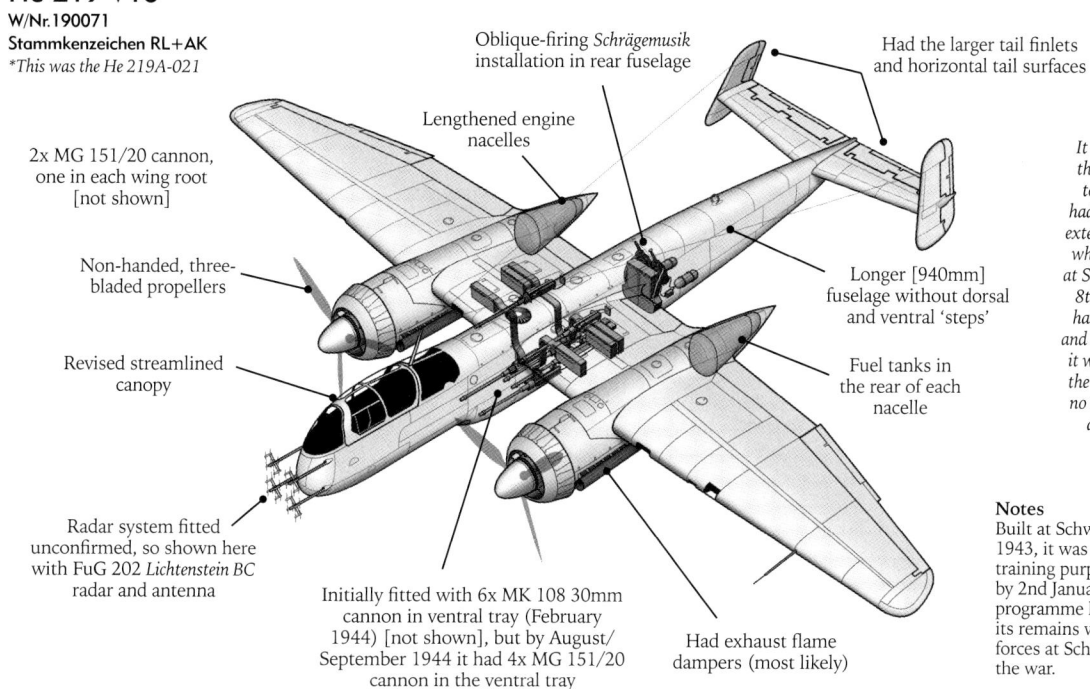

It is stated by many sources that this machine was used to test Jumo 222 engines, had four-blade propellers and extended span wings, however when found by British forces at Schwechat the report (dated 8th August 1945) stated it had a standard 18.5m wing and DB 603 engines. Although it was allocated for fitment of the three-seat cockpit, there is no evidence to prove that this actually ever took place.

Notes
Built at Schwechat in November 1943, it was eventually intended for training purposes at Jüterbog, but by 2nd January 1945 the V18's test programme had been shut down and its remains were found by British forces at Schwechat at the end of the war.

He 219 V19*
W/Nr.190073
Stammkenzeichen DV+DI
Same as He 219 V18 except:

- Initially intended for projected 3-man cockpit, cancelled 21/04/44
- FuG 220 SN-2 radar with four antler/dipoles on nose
- FuG 212 radar radar with antenna in centre of nose cap

Notes
This configuration was cancelled and the standard airframe was issued to I./NJG 1 at Venlo, where it was lost on the 11th/12th April 194.
The Versuchsnummer 'V19' was never allocated to this airframe

He 219 V20
Same as V19 (above)
Notes
Earmarked for pressurised cockpit experiments, however the project never got beyond the planning stage.

He 219 V21*
W/Nr.190117
Stammkenzeichen DV+DM
Same as V19 (above)
This was the He 219A-046
Notes
Earmarked for trials with internal exhaust flame dampers on the DB 603A engines (not known if trials were ever undertaken and as no documents or images survive, we cannot depict it in an isometric). Ultimate fate unknown.

He 219 V22*
No actual aircraft was ever assigned to this Versuchnummer
Notes
Earmarked for trials with internal exhaust flame dampers on the DB 603G engines, however these were never undertaken, probably due to non-production of the that engine series.

He 219 V23
Same as V19 (above)
Notes
Images exist of a wrecked airframe with 'V23' stencilled on the port side of the nose, at Cheb in April 1945. This machine lacks the 21.5m wing intended for testing by this machine or the Jumo 222 engines and four-blade counter-rotating propellers. The tail marked as 'V23' was found by British forces at Heinkel's Schwechat facility (confirmed by a British report dated 8th August 1945). Heinkel's list of Versuch He 219s dated 2nd January 1945 stated that the V23 had been broken up, with the fuselage sent to Cheb (a repair depot), while the wings had been retained by Heinkel as spares for the V16. The images of the 'V23' marked machine at Cheb most likely confirms that the forward fuselage of this machine had been attached to the rest of the V32 as part of the repair programme.

He 219 V24*
No actual airframe was assigned to this Versuchnummer
Notes
Earmarked for trials with two 30mm MK 103 cannon in the ventral tray, project did not progress beyond the planning stages, due to the MK 103 being unsuitable for night operations. The specifications for the V24 also listed an underslung BMW 003 jet engine as a 'possibility', but such fitment was only ever trialled by the A-010/TL and the V30.

He 219 V25*
W/Nr.190122
Stammkenzeichen DV+DR
Same as V19 (above)
This was the He 219A-051
Notes
This airframe was used for the testing of single-core electrical cables and was tested at E-Stelle Rechlin in 1944, along with possible trials by Telefunken at a later date. Single-core cables were introduced at Schwechat from W/Nr.190223.

He 219 Evolution 2
Prototypes

He 219 V26*
W/Nr.190120
Stammkenzeichen: DV+DP
Verbandskennzeichen: G9+EB
*This was the He 219A-049
Same as he 219 V19 except:

Notes
Left the Schwechat factory in March 1944 and then tested the oblique-firing cannon at *E-Stelle* Tarnewitz. It is claimed that it was also used by I./NJG1 at Venlo, but there is no evidence to support this. Lost in a crash at Prague on the 11th June 1944 during a ferry flight from Tarnewitz to the Heinkel factory at Schwechat, Vienna.
Note: This is the machine photographed by USAAF fighters during a low-level attack on Tarnewitz on the 13th May 1944.

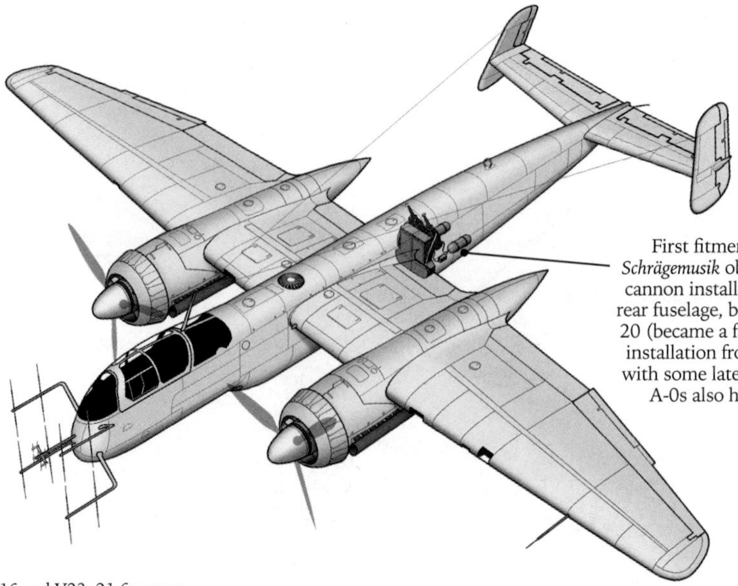

First fitment of the *Schrägemusik* oblique-firing cannon installation in the rear fuselage, behind Frame 20 (became a factory-fitted installation from the A-2, with some late production A-0s also having it)

He 219 V27*
*No airframe was assigned this Versuchnummer
Notes
To be built to a specification almost identical to the V16 and V23; 21.6m span, Jumo 222E/F engines with counter-rotating wide-chord four-blade propellers, no wing-mounted cannon and only 4x MG 151/20 cannon in the ventral bay. The type is often quoted as being the prototype for the planned B-1 series, but the V27 was to have been converted from an A-2-series airframe and thus would have retained the two-seat cockpit, whilst the B-1 series was to have had the three-seat cockpit.

He 219 V28*
W/Nr.190068   Stammkenzeichen: RL+AH
Same as V19 (page 101)
*This was the He 219A-018
Notes
Initially built in January 1944 with DB 603A engines, but converted in April 1944 to DB 603Es. *Many sources state this was used for 'tactical braking' (braking parachute) trials, but that is incorrect. Some sources state this was later converted with shorter span, but this is also incorrect and it retained the standard 18.5m span (confirmed by British report dated 8th August 1945).*
Retained by Heinkel as a Musterflugzeug and used in endurance trials with the DB 603E engine. Some incorrectly list as VO+BC (that was the V11). Used briefly by I./NJG 1 at Venlo (as G9+SH) in June 1944. By 2nd January 1945 the V28's test programme had been closed down and it was one of five He 219s found by Allied forces at Scwechat at the end of the war (could not be examined in detail though, as it had been bulldozed into a crater and covered over).

A still from the gun camera of a USAAF fighter as it sweeps across the field at Tarnemitz on the 13th May 1944 captured the V26 in the only known image of the type

He 219 V29*
W/Nr.190069   Stammkenzeichen: RL+AI
Same as V19 (page 101)
*This was the He 219A-019
Notes
Used for de-icing (wings, tails and propellers) and hot water heating trials by *E-Stelle* Rechlin detachment at at Munich-Riem and found wrecked there at the end of the war.

He 219 V30*
W/Nr.190101
Stammkenzeichen: RL+AT
*This was the He 219A-030

Notes
Built at Schwecaht in late 1943, but not fitted with the ventral BMW 003 engine until the summer of 1944. May have been trialled with I./NJG 1 at Venlo, as their readiness report of the 1st September 1944 lists a 'Flöte', which is thought by Allied intelligence to be a code-name for a jet-powered He 219? Some sources list this W/Nr. as shot down on the night of the 13-14th April 1945, but that is incorrect and the aircraft shot down may well have been a Mosquito (NT494) from No.157 Squadron lost in the area the same night.

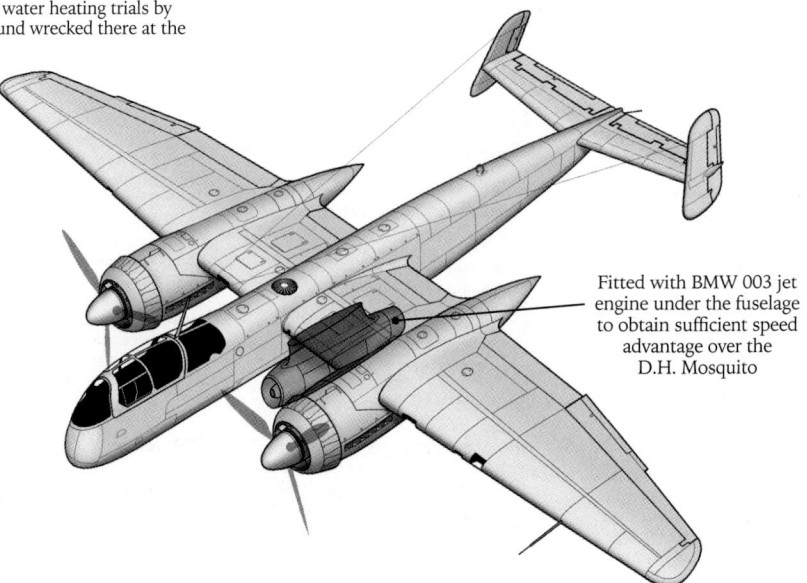

Fitted with BMW 003 jet engine under the fuselage to obtain sufficient speed advantage over the D.H. Mosquito

He 219
Evolution
Prototypes

He 219 V31*
W/Nr.190106
Stammkenzeichen: DV+DB
This was the He 219A-035

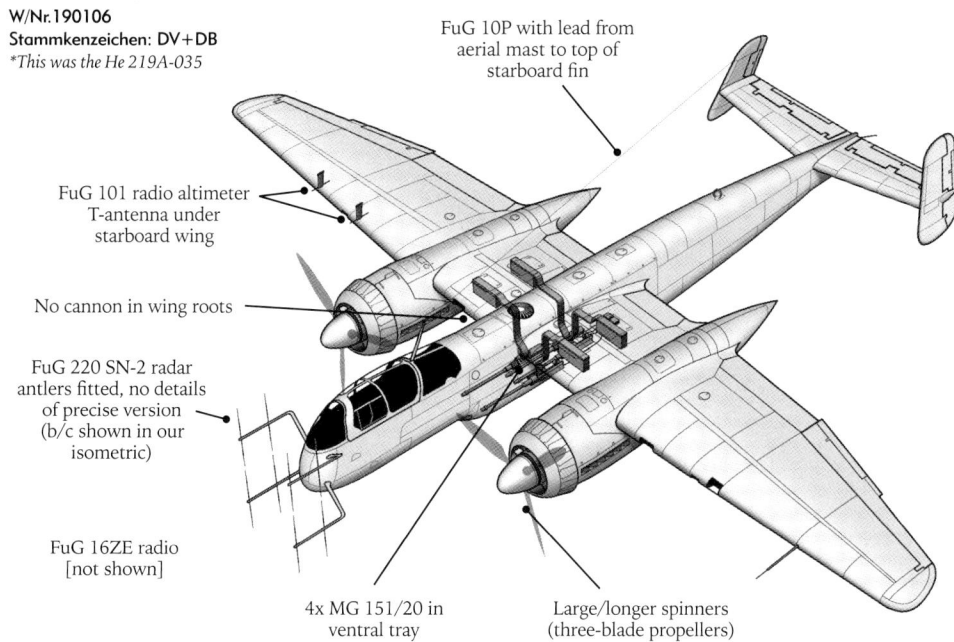

- FuG 10P with lead from aerial mast to top of starboard fin
- FuG 101 radio altimeter T-antenna under starboard wing
- No cannon in wing roots
- FuG 220 SN-2 radar antlers fitted, no details of precise version (b/c shown in our isometric)
- FuG 16ZE radio [not shown]
- 4x MG 151/20 in ventral tray
- Large/longer spinners (three-blade propellers)

Involved in flight testing (during November 1944) the DB 603G engine, of which only 100 zero-series examples were ever built

Notes
Used for load measurements and special loading trials during May 1944. Many state that this machine was later used for 'tactical braking' (braking parachute) trials, however when its wreck was found by Allied forces at Schwechat in 1945 the type exhibited no sign of the system although the British report stated that the V11 was used for such trials.

He 219 V32*
W/Nr.190121
Stammkenzeichen: DV+DQ
This was the He 219A-050
Same as He 219 V31 except:

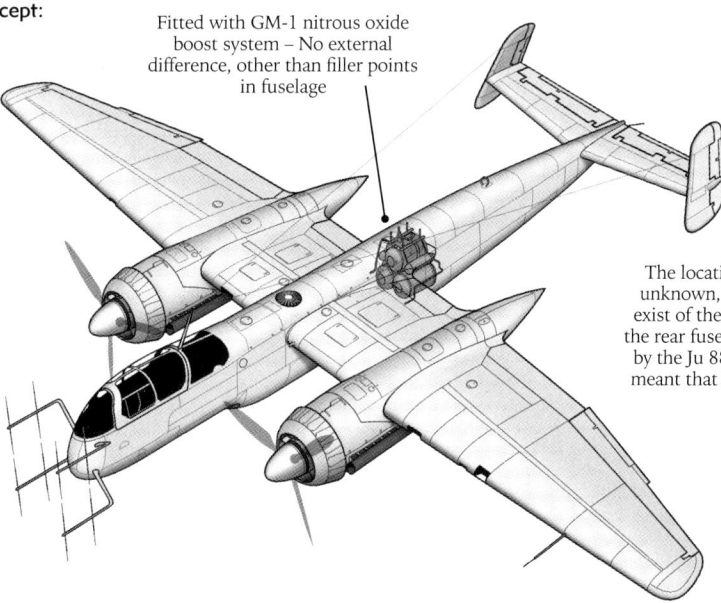

- Fitted with GM-1 nitrous oxide boost system – No external difference, other than filler points in fuselage

The location and size of the GM-1 tanks is unknown, as no documents or photographs exist of the V15/V32, but were most likely in the rear fuselage and similar to the system used by the Ju 88 – fitment of GM-1 in any He 219 meant that Schrägemusik could not be installed

Notes
Used for service trials of the GM-1 boost system, undertaken by I./NJG1 at Venlo in mid-1944. The wreck of this airframe (fitted with the forward fuselage of the V23) was found along with nine others by US forces at Cheb (German name Eger) in April 1945.

The wreck of the V32 found at Cheb at the end of the war, fitted with the forward fuselage of the V23 (©USAAF)

He 219 Evolution 2
Prototypes

He 219 V33*
W/Nr.190063
Stammkenzeichen: RL+AC
*This was the He 219A-013

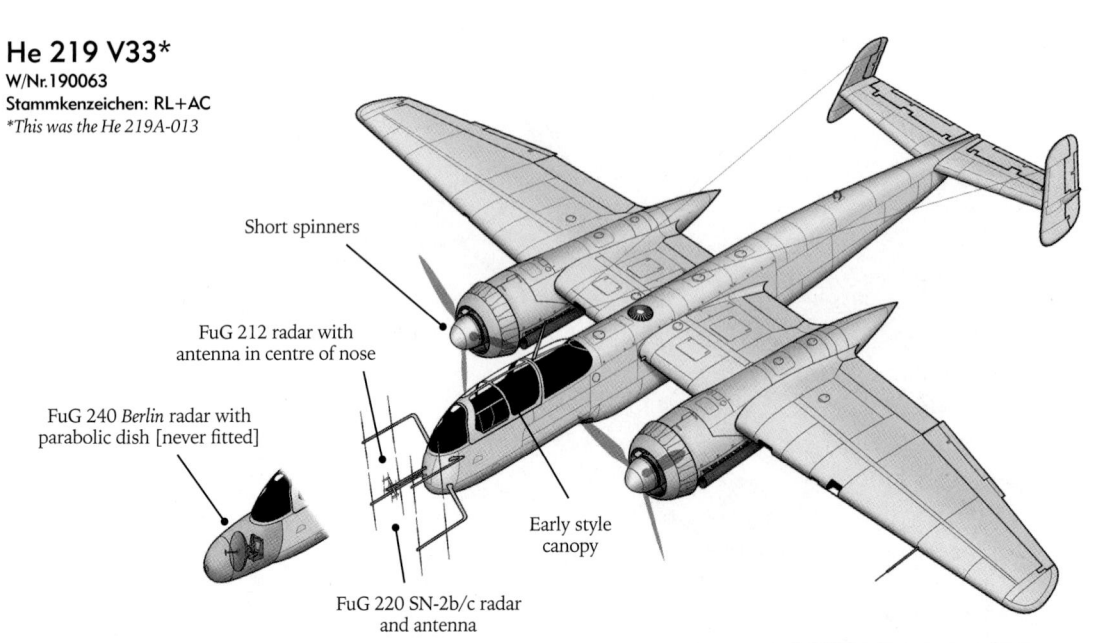

Callouts:
- Short spinners
- FuG 212 radar with antenna in centre of nose
- FuG 240 *Berlin* radar with parabolic dish [never fitted]
- Early style canopy
- FuG 220 SN-2b/c radar and antenna

Notes
Built at Schwechat in the summer of 1943 and first flew on the 1st October that year. By February 1944 it was at *E-Stelle* Tarnewitz involved in airborne weapons firing (exact nature of tests unknown, but unlikely to be any experimental armament type). It was intended for testing the FuG 240 *Berlin* radar with its parabolic dish [see isometric] and was to be returned to Heinkel for fitment before it moved to the Telefunken facility at Diepensee for trials. Unlikely that this installation or fitment every took place, as it was damaged in a non-fatal crash on the 23rd April 1944, with its remains used as a source of spares (tail unit later fitted to W/Nr.190061). Only twenty-five FuG 240 radar units were built by the end of the war, with ten of these being fitted to Ju 88s, there is no evidence to prove that any of the remainder were allocated to the He 219 programme.

This shot of the He 219 V33 (A-013), W/Nr.190063, RL+AC taken in early 1944 confirms the radar equipment, early cockpit and short spinners fitted to this machine

He 219 V34*
W/Nr.190112
Stammkenzeichen: DV+DH
*This was also the A-041

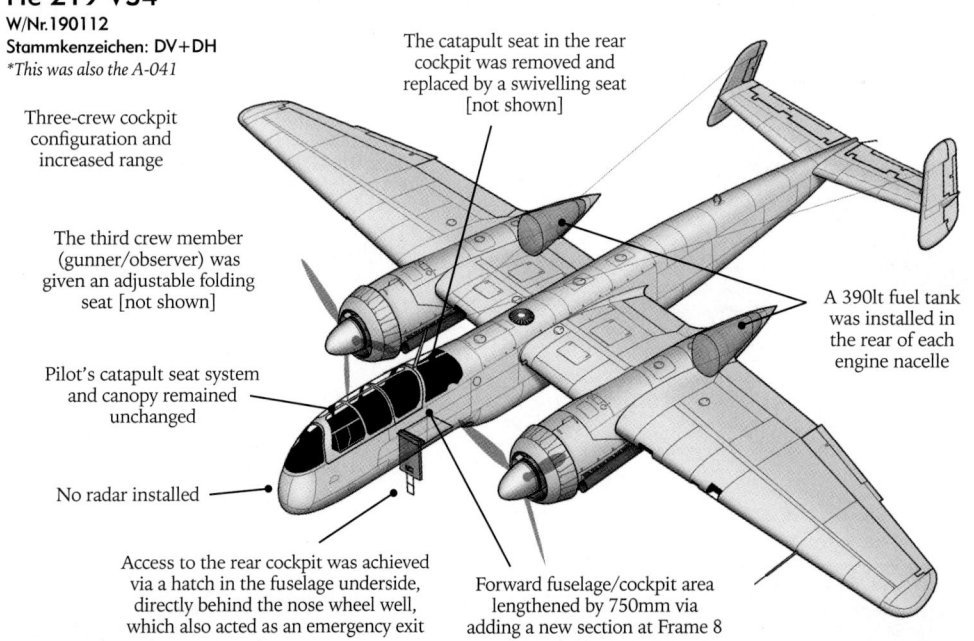

Callouts:
- Three-crew cockpit configuration and increased range
- The third crew member (gunner/observer) was given an adjustable folding seat [not shown]
- Pilot's catapult seat system and canopy remained unchanged
- No radar installed
- Access to the rear cockpit was achieved via a hatch in the fuselage underside, directly behind the nose wheel well, which also acted as an emergency exit
- The catapult seat in the rear cockpit was removed and replaced by a swivelling seat [not shown]
- A 390lt fuel tank was installed in the rear of each engine nacelle
- Forward fuselage/cockpit area lengthened by 750mm via adding a new section at Frame 8

Notes
Built at Schwechat in the winter of 1943/44 and was ferried from there to Rostock-Marienehe on the 23rd February 1944 for conversion to a three-seater. This was done over the next few weeks. Ferried to Werneuchen and first flown there on the 7th June 1944. Flew to *E-Stelle* Rechlin and on the 15th June flown from their to Vienna, returning to Rechlin later, as it was reported as being test flown there on the 26th June. The ultimate fate of this aircraft is unknown.

He 219 V35 & V36*
*No airframes were assigned to either Werknummer
Notes
Intended to have the new three-seat cockpit, DB 603E engines, 18.5m wooden wings and a wooden tail unit. Neither were ever built.

He 219 V37 & V38*
*No airframes were assigned to either Werknummer
Notes
Intended to have the new three-seat cockpit, Jumo 222E/F engines, 21.6m wooden wings and a wooden tail unit. Neither were ever built.

He 219 V39 & V40*
*No airframes were assigned to either Werknummer
Notes
The only data on these two is that they were the 'third model/prototype, like the V27', so would most probably have had the new three-seat cockpit, Jumo 222E/F engines with counter-rotating wide-chord propellers, 21.6m wings and no wing root armament, but 4x MG 151/20 in the ventral tray. Neither were ever built.

He 219 V41
W/Nr.420325 (production A-2 airframe) – prototype for planned D-1 series

Fitted with Jumo 21E engines (most likely in annular cowls) with MW50 water/methanol injection

Schrägemusik removed to make space for MW50 tank in rear fuselage

Retained FuG SN-2b/c radar

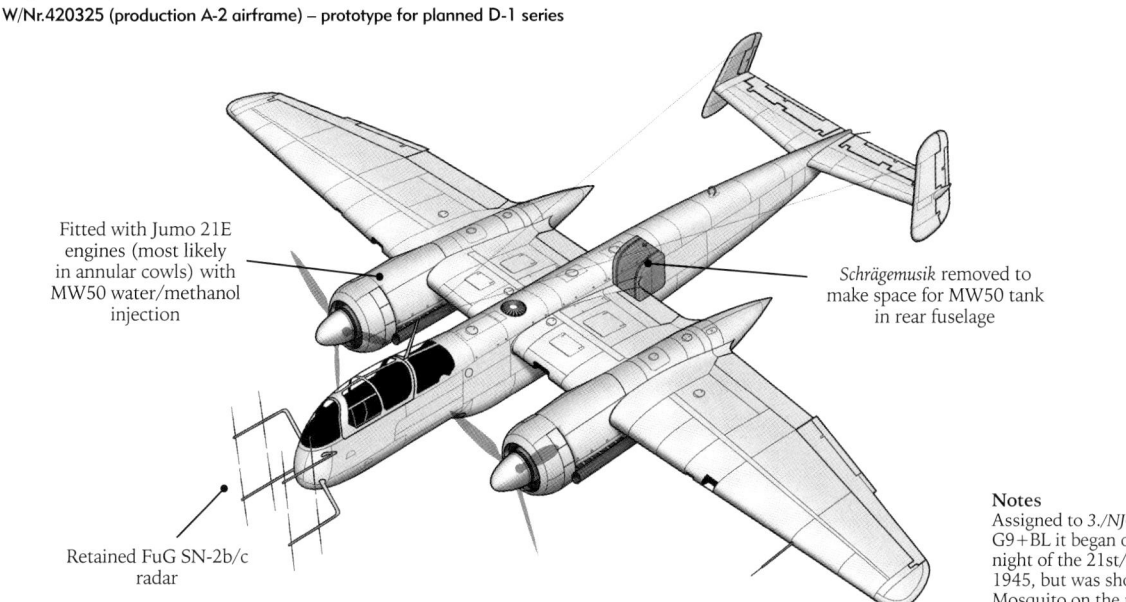

Notes
Assigned to 3./NJG 1 at Venlo as G9+BL it began operations on the night of the 21st/22nd February 1945, but was shot down by a Mosquito on the night of the 20th/21st March 1945.

He 219 V76
Please note any reference to this *Versuchnummer* is incorrect, as it was the He 219A-076.

No Assigned V-series Number

A number of He 219s were used for trials work, but were never assigned a *Versuchnummer*, with those known to date as follows:

He 219A-012
W/Nr.190062
Stammkenzeichen: RL+AB & PK+QL*

*The use of this primary identification code was in error, as the PK+Q-series was allocated to the Me 163 programme, and thus W/Nr.190062 flew for at least two months with the wrong codes applied

He 219A-042, W/Nr.190113, DV+DI at Rechlin during catapult seat seat trials in 1944

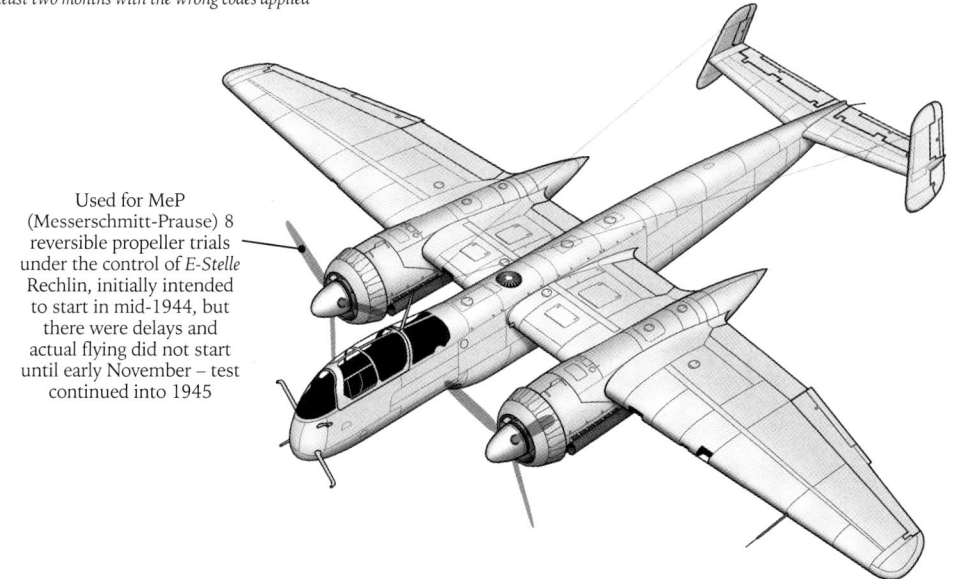

Used for MeP (Messerschmitt-Prause) 8 reversible propeller trials under the control of *E-Stelle* Rechlin, initially intended to start in mid-1944, but there were delays and actual flying did not start until early November – test continued into 1945

Notes
Initially allocated to I./NJG 1 at Venlo (24th October 1943), but if it ever actually got there was only for a brief spell, as it was at Rechlin in mid-January 1944 and remained there for the next twelve months engaged in endurance trials.
Used for flame damper and de-icing trials with the Kärcher heating system.
Listed as scrapped at 'Vienna' in May 1945, but the five He 219s found by Allied forces at Schwechat (Vienna) did not include W/Nr.190062, so it may be that it was scrapped elsewhere such as Aspern or Zwölfaxing?

He 219
Evolution 2
No V-series Number

He 219A-042
W/Nr.190113
Stammkenzeichen: DV+DI

Delivered to *E-Stelle* Rechlin on the 23rd February 1944 for catapult seat trials and modified as follows:

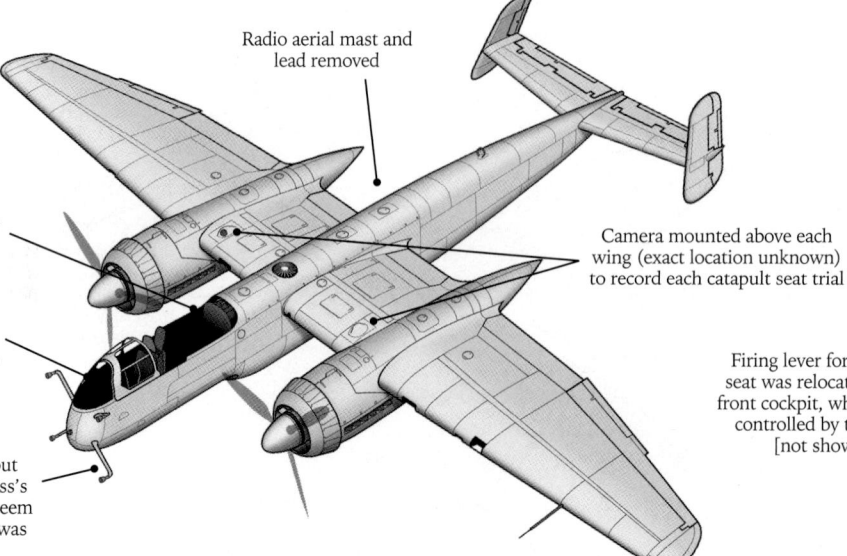

- Rear canopy section removed
- Front section of canopy removed and replaced with a much shorter version that only covered the pilot's position
- Retained FuG 220 antlers, but no dipoles; from Wilhelm Buss's report in May 1944 it would seem that all the radar equipment was still in the rear cockpit
- Radio aerial mast and lead removed
- Camera mounted above each wing (exact location unknown) to record each catapult seat trial
- Firing lever for the rear seat was relocated to the front cockpit, where it was controlled by the pilot [not shown]

Notes
Although a *Versuchnummer* was to have been allocated to it (telex from Heinkel to the RLM 24-02-44), its allocation has never been traced (some state it is the A-019 and/or V19, but both are in error). Found scrapped at Munich-Riems at the end of the war.
This machine was intended for conversion to a 3-man cockpit layout, but there is no evidence to prove that this modification was ever undertaken.

He 219A-042, W/Nr.190113, DV+DI seen during catapult seat trials at Rechlin in 1944. The red/white panels are calibration marks used during high-speed filming of test firings of the seat

He 219A-016, W/Nr.190066, RL+AF seen with the initial FuG 220 and FuG 212 radar, this image also shows the early style canopy and shot spinners fitted to this airframe

He 219A-016
W/Nr.190066
Stammkenzeichen: RL+AF (often mis-quoted as being the V16)

- It was apparently the first He 219 to be fitted with the improved FuG 220 SN 2c/d v/r (forward and rearward-facing) radar
- Last recorded at Weneuchen on the 6th August 1944 with *Naxos Z-4* system installed (this would have most likely resulted in a bulge in the top of the front canopy section to house it)
- In the summer of 1944 it was fitted with FuG 218 *Neptun* radar (with small antlers and dipoles) in place of the FuG 220/212
- Initially fitted with FuG 220 SN-2 and FuG 212C-1 radar and antenna
- This machine was apparently fitted with enlarged air intakes whilst with *NJGr.10* and this may indicate that it also had upgraded engines fitted at this stage as well [not shown]

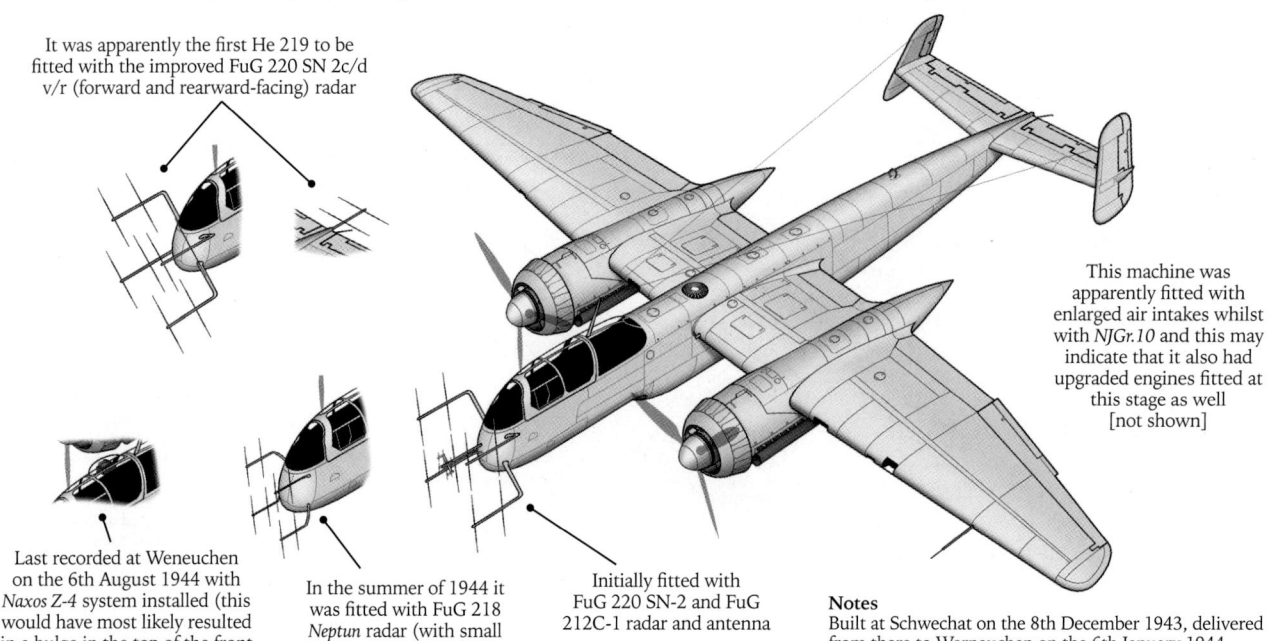

Notes
Built at Schwechat on the 8th December 1943, delivered from there to Werneuchen on the 6th January 1944. Used by Telefunken at Werneuchen to test radar equipment. Reported on the strength of *NJGr.10* at Werneuchen and Finow in the summer of 1944

He 219A-2
W/Nr.290062
Stammkenzeichen: CS+QI
Same as He-219A-012 (page 105)
Notes
Built at Rostock-Marienehe in September 1944 and assigned to *E-Stelle* Rechlin for MeP 8 reversible-pitch (braking) propeller trials. Was at Staaken in November 1944 and had flown there by the 9th December, after which it transferred to Rechlin. The ultimate fate of this machine is unknown.

He 219A-0, W/Nr.190188, BE+JA flown by Hptm Paul Förster (on left) and *Fw.* Ernst Böhmer (on right), seen at Venlo in May 1944 not long after delivery

Pre-Production

He 219A-0 – Early
Based on the V7 to V12

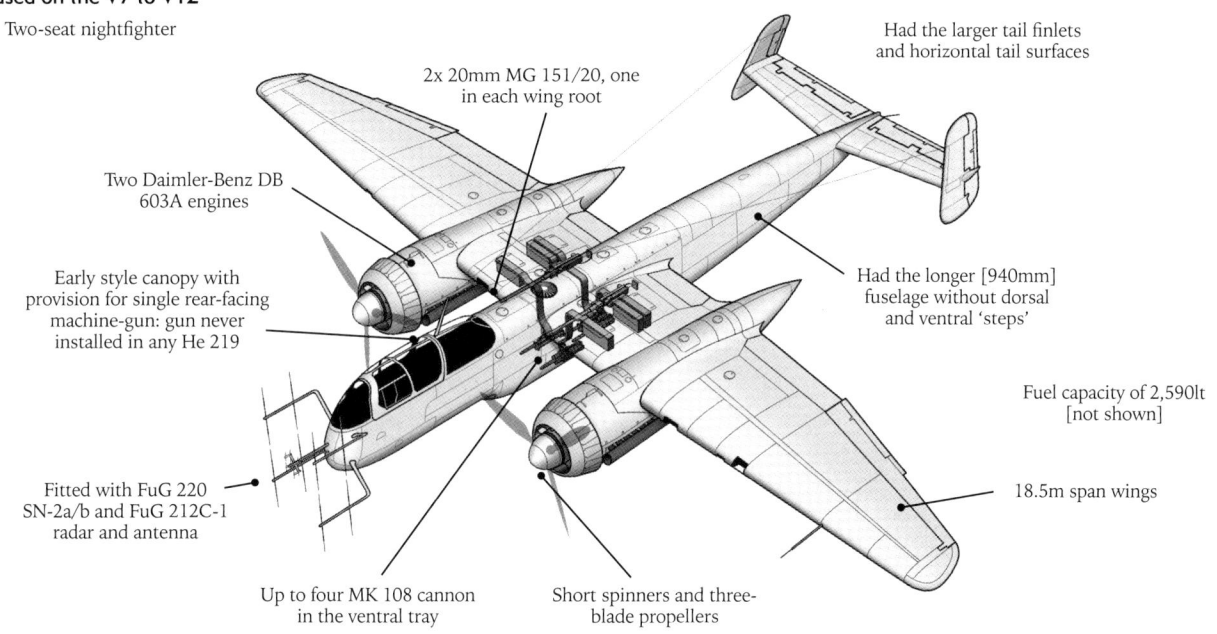

Two-seat nightfighter

- 2x 20mm MG 151/20, one in each wing root
- Two Daimler-Benz DB 603A engines
- Early style canopy with provision for single rear-facing machine-gun: gun never installed in any He 219
- Fitted with FuG 220 SN-2a/b and FuG 212C-1 radar and antenna
- Up to four MK 108 cannon in the ventral tray
- Short spinners and three-blade propellers
- Had the larger tail finlets and horizontal tail surfaces
- Had the longer [940mm] fuselage without dorsal and ventral 'steps'
- Fuel capacity of 2,590lt [not shown]
- 18.5m span wings

He 219A-0 – Late
Same as He 219A-0 – Early except:

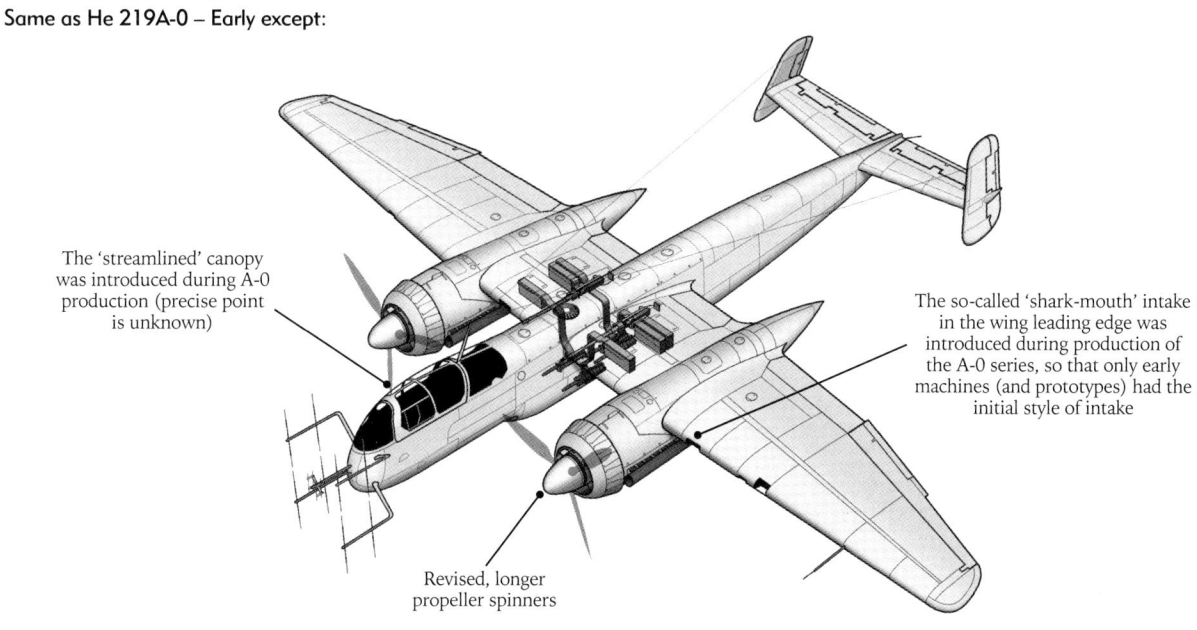

- The 'streamlined' canopy was introduced during A-0 production (precise point is unknown)
- Revised, longer propeller spinners
- The so-called 'shark-mouth' intake in the wing leading edge was introduced during production of the A-0 series, so that only early machines (and prototypes) had the initial style of intake

He 219 Evolution 2
Notes

Rüstsätze
The only Rüstsätze (equipment sets) applicable to A-0 series were designated 'I', 'II' and 'III', although these were later changed to 'M1', M2' & 'M3' (the 'M' standing for munition)

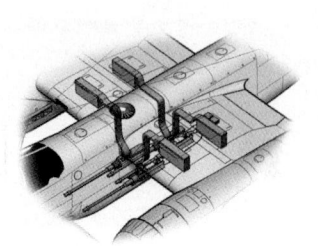

M1 – 4x MG 151/20A in ventral tray with 300rpg each

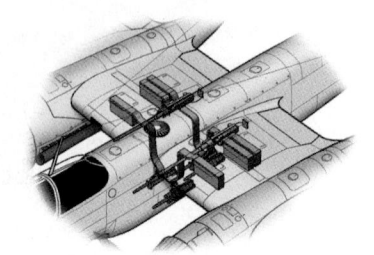

M2 – 4x MK 108 30mm in ventral tray with 300rpg each

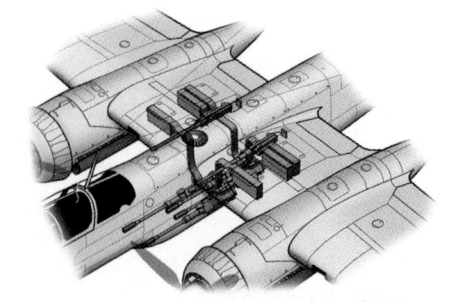

M3 – 4x MK 103 30mm with 300rpg each – Unlikely few, if any He 219s, were ever fitted with this weapon, as its range of 1,200m was far beyond visual range for night interception, plus it was continually in short supply and was nearly three times the weight of the MK 108

Notes on Pre-production Series Airframes
The pre-production series (the first being completed at Schwechat in September 1943) comprised the following airframes:
- A-01 to A-10, W/Nrs.190051-190060, PK+QA to PK+QJ
- A-011 to A-025 W/Nrs.190061-190075, RL+AA to RL+AO
- A-026 to A-033 W/Nrs.190097-190104, RL+AP to RL+AW
- A-034 to A-059 W/Nrs.190105-190130, DV+DA to DV+DZ
- A-060 W/Nr.190131, GU+BA*
- A-061 to A-073 W/Nrs.190175-190187, GU+BB to GU+BN*
- A-074 to A-080 W/Nrs.190188-190194, BE+JA to BE+JG*
- A-081 to A-097 W/Nrs.190210-190226, BE+JH to BE+JX*
- A-098 to A-106 W/Nrs.190227-190235, unknown

The W/Nr.210901-210905 and 211116-211125 production batches did not receive A-0xx numbers.

These allocations are not confirmed by surviving documents, but are reasonably inferred from other confirmed period information

Notes on specific airframes
- A-010/TL W/Nr.190060, PK+QJ. This airframe was first used to test the carriage of a BMW 003 jet engine in a nacelle under the fuselage. First flew in this configuration with the jet at idle took place on the 23rd September 1943. It sustained 40% damage in a heavy landing at Aspern (Vienna) on the 13th November 1943. Repaired and became the V17 (see elsewhere), where it undertook DB603 engine (with G-supercharger) trials. Found intact by American troops at Hörsching/Linz airbase, Austria at the end of the war. The V30 (A-030, W/Nrs.190101, RL+AT) was also used for such trials (see elsewhere).

He 219A-0, W/Nr.190116, DV+DL prior to delivery to I./NJG 1 in April 1944, note the longer spinners and later style of canopy fitted to this airframe

- A-046, W/Nr.190116, DV+DL, allocated to I./NJG 1 on the 14th April 1944, then transferred four weeks later to II./NJG 1 at Deelan. Lost on the night of the 20th/21st May 1944, crashing three km south of Hertogenbosch in the Netherlands.

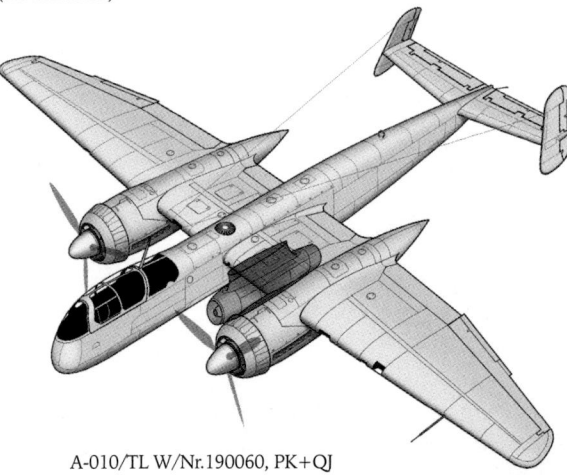

A-010/TL W/Nr.190060, PK+QJ

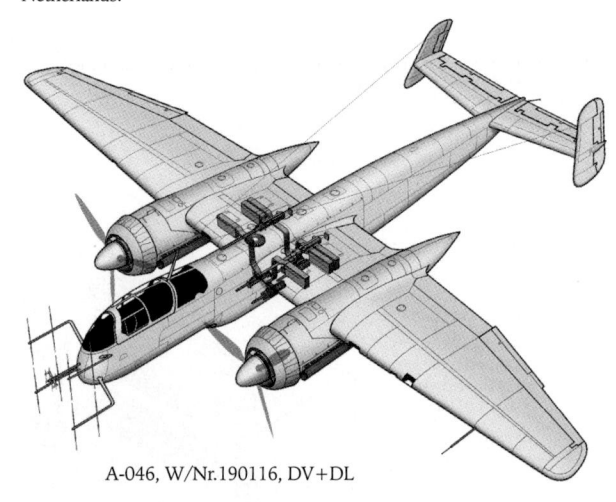

A-046, W/Nr.190116, DV+DL

- A-01, W/Nr.190051, PK+QA, used for long-term testing by E.Kdo, Lärz in 1944
- A-03, W/Nr.190053, PK+QC, used for long-term testing by E.Kdo, Lärz in 1944
- A-07, W/Nr.190057, PK+AG, used for long-term testing by E.Kdo, Lärz in 1944
- A-09, W/Nr.190059, PK+AI, used for long-term testing by E.Kdo, Lärz in 1944
- A-011, W/Nr.190061, RL+AA, used for long-term testing by E.Kdo, Lärz in 1944, crashed near Mirow on the 16th June 1944 due to tailplane failure (was fitted with the fin/rudders from W/Nr.190063 at this time)
- A-018, W/Nr.190068, RL+AH, converted with shorter-span wings
- A-076, W/Nr.190190 BE+JC, assigned to 6./NJG 1 at Deelan in May 1944 (as G9+PP), transferred to 1./NJG 1 at Venlo in July 1944
- W/Nr. not known, CS+QI, used for MeP.8 reversible-propeller tests by E-Stelle – See V3
- W/Nr.190004, G9+AB, used by Stab. NJG1 at Venlo (flown by Hptm. Förster)
- W/Nr.190012, G9+FK, used by 2./NJG1 at Venlo (flown by Oblt Modrow) – Had both FuG 220 SN-2 and FuG 212C1 radar

Production

He 219A-1

Notes
High-speed bomber, cancelled before production began, was to have had DB 603A/B counter-rotating engines* and FuG 220 radar.
Note that the DB603B engine never reached production, so the type, had it ever been put into production, would more likely have used the DB 603A or AA

He 219A-2, W/Nr.290004, G9+DH wreck found at Paderborn by US forces in May 1945 (©USAAF)

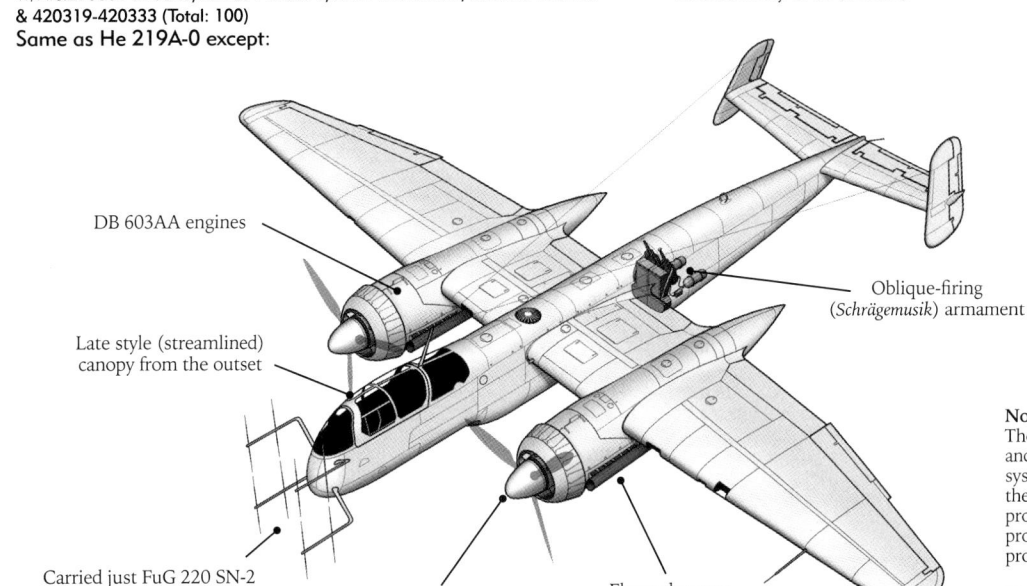

He 219A-2
W/Nrs.290001-290020, 290054-290078, 290110-290129, 290186-290205 & 420319-420333 (Total: 100)
Same as He 219A-0 except:

- DB 603AA engines
- Late style (streamlined) canopy from the outset
- Carried just FuG 220 SN-2 radar with antenna on nose
- Elongated propeller spinners
- Flame dampers as standard
- Oblique-firing (*Schrägemusik*) armament

Notes
The A-2 had fuel delivery problems and the A-5 version with revised fuel system was thus intended to replace the A-2, although it never went into production – The first Schwechat-produced A-2s came off the production line in September 1944.

Note: All of the Rüstsatz sets mentioned in many published sources for the A-2 series are erroneous and again originate from the unattributed post-war title Entwicklung de He 219 Baureihen, so they have not been included here.

He 219A-3

Notes
Planned development of A-2 with DB 603E engines that is listed in German documentation as having 'miniaturised standard equipment and additional container' – the later item most likely being a 900lt external fuel tank, which was never adopted by the He 219. Some sources quote the DB603A/B as the powerplant, but that is incorrect – series cancelled before production began (no prototypes).

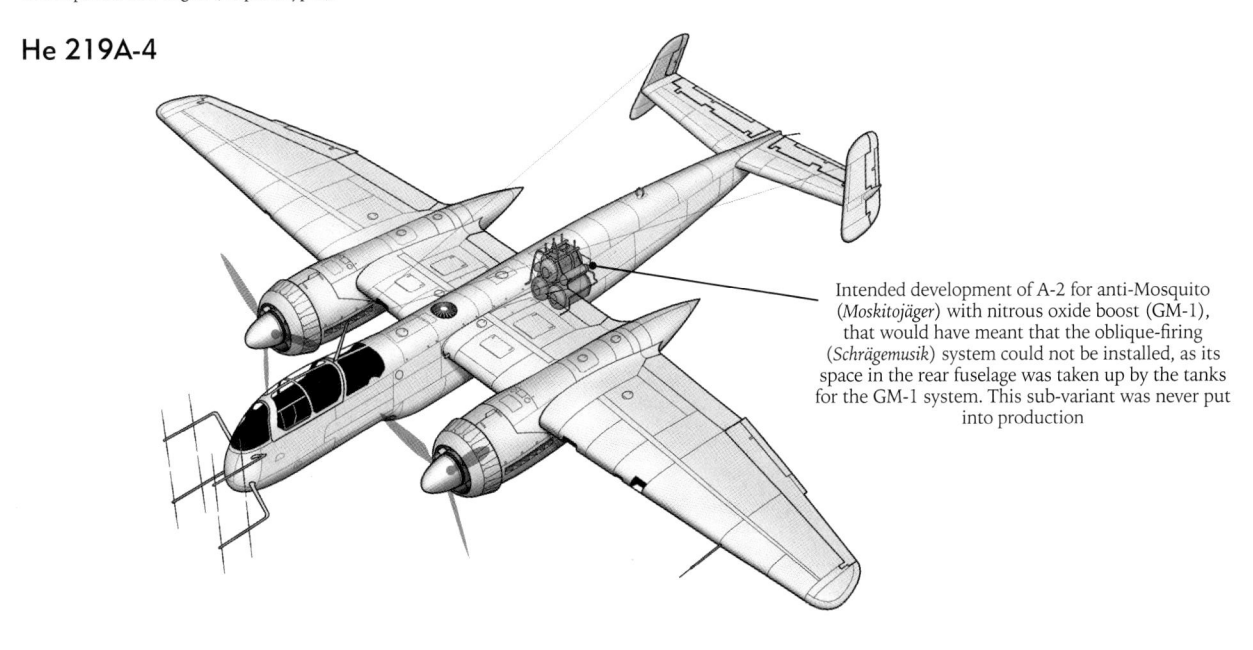

He 219A-4

Intended development of A-2 for anti-Mosquito (*Moskitojäger*) with nitrous oxide boost (GM-1), that would have meant that the oblique-firing (*Schrägemusik*) system could not be installed, as its space in the rear fuselage was taken up by the tanks for the GM-1 system. This sub-variant was never put into production

He 219
Evolution
Production

He 219A-5

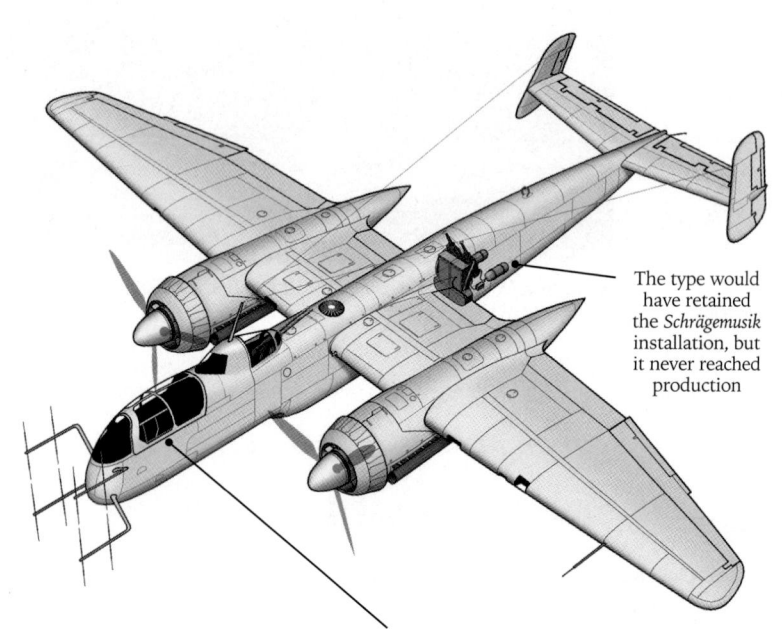

The type would have retained the *Schrägemusik* installation, but it never reached production

Note: All of the Rüstsatz sets mentioned in many published sources for the A-5 series are once again erroneous and originate from the unattributed post-war title *Entwicklung de He 219 Baureihen*, so they have not been included here.

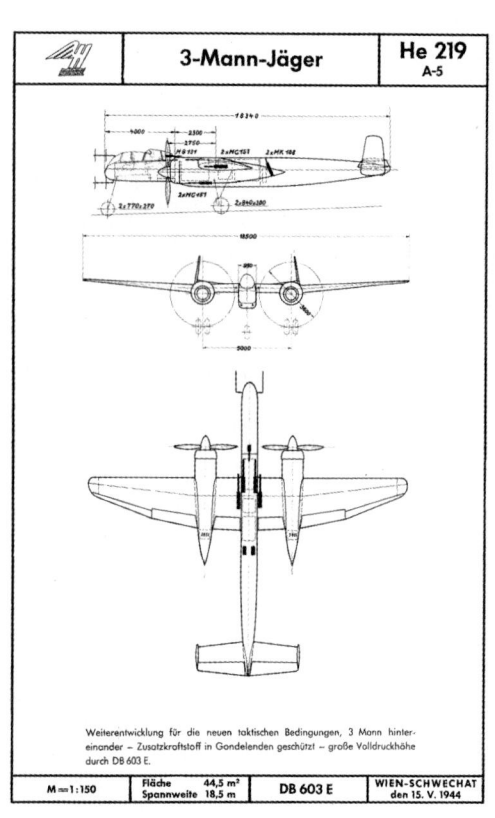

Further development of A-3 as a three-seater (tandem layout) with cockpit (rear-facing) armament (most likely an MG 131Z), standard 2,590lt of fuel in the fuselage and an additional 780lt via tanks in the rear of each engine nacelle

Dated 15th May 1944, this is the general arrangement diagram for the A-5 series

He 219A-6

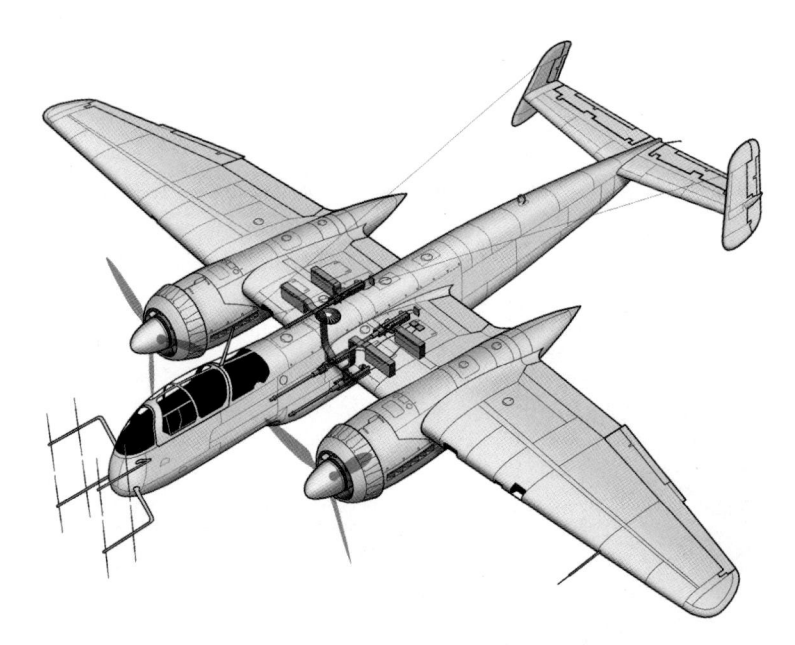

Notes
Another anti-Mosquito (*Moskitojäger*) based on the A-2, with DB 603AA engines, reduced armour and armament (only 2x MG 151/20 in ventral tray with one each in the wing roots) and no *Schrägemusik* system – type never reached production*.
*The often published image quoted as an A-6, is most likely an A-0 with reduced armament, photographed at Venlo in the autumn of 1944

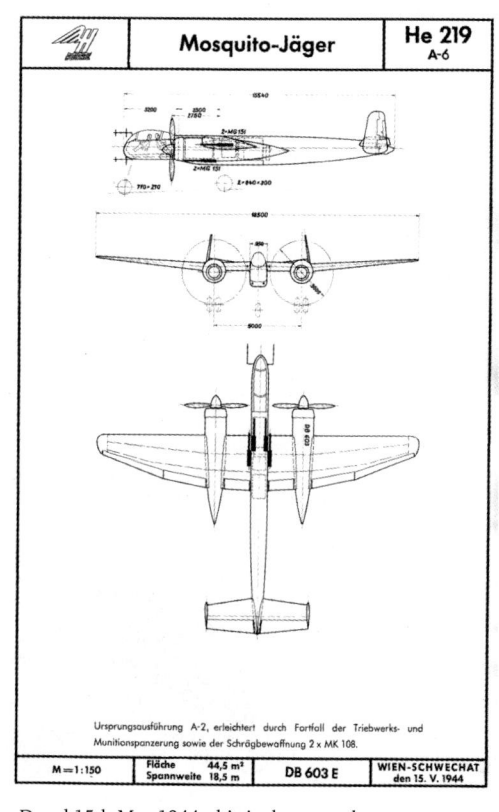

Dated 15th May 1944, this is the general arrangement diagram for the proposed A-6 series

He 219
Evolution
Production

He 219A-7
W/Nrs.310106-310210, 310182-310192, 310200-310215, 310220-310230, 310312-310313 & 310322-310328 (Total = 63)
Development of A-2, same except:

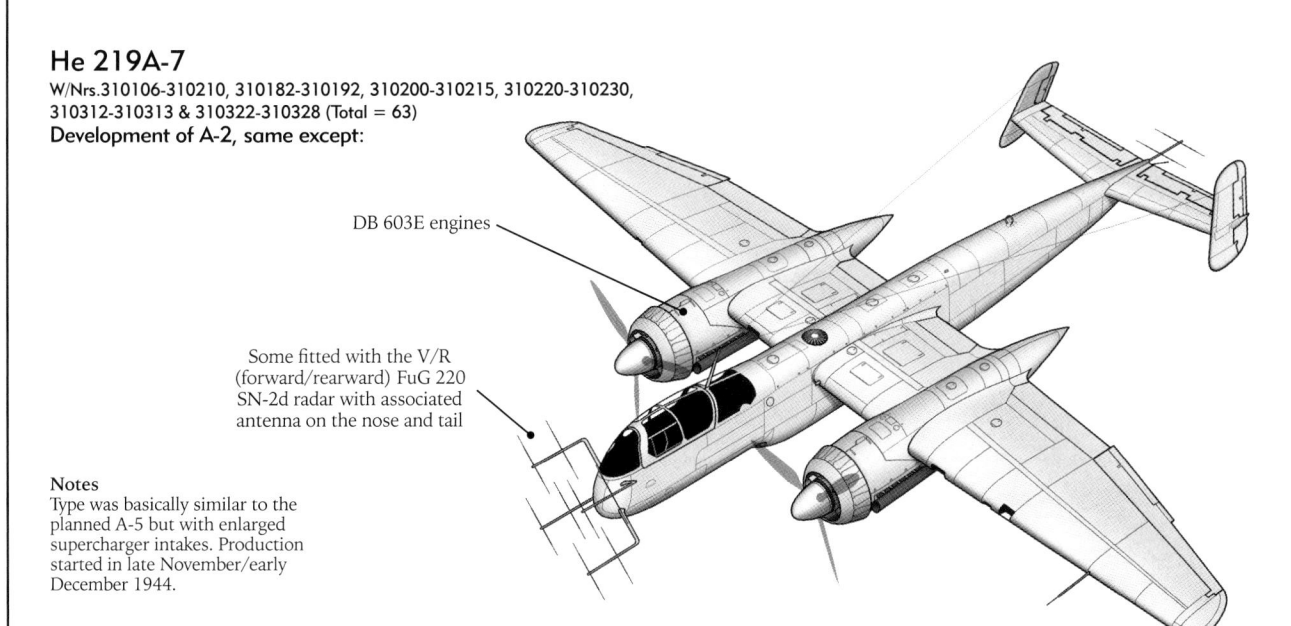

DB 603E engines

Some fitted with the V/R (forward/rearward) FuG 220 SN-2d radar with associated antenna on the nose and tail

Notes
Type was basically similar to the planned A-5 but with enlarged supercharger intakes. Production started in late November/early December 1944.

He 219A-7 FuG 218
(W/Nr.310106)
Same as He 219A-7 except:

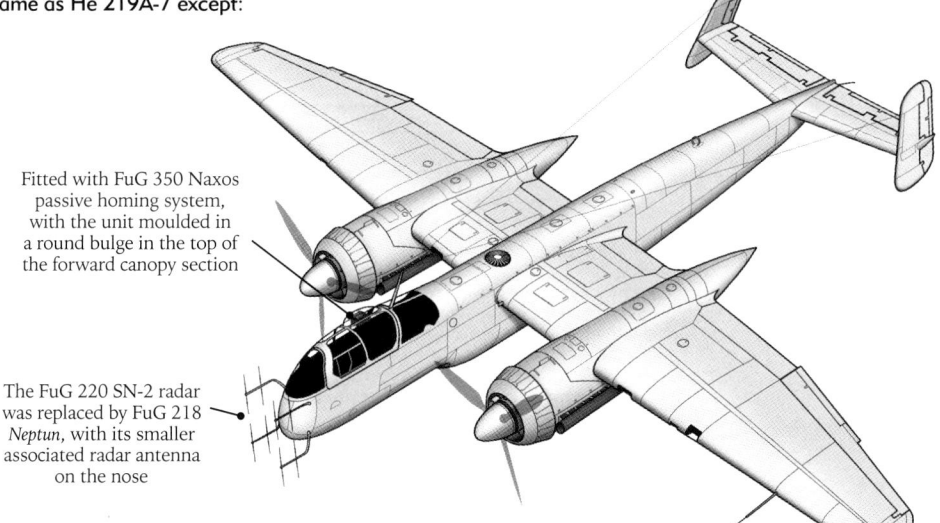

Fitted with FuG 350 Naxos passive homing system, with the unit moulded in a round bulge in the top of the forward canopy section

The FuG 220 SN-2 radar was replaced by FuG 218 *Neptun*, with its smaller associated radar antenna on the nose

Notes
As far as is known, this is the only A-7 to have been fitted with this radar system (it became AirMin 44 when captured by British forces in 1945).

Total He 219 production: Heinkel documents state 294, the report prepared in June 1945 by the Quartermaster 6.Abeilung and the Air Inspector General stated only 274 were delivered.

Note: All of the Rüstsatz sets mentioned in many published sources for the A-7 series are once again erroneous and originate from the unattributed post-war title Entwicklung de He 219 Baureihen, so they have not been included here.

He 219D-1
Night fighter converted from A-2s:

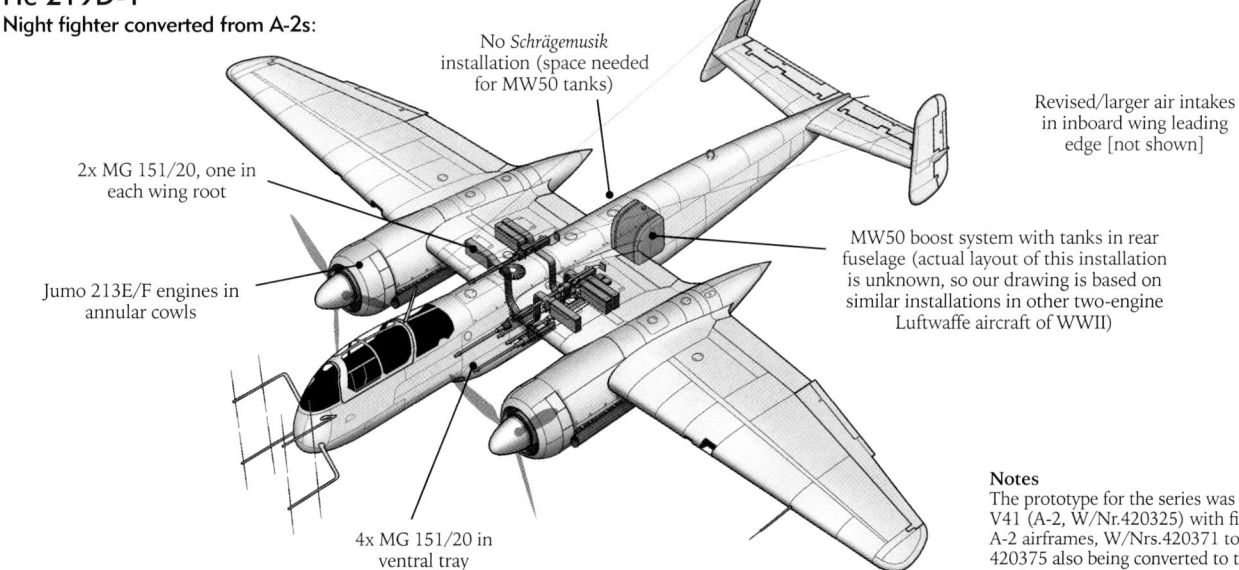

No Schrägemusik installation (space needed for MW50 tanks)

Revised/larger air intakes in inboard wing leading edge [not shown]

2x MG 151/20, one in each wing root

Jumo 213E/F engines in annular cowls

MW50 boost system with tanks in rear fuselage (actual layout of this installation is unknown, so our drawing is based on similar installations in other two-engine Luftwaffe aircraft of WWII)

4x MG 151/20 in ventral tray

Notes
The prototype for the series was the V41 (A-2, W/Nr.420325) with five A-2 airframes, W/Nrs.420371 to 420375 also being converted to this configuration at Schwechat.

He 219 Evolution 2
Projected Versions

Projected Versions

He 219B-1

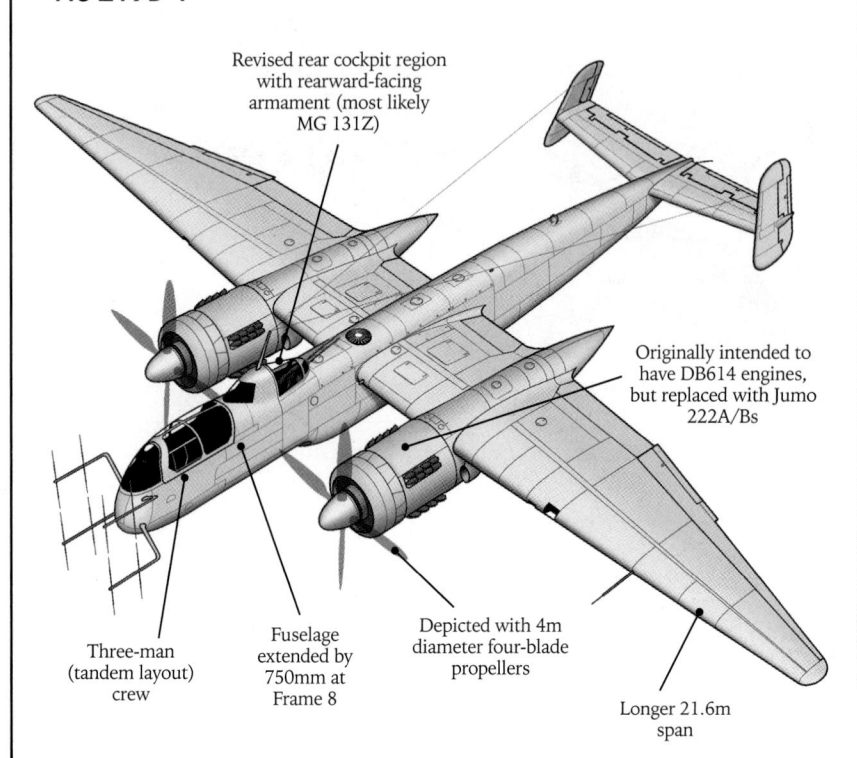

- Revised rear cockpit region with rearward-facing armament (most likely MG 131Z)
- Originally intended to have DB614 engines, but replaced with Jumo 222A/Bs
- Three-man (tandem layout) crew
- Fuselage extended by 750mm at Frame 8
- Depicted with 4m diameter four-blade propellers
- Longer 21.6m span

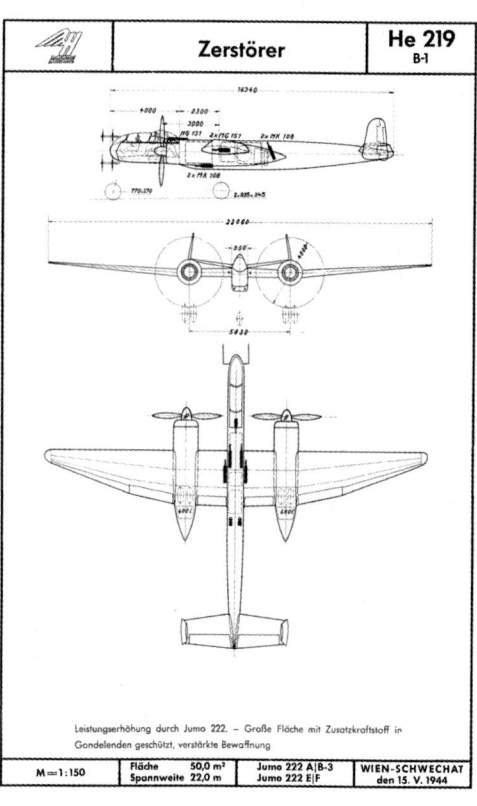

Not Shown
- Enlarged/strengthened undercarriage
- Standard fuselage fuel capacity of 2,590lt, but an additional 1,200lt was to be carried via a tank in the rear of each engine nacelle
- Two MG 151/20, one at each wing root
- 2x MK 108 in ventral tray
- 2x MK 108 as oblique-firing *Schrägemusik* installation in rear fuselage

Dated 15th May 1944, this is the general arrangement diagram for the proposed B-1 series

Notes
One prototype completed but powered by DB 603Aa due to lack of Jumo 222s.
Factory drawings show no exhaust stacks, as internal exhaust dampers were envisaged, but as no detail drawings of such a system survive, we have depicted it with just standard exhausts and no flame dampers.

He 219B-2
Höhen-jäger (High-altitude fighter)

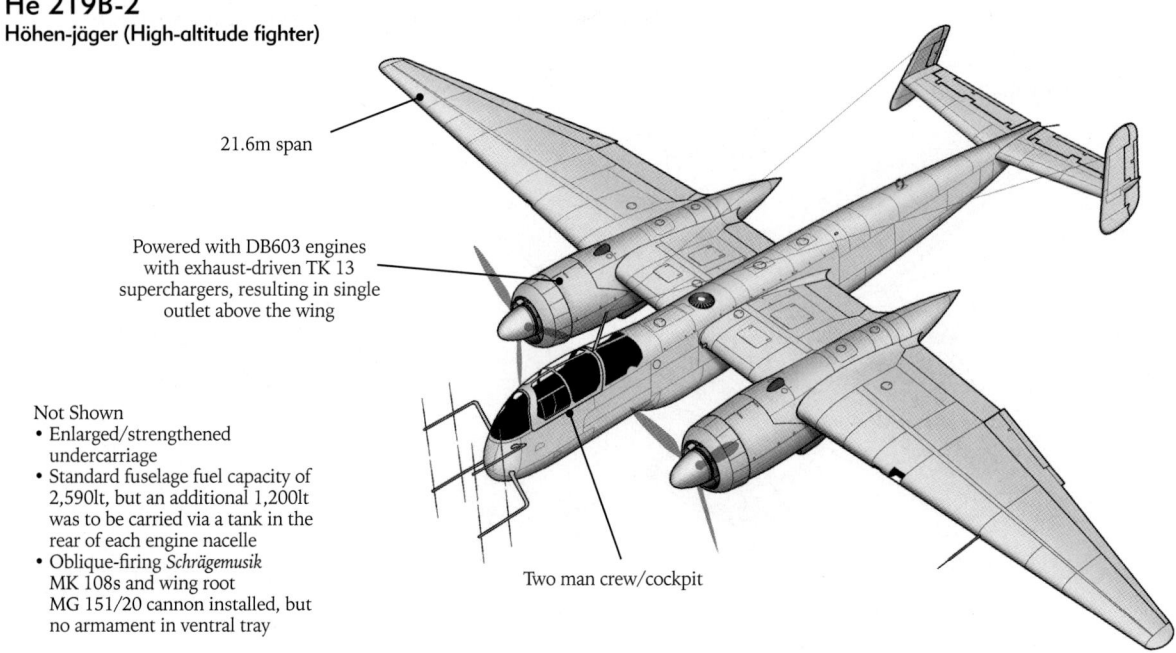

- 21.6m span
- Powered with DB603 engines with exhaust-driven TK 13 superchargers, resulting in single outlet above the wing
- Two man crew/cockpit

Not Shown
- Enlarged/strengthened undercarriage
- Standard fuselage fuel capacity of 2,590lt, but an additional 1,200lt was to be carried via a tank in the rear of each engine nacelle
- Oblique-firing *Schrägemusik* MK 108s and wing root MG 151/20 cannon installed, but no armament in ventral tray

He 219
Evolution
Projected Versions
2 | 113

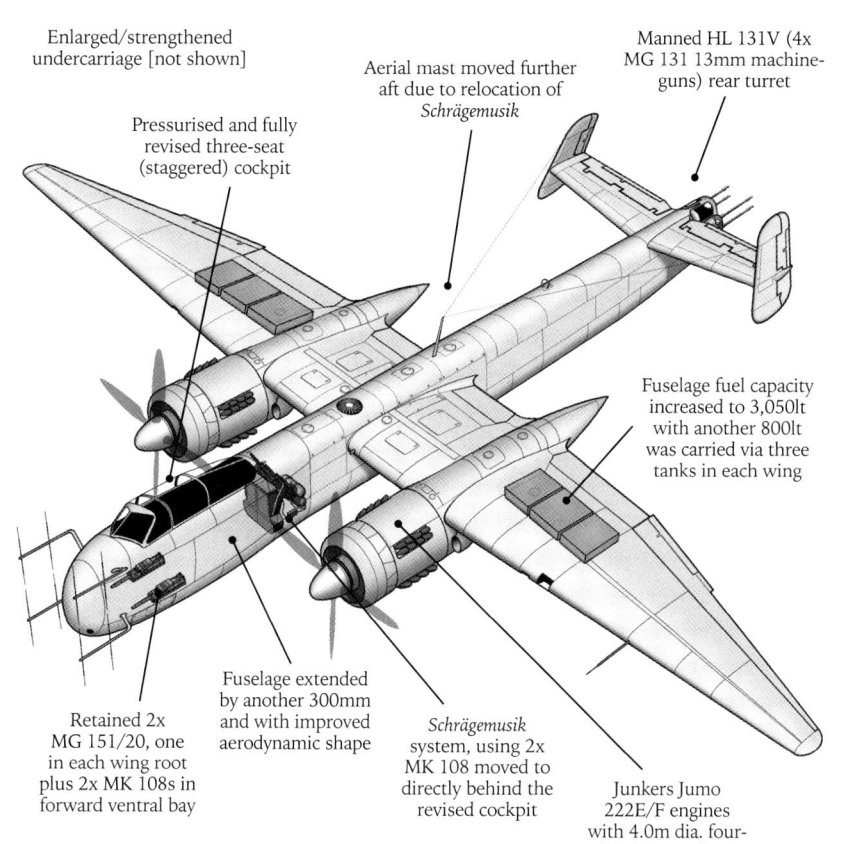

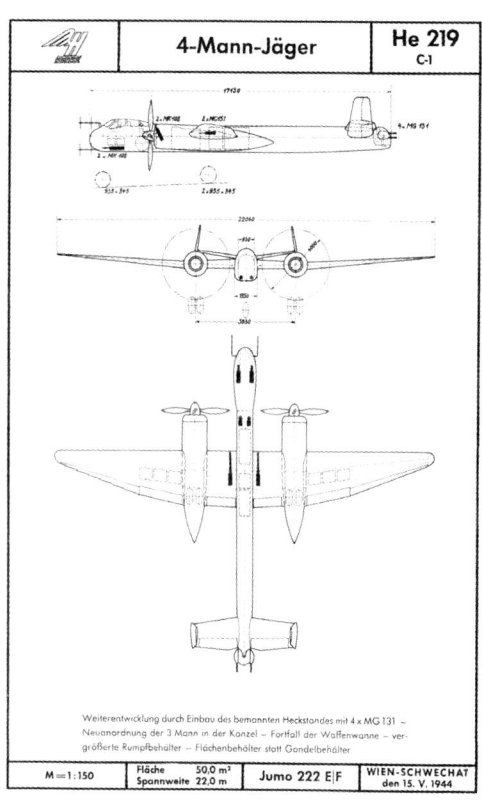

He 219C-1
Basically similar to the B-1 except:

- Enlarged/strengthened undercarriage [not shown]
- Pressurised and fully revised three-seat (staggered) cockpit
- Aerial mast moved further aft due to relocation of *Schrägemusik*
- Manned HL 131V (4x MG 131 13mm machine-guns) rear turret
- Fuselage fuel capacity increased to 3,050lt with another 800lt was carried via three tanks in each wing
- Retained 2x MG 151/20, one in each wing root plus 2x MK 108s in forward ventral bay
- Fuselage extended by another 300mm and with improved aerodynamic shape
- *Schrägemusik* system, using 2x MK 108 moved to directly behind the revised cockpit
- Junkers Jumo 222E/F engines with 4.0m dia. four-blade propellers

Dated 15th May 1944, this is the general arrangement diagram for the proposed C-1 series

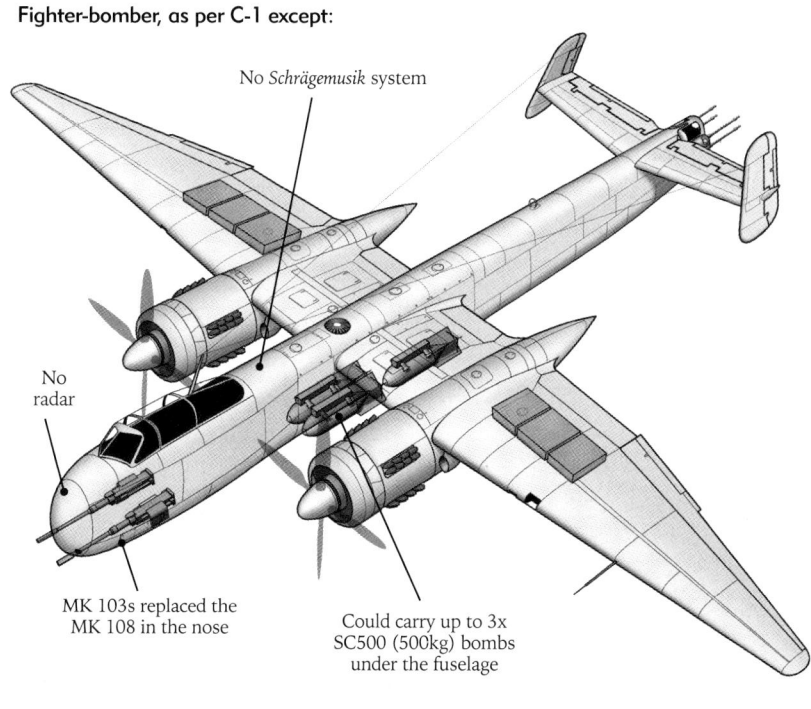

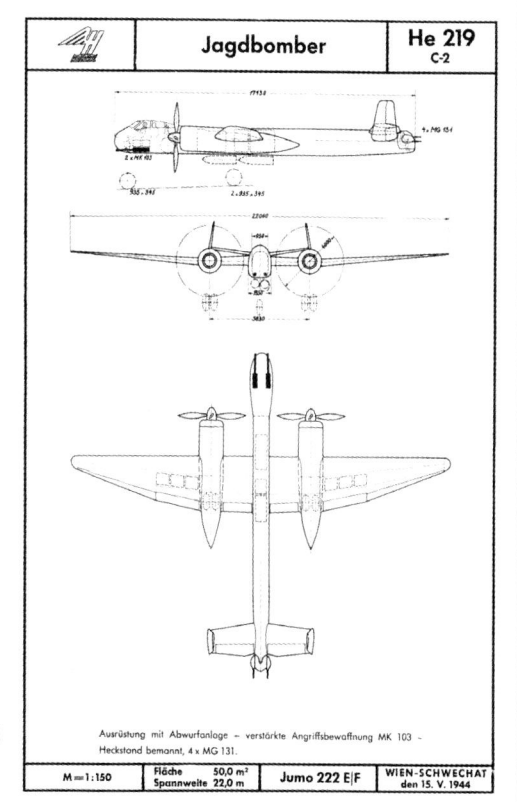

He 219C-2
Fighter-bomber, as per C-1 except:

- No *Schrägemusik* system
- No radar
- MK 103s replaced the MK 108 in the nose
- Could carry up to 3x SC500 (500kg) bombs under the fuselage

Dated 15th May 1944, this is the general arrangement diagram for the proposed C-2 series

He 219 Evolution 2
Projected Versions

He 219E
Similar to the He 219A-5 except:

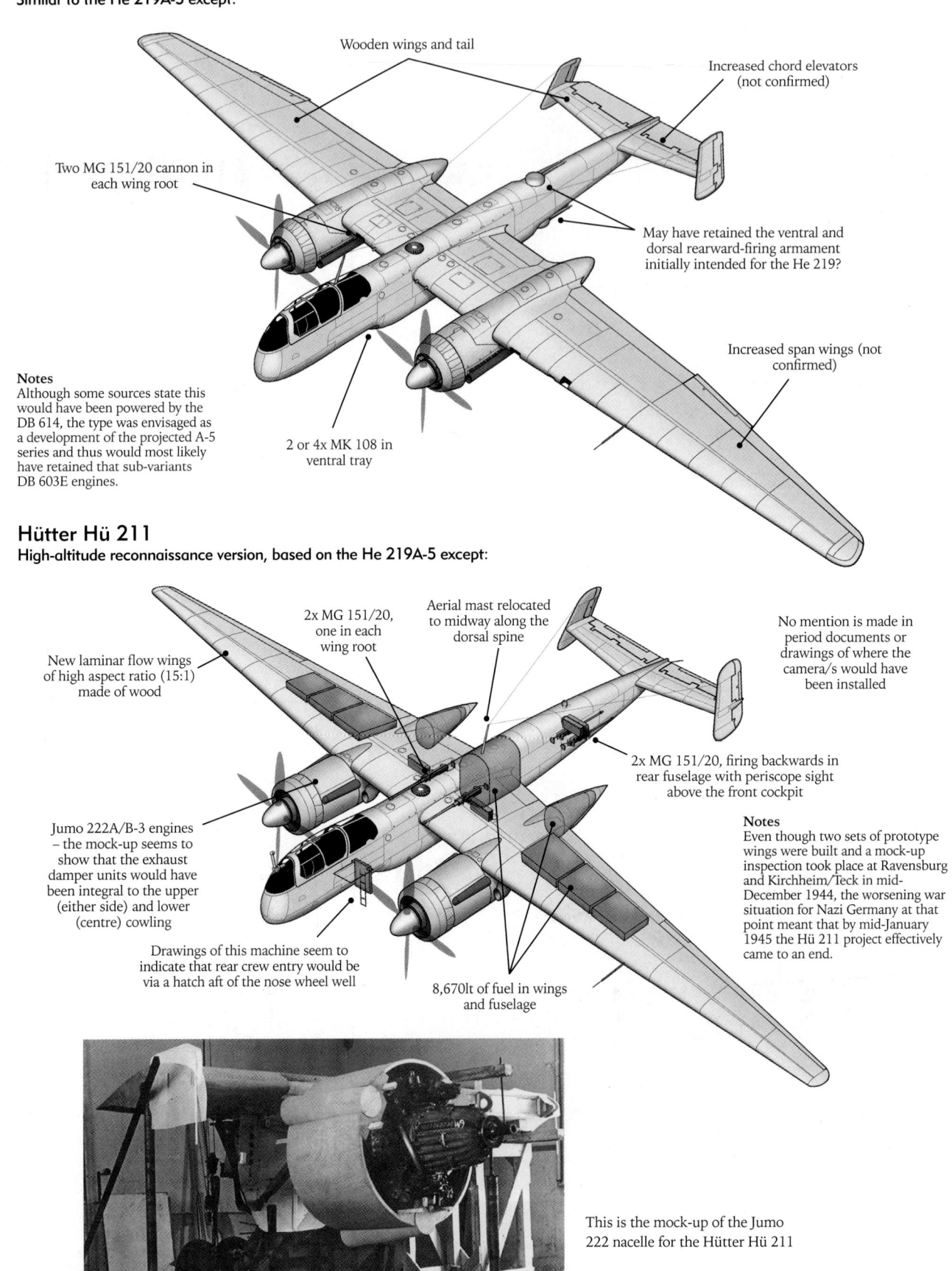

- Wooden wings and tail
- Increased chord elevators (not confirmed)
- Two MG 151/20 cannon in each wing root
- May have retained the ventral and dorsal rearward-firing armament initially intended for the He 219?
- Increased span wings (not confirmed)
- 2 or 4x MK 108 in ventral tray

Notes
Although some sources state this would have been powered by the DB 614, the type was envisaged as a development of the projected A-5 series and thus would most likely have retained that sub-variants DB 603E engines.

Hütter Hü 211
High-altitude reconnaissance version, based on the He 219A-5 except:

- New laminar flow wings of high aspect ratio (15:1) made of wood
- 2x MG 151/20, one in each wing root
- Aerial mast relocated to midway along the dorsal spine
- No mention is made in period documents or drawings of where the camera/s would have been installed
- Jumo 222A/B-3 engines – the mock-up seems to show that the exhaust damper units would have been integral to the upper (either side) and lower (centre) cowling
- 2x MG 151/20, firing backwards in rear fuselage with periscope sight above the front cockpit
- Drawings of this machine seem to indicate that rear crew entry would be via a hatch aft of the nose wheel well
- 8,670lt of fuel in wings and fuselage

Notes
Even though two sets of prototype wings were built and a mock-up inspection took place at Ravensburg and Kirchheim/Teck in mid-December 1944, the worsening war situation for Nazi Germany at that point meant that by mid-January 1945 the Hü 211 project effectively came to an end.

This is the mock-up of the Jumo 222 nacelle for the Hütter Hü 211

He 319

Notes
Night fighter project developed in parallel with the He 219, it only differed in having a single vertical fin and standard tailplanes, design abandoned in November 1942 in favour of the He 419

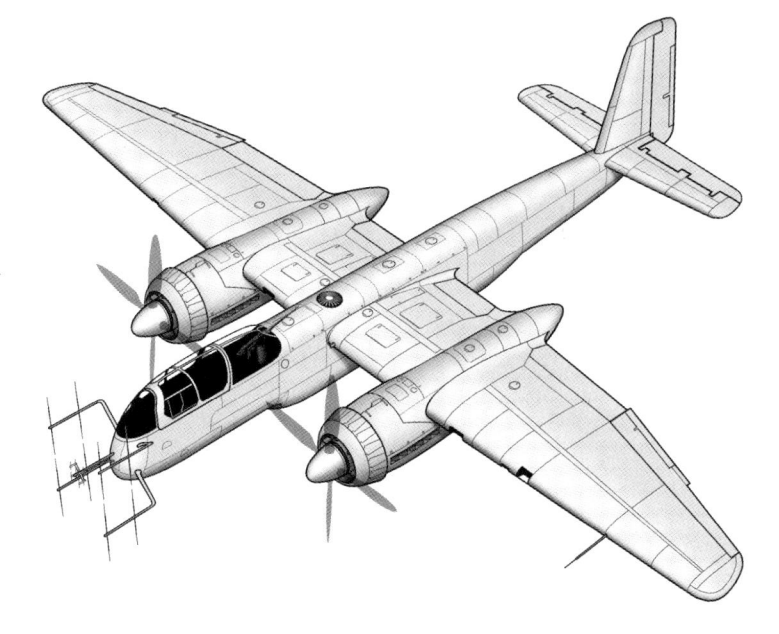

He 419

Notes
High-altitude fighter development of He 219, wing centre section increased to make span greater.

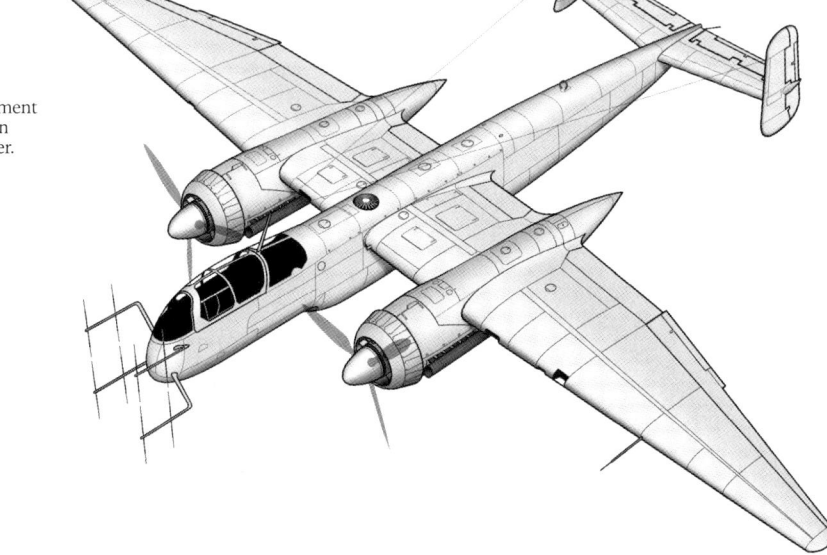

The series was envisaged in the following sub-variants:

He 419A-0* – Basically an He 219A-5 except:
- Long-span wings
- DB603G engines
- 4x MG 151/20 in ventral tray
- 2x MG 151/20, one in each wing root

*This was not a pre-production version it would have been seen as a new sub-variant based on the He 219A-5

He 419A-2
- DB603U engines
- 4x MG 151/20, MK 108 or 2x MK 103* in ventral tray – *Unlikely it would have been adopted as it was continually in short supply and was nearly three times the weight of the MK 108!
- 2x MG 151/20, one in each wing root

He 419B-1
- DB603G engines
- 4x MK 108 in ventral tray
- 2x MG 151/20, one in each wing root
- 2x MK 108 in *Schrägemusik* installation

He 419B-1/R1 – Same as B-1 except:
- Exhaust-driven turbo-superchargers
- Wings of 59m²

He 419B-1/R2 – Same as B-1 except:
- 4x MG212s in ventral tray

He 419B-1/R3 – Same as B-1 except:
- 4x MK 103s in ventral tray – Unlikely it would have been adopted as it was continually in short supply and was nearly three times the weight of the MK 108!

He 419B-2
- DB603U engines
- 4x MG 151/20 in ventral tray
- 2x MG 151/20, one in each wing root

He 419C
- DB603G engines
- 4x MG 151/20 in ventral tray
- 2x MG 151/20, one in each wing root
- 2x MK 108 in *Schrägemusik* installation

Camouflage & Markings

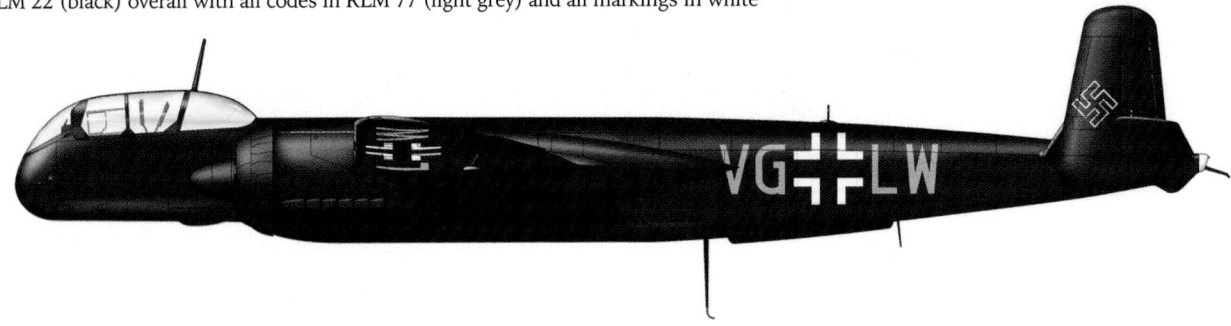

He 219 V1, VG+LW
RLM 22 (black) overall with all codes in RLM 77 (light grey) and all markings in white

As always, I will start by saying that nothing is certain when trying to determine colours from old black and white photographs. The best you can make is an educated, and with luck, intelligent guess using both photographic and documentary evidence. The regulations with regard to the camouflage and markings of Luftwaffe aircraft during the war period are well known and most survive, the problem is that at the front line when the regulations changed it was highly unlikely that the ground crew rushed out to paint every aircraft in their charge, it was simply not practical. Also, in Nazi Germany, as the war situation worsened during 1944 and 1945 the haste with which machines were needed at the front and the lack of paints when they got there meant that inevitably the regulations were adhered to less and less. This whole subject is massive, you can write volumes

This wartime image of G9+FK in flight clearly shows the initial underside split of black (RLM 22) and light blue-grey (RLM 76). The wing leading edge demarcation for the black is of note, as is the heavy exhaust staining visible on both nacelles and back onto the underside of the tailplane

Always be aware of retouched images, this is another shot of He 219A-0 G9+FK in flight on the 18th April 1944, but in retouching the images, the 'G' under the starboard wing has been changed to a 'D'!

Camouflage & Markings 3

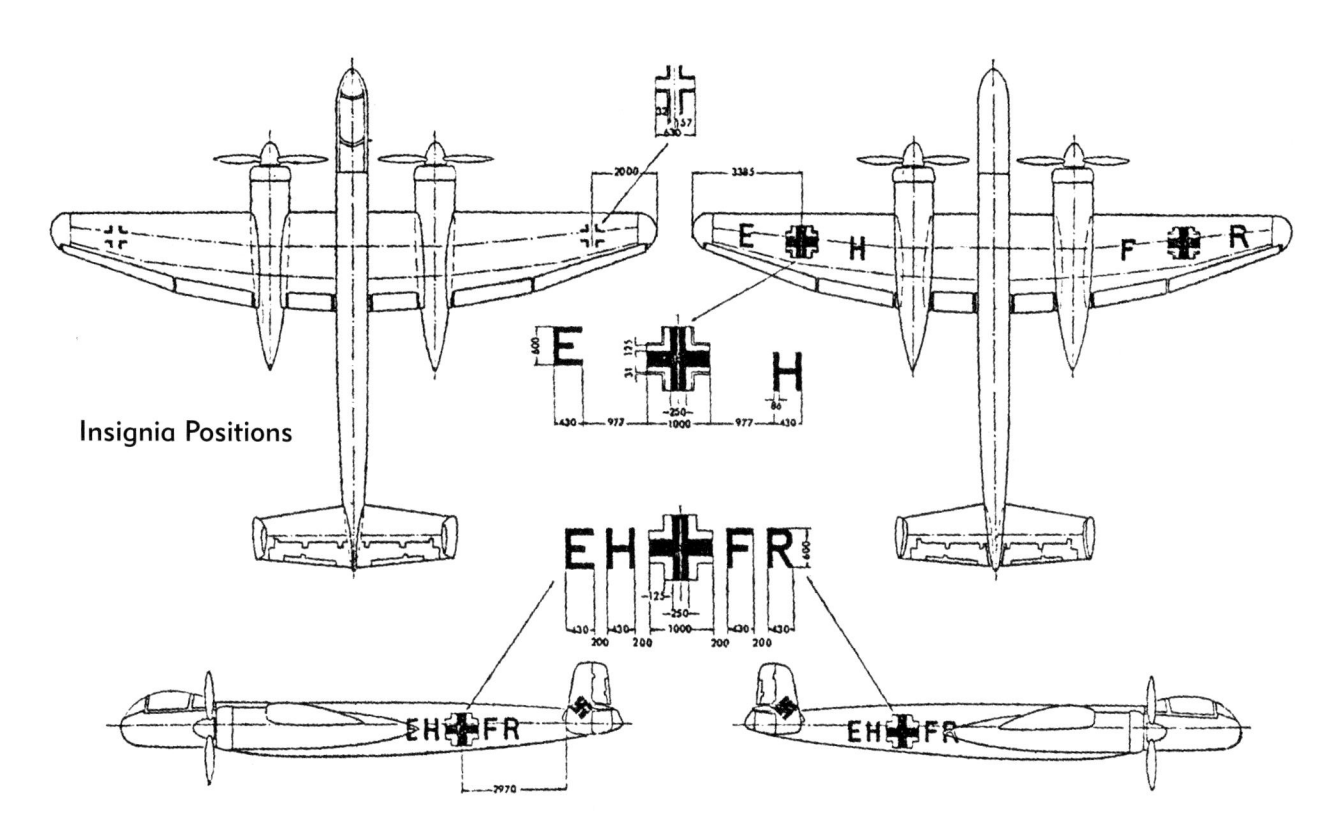

Insignia Positions

on the subject, but we will try and keep it concise. Just remember, nothing is an absolute when it comes to camouflage and markings, and nothing illustrates that more graphically than late-war Luftwaffe C&M!

Although we all use the term 'RLM' to prefix Luftwaffe colours it should be noted that in period documents the only colour designated in this manner was RLM 02, the rest were simply prefixed 'Farbton' (shade/tone/hue of a colour). The confusion lies in the fact that the main paint manufacturer (Warnecke und Böhm) issued paint charts that prefixed all colours with 'RLM', followed by Farbton 74, 75, 76 etc. However for consistency throughout this book we will prefix all colours with 'RLM'

He 219 Prototypes (V-series)

The series of images that are often published claiming to show the He 219 V1 (VG+LW) in flight in early 1943 wearing 'day fighter camouflage' are quite spurious. They were all retouched by Heinkel at the time, probably to remind the RLM that the type was still being considered for as a multi-role type for both day and night operations. The claims that this aircraft wore RLM 74 *Graugrün* (Grey-green) and RLM 75 *Grauviolett* (Grey-violet) over RLM 76 *Lichtblau* (Light Blue) are therefore without foundation.

The first six prototypes all adopted the same scheme, that being black (RLM 22) overall with the fuselage code letters applied in grey (RLM 77). It seems that the swastika on the vertical fins, plus the fuselage and upper and lower wing crosses were in white, as they were all simple 'outline' versions – Type H4 swastika, with Type B6 cross for the fuselage and Type 5 below the wings; there are no period images to confirm the upper wing crosses, but they were most likely also Type B5 (or B6?). The code

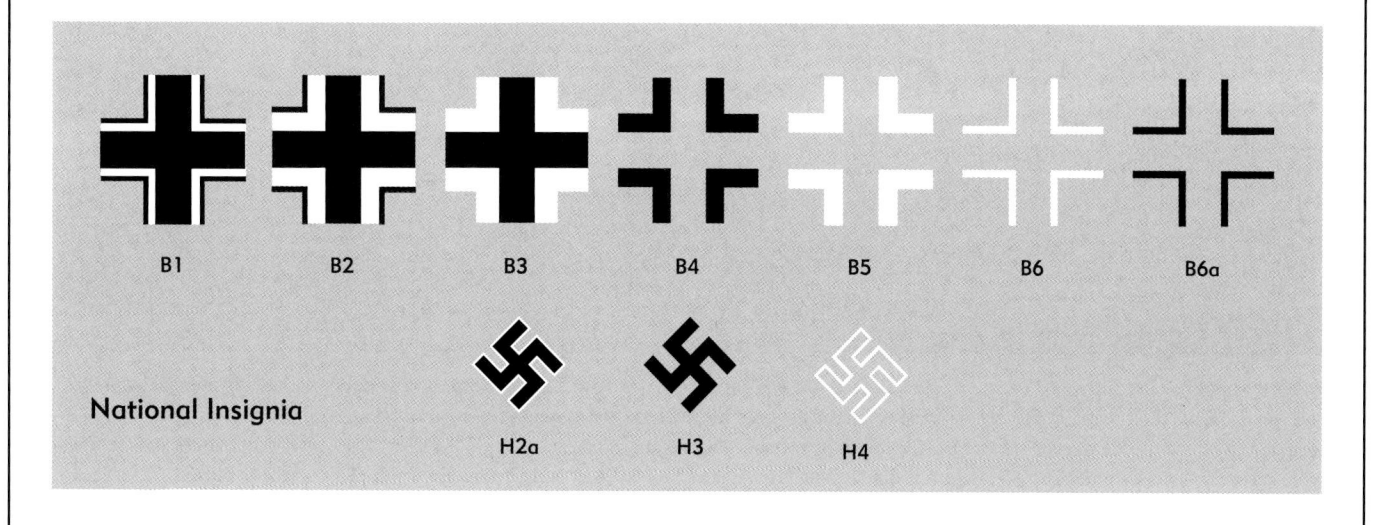

National Insignia

B1 B2 B3 B4 B5 B6 B6a

H2a H3 H4

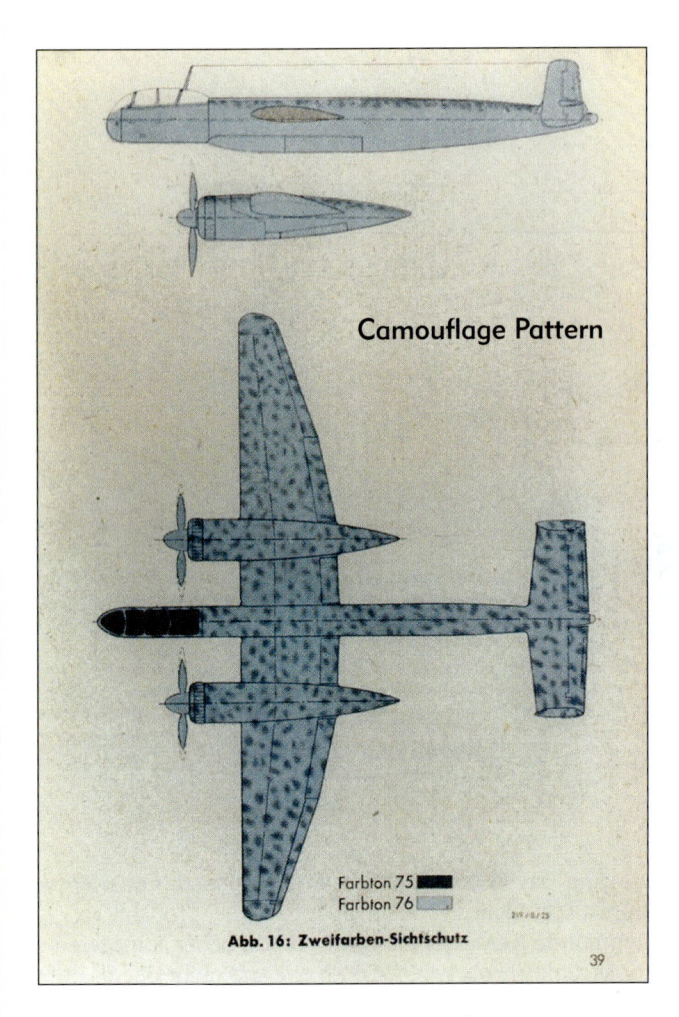

Camouflage & Markings 3

Camouflage Pattern

Farbton 75
Farbton 76

Abb. 16: Zweifarben-Sichtschutz

This shot taken by a member of the USAF at the end of WWII shows the V17 as found by Allied troops. Items of note include things like the rear nacelle being black, but the front section and the outer wing panels seem to be light blue/grey (RLM 76)? The codes (PK+QJ) show the typical German style for letters such as J. The scalloped dark area on the lower edge of the vertical fin is of interest, as this is not a shadow? (©USAF)

letters (e.g. VG+LW) were repeated under the wings, probably also in RLM 77, with the first two (e.g. V+G) under the starboard and the other two (e.g. L+W) under the port, read from the trailing edge looking forward. The V3, V5 and the V6 are also both confirmed as carrying a small (white or grey) version of their V-number on the extreme (upper) tip of the nose cone (the actual position of this varies, as the V3 & V5 had it above the centreline positioned on the horizontal panel line in this region, whilst the V6 had it a lot higher, just below the edge of the windscreen frame).

Very few images exist of most of the V-series, so knowledge of their C&M is thus limited. The vertical fin of the V3 when found by Allied forces at Schewchat at the end of the war certainly does not look to be black, as the swastika and 'V3 are in black yet show high contrast against the base colour, but guessing its overall scheme from one small component would be unwise. The V11, also found at Schwechat at the end of the war, seems to have a scheme that again shows a dark overall shade? The problem is that only the fuselage was found, and the images are all from the Allied technical report created on the aircraft found at Schwechat, so their quality is poor. This results in what looks like a mottle effect, as if these machines were RLM 76 on the undersides, with the demarcation lower down on the fuselage sides, and the upper surface were probably grey or green, possibly RLM 02 or RLM 75 with squiggles of RLM 02 (is that where this often-stated He 219 'scheme' comes from?). The V5 was repainted by the time it was photographed at Tarnewitz

A lovely shot of W/Nr.310189 at Farnborough in late 1945. The consistent nature of the 'speckles' on the upper surfaces is of great interest, as is the fact that their demarcation seems to be on a straight line that cuts many off mid-way. This can be seen on the rear fuselage, and it is true that this may be due to over-spraying of the codes by the RAF, but it can also be seen on the forward nose, below the canopy sills, which were certainly not repainted. The 'V1' does not denote this is a V-series prototype, it is the frequency of the SN-2 radar it carried

in the summer of 1943, adopting the operational scheme described later in this section. The fuselage cross looks to be the simplified Type B1b, but may have a slight white edge, so could be a B1a. Nothing else can be seen other than the 'PU' of its codes, but the scheme probably meant it has Type B4 crosses above and Type B1a underneath the wings.

Production He 219 Series

From the V7 onwards and with all the pre-production (A-0) series, the colour scheme adopted was RLM 76 *Lichtblau* lower surfaces, with RLM 75 *Grauviolet* on the upper surfaces, over which was applied lines/loops of RLM 76 to create a mottle effect. The undersides of the wings were initially painted RLM 76 and the underwing cross seems to be a Type B2, which had its centre 3385m inboard of the tip. The *Stammkenzeichen* was applied in black characters as already noted in the previous section for the first six prototypes and this was repeated, also in black, on each fuselage side, straddling the cross. The style of the fuselage cross varies, although images are limited as that region was often blocked by the wing/nacelle. Certainly the V11 when found had what looks to be a basic Type B1a fuselage cross, whilst the V9 when flown and crashed by Maj. Streib in June 1943 had a Type B4 in this region. Many of the machines found at the end

The upper wing cross is a little different, as it seems to once again not be parallel with the wing leading edge, but this time nor is it parallel to the first (inboard) panel line – it seems to line up with the panel line directly behind the first one [highlighted by a red line] (©S. Willey)

Whilst the NASM He 219 wings were undergoing stripping great care was taken to preserve the correct markings. Here you can see the underwing cross of the starboard wing – note that it is not parallel with the wing leading edge, it lines up with the first (inboard) panel line (©S. Willey)

Once all the paint was removed from the wings of the NASM machine many other markings were discovered. Here you can see one such number, found on the trailing edge, above the flap section outboard of the engine nacelle on the starboard wing (©S. Willey)

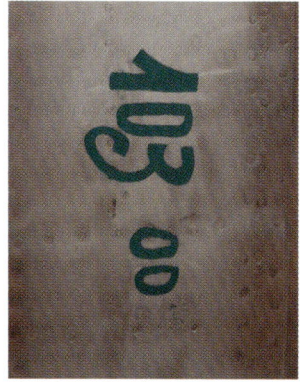

of the war had a Type B1a cross under the wings and on the fuselage sides and certainly W/Nr190116 had these markings prior to delivery in April 1944, so they are most common for in-service machines. The fuselage cross was positioned 2970mm from the furthest forward point of the leading edge of the vertical fin. The swastika on each vertical fin was Type H3, positioned at mid-way up, so that the rear arm was just above the bulged fairing in the rear portion of the fin (the bit that projects back over the elevators). The W/Nr. was applied in black, low down on each vertical fin, using the panel line above it to orientate it. The upper wing cross also seems to go through some variations, as the V9 at the time Maj. Streib crashed it in June 1943 had a Type B6a, however most aircraft found at the end of the war had the Type B4 upper wing cross, positioned 2000mm inboard of the wing tip. Propeller blades were finished in RLM 70 *Schwarzgrün* (Black-Green) with the spinners in RLM 76, although some machines were supplied with the spinners in RLM 70. There are photos to also confirm that some operational He 219s had spirals (either white or yellow) applied to the spinners over the base RLM 70 and, in once instance

Many other numbers were found on the wing upper surfaces of the NASM machine, and each was reproduced faithfully (©S. Willey)

Camouflage & Markings 3

He 219A-0 (V9), G9+FB, I./NJG 1, Venlo (Holland), June 1943
RLM 76 underside with 'reverse mottling' of RLM 76 over the upper RLM 75. Code 'F' in *Hellgrün* RLM 25. Shot down five Lancasters on the night of the 11th/12th June whilst flown by *Maj.* Werner Streib but written off in subsequent crash-landing on returning to base

He 219A-0 (V17), W/Nr.190060, PK+QJ, found at Hörsching-Linz, Austria in May 1945
RLM 76 underside with 'reverse mottling' of RLM 76 over the upper RLM 75. All fuselage markings in black except centre of fuselage crosses, which are in RLM 75

He 219A-2, W/Nr.420331, G9+DB of Stab I./NJG 1, Westerland/Sylt, spring 1945
RLM 76 with 'reverse mottling' over the upper RLM 75. Black of fuselage crosses overpainted in RLM 74, all other national markings in black. 'D' of code in black, outlined in white; 'B' in RLM 24 *Dunkelblau* (Dark Blue)

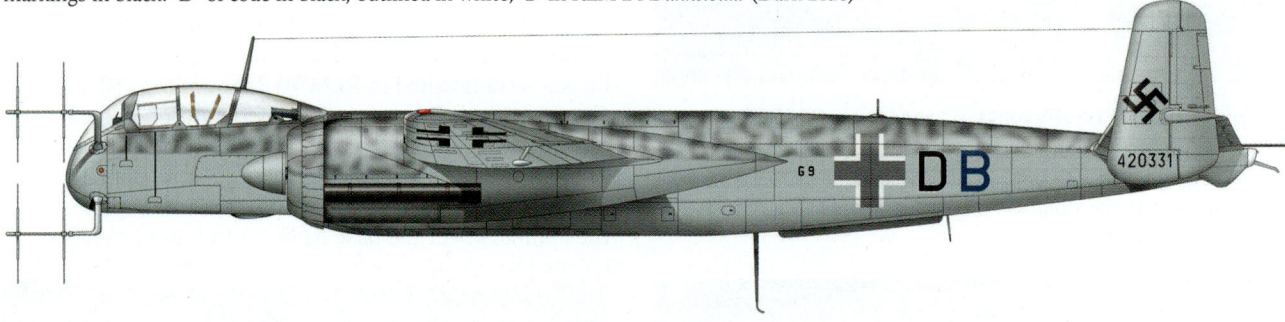

He 219A-7, W/Nr.310189, D5+CL of 3./NJG 1, Grøve, 1945
RLM 76 with 'reverse mottling' over the upper RLM 75. All markings in black, except 'C' of code which is RLM 04 *Gelb*

Camouflage & Markings

Now many modellers today take great care highlighting panel lines, well with the He 219 many were filled as can be seen here with the application of a filler/primer to all the panel lines on the wing leading edge (©S. Willey)

The end result of the filler/primer. The item painted in grey-green primer to the right is part of the wing spar and as such was steel, not aluminium and thus needed corrosion protection (©S. Willey)

at least, a RLM 76 spinner with a wide green spiral (W/Nr.290004, G9+DH of NJG1).

The most interesting aspect of the upper camouflage scheme is the variations in the intensity of the resulting 'mottle', with both dense and very light areas being seen in period photographs. It seems that in most instances the canopy framework was initially solid RLM 75, but later this area tended to get lightened with RLM 76, although you can't tell from images if the whole framework was painted this colour, or if it's an extension of the lines/loops (we are guessing the former, as it would be easier). Unit codes were in black, with the first two always smaller than the others (e.g. G9) and the individual aircraft number (the last of the code) was usually black, although there are variations, such as G9+HK of 2./NJG1 with the 'H' in red, G9+BA of I./NJG1 with the 'B' in blue and D5+CL of 3./NJG3 with the 'C' in yellow because these colours denote the *Staffel* or Gruppe. On top of this there are instances where the second letter was in a different colour, such as G9+DB of I./NJG1, where the 'B' was in blue and those machines which carried just an individual coloured letter, such as 'Yellow C' of NJGr.10.

Identification Colors

From some stage in 1944, to aid identification with ground anti-aircraft forces, the starboard wing was painted RLM 22. There seems to be some variation in how the black was applied to the engine nacelle though, as some had just the aft section in this colour, with the rear edge of the lower engine cowling being the demarcation point

He 219A-0 W/Nr.190012, G9+FK flown by Oblt (later Hptm.) Ernst-Wilhelm Modrow
As photographed during a test flight near Venlo on the 18th April 1944. RLM 76 underside with 'reverse mottling' of upper surface RLM 75. All markings in black/white, except for 'F' code which is believed to be *Hellgrün* RLM 25. The starboard view shows all the wing and rear section of the engine cowling in RLM 22 (black). White letter 'G' outboard of starboard underside cross; no letter below port wing. Unit badge on nose (both sides)

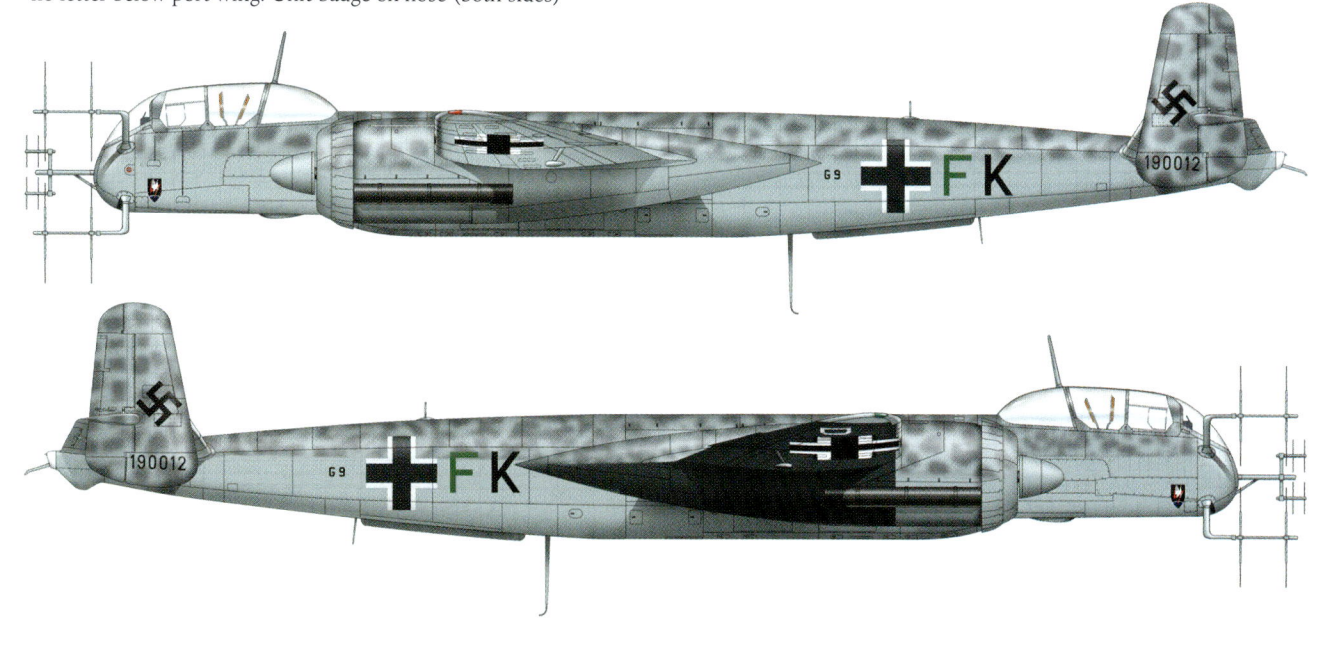

Camouflage & Markings 3

He 219A-0, W/Nr.190063, DV+DL
RLM 76 overall with RLM 75/76 'reverse mottling' on upper surfaces. Codes in black, repeated below the wings, D+V below starboard and D+L below port

He 219A-2 W/Nr.290004, G9+DH of NJG 1
RLM 76 underside with 'reverse mottling' of upper surface RLM 75. RLM 22 below starboard wing and cowling, and below port cowling only. Codes and centre of fuselage cross RLM 74 (or 75?); 'D' of code in black outlined in white. Plain white cross below starboard wing, plain black cross below port

He 219A-2, W/Nr.290010, G9+MK, flown by Lt Kurt Heinz Fischer, 2./NJG 1, Münster-Handorf (Germany), November 1944
RLM 76 overall with 'reverse mottling' of upper surface RLM 75. Codes in black, with 'M' in red. Unit badge on nose both sides. Note 'VI' above serial on fin and below windscreen

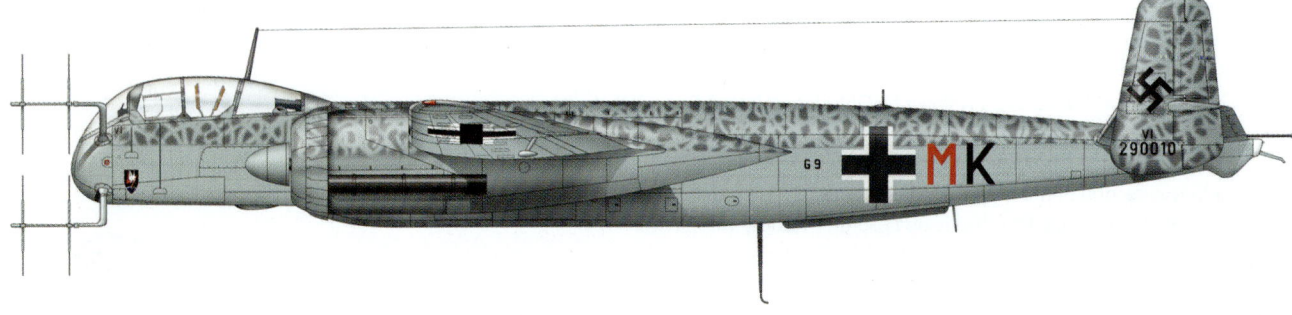

(the front remained in RLM 76), while others had the lower cowling in black, with the front cowl ring remaining in RLM 76 and the upper edge of the black being defined by the upper hinge line of the lower access panel. The black of the wing did not extend fully to the leading edge, instead RLM 76 wrapped round the leading edge by a width probably defined by the length-wise panel line in this region. As the upper surfaces had a base of RLM 75 with the RLM 76 lines/loops, the light blue region under the wing leading edges etc. confirms that the RLM 22 was applied over the existing RLM 76. This probably goes some way to explaining why there are variations in how the demarcation was dealt with between the RLM 22 and 76 around the engine nacelles. To gain contrast with the black starboard wing underside, the cross here was a Type B5, all other markings remained unchanged.

RLM 22 Undersides

The He 219 also adopted the night close-support scheme during its operational career, even though it was never used in this role. This saw the lower surfaces, fuselage sides and vertical fins in RLM 22 (black) and the remaining upper surfaces in RLM 75 with the lines/loops of RLM 76, as per the original scheme. Some published sources state that this scheme was RLM 22 overall with dots of RLM 75 and 02 on the upper surfaces, however the original scheme found on NASM's A-2 prove that the 'dots' were in fact created by applying lines/loops of one colour (RLM 76) over a solid base colour (RLM 75). National insignia for this scheme would have the Type B5 crosses under the wing and the Type B4 (or B6a) on top. The fuselage cross was Type B5 and the swastika was Type H4; the W/Nr. on the vertical fins was applied in white. If unit

He 219A-2, W/Nr.290070, G9+CH, 1./NJG 1
RLM 22 (black) on all undersides; top surfaces in RLM 75/76. All markings in white, except 'H' of code which is probably in RLM 77. Cowlings are RLM 75. Spinner is black/white. Note 'VI' in black below windscreen

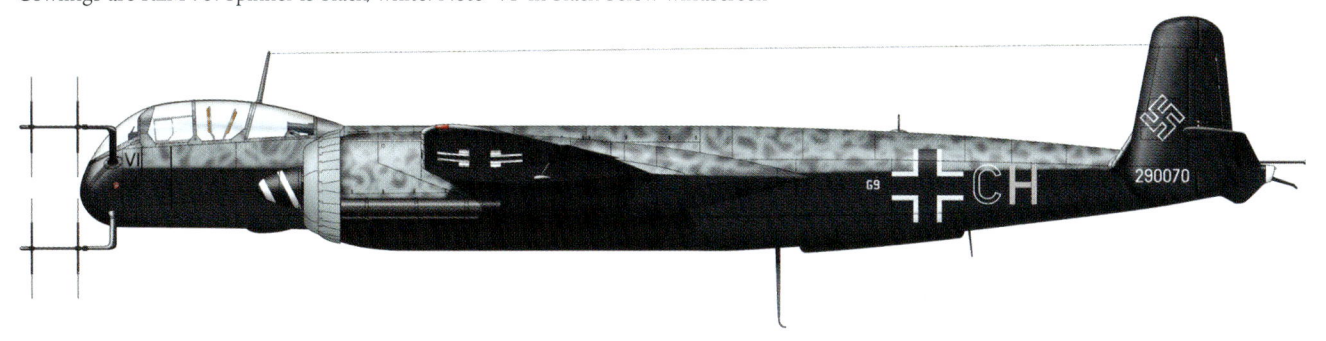

He 219A-2, W/Nr.290068, NJG.1
RLM 22 (black) overall with RLM 76 reverse mottling' of upper surface RLM 75 White spiral on spinners, white serial on fins. B6 Balkankreuz on fuselage sides filled with black, B5 below wings; H4 swastikas on fin

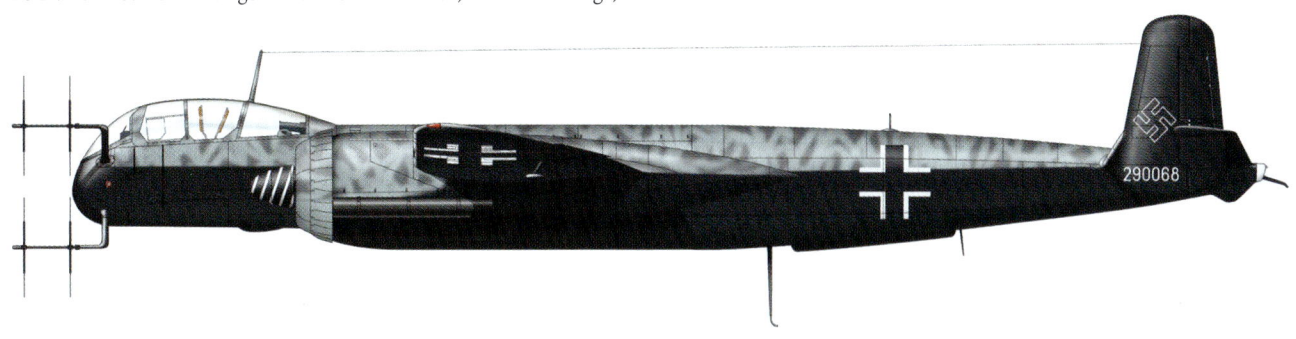

He 219A-2 W/Nr.290126, D5+BL of 3./NJG 3 and captured at Grøve in May 1945
RLM 22 (black) on all undersides; top surfaces in RLM 75/76 'reverse mottling'. All markings in white, except 'BL' of code which is probably RLM 77 (some sources quote RLM 04 Gelb). Cowlings fronts are RLM 76. Spinner is black/white

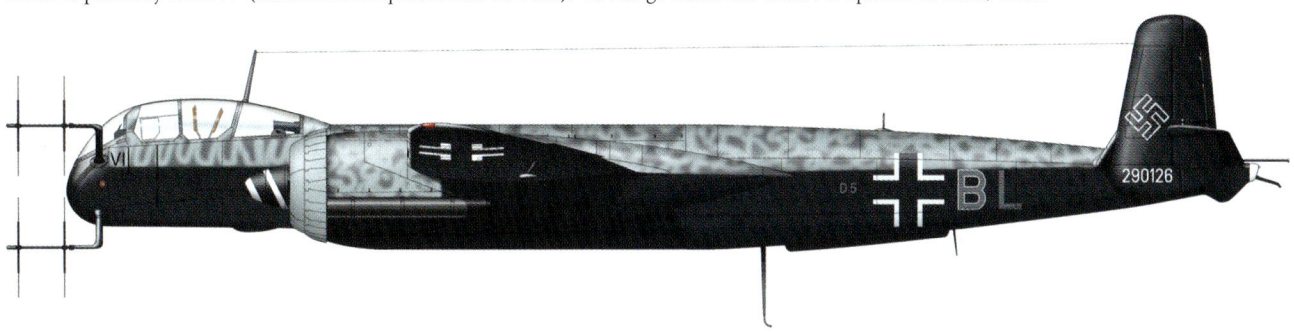

He 219A-2 W/Nr.290123, G9+TH of 1./NJG 3 and captured at Westerland/Sylt in May 1945
RLM 22 (black) on all undersides including all sides of fin and rudders; top surfaces in RLM 75/76 'reverse mottling'. Code 'T' in white outline; 'H' in RLM 75 or RLM 77

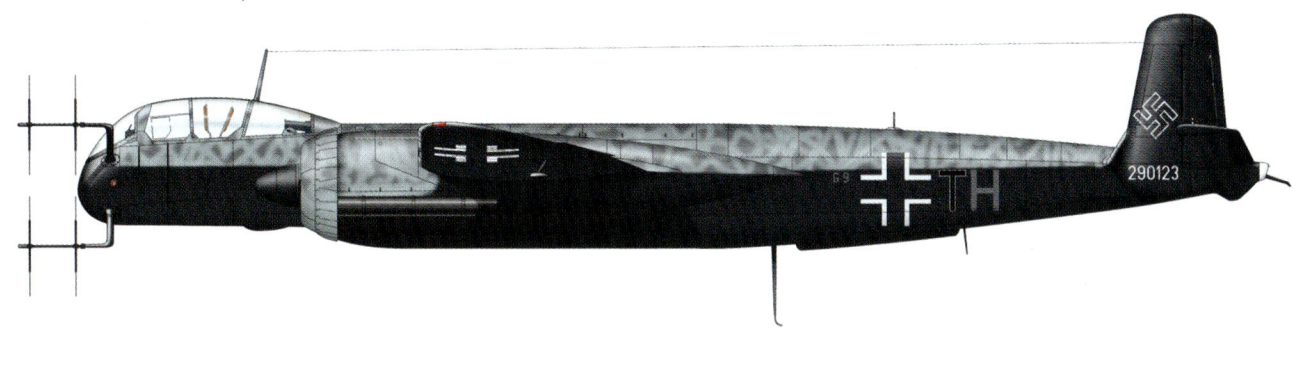

Camouflage & Markings 3

Here you can see the various numbers found under the paint of the NASM He 219's wings, along with the steel spar cap to the far right, which will be primed with RLM 02 grey-green (©S. Willey)

When the technicians removed the paint from the fuselage they discovered the inner wing root still had the original light blue (RLM 76) squiggles that created blotches of the underlying grey-violet (RLM 75), so it was preserved. The newly applied scheme on the rest of the fuselage is a close match, but as you will see the width of the squiggles is a little too dense/wide in comparison with the original (©S. Willey)

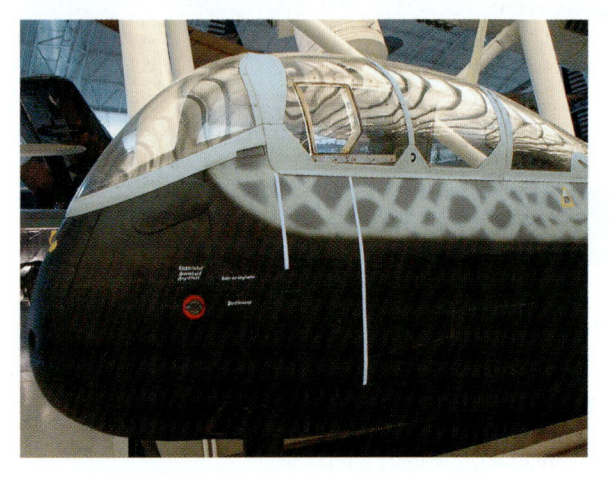

Up the front of the fuselage on the NASM example you can see that the canopy framing was a solid colour, in this instance light blue (RLM 76). This machine did not have radar when tested in the USA, so the mounting points for the antennae have been blanked with oval plates (©S. Willey)

On the fuselage side, under the wing at its mid-point is this marking – it reads "Achtung! Vor Bugrad Einzieheh Fahrwerkschalter auf "Aus" stellen!", which basically means "Attention! Prior to nose gear retract, switch to "Off"

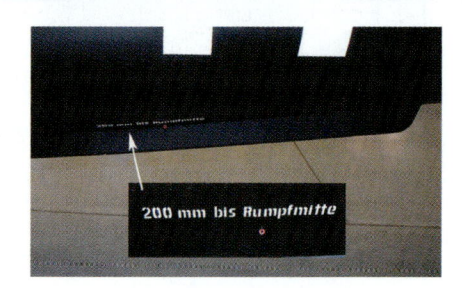

On the port side of the aft fuselage, just above the antenna that runs along the centreline, you will find this marking, which reads "200mm bis Rumpfmitte" (200mm to centre of the fuselage) (©S. Willey)

Stencils on the nose of the He 219 include the white lines denoting where the crew access steps are (©S. Willey)

Here is a close-up of the markings on the port nose of the He 219. The red-rimmed socket has 'Elektrischer Aussenbord Anschluss' (Electric Outboard Connection) written above it and this is for connection for a ground power unit. Just behind it is 'Halter der eingebauten' and 'Zerstöranlage', these denote that there is a jacking/lifting point for the entire airframe covered by doped linen between these two stencils (©S. Willey)

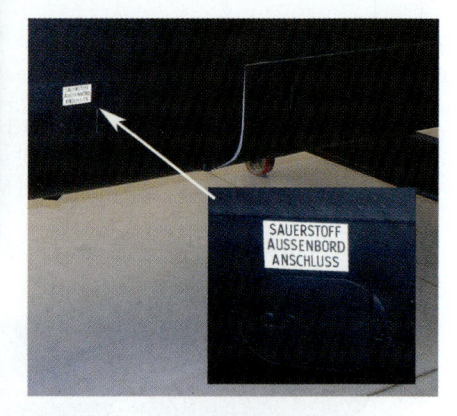

On the starboard lower fuselage side, aft of the wing trailing edge is this marking. It reads "Sauerstoff Aussenbord Anschluss" (Oxygen outboard port), which is basically an external charging point for the onboard oxygen bottles (©S. Willey)

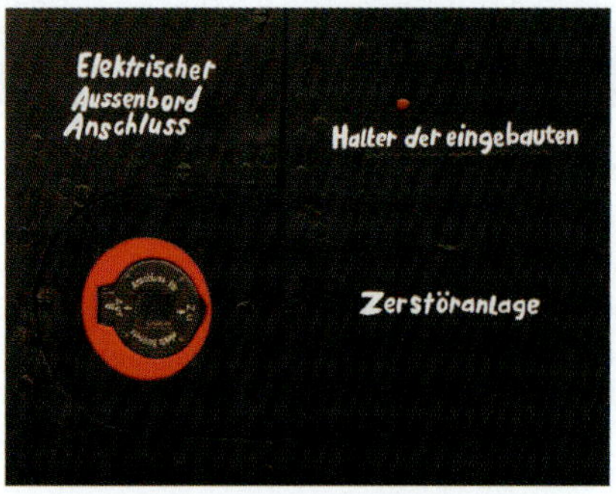

AA01/30/124 — Valiant Wings Publishing — Issued: July 2021

codes were applied to aircraft with this scheme, the usually black characters would have been outlined in white, whilst the individual aircraft letter was usually white – all to gain some contrast with the black undersides. There are also instances captured on film with these machines having the spinners in black (or RLM 70) with white spirals.

It has for many years been stated that this scheme was sporadically applied, however current research seems to show that this scheme was not applied in a random manner, but to specific production blocks. All surviving images of He 219s in this scheme fall within the W/Nr.290057 to 290126 range, none have (thus far) been seen outside of this range. Comparing this with know production blocks it can be deduced that aircraft in the W/Nr.290054 to 290078 and 290111 to 290129 ranges were all finished in the night close-support scheme off the production line. It should be noted though, that some machines seem to have been repainted in service in the RLM 76/75 scheme previously stated, as W/Nr.290059 found wrecked at Münster-Handorf at the end of the war falls into the night close-support scheme range of airframes, but it was certainly in the RLM 76/75 scheme when found.

Ground Concealment

As the war situation worsened for Nazi Germany, the need to conceal aircraft on the ground from marauding Allied fighters became necessary. With the He 219 the '*Liegeplatz Tarnung*' scheme saw darker shades applied over the base colours to hide the aircraft on the ground. The denser/darker areas were most likely green (although some state dark greys), something like RLM 83 dark green, but may have included RLM 81 or even RLM 70 and these were applied in random squiggles across all upper surfaces, with this varying greatly in both density and the regions covered. Certainly some machines were photographed when found by Allied forces with a very dark overall look to the entire upper surfaces, whilst others seemed to have quite a restrained application and some seem to only have it applied around the nose and engines? The exact nature of this type of paint application was entirely down to the unit and/or people involved and the colours used were probably more a case of what was available rather than following a prescribed set of shades.

This top view of the completed fuselage on the NASM example illustrates how the underlying grey (RLM 75) is broken up by squiggles of light blue (RLM 76). The NASM technicians have left the extreme tail cone black and the scallop shapes you can see inside the hinge area of the elevators are caused by the holes in the structure being blanked off with doped, but unpainted, linen as this was how this area was covered originally (©S. Willey)

Here is another shot, taken whilst NASM was respraying the wings of their machine, you can clearly see how the loops of RLM 76 over the base RLM 75 form 'blotches'; note how they reach the leading and trailing edges, but the nature of the loops means that both areas are solid RLM 75 really. The early machines with the starboard wing in RLM 22, would have initially had that wing in RLM 76, so the 'overlapping' area of that colour along the leading edge, it not actually as such, because the upper wing remains as here with RLM 75 and the loops of RLM 76 (©NASM)

A nice wartime image of He 219A W/Nr.290004 G9+DH found wrecked at Paderborn by US forces in May 1945. The upper surfaces you can clearly see have a squiggle of the lighter colour applied on top of a dark base colour, it is not a case of speckles created with a darker shade on a light background. Note the different colours along the upper leading edge of each vertical fin, probably caused because these areas were most likely made of wood. The 'IV' above the W/Nr. on the fin denotes the SN-2d radar fitted and you can see that the 'D' of the codes is outlines in white, whilst the 'G9' has a very specific style of character (©USAAF)

Camouflage & Markings 3

This image of He 219A W/Nr.290112 found at Hildesheim at end of war nicely illustrates the night close-support scheme applied to aircraft in the W/Nr.290057 to 290126 production batches. The upper and lower demarcation is soft, indicating that the RLM 22 was applied over the RLM 76, the inside faces of the fin/rudders are also RLM 22 and this machine lacks any squadron codes, so was probably not operational (used for training etc.). Although the upper surfaces do not look to be mottled, the patterns visible on the tailplanes are not caused by the shadow of the netting above, so it is RLM 75 base with the RLM 76 loops to create mottling, although the style/intensity of the RLM 76 differs

This is another good example of the night close support scheme on a He 219A, this unidentified machine was found wrecked at end of war and you can clearly see just how small the 'blotches' of RLM 75 are on the upper surfaces of the wing and along the fuselage. This type of application is probably why so many state that the darker areas were applied as a speckled effect, rather than created by the lighter shade being applied on top

Captured & Czech AF Markings

When Allied forces at the end of WWII captured machines they usually remained in their overall ex-Luftwaffe operational scheme. All that was changed was that their codes and national insignia were over-painted. The shades seen in black and white images make it difficult to determine the colours used, but considering the stage of the war machines captured and repainted by British forces would probably have used RAF Ocean Grey to blot out the markings, or maybe Dark Green. It is also possible, if stocks existed, that contrasting Luftwaffe colours were used, such as RLM 74 or 75? British roundels were applied to the fuselage sides and lower wings, using the yellow-rimmed 36in diameter Type C1 roundel. There is only one image we could find that shows the upper wings of a British-captured example, and only then a partial one, so from what is visible we assume that a 50in diameter Type C roundel was applied, as a white ring can be seen inboard of the outer dark (blue) section, so it is not a Type B roundel. The swastika was overpainted and a 24in x 24in Type C fin flash applied, although in all instances the W/Nr. remained intact on the fin.

The American-captured machines seem to have used either Olive Drab or Neutral Grey to blot out the

This shot of He 219A-2 W/Nr.290013 taken at Rostock-Marienehe in July or August 1944 is interesting, in that the camouflage is unfinished around the upper nose, with the base RLM 75 evident, but lacking the loops of RLM 76 to create the 'blotches'. This machine is pre-delivery, as it lacks radar dipoles and exhaust flame dampers

markings. Stars and bars were applied on the fuselage sides and above the port and below the starboard wings. Most of these machines seemed to have also had a small 'U.S.A.' applied in black characters aft of the fuselage crosses location. This initial scheme was applied whilst the aircraft were still in Europe, once they arrived in the USA, however, the 'FE' number was applied in white to the vertical fins and under the starboard wing. You will also note in period photos that all of these machines seem to have patchy areas of colour along the panel

This unidentified He 219A is photographed at Münster-Handorf in the winter of 1944-45, it has the starboard lower wing in black to aid identification, but the demarcation is at the front cowl ring, with the side demarcations simply done via following the upper hinge line of the lower cowling

Camouflage & Markings 3

He 219A, 1L+MK of 2./NJGr 10 found at Halle in April 1945
Standard RLM 76 with 'reverse-mottling' on the upper RLM 75 but with a dense mottling of a dark colour, either RLM 82 (Dark Green) or RLM 74 (Dark Grey) applied over all the upper surfaces and fuselage sides to conceal the aircraft on the ground. Spinners were black with yellow (RLM 04) spirals

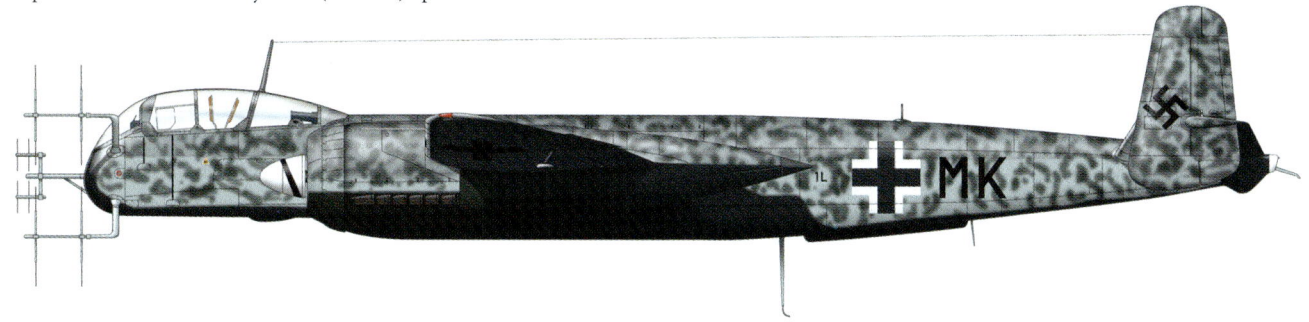

He 219A-7, W/Nr.310189, ex-D5+CL of 3./NJG 1
Retained original RLM 76 with 'reverse mottling' over the upper RLM 75. All original markings overpainted possibly in Medium Sea Grey or similar, RAF Type C1 markings applied are of non-standard sizes

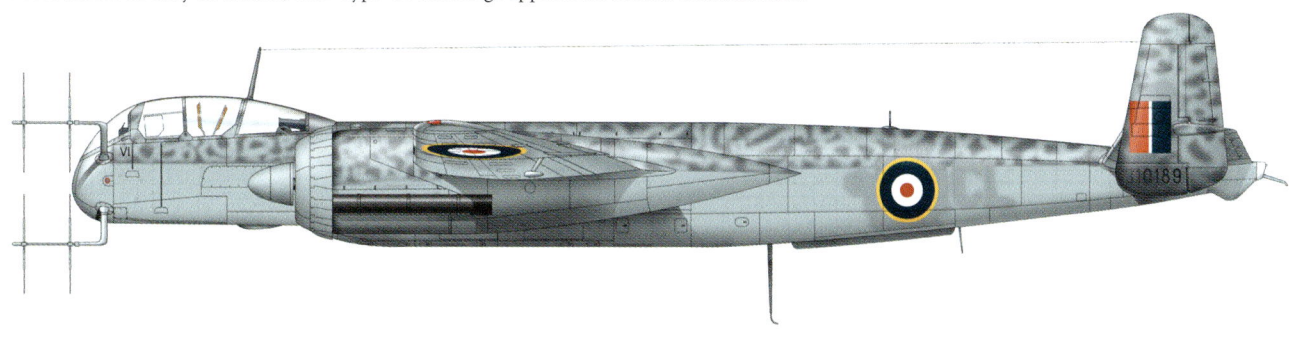

He 219A-0, W/Nr.210903 as FE-612 at Freeman Field in late 1945
Retained original Luftwaffe RLM 76 with 'reverse-mottling' on the upper RLM 75

LB-79/II, 'White 34' of the Czech Air Force
Dark Green upper surfaces with Light Blue undersides. National markings above and below both wings and on the vertical tail surfaces, outlined in white

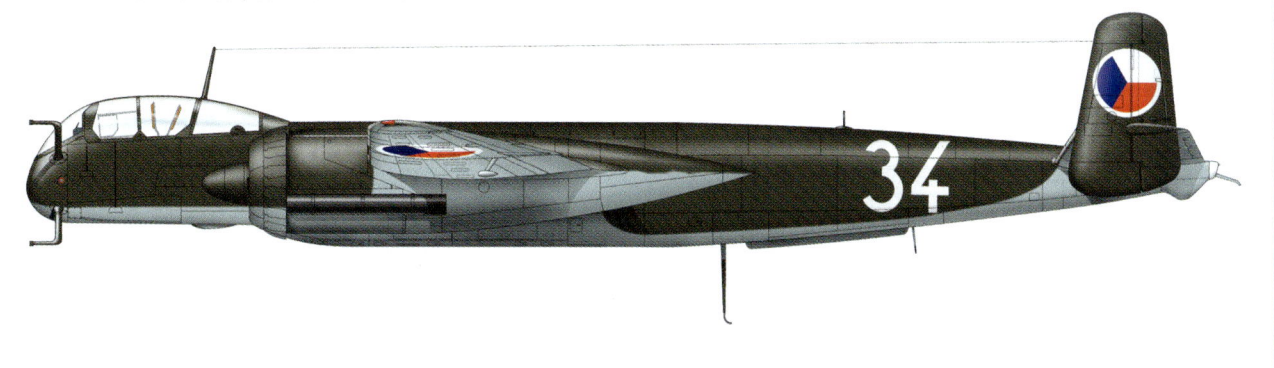

Camouflage & Markings 3

This period colour image shows W/Nr.290059, G9+BH as found at Münster-Handorf at the end of the war, you can see how some claim the camouflage was a 'speckle' or mottle of colour applied on a light base when you look at the tail, but move forward and although the aircraft has been subject to fire (note nose wheel hub is just a mass of burnt aluminium) actually determining what scheme this aircraft had (RLM 75 base with RLM 76 lines/loops or dark greens over that as well), is impossible to say. This is one of the reasons He 219 camouflage and markings is so hotly debated, just about any theory can be 'supported' by images! (©USAAF)

lines, this is simple due to the 'pickling' process used to protect them on their long sea voyage, and the chemicals used to remove it once back in the USA, which also removed the upper layer of the original paint, resulting in a very patchy appearance.

Two He 219A-5s were used in Czechoslovakia in the immediate post-war period, with each being made from parts found at Zatec. Just one image has come to light as far as we know, and this only shows one (partially) in the distance. Modern Czech titles have depicted these machines in two schemes, the first being one of the Czech pre-war Dark Green over Light Blue scheme, with the Czech roundels high on the vertical fins and above and below each wing, all outlined in white. No roundel was applied to the fuselage, instead a large number in white characters was applied – these being '32' or '34'. The demarcation between the two main colours was soft-edged and ran low down on the fuselage sides, curving up to meet the leading/trailing edges of wing and tailplanes. It is presumed that the inner faces of the vertical fins were in Dark Green as the spinners were certainly in this colour. Demarcation on the engine nacelles was again soft-edged and the rear section was split along a wavy line parallel to the wing trailing edge, whilst the front section was low down, with a sweeping line up to the wing leading edge. It is claimed that the first machine ('32') was repainted in 1950 in what looks like an overall scheme of RLM 02 (like their Me 262s – *See Airframe and Miniature No.1 from Valiant Wings Publishing*), retaining the roundels but with the code number now in black. The second machine ('34') was apparently intended to test BMW 003 and Jumo 004 engines captured at the war's end, but its conversion for this role was never completed and it never flew. This machine carried the same overall scheme as first applied to '32', and although '32' carried radar antenna '34' only had the base of the antlers installed. Note: Many artists since seeing the one blurred image of '34' created profiles that showed a machine with an area of the upper mid-fuselage exposed and some sort of odd framework in the aft area. It would seem the image showed the machine being serviced, with the upper fuel cells uncovered and that is what they have mistaken for a revision to this area of the dorsal spine. As the machine was intended to air-test jet engines, slung underneath, they would require fuel and it is most likely therefore that one or more of the cells in the fuselage would have been set aside for jet fuel and this may/may not have resulted in revisions, but these were unlikely to have resulted in major changes to the upper spine structure or shape.

We would also recommend the following titles for those wishing to read more on the complex subject of Luftwaffe camouflage and markings:
- Luftwaffe Camouflage & Markings 1933-1945 Volume Two by K.A. Merrick & J. Kiroff (Classic Publications 2005 ISBN: 1-903223-39-3)
- Luftwaffe Camouflage & Markings 1933-1945 – Photo Archive 1 by K.A. Merrick, E.J. Creek & B. Green (Midland Publishing 2007 ISBN: 978-1-85780-275-7)
- The Official Monogram Painting Guide to German Aircraft 1935-1935 by K.A. Merrick & T.H. Hitchcock (Monogram Aviation Publications 1980 ISBN: 0-914144-29-4)

W/Nr.210903 later to become USA8 (then FE-612) seen at Grøve in June 1945 before being painted in American markings

Heinkel He 219
Stencil Marking Details

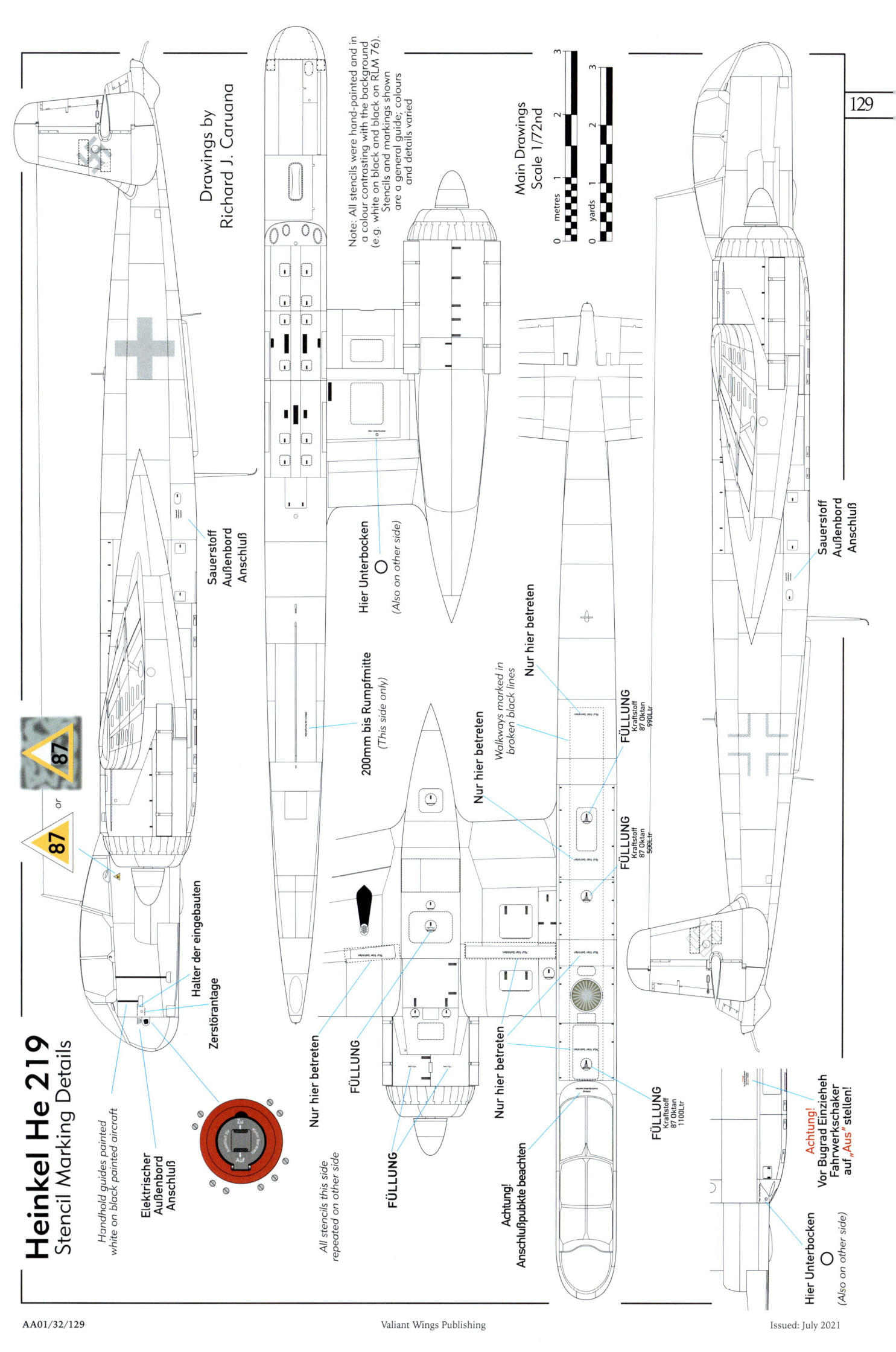

Drawings by Richard J. Caruana

Note: All stencils were hand-painted and in a colour contrasting with the background (e.g. white on black and black on RLM 76). Stencils and markings shown are a general guide; colours and details varied

Main Drawings Scale 1/72nd

Handhold guides painted white on black painted aircraft

Elektrischer Außenbord Anschluß

Halter der eingebauten Zerstörantage

All stencils this side repeated on other side

Sauerstoff Außenbord Anschluß

Hier Unterbocken
(Also on other side)

200mm bis Rumpfmitte
(This side only)

Nur hier betreten

FÜLLUNG

Achtung! Anschlußpubkte beachten

FÜLLUNG
Kraftstoff
87 Oktan
1100Ltr

Nur hier betreten

FÜLLUNG
Kraftstoff
87 Oktan
500Ltr

Walkways marked in broken black lines

Nur hier betreten

FÜLLUNG
Kraftstoff
87 Oktan
990Ltr

Sauerstoff Außenbord Anschluß

Hier Unterbocken
(Also on other side)

Achtung!
Vor Bugrad Einzieheh
Fahrwerkschaker
auf „Aus" stellen!

AA01/32/129 — Valiant Wings Publishing — Issued: July 2021

He 219
Model 4
1/72 He 219A-2

Building the Uhu

Dragon 1/72nd
He 219A-2
by Libor Jekl

With the He 219 now available as mainstream injected kits in 1/144th, 1/72nd. 1/48th and 1/32nd, we thought it would be a good idea to build a couple. Apologies for not doing the type in 1/144th or 1/32nd, but we have published a complete guide on building the Zoukei-Mura 1/32nd example and because that is still available, we have just included some spreads and an image of the built example here to whet your appetite.

All photos © the authors 2021

It has been 30 years since the 'Golden Wing Series' started to appear from Dragon in 1/72nd scale. It featured some interesting WWII aircraft types that had not been covered before, and the He 219 series were some of the first released. The initial boxings of the A-0 and A-7 versions were later supplemented with the projected A-5/R4 and B-series. These kits still command a high price, which is not surprising considering the attractiveness of the type and lack of competition in the market in this scale. In 2016 Platz did a reboxing of the original mouldings with etched parts from Eduard, integrated ballast components and quality decal sheet, which all combined to give a rather high asking price, twice as much or higher when compared to Dragon's initial releases.

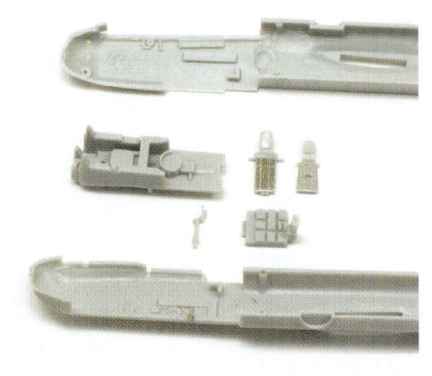

The basics of the interior, with just the backs of each seat corrected with some self-adhesive foil

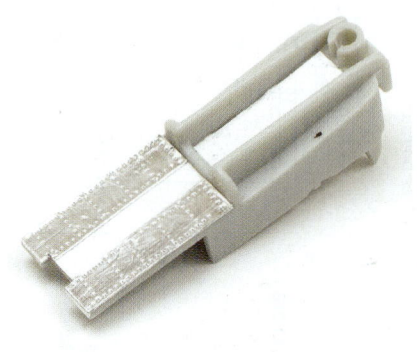

The interior of the nose wheel well is underneath the cockpit, so this was also lined with a combination of plasticard and foil, to cover the prominent ejector pin marks

The cockpit tub was painted RLM 66 and the pre-painted etched details from the Eduard set added

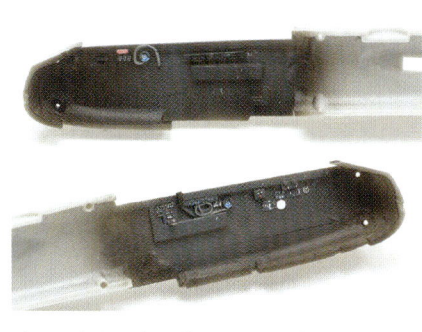

He 219 Model 4
1/72 He 219A-2

The cockpit sidewalls were also done in RLM 66 before the etched components were added

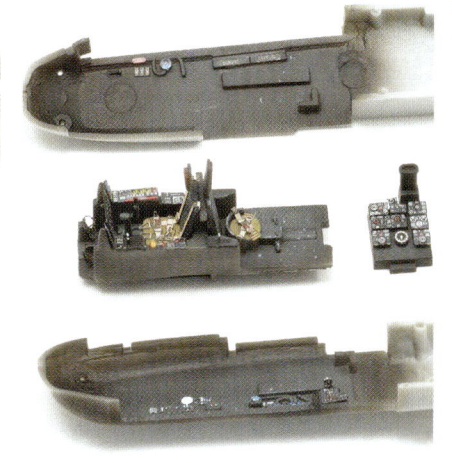

The four main elements of the cockpit interior, all ready to be assembled

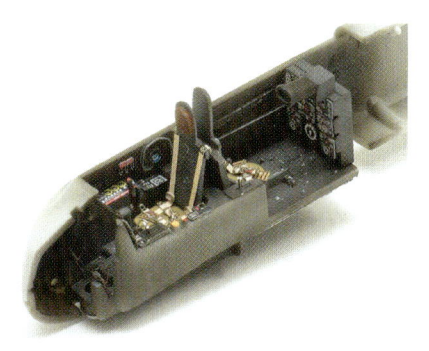

The tub and bulkhead are first attached to the starboard fuselage half

The original He 219A-7 kit was released in 1991 and consisted of 104 parts, the majority of them moulded in a light grey-coloured plastic combined with a couple of components on the small etched fret, such as the instrument panel, radar dipoles and aerials etc. Judging the kit by the standards of the time it truly was the best example on the market, being generally well moulded with fine engraved panel lines and very good interior detail. However, on closer inspection you may find some of the panel lines are softly defined, with some almost disappearing on rounded or similar transitional areas, even though these are new mouldings. On some of the thicker parts such as the fuselage halves and nacelles you will find some sink marks, while some of the ejector pin marks are located in visible places and the tooling seam lines are apparent on smaller parts as well as the surface being somewhat 'gritty' on some of the larger components. Looking at the wing I think the trailing edge is reasonably thin, however, on the horizontal tailplanes it seems to be overscale and I would recommend thinning it down a bit. The cockpit detail is generally nice, the base consists of the tub with pilot and radio operator stations, while its outer part forms the nose wheel bay. Besides the regular components there are also petite details on the sidewalls, a set of radio equipment along with radar screen and its glare guard and the internal armoured glass. Speaking of the clear parts, these are reasonably thin and shows no distortion. You get a single-piece canopy with finely defined framing, DF loop clear cover, gunsight and posi-

You are going to need a lot of weight adding to this kit, here is stage one with it added ahead and behind the cockpit – it would not be enough though and more would be added to the ventral tray and each engine nacelle

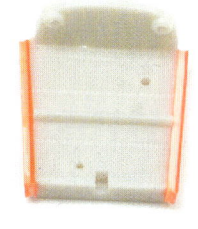

tion lights along with the rear fuselage tip. However, some details are omitted such as the folding armour plate mounted in front of the armoured glass in the windscreen, the gunsight for the oblique-mounted cannon and the radio-altimeter aerials under the starboard wing. While the main undercarriage legs are well detailed and show even the weld seams on them, the wheel bays are simplified with the rear compartments being completely devoid of any detail, allowing you to see inside the wing. I'm afraid the main gear covers look too thick and plain and on their inner faces there are deep ejector pin marks. The instructions do not give any details with regard armament configuration, so I recommend checking images for the particular aircraft you intend to build in order to match

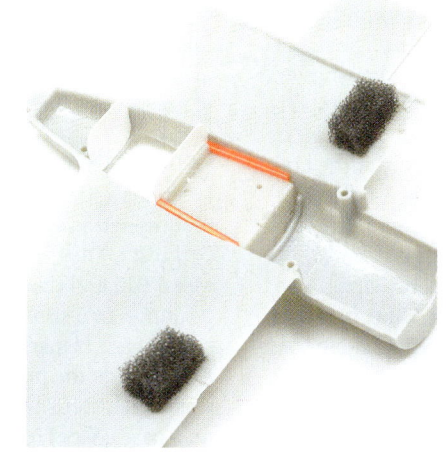

The main bays need mid and aft bulkheads making from scratch, while the foam is to just block off the intakes so you can't see inside the wings once assembled

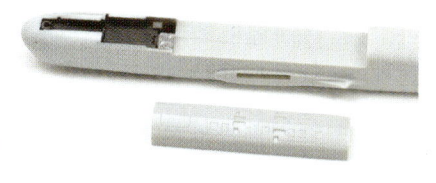

The first stage of the main wheel well upgrade, with some details added to the only bulkhead/floor elements in the kit

The ventral tray about to be fitted, it doesn't, plus the keel has far too pronounced a 'point' to it

He 219
Model 4
1/72 He 219A-2

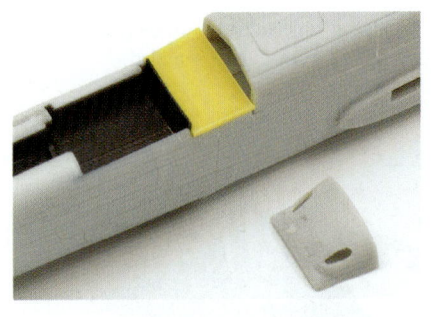

The front of the ventral tray, modified to the twin cannon installation, does not fit either, so plasticard was used to bulk the area before it was added

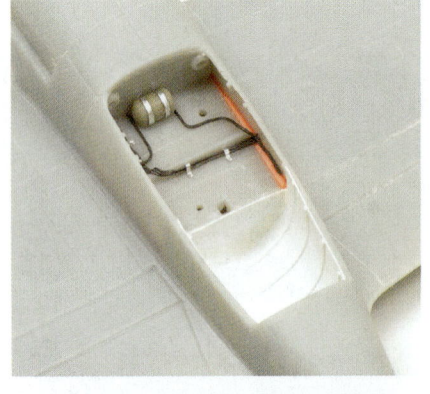

Detailing continued in the main wheel wells, with the bottle and pipework all added from scratch

As well as the mid and aft bulkheads, a 'roof' was added to the aft region of each main wheel well, along with ribs, all from plasticard

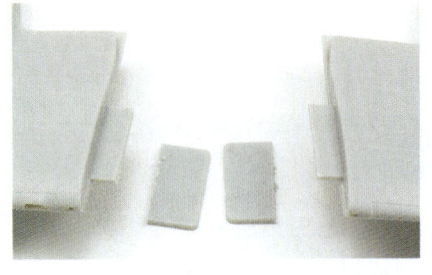

The wings are supposed to use interlocking tabs for alignment, they don't work, so the upper half from one and the lower from the other was removed, then they worked better

Wings and fuselage together, the root joints are not too bad

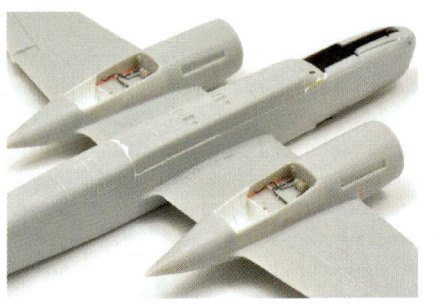

Underneath the wing root joints are also not bad, the same cannot be said for the ventral tray though, as witnessed by the filler

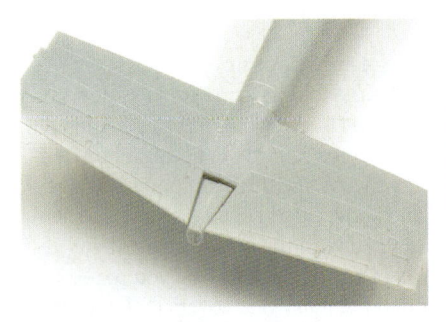

The fit of the horizontal tailplane unit it..., poor

To overcome this, a piece of plasticard was cut to shape and glued in place

The fit of the tailplanes underneath is not good either, so out with the filler again

the individual additional armament sets (*Rüstsätze*) that were used, e.g. the number of weapons in the ventral tray in combination with the obliquely mounted cannon. The main dimensions and shapes correspond well to scale drawings and photographs, although I noted some minor differences such as the suspicious slope and shape of the windscreen and the fuselage ventral cross-section, which is too pointy at the bottom. The small airframe variations between the A-0 and A-7 versions which are both covered by the same tooling are not catered for either, as the kit really depicts the latter version (e.g., shape of the air intakes in the wing leading edge). Also, it seems the panel lines do not match the real thing in places either, especially on the rear fuselage and nacelles where some are evidently missing. The kit provides markings for two A-7 machines; W/Nr.310189 of 3./NJG 3 and W/Nr.290123 of I./NJG 1, both dated as being in the spring of 1945. However, the latter I suggest should be an A-2, considering its *Werknummer*. The decal sheet is well printed, although it has rather thick carrier film, but that is common with other Japanese kit manufacturers of that time; anyway, after 30 years the decals in my example had yellowed a bit.

Construction

I commenced the build with the cockpit assembly, where I first needed to thin down the thickness of both ejection seat backrests. They were further coated with self-adhesive Bare Metal Foil and rivets added in order to give them a better appearance. In a similar manner I continued in the nose wheel bay where I blanked off its front compartment using a plastic strip to hide the prominent ejector pin marks. The interior was then airbrushed with H416 RLM 66 *Schwarzgrau* applied on a base coat of Mr Finishing Surfacer 1500 (black) to give

He 219 Model
1/72 He 219A-2

this region some high and low lights and then I brushed painted the details with Vallejo acrylics. I utilised the Eduard self-adhesive etched set (SS286), which is sadly no longer in production, but which has been replaced with a new set (#73670), and added the pre-painted faces to the radar and radio components as well as the instrument panel, seat belts and sidewall panels. After fixing the cockpit tub to a fuselage half I started to add the ballast, and there is a lot of it needed! Besides all the free space in the nose and behind the cockpit I eventually glued it also in the engine nacelles and fuselage ventral tray. The halves could be then joined, cleaned up and then I rectified any damaged or shallow panel lines with a fine razor saw. I continued with the attachment of the ventral tray, which did not match the fuselage profile well plus its cross section did not follow the fuselage outline. This had to be addressed with some Milliput Superfine White epoxy putty that formed new transitions that were further smoothed out and sanded to shape. Even worse was the fit of the tray's front part with the cannon apertures, so I used a spacer cut from 0.5 mm thick plastic sheet glued beneath it and again filled the joints and sanded everything smooth. The inner cannon openings were plugged with pieces of plastic to depict the particular version I was building. Also, the separately moulded panel covering the oblique-firing cannon did not accurately match the corresponding hole in the fuselage spine, but this was solved with a few drops of thick cyanoacrylate.

Now I focused my attention on the simplified wheel bays. First, I extended the bays floors with 1mm thick plastic strips as these parts were too narrow. Also from plastic sheet I cut new front and rear bulkheads, blanked off the intakes in the wing with pieces of foam to avoid looking into the empty wing and then joined the halves together. However, I had to use filler again, in fact I combined it with pieces of scrap plastic to fill the large gaps in the front part of the nacelles. In each of the rear bay compartments I glued in twisted strips of 0.13 mm plastic creating the floor and on it I added the ribs cut from the same plastic sheet. Using various gauges of brass wires I further added the brake and fluid lines and attached them via thin strips of self-adhesive foil. The separately moulded rear conical tips of the nacelles did not fit well either and had to be levelled and the joints filled with cyanoacrylate. Then I scribed in new panel lines to replicate those on the real thing at this point, which were omitted in the kit. The trial fitting of the wing halves to the fuselage showed yet more poor fit, this was caused by the wing tabs which should interlock, thus setting the wing position, but in reality this just did not work. I therefore cut half from each tab and matched each halve separately and that eventually worked fine. The horizontal stabiliser did not bring any relief either as it needed a lot of trial fits, adjustment and eventually some filler as well. Some Milliput was also needed to smooth out the joints of the vertical stabilisers.

I continued with scratch building the missing airframe details. From a piece of stretched sprue I prepared a sufficient amount of actuating rods for the engine cooling flaps and glued them in pre-drilled (0.2 mm) holes; after trial fitting the engine front faces these these had to be cut to about 1.5 mm in height. In the nose on the front decking I

The actuating linkage for the cowl flaps was depicted via lengths of fine wire, which would later be cut to length

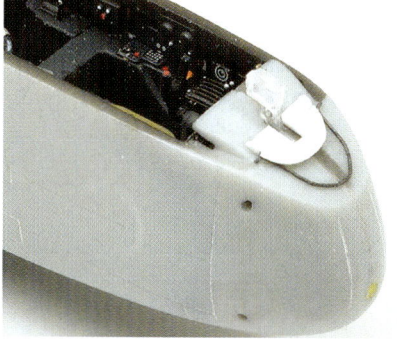

The missing armoured plate in the nose was added from plasticard

Yep, more filler around the vertical fins as well

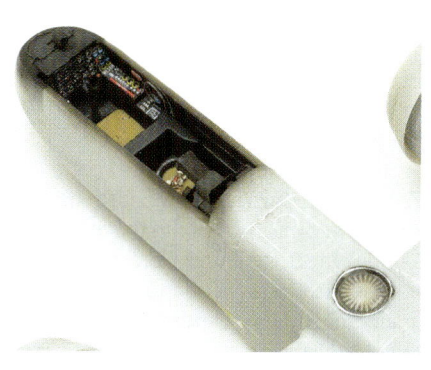

Even the clear cover for the dorsal D/F loop did not fit and needed filler

Should have checked the fit of the canopy to the fuselage earlier, as it did not follow the profile of the dorsal spine and I ended up having to build the area up with plasticard and filler

Once the radar antlers are in place, fit a piece of plastic rod into the socket for the nose oleo leg to ensure the lower two antlers don't touch the worktop, otherwise they will get damaged

He 219 Model 4

1/72 He 219A-2

The model was primed with Mr Surfacer 1000 (grey)

The soft nature of the primer allows you to add all the rivet detail later

Colour starts with the underside and as black is too intense for a model, this was done with Tyre Black, with low-lights done with pure black and some contrasts added with blue and Radome Tan

The upper surface is sprayed RLM 75 with a darkened version used to highlight panel lines

The complex 'spider's web' of RLM 76 begins, working from different points in an attempt to stop the pattern becoming too regular

The lines added, resulting in a 'mottle' effect that is very effective

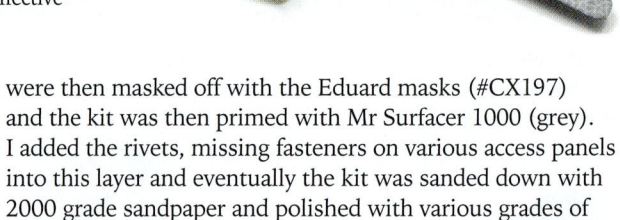

added some cabling and from thin plastic sheet I cut the folding armoured plate that was fixed in front of the armoured glass. In the fuselage spine I installed the etched aerial of the *Peilgerät E26* and secured the clear cover; however, this part did not perfectly match the opening, so the gap around it was filled with Milliput. Now I could cement the single-piece canopy in place, but before that I added the gunsight body with a separate sighting glass for the *Schrägemusik* oblique armament, with both pieces fixed to the upper canopy frame. Unfortunately, the rear canopy component had a step in the transition to the fuselage and Milliput had to come to rescue once again. I guess I should have checked this construction step much sooner and use a 0.5 mm spacer under the rear cockpit part (#A9) as that would has helped to level up the joint. Finally I glued the antlers for the radar dipoles and in order to prevent damage of the bottom pair, I put in the opening for the front undercarriage leg a piece of a sprue on which the model could safely stand. The transparent parts were then masked off with the Eduard masks (#CX197) and the kit was then primed with Mr Surfacer 1000 (grey). I added the rivets, missing fasteners on various access panels into this layer and eventually the kit was sanded down with 2000 grade sandpaper and polished with various grades of Gunze-Sangyo fine 'grinding' cloths.

Camouflage & Markings

As the kit decal sheet was old I opted for one of the sheets from Owl (#QWL72024) and the particular aircraft I selected was the A-2 version which could easily be built straight from the box because the A-7 airframe's attributes were practically identical. This machine belonged to *1./NJG 1* and was lost in February 1945 after shooting down a Lancaster; however, one of its gunners hit the Heinkel with return fire so the crew had to eject. I started spraying the camouflage colours with the lower and side surfaces, which were done with H77 Tire Black as the base colour for original RLM 22 *Schwarz* and this

He 219 Model

1/72 He 219A-2

was subsequently post-shaded with H12 Black, H15 Blue and H318 Radome Tan applied in irregular patches in order to break up the uniform dark background. The upper surfaces wore the camouflage scheme consisting of RML 75 *Grauviolet* with a mottle effect created by airbrushed lines of RLM 76 *Lichtblau* (some sources state this also could be RLM 02 *Grau*). I followed the way the camouflage was applied on the real plane and sprayed the H69 RLM 75 first followed by a 'spider's web' created with well diluted H417 RLM 76. I started applying the lines from several sides to avoid similar patterns and tried to keep their thickness consistent. The surface was then fixed with gloss Mr Color Superclear varnish as the base for the decals. They worked fine and whilst being thin, they were sufficiently rigid to allow them to be moved about on the surface and they did not curl up. After application of a dark wash in the panel lines on the upper surfaces and mid-grey underneath I gave the kit a final layer of semi-matt varnish and then brushed on traces of dust and fluid leaks mixed from oil paints diluted with Testors synthetic thinner.

Final Details

Since the wheels from the kit did not meet my expectations, I replaced them with resin items from Rescue Model (#72008 Heinkel He 219 Wheel Set). Besides having more detailed hubs for the main wheels and alternative types for the nose wheel (plain or spoked) they all featured extremely fine and convincing tread patterns. On the main wheel bay covers I filled the ejector pin marks, whilst the nose gear covers were completely replaced with new items cut from 0.3 mm plastic sheet, including their actuating rods that were omitted in the kit. The oleo legs were completed with brake lines added from brass wire, along with etched labels and then they were painted H70 RLM 02 *Grau*. Their slider elements were accentuated with a Molotow Chrome 1mm pen and fixed in the bays. Next, I assembled the exhaust flame dampers and painted them in a black-brown shade. Whilst assembling the propellers I left off the spinner rear exten-

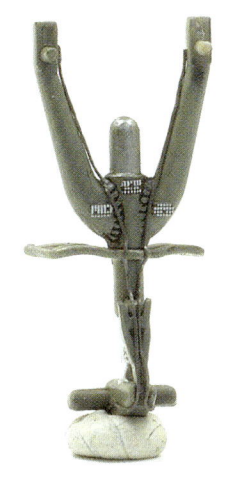

The main oleo legs were painted, then detailed with brake lines and data placards

The crew access ladder was built from plasticard

All the undercarriage parts ready for attachment

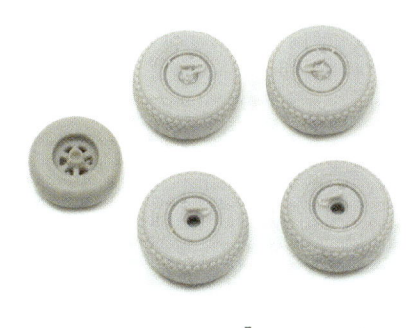

Rescue Models' resin main and nose wheels were used to replace the kit parts, as they had better hub and tread detail

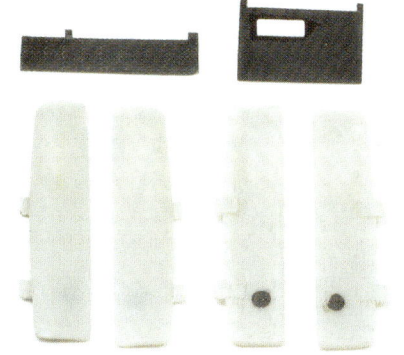

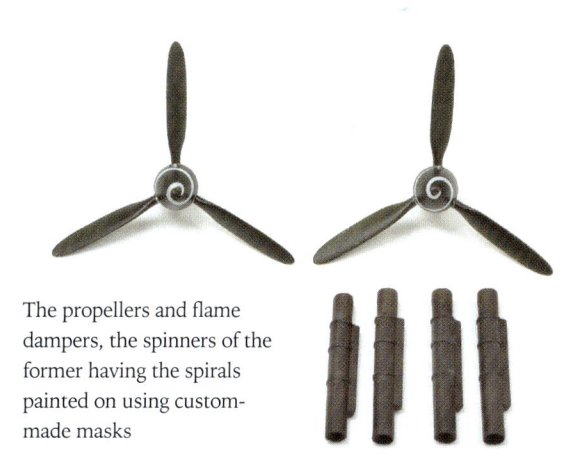

The propellers and flame dampers, the spinners of the former having the spirals painted on using custom-made masks

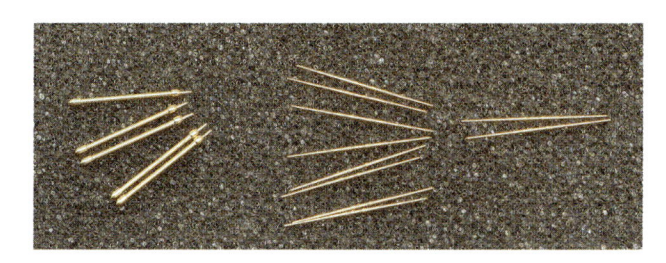

The main doors had the ejector marks filled, whilst the nose wheel doors were completely replaced with scratchbuilt examples

The dipoles of the radar need replacing (the kit uses two-dimensional etched), so the excellent brass ones from Master were used instead

sion rings because they only apply to the A-7 version and so I could airbrush on the white spirals I used custom cut masks. To give the kit a little more spirit I opened the access ladder, which was scratch built from plastic stock. The other kit's components that needed further refinement were the radar dipoles and so these were replaced with brass turned parts from Master (#AM-72-016 German Radar FuG 220 Lichtenstein SN-2), which includ a spare antler and pair of dipoles that could be used for the rearward-facing component of the FuG 220. The brass parts were primed with Mr Surfacer 1000 and the bottom dipole pairs painted with white-red warning strips. The dipoles were then carefully attached to the antlers with thick cyanoacrylate and using a simple paper template cut at 45°, I adjusted their final position. Finally I fixed the antennae mast and from elastic fine thread, added the aerial leads while the pitot was replaced with Albion Alloys fine interlocking tubing.

Conclusion

In my opinion the He 219 kit from Dragon is getting a bit old now, but it is still sound and a reasonable kit, though the price is unusually high. Honestly, most of us purchase it because there is no other available option in the market in this scale. Whist the kit can offer good levels of detail, its construction is too complex so I would recommend it primarily to more experienced and determined modellers because building it will test your modelling skills! I hope the situation will change soon and we can look forward to a modern and precise new tooling of this unique Luftwaffe nightfighter.

He 219
Model **4**

1/48 He 219A-7 Uhu | 137

Tamiya 1/48 (#61057)
He 219A-7 Uhu
by Steve A. Evans

This box has become something of a legend and is instantly recognisable. Top-class stuff from 1997

The Heinkel manufacturer came up with some great designs during WWII, many of which were icons of their time. The He 219 may not have been as well received back in 1944 but today all of these late-war Luftwaffe machines have taken on a kind of mythical status, none more so than the mighty 'Uhu'. Tamiya took the decision, back in 1997, to give the world it's own rendering of the great fighter and it went on to be an instant success and still sells well, all these years later. That's because it not only has the legendary Tamiya quality but also that added bonus of being a kit of an amazing looking aircraft. Inside the well-decorated box, there are five large sprues of dark grey-coloured plastic and a single sprue of very clear transparencies. The plastic is well formed, with very neat recessed panel lines and limited fastener detail. There is some flash on a few parts but it's very slight and any mould lines that are visible are very easily removed.

Option wise, you get two crew figures to put into place, or not and the radiator flaps on the engine nacelles can be open or closed, as can the canopy. There is also the odd-looking crew access ladder that can be fitted but if you do that you should really modify the fuselage piece to have the stowage cut-out clearly visible. The most visible option is the main wing flaps as you can have them in the up or down position. You get three marking options in the box and although the instructions, with their multiple-view drawings and a separate camouflage sheet, are a thing of beauty, the decals are not. Basically the older style of printing and presentation of the decals hasn't aged well and they are not very sharp and of dubious register. I'm going to ignore the decals and use my Silhouette cutter to make some new ones but there are a number of aftermarket sets out there anyway. I've had this particular kit hidden away in my 'stash' for the best part of 15 years, so I think it's about time I built it, don't you?

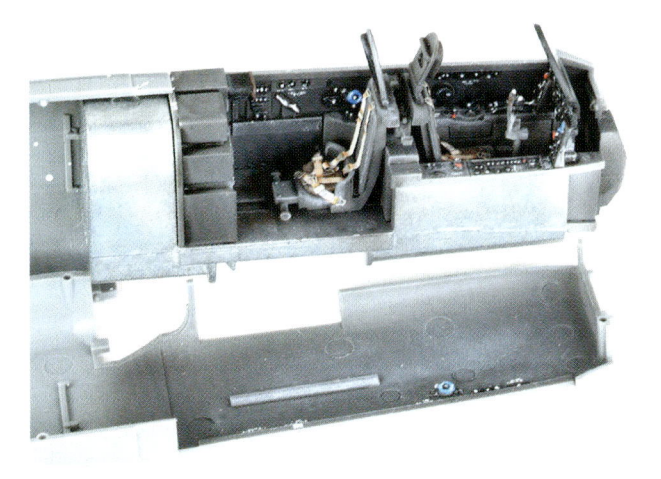

The cockpit comes with a handy little white metal nose weight as it's base, so that takes care of the balance problems

The moulded detail is actually very nice, only needing some seatbelts to finish it off but there are two crew figures included of you'd like to go that route

He 219 Model 4
1/48 He 219A-7 Uhu

The oblique firing cannon are included but the sighting system in the roof of the canopy is not

The nose is completed with a clever arrangement to get the struts for the radar unit in place

The insert for the cannons in the belly will need to be modified to add blast tubes; otherwise they're just open holes

Construction

It all starts with the interior and the very compact two-man cockpit. Tamiya do the modeller a huge favour by making the cockpit floor a large white metal unit, which immediately takes care of the nose weight problem. It weighs in at about 50 grams so it's more than enough to stop this one tottering back onto it's own tail. The plastic parts for the interior are reasonably well moulded, with some good, sharp detail. It's a little basic in places and nowhere near up to the modern standard of such things, but with the canopy closed and some seatbelts in place of the crew figures, it'll look just fine. One major omission that needs to be corrected is the overhead sighting system used for the *Schräge Musik* oblique cannons. It's pretty easy to do with a spare sight, cut to the correct size and a little bit of plasticard for the mounting and generator system. The metal and plastic parts fit together just like they're supposed to and once painted they slot into place in the fuselage without any difficulty as well. It looks a bit odd to begin with but as soon as you wrap the nose halves around the metal projection at the front it all

The wings are a simple build, maybe a little too simple by todays standard, especially the wheel bays

As usual with Tamiya, there are very few fit problems in before you know it; you've got yourself a pretty sizeable model

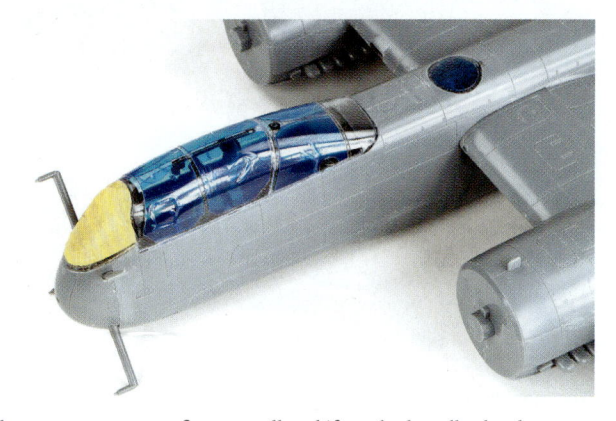

The transparent parts fit very well and if you look really closely you can see the added sight in the roof for the 'Schräge Musik' guns

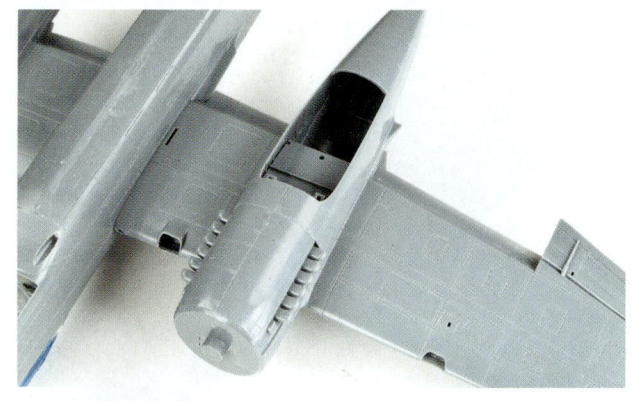

The fit of the parts is good and I added some rivet detail to the surfaces but the undercarriage bays are the kits real weak-spot

He 219 Model 4
1/48 He 219A-7 Uhu

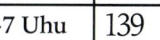

Halfords Grey Plastic Primer is my favourite place to start the paint process

RLM 76, in this case it's the very good-looking Hataka version, layered for a slightly shaded effect

Random blotches of RLM 75 as per the instructions. I'm not sure if this is the real paint job for this actual aircraft but I'm not going to fight with this one. All done freehand with my trusty Iwata HP-BH

The black underside is made up of three shades of Tamiya paint, Rubber, NATO and Flat Black; this gives it some variation without going over the top

makes perfect sense. The long and rather skinny fuselage halves close up well, with not much of a joint to deal with, although there are a lot of little panels and such like on the underside to be careful of. The Mk108 cannon in the rear are a clever little addition and the hatch fits reasonably well, although care is needed and of course you could leave it loose if you're going to do some detail work in the back. The only other alterations are the cannon openings in the ventral gun-pack insert. This one only has the two MG 151 20mm cannon fitted but the muzzle openings are just open holes and lack the blast tubes that can be seen on the real thing. It's a simple job to fix with a little bit of tubing, but it does make a difference.

Then it's time for the wings and engine nacelles. These are a very simple build, only five parts per side and to be honest the interior of the wheel bays is the biggest disappointment on this kit. There is next to nothing in there and even the rear bulkheads are missing. If I'd known just how obvious this is when it's all finished I would definitely have added a lot more to it. The wings themselves fit superbly, especially with the tubular spars in place for added strength and the tail is the same. There are no gaps, no misaligned parts and no filler needed at any point here. It's this kind of fit and finish that made the Tamiya reputation.

Colour & Markings

In the box you get three options, the one with the black underside, as per the box lid art, and two in the lighter, all RLM 76 versions. It was always my intention to do the black version but any of them will do. Interestingly the camouflage and markings guides show two distinct camouflage patterns for the upper surface. One has just 'splotches' of RLM 75 over 76, whilst the other has an intricate pattern of RLM 76 over 75. The photographs of W/Nr.290123 are completely ambiguous as to which one it should be so I went with the simple option of the RLM 75 splotches. That meant the first thing to do was get a nice coat of the RLM 76 in place. For the upper surface I used Hataka (Orange Line) lacquers as they spray very finely. Their version of RLM 76 has a pleasant blue tinge to it and layered up over the grey primer I began with, it makes a good starting point with the shading. RLM 75 'splotches' were then applied, freehand with the airbrush and I went for quite heavily applied ones as well, keeping it in line with the box top art. As always, there are lots of differing

He 219 Model 4
1/48 He 219A-7 Uhu

In close up you can see the variation in tones quite nicely and some very limited sponge chipping with RLM 76, this one is actually going to stay quite clean

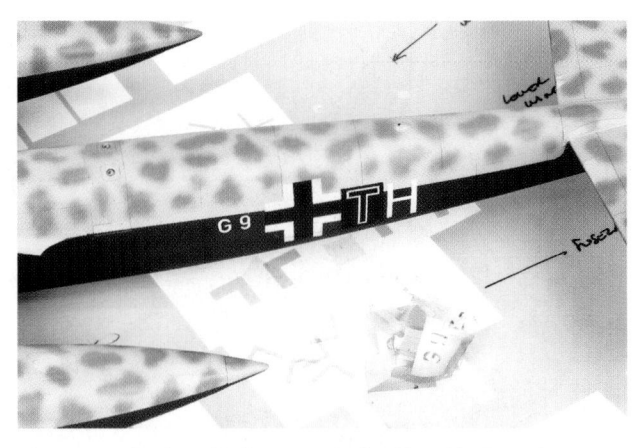

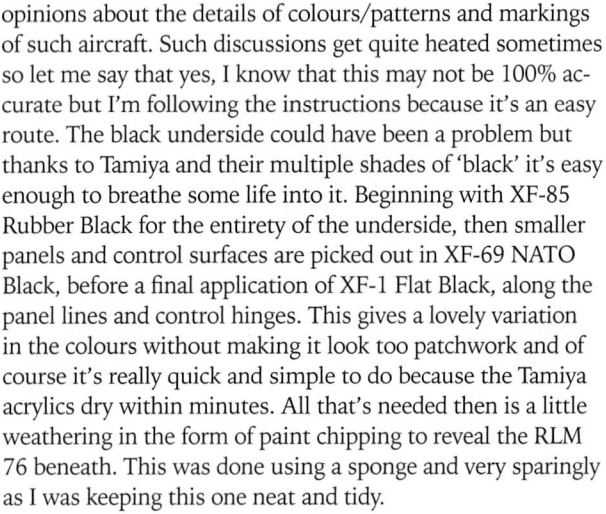

The Tamiya decals in this kit are, quite frankly, rubbish, so this was the perfect opportunity to get the mask cutter out and do some design work of my own

opinions about the details of colours/patterns and markings of such aircraft. Such discussions get quite heated sometimes so let me say that yes, I know that this may not be 100% accurate but I'm following the instructions because it's an easy route. The black underside could have been a problem but thanks to Tamiya and their multiple shades of 'black' it's easy enough to breathe some life into it. Beginning with XF-85 Rubber Black for the entirety of the underside, then smaller panels and control surfaces are picked out in XF-69 NATO Black, before a final application of XF-1 Flat Black, along the panel lines and control hinges. This gives a lovely variation in the colours without making it look too patchwork and of course it's really quick and simple to do because the Tamiya acrylics dry within minutes. All that's needed then is a little weathering in the form of paint chipping to reveal the RLM 76 beneath. This was done using a sponge and very sparingly as I was keeping this one neat and tidy.

At last, it's time to get on with spraying the markings. Having only recently bought a cutter, I'm still only doing some relatively easy subjects and because the decals in this one are so poor, this was the perfect opportunity. It took a little while and more than a few false starts but in the end I think the sprayed on markings look far better than the decals ever could have.

Weathering is then the order of the day and just a smear or two of pastel dust will do, as well as a light spray of X-19 Smoke along the panel lines and around the engines. That lot is then sealed in under a coat of gloss and it's time for the oil wash. The upper surface got a coat of very dark brown oil and then the black underside I did with a light grey oil to do a reverse panel line highlight. It was a bit of an experiment for me and I hated it, so just washed it all off again and left it plain, much better.

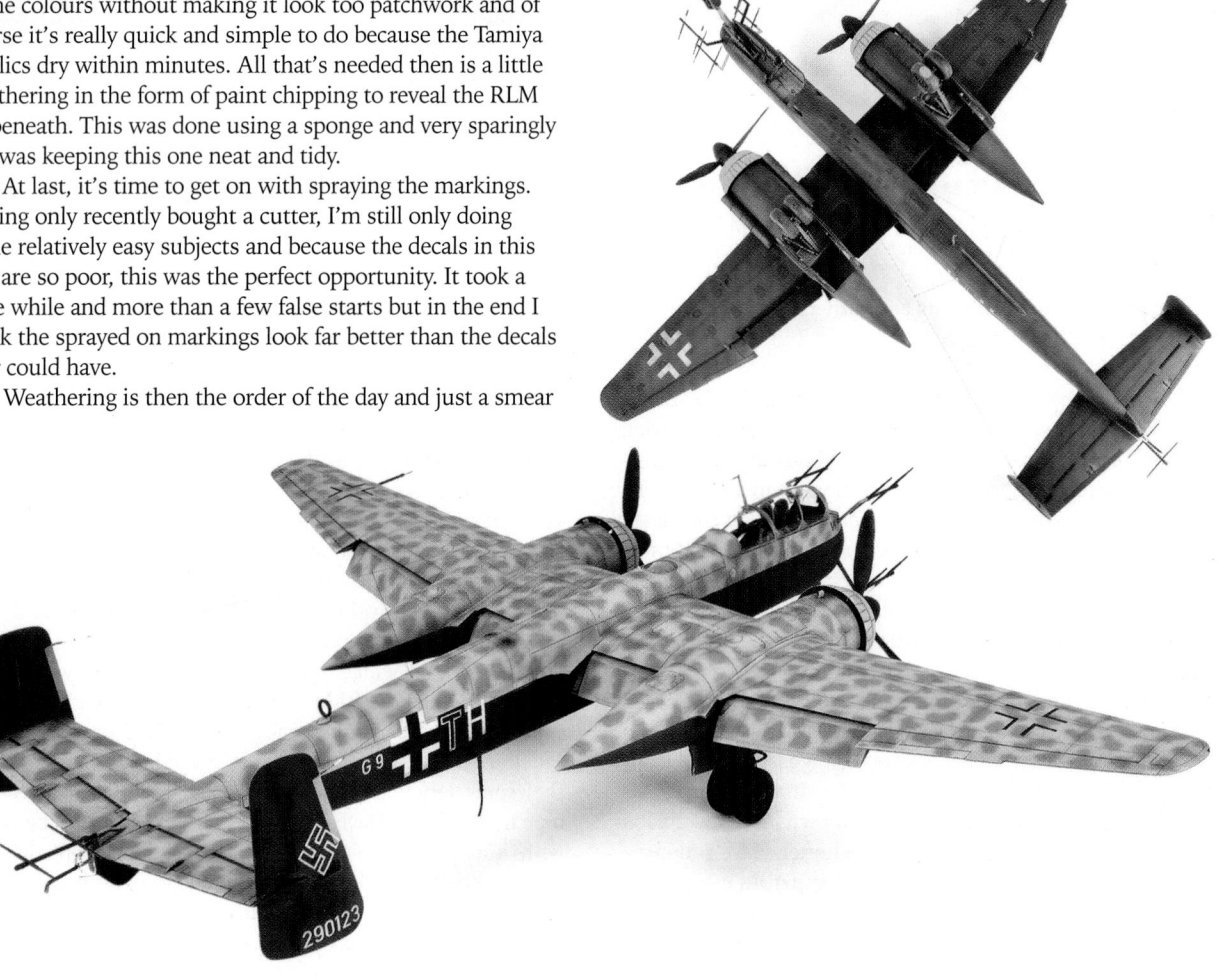

Final Assembly

There is still a lot to do and I now have to offer my sincere apologies to you, dear modeller, because due to some technical difficulties I lost a whole bunch of photographs of the final assembly. Use your imagination and conjure up a picture of the model with no less than half the box contents still to be attached. The undercarriage, complete with added brake lines are the most important and it takes a little time to get all the wheels to sit on the ground at the same time. The nose wheel assembly and the associated doors and actuators are next, followed closely by all the remaining doors and the main wing flaps. Then it's time for the aerials and it seems to be a never-ending parade of these things from nose to tail, making this a very prickly model indeed. This is not helped by the fact that all of the aerials are delicate and need careful handling. The propellers and spinners are one of the last things to be fitted and it's here that there is some doubt over the accuracy of the shapes. The spinners are a little too long and pointy, while the propeller blades themselves are too thin. This is no huge error but it's something to think about if you're looking to upgrade the kit with some aftermarket stuff. Finally the whole thing gets a coat of matt varnish, the masking is removed and the aerial wires added with Uschi 'Rig That Thing', elastic thread. A few touch ups with the paint and I'm calling this one finally, after 15+ years, done!

Conclusion

Here we are in 2021 and Tamiya are still taking us to school from way back there in '97. This kit is still gorgeous, the fit and finish is just about perfect and while there are some detail areas that can be improved, it is still streets ahead of many of the 'new-tooled' kits being thrown at us today. Well done Tamiya and if anyone has one of these in their own stash, then build it right now, you won't be disappointed.

Paints Used	
Alclad 2:	
ALC-600 Aqua Gloss	
Hataka Orange Line:	
HTK-CS110 Mid-War Luftwaffe Set	
C040 RLM 66	C049 Insignia White
Tamiya Color acrylic:	
XF-1 Flat Black	XF-69 NATO Black
XF-85 Rubber Black	X-19 Smoke
Xtracolor enamel:	
XDFF Matt Varnish	

Zoukei-Mura 1/32nd

He 219A-0

by Daniel Zamarbide

Dani did an in-depth, stage-by-stage build of the Zoukei-Mura kit in the second of our Airframe Constructor series, which you can still buy from us. To order this book, either visit our website www.valiant-wings.co.uk or call on 01234 413843

He 219 Kits
Appendix I

AMT A-630 100

AMT-Frog 3702-80l

Dragon 5005

Dragon 5006

Dragon 5029

Dragon 5041

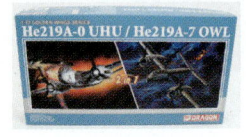

Dragon 5121

Frog F177 early

Mark I MKM14419

Mark I MKM14425

Mark I MKM14449

Mark I Models MKM14427

Revell 03928

Revell 04666

Revell 04690

Revell 4127

Revell 54690

Revell H-112

Revell H-112

Revell H-160

Tamiya 61057

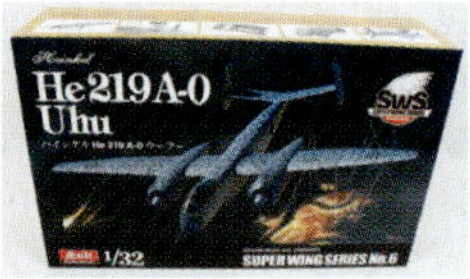

Zoukei-Maru SWS No.6

Below is a list of all static scale construction kits produced to date of the He 219 series. This list is as comprehensive as possible, but if there are amendments or additions, please contact the author via the Valiant Wings Publishing address shown at the front of this title.

All are injection-moulded plastic unless otherwise stated.

1/144th
- FE Resin [res] He 219A-7 Uhu #14446 (Announced 2004/5, released 2008)
- Kami de Korokoro [res] He 219A-7 Uhu #P-001 (200?)
- Mark I Models He 219A-2 #MKM14419 (2014) – *New tooling*
- Mark I Models He 219A-5 #MKM14425 (2014) – *New tooling*
- Mark I Models He 219A-7 #MKM14427 (2014) – *New tooling*
- Mark I Models He 219A-0/LB-79 'Flying Laboratory' #MKM14449 (2016)

1/72nd
- Alanger (ex-Revell) He 219A Uhu #49029 (200?)
- AMT (ex-Frog) He 219A-7 #3702-801 (1967-early 1970s) – Also issued as #A-630:100
- Dragon He 219A-0 Uhu #5005 (Announced for December 1991 – not released until 1992) – Reissued in 2004, same kit number and again in 2009
- Dragon He 219A-0/A-7 Uhu '2 in 1' #5121 (2021)
- Dragon He 219A-7 #5006 (1992)
- Dragon He 219B-1 #5029 (2007)
- Dragon He 219A-5/R4 #5041 (2008)
- Flugzeug [ltd inj] He 219 Owl #1016 (1989->)
- Frog He 219 'Uhu' Night Fighter #F177 (1966-1973) – Reissued, also as #F177, 1974-1977
- Hasegawa (ex-Dragon) He 219A-0 Uhu #HD23 [and #86823] (2000) – *Limited edition*
- Lindberg He 219 #575 (1967-1975) – Reissued as #2315 (1975-1997)
- Matchbox (ex-Frog) He 219 #40202 (1996)
- Minicraft (ex-Frog) He 219 #177 (1972)
- Platz (ex-Dragon) He 219A-0 Uhu 'Werner Streib' #AE-3 (2016)
- Platz (ex-Dragon) He 219A-7 (A-2/5/7) Uhu #AE-1 (2016)
- Platz (ex-Dragon) He 219A-0 Uhu w/Kübelwagen #AE-9 (Due 2018) – *Limited edition*
- Revell He 219 'Owl' #H-112 (1967) – Reissued as #H-160 Heinkel 'Nachtjäger' (Night Fighter) He 219 'Owl' in 1974 to 1977, reissued in late 1981 as Heinkel He 219 'Uhu' (#4127) and again in 1983 also as #4127 (different box top)
- Revell (ex-Frog) He 219A-5/R1 'Uhu' #4116 (1992) – *This kit was one of nineteen Axis types sold to Revell Inc by Novo in 1977, it was not initially produced by Revell as they already had their own mould for the type in their own range* – Reissued as He 219 'Uhu' (#04690) in 2010 and as a 'Model-Set' with paints and glue as #64690 in 2011
- Revell-Japan He 219 Owl #H-112 (1967) – Reissued, same box art and item number in 1970
- Revell/Kikoler He 219 Owl #H-112 (1967) – Reissued, same box art and item number in 1979
- Revell/Lodela He 219 Owl #H-112 (1979)
- Volks [res] He 219 Uhu #SD13 & #SDB02 (1984-1994)

1/48th
- Airmodel [vac/res] He 219A #AM-4810 (1969-2000)
- Arba Products [res] He 219A-5 #N/K (1993)
- Blue Max – *See Schmidt Vacu-modellbau*
- Flugzeug (ex-Karo-AS Modellbau) [vac/res] He 219 Uhu #N/K (1990s)
- Karo-AS Modellbau [vac/res] He 219 Uhu #AM-48.10 (1990)
- MHW Models Ltd [res] (ex-Volks) [res] He 219 Uhu #N/K (1987)
- MPM [ltd inj] He 219A Uhu #48001 – *Planned but never released*
- MPM/HML [res/vac/pe/mtl] He 219A-0 #HML 001 (1996)
- R&D Replicas [vac] (ex-Karo-AS) He 219 Uhu #48.10 (1994-1999)
- Right Staff Products Inc. [res/inj/mtl/pe] He 219 – *Announced 1990, never released*
- Tamiya He 219A-7 Uhu #61057 (1997)
- Tamiya He 219A-7 Uhu & Kettenkraftrad #89682 (2006) – *Limited edition*
- Volks [res] He 219 Uhu #SD02 (1984-1994)

1/32nd
- Combat Models [vac] He 219B-2/R1 Uhu #32-008
- ID Models [vac] He 219 Uhu #3227 (1981-1999)
- Revell He 219A-7 (A-5/A-2 late) 'Uhu' #04666 (2012) – *New tooling*
- Revell He 219A-0/A-2 Nightfighter #03928 (2017) – *Revised tooling*
- Schmidt Vacu-Modellbau [vac] (ex-Combat Models) He 219 #3206 (1984-2000) – *Issued under their Blue Max label*
- Tigger Models (ex-ID Models) He 219 #46 (2005->)
- Zoukei-Mura Inc. He 219A-0 Uhu #Super Wings Series No.6 (Announced 2012, released 2013) – *New tooling*

Notes

inj – Injection moulded plastic
ltd inj – Limited-run injection moulded plastic
mtl – White-metal (including Pewter)
pe – Photo-etched metal
res – Resin
vac – Vacuum-formed Plastic
(1999) – Denotes date the kit was released
(1994->) – Dates denote start/finish of firm's activities, the exact date of release of this kit is however unknown
ex- – Denotes the tooling originated with another firm, the original tool maker is noted after the '-'

He 219
Access/Masks
Appendix II

Below is a list of all accessories and masks for static scale construction kits produced to date for the He 219 series. This list is as comprehensive as possible, but if there are amendments or additions, please contact the author via the Valiant Wings Publishing address shown at the front of this title.

1/144th

- Peewit [ma] He 219 Canopy & Wheel Masks #M144001 {Eduard/Mark I}

1/72nd

- Airmodel [vac] He 219A-5/R4/B-1 Conversion #AM-003 {Frog}
- Airwaves [pe] He 219 Detail Set #AEC72070 {Dragon}
- Cooper Details [res/pe] He 219 Detail Set #CD7210 {Dragon}
- Cutting Edge Modelworks [vma] He 219 Wheel Hub Masks #CEBM72028 {Dragon}
- Detail Model [res/pe] He 219 Wheel Bays #7034 {Dragon}
- Detail Model [res/pe] He 219 Control Surfaces #7015 {Dragon}
- Detail Model [res/pe] He 219 Detail Set #7016 {Dragon}
- Eduard [pe] He 219 Detail Set #72054 {Dragon}
- Eduard [pe] He 219 Interior Detail Set #73286 {Dragon}
- Eduard [pe] He 219 Interior Detail Set 'Zoom' #SS286 {Dragon}
- Eduard [pe] He 219 Detail Set #73670 {Dragon}
- Eduard [pe] He 219 Interior Detail Set 'Zoom' #SS670 {Dragon}
- Eduard [vma] He 219 Canopy Mask #XS192 {Dragon}
- Eduard [vma] He 219 Canopy Mask #XS192 {Dragon}
- Eduard [ma] He 219A Canopy & Wheel Masks #CX197 {Dragon}
- Eduard [ma] He 219B Canopy & Wheel Masks #CX195 {Dragon}
- Entropy Models [pe] He 219A-0-A-7 Detail Set #EP-A3 {Dragon}
- Equipage [res/rb] He 219A/B Wheel Set #72056
- Falcon [vac] Luftwaffe WWII Part 1 inc. He 219 #Clear-Vac Set 05 {Revell}
- Falcon [vac] Luftwaffe Part 3 inc. He 219A-2 & A-7 #Clear-Vac Set 07 {Dragon}
- Hawkeye Designs [res] He 219 Detail Set #115 {Dragon}
- LF Models [res] He 219 Weighted Wheels #D7210

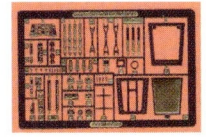

Airwaves AEC72070

Cooper Detail CD7210

Hawkeye Design 115

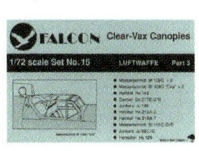

Falcon Set No 15

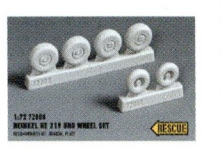

Detail Model 7016

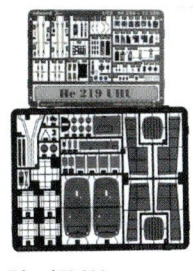

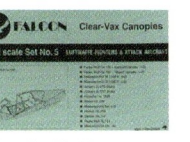

Falcon Set No.05

Rescue Models 72008

Eduard 73-286

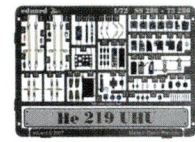

Eduard SS286

- Owl [res] Four-Blade Propellers for V3 to V8 #OWLR72041 {Dragon}
- Owl [res] Radar Aerials FuG 202/212 for V4 to V11 #OWLR72037 {Dragon}
- Platz [pe] He 219 Detail Set #M-72-36 {Dragon/Platz} – *Made by Eduard*
- Platz [ma] He 219 Canopy & Wheel Masks #MS72-1 {Dragon/Platz} – *Made by Eduard*
- Rescue Models [res] He 219 Wheel Set #72008 {Dragon/Platz}
- Squadron [vac] He 219A-5 Canopy #9152 {Tamiya}
- True Details [res] He 210A-0/A-7/B-1 Wheels #72013 {Dragon}

1/48th

- Aires [res/pe] He 219A-7 Detail Set #4042 {Tamiya}
- Aires [res/pe] He 219A-7 Cockpit Set #4046 {Tamiya}
- Aires [res/pe] He 219A-7 Gun Bays #4127 {Tamiya}
- Aires [res/pe] He 219A-7 Main Wheel Bays #4426 {Tamiya}
- AML [res] FuG 220 SN-2c/d Radar Antenna for He 219A-074 & A-2 #AMLA48068 {Tamiya}

Aires 4042

Aires 4127

Aires 4426

Birdman He 219 masks

Brassin 648328

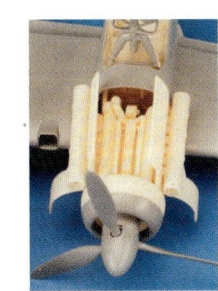

CMK 4002

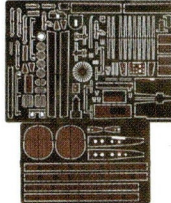

Eduard 48-231

CMK 4001

Eduard 49-392

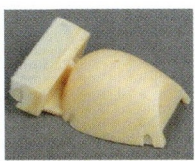

Cooper Details CD4832

Eduard EX161

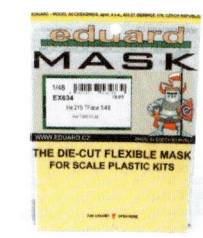

Eduard EX634

- Andreas Duda [res] He 219 Carburettor Intakes #N/K
- Andreas Duda [res] He 219 Propeller Blades #N/K
- Brassin [res/ma] He 219 Wheels #648328 {Tamiya}
- Birdman [ma] He 219A Canopy Masks #Vol.6 {Tamiya}
- CMK [res] He 219 Interior Set #4001 {Tamiya}
- CMK [res] He 219 Engine Set #4002 {Tamiya}
- CMK [res] He 219 Exterior Set #4003 {Tamiya}
- CMK [res] He 219 Engine Set #4128 {Tamiya}
- Cooper Details [res] He 219A-7 Corrected Nose Cap #CD4832 {Tamiya}
- Cutting Edge Modelworks [res/br] FuG 227 Flensburg Wing Tip Radar Antenna #CEC48207
- Cutting Edge Modelworks [res/br] FuG 220 Lichtenstein BC radar #CEC48210
- Cutting Edge Modelworks [vma] He 219 Wheel Hub Masks #CEBM48254 {Tamiya}
- Eduard [vma] He 219 Canopy Masks #XF033 {Tamiya}
- Eduard [ma] He 219 Canopy & Wheel Masks #EX161 {Tamiya}
- Eduard [ma] He 219A-7 'TFace' Canopy & Wheel Masks #EX634 {Tamiya}
- Eduard [pe] He 219 Uhu Detail Set 'Zoom' #FE947 {Tamiya}
- Eduard [pe] He 219 Uhu Seat Belts – Steel #FE948 {Tamiya}
- Eduard [pe] He 219 Uhu Interior Detail Set 'Zoom' #FE392 {Tamiya}
- Eduard [pe] He 219 Uhu Detail Set #49392 {Tamiya}
- Eduard [pe] He 219A-7 Detail Set #48231 {Tamiya}
- Eduard [pe] He 219A-7 Detail Set #49947 {Tamiya}
- Eduard [pe/ma] He 219A-7 'Big Ed' Detail & Mask Set #BIG49217 {Tamiya}
- Eduard [ma] He 219 Canopy & Wheel Masks #EX161 {Tamiya}
- Eduard [pe] He 219 Uhu Detail Set #49-392 {Tamiya}
- E-Z Masks [vma] He 219 Canopy & Wheel Hub Masks #60 {Tamiya}
- Maketar [ma] He 219A-7 Masks #MM48100 {Tamiya}
- MB Model Inc. [pe] He 219 Cockpit Detail Set #2007 {Tamiya}
- Metallic Details [pe] He 219A-7 Detail Set #MD4806 {Tamiya}
- Montex [vma] He 219A-7 Canopy & Marking Masks #MM480838 {Tamiya}
- Montex [vma] He 219A-7 Canopy (Interior & Exterior) Masks #SM480838 {Tamiya}
- Owl Decals [res] Radar Aerials FuG 220 SN-2c/d for He 219 # OWLR48010 {Tamiya}
- Pend Oreille Model Kits [res] He 219A-7 Control Surfaces #48PO-A149 {Tamiya}

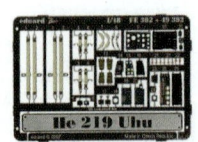

He 219
Decals
Appendix II

Eduard FE392

Eduard FE947

Quickboost QB48072

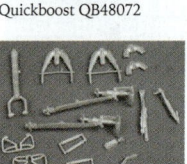

Vector VDS48-054

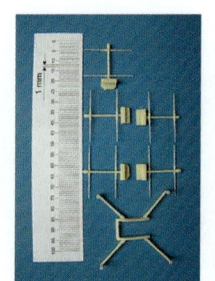

SAC 48123

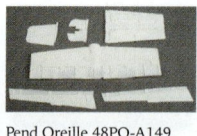

Pend Oreille 48PO-A149

Owl Decal 48010

Squadron 9599

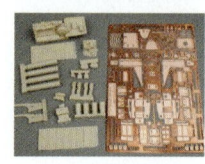

Verlinden 1323

SBS Model 48001

- Pmask [vma] He 219A-7 Canopy Masks #Pk48088 {Tamiya}
- Q-M-T [res] He 219 Exhausts #R48004 {Tamiya}
- Quickboost [res] He 219A-0 Conversion #QB48072 {Tamiya}
- Res-IM [vma] He 219A-7 Masks #GM48004 {Tamiya}
- SBS Model [res] He 219 Propeller Set #48001 {Tamiya}
- SBS Model [res] He 219 Short Spinners and Propeller Blade Set #480005 {Tamiya}
- Scale Aircraft Conversions [mtl] He 219 Uhu Landing Gear #48123 {Tamiya}
- Squadron [vac] He 219A-0 Canopy #9599 {Tamiya}
- True Details [vma] He 219 Fast Frames #41033 {Tamiya}
- Vector [res] He 219A-0/A-5 Conversion #VDS48054 {Tamiya}
- Verlinden Productions [res/pe] He 219A-7 Upgrade #1323 {Tamiya}

1/32nd
- AML [res/pe/dec] He 219A-0 B4+AA or DV+DL Conversion #AMLA32028 {Revell}
- AML [res/pe/dec] He 219A-0 G9+FB or 2./NJG 10 Conversion #AMLA32027 {Revell}
- AML [res/pe/dec] He 219A-0/R6 or A-2 Conversion #AMLA32026 {Revell}
- AML [res/pe/dec] He 219A-0 or A-2 Conversion #AMLA32025 {Revell}
- BarracudaCast [res] He 219A-7 Main Wheels – Diamond Tread #BR32062 {Revell}
- BarracudaCast [res] He 219A-7 Open Cowl Flaps #BR32063 {Revell}
- Brassin [res/ma] He 219 Wheels #632016 {Revell}
- CMK [res] He 219A Armament Set #5081 {Revell}
- CMK [res] He 219A Engine Set #5082 {Revell}
- CMK [res] He 219A Dorsal Fuel Tanks #5083 {Revell}
- Eduard [ma] He 219A-7 'Big Ed' Detail & Mask Set #BIG3397 {Revell}
- Eduard [ma] He 219A-2/A-5 'Big Ed' Detail & Mask Set #BIG3324 {Revell}
- Eduard [ma] He 219A-0/A-2/A-7 Canopy & Wheel Masks #JX145 {Revell}
- Eduard [pe] He 219A-7 Exterior Detail Set #32324 {Revell}
- Eduard [pe] He 219 Interior Detail Set #32757 {Revell}
- Eduard [pe] He 219A-7 Interior Detail Set #32937 {Revell}
- Eduard [pe] He 219A-7 Interior Detail Set 'Zoom' #33115 {Revell}
- Eduard [pe] He 219A-7 Detail Set 'Zoom' #33210 {Revell}

- Eduard [pe] He 219 Seat Belts #32755 {Revell}
- Eduard [pe] He 219A-7 Seat Belts – Steel #33211 {Revell}
- Eduard [pe] He 219A-7 Undercarriage Detail Set #32325 {Revell}
- G Factor [br] He 219 Landing Gear #00002 {Revell}
- GCLaser (ex-HGW) [pe/pa] He 219 Seat Belts #132510 {Revell}
- Halbert Models [res] He 219 Wheel Set No.2 #3217
- HGW [pe/pa] He 219 Seat Belts #132510 {Revell}
- HGW [pe/pa] He 219 Seat Belts #132515 {Zoukei-Mura}
- Jerry Rutman [res/mtl/pe] He 219A Detail Set #N/K {Combat Models}
- Mk I Design [res/mtl/br] He 219A-7 Detail Up Set #MA-32004 {Revell} – Also issued, same item number, by KA Models
- Marine Air Products [res/mtl/pe] He 219A Detail Set #N/K {Combat Models}
- Model Design Construction [res] He 219 Seat Upgrade #CV32070 {Revell}
- Model Design Construction [res/br] He 219 Gun Pack with Sights #CV32065 {Revell}
- Montex [vma] He 219A-2/A-5/A-7 Canopy Masks #SM32132 {Revell}
- Montex [vma] He 219A-2/A-5/A-7 Canopy & Marking Masks #MM32132 {Revell}
- New Ware [ma] He 219A-0/A-2 National Insignia Masks #NWAM0408 {Revell #03928}
- New Ware [ma] He 219A-7 National Insignia Masks #NWAM0407 {Revell #04666}
- New Ware [ma] He 219A-0/A-2 Masks 'Expert Set' #NWAM0406 {Revell #03928}
- New Ware [ma] He 219A-7 Masks 'Expert Set' #NWAM0404 {Revell #04666}
- New Ware [ma] He 219A-0/A-2 Masks 'Basic Set' #NWAM0405 {Revell #03928}
- New Ware [ma] He 219A-7 Masks 'Basic Set' #NWAM0403 {Revell #04666}
- Owl [res] He 219A-0 Conversion Set #OWLR32010 {Revell}
- Owl [res] Radar Aerials FuG 220 SN-2c/d for He 219A #OWLR32009 {Revell}
- Owl [res/pe] He 219A-0 Air Intake #OWLR32013 {Revell}
- Owl [res] He 219A-0 Basic Conversion Set #OWLR32012 {Revell}
- Pmask [vma] He 219A-7 (A-5/A-2 Late) Canopy Masks #Pk32014 {Revell}
- Profimodeller [br] He 219Ggun Barrels & Pitot Tube Set #32119P {Revell}
- Profimodeller [br] He 219 Neptun Radar Antenna #32120P {Revell}
- Profimodeller [br] He 219 SN2 Radar Antenna #32121 {Revell}

- Profimodeller [br] He 219 Undercariage Strengthening #32118 {Revell}
- RB Productions [pe] He 219 Radiator Cowl Gills #RB-P32029 {Revell} – Also issued, with same part number, by EagleParts
- Red Fox Studio [dec] He 219A-0/A-2 Quick Set 3D Instrument Panel #RFSQS-32028 {Revell}
- Revell [pe] He 219A-7 Detail Set #00725 {Revell} – Made by Eduard
- Quickboost [res] He 219A-0/A-2 Gun Barrels #QB32199 {Revell}
- Quick & Easy [res] He 219A Seat with Harness #Q32182 {Revell}
- Scale Aircraft Conversions [mtl] He 219 Uhu Landing Gear #32069 {Revell}
- Zoukei-Mura [res/br] MK 103 Gun Set [4x Barrels & Bodies] #SWS06-M11 {Zoukei-Mura}
- Zoukei-Mura [res/br] MK 108 Gun Set [6x Barrels & Bodies] #SWS06-M10 {Zoukei-Mura}
- Zoukei-Mura [res/br] MG 151 Gun Set [6x Barrels & Bodies] #SWS06-M09 {Zoukei-Mura}
- Zoukei-Mura [res] Machine-Gun Set #SWS06-M04 {Zoukei-Mura}
- Zoukei-Mura [pe] He 219A-0 Frame Set #SWS06-M07 {Zoukei-Mura}
- Zoukei-Mura [pe] He 219A-0 Access Panel Set #SWS06-M08 {Zoukei-Mura}
- Zoukei-Mura [pe] He 219A-0 Interior Detail Set #SWS06-M06 {Zoukei-Mura}
- Zoukei-Mura [res] He 219A-0 Weighted Tyres with Tread #SWS06-M03 {Zoukei-Mura}
- Zoukei-Mura [res] He 219A-0 Weighted Tyres without Tread #SWS06-M02 {Zoukei-Mura}
- Zoukei-Mura [mtl] He 219 Uhu Landing Gear #SWS06-M01 {Zoukei-Mura}
- Zoukei-Mura [res] Heroic Return Figure Set #SWS06-F06 {Zoukei-Mura}
- Zoukei-Mura [res] Tactics Discussing their Strategy Figure Set #SWS06-F04 {Zoukei-Mura}
- Zoukei-Mura [res] Engine Maintenance (Figure) Set #SWS06-F03 {Zoukei-Mura}
- Zoukei-Mura [res] Barrel Cleaning (Figure) Set #SWS06-F02 {Zoukei-Mura}
- Zoukei-Mura [res] He 219A-0 Radar Operator Figure #SWS06-F06 {Zoukei-Mura}
- Zoukei-Mura [res] He 219A-0 Facing Forward Pilot Figure #SWS06-F01 {Zoukei-Mura}
- Zoukei-Mura [res] Uhu Crew & Lights Set #SWS0000 {Zoukei-Mura}

Marine Air Products He 219A Detail Set #N/K

Jerry Rutman He 219A Detail Set #N/K

He 219
Decals
Appendix III

Since we initially covered the type there have been quite a few decal sheets produced for the He 219, mainly due to the arrival of the type in 1/32nd from Revell and Zoukei-Mura, so below is a list of those that we could identify. This list is as comprehensive as possible, but there are bound to be omissions so if there are amendments or additions, please contact the author via the Valiant Wings Publishing address shown at the front of this title.

1/72nd

AIMS
#72D023 Heinkel He 219A
- He 219A-0, G9+FK, 2./*NJG 1*, flown by *Hptm*. Ernst-Wilhelm Modrow
- He 219A-2, G9+BA, *1./NJG 1*
- He 219A-2, G9+DH, *1./NJG 1*, Paderborn, April 1945
- He 219A-2, D5+BL, *1./NJG 1*, Grøve, Denmark, 1945
- He 219A-5, G9+DB, *1./NJG 1*
- He 219A-7, G9+EH, *1./NJG 1*
- He 219 V2, W/Nr.219002, G9+LW, flown by *Maj*. Werner Streib, *Stab./NJG 1*, Venlo, The Netherlands, January 1943

Aviation Usk
#7202
- He 219A-2, W/Nr.290129, G9+TH, *1./NJG 1*, early 1945
- He 219A-5/R2. W/Nr.310189, D5+CL, *3./NJG 3*
- He 219A-0, G9+DH, *1./NJG 1*, which crashed in late 1944
- He 219A-0, G9+DK, *2./NJG 1*

Esci
#27 Heinkel He 177 Greif & He 219 Uhu Inc.
- He 219A-7, G9+HB, *1./NJG 1*

Owl Decals
#OWLD72001
Die Nachtjäger Pt.1
Inc;
- He 219A-0/R6, G9+FK, 2./*NJG 1*, flown by *Hptm*. Ernst-Wilhelm Modrow, Venlo, The Netherlands, April 1944

#OWLD72007
Die Nachtjäger Pt.3
Inc;
- He 219A-2, W/Nr.290126, D5+BL, *3./NJG3*, Grøve, Denmark, 1945

#OWLDS72023
- He 219A-0/R6, G9+FK, flown by *Hptm*. Erst-Wilhelm Modrow, 2./*NJG 1*

#OWLDS72024
- He 219A-2, W/Nr.290070, G9+CH, *1./NJG 1*

#OWLDS72025
- He 219A-0, 1L+MK, 2./*NJG 10*

#OWLDS72026
- He 219A-2, W/Nr.290004, G9+DH, *1./NJG 1*

#OWLDS72027
- He 219A-045, DV+VL, Werneuchen test establishment

#OWLDS72028
- He 219A-02 (V9), W/Nr.190009, G9+FB, flown by *Maj*. Wener Streib, Stab. *1./NJG 1*

#OWLDS72029
- He 219A-019, DV+DI, *E-Stelle* Rechlin

#OWLDS72030
- He 219A-0, W/Nr.210901, B4+AA, *Nachtjägerstaffel Norwegen*

#OWLDS72031
- He 219A-074, W/Nr.190188, BE+JA, *3./NJG 1*, flown by *Hptm*. Paul Förster

Peddinghaus Decals
#EP2721
- He 219A-2, W/Nr.290009, G9+MK, 2./*NJG 1*, flown by *Lt* Fischer

Owl Decals 48007

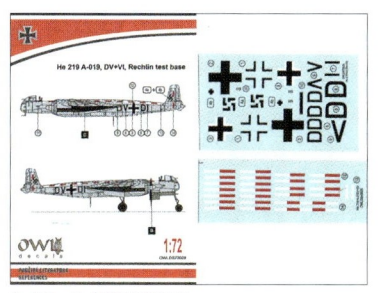

Owl Decals OWLDS72029

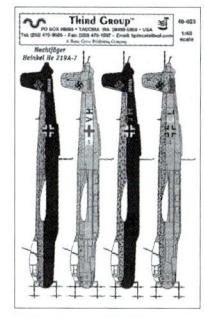

1/48th

AIMS
#48D012 Heinkel He 219A
- He 219A-0, G9+FK, 2./*NJG 1*, flown by *Hptm*. Ernst-Wilhelm Modrow
- He 219A-0, G9+FB, *Stab./NJG 1*, flown by *Maj*. Werner Streib, Venlo, The Netherlands, July 1943
- He 219A-2, D5+BL, *1./NJG 1*, Grøve, Denmark, 1945
- He 219A-2, G9+BA, *1./NJG 1*
- He 219A-5, G9+DB, *1./NJG 1*
- He 219A-7, G9+EH, *1./NJG 1*

APC Decals
#48138 LB-79/He 219 Uhu
- LB-79, '32', LVU Aviation Research Institute, Czechoslovakian Air Force, 1950s
- LB-79, '34', LVU Aviation Research Institute, Czechoslovakian Air Force, 1950s

EagleCals
#EC48-147 He 219 Uhu
- He 219A-0, G9+FK, flown by *Hptm*. Ernst-Wilhelm Modrow, *1./NJG 1*
- He 219A-2, W/Mr.290126, D5+BL, 3./*NJG 3*, Grove (later selected for testing in UK)
- He 219A-7, W/Nr.310193, found wrecked at the end of the war

Owl Decals
#OWLD48001
Die Nachtjäger Pt.1
Same option as #OWLD72001

#OWLD48007
Die Nachtjäger Pt.3
Same option as #OWLD72003

#OWLD48022
Same option as #OWLD72003

#OWLD48023
- He 219A-0/R6, W/Nr.190012, G9+FK, 2./*NJG 1*, flown by *Hptm*. Ernst-Wilhelm Modrow

#OWLD48024
Same option as #OWLD72024

#OWLD48025
Same option as #OWLD72025

#OWLD48026
Same option as #OWLD72026

#OWLD48027
Same option as #OWLD72027

#OWLD48028
Same option as #OWLD72028

#OWLD48029
Same option as #OWLD72029

#OWLD48030
Same option as #OWLD72030

#OWLD48031
Same option as #OWLD72031

Peddinghaus Decals
#EP2725
- He 219A-019, DV+DI, *E-Stelle* Rechlin

#EP2723
- He 219A-02 (V9), W/Nr.190009, G9+FB, *Stab. 1./NJG 1*, flown by *Maj*. Werner Streib

Third Group 48-023

#EP2720
- He 219A-2, W/Nr.290009, G9+MK, 2./*NJG 1*, flown by *Lt* Fischer

Third Group
#48-023 *Nachtjäger*
- He 219A-7, W/Nr.290068
- He 219A-7, W/Nr.310012, G9+VH
- He 219A-7, W/Nr.290123, G9+TH, flown by *Hptm*. Schirmacher & *Fw*. Waldmann, Feb. 1945
- He 219A-7, W/Nr.310189, G9+CL

1/32nd

AIMS
#32D006 Heinkel He 219
- He 219A-2, G9+DH, *1./NJG 1*, found burnt out at Paderborn, Germany, 10th April 1945
- He 219A-0, G9+BA, *Stab./NJG 1*
- He 219A-2, D5+BL, 3rd *Staffel*, *1./NJG 1*, Grøve, Denmark, 1945
- He 219A-5, W/Nr.420331, G9+DB, *1./NJG 1*
- He 219A-0/R2 (V2), W/Nr.219002, G9+FB, *Stab./NJG 1*, flown by *Maj*. Werner Streib, Venlo, The Netherlands, 11/12th June 1943
- He 219A-0, G9+FK, 2./*NJG 1*, flown by Hptm. Ernst-Wilhelm Modrow
- He 219A-7, G9+EH, *1./NJG 1*

EagleCals
#EC32-147 He 219 Uhu
Same options as #EC48-147

Owl Decals
#OWLD32013
Same option as #OWLD72007

#OWLD32014
Same option as #OWLD72023

#OWLD32015
Same option as #OWLD72024

#OWLD32016
Same option as #OWLD72025

#OWLD32017
Same option as #OWLD72026

#OWLD32018
Same option as #OWLD72027

#OWLD32019
Same option as #OWLD72028

#OWLD32020
Same option as #OWLD72029

#OWLD32021
Same option as #OWLD72030

#OWLD32022
Same option as #OWLD72031

Zoukei-Mura
#SWS06-D01
- He 219A-019, W/Nr.190063, DV+DI, *E-Stelle* Rechlin

He 219 Bibliography
Appendix IV

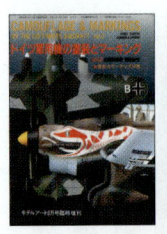

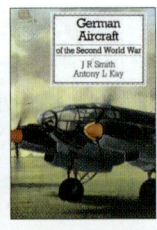

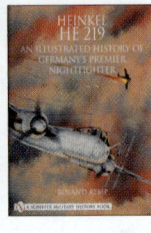

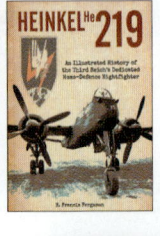

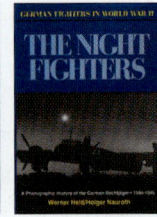

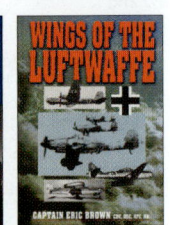

The below list of Heinkel He 219 related publications is as comprehensive as possible, but there are bound to be omissions so if you have amendments or additions, please contact the author via the Valiant Wings Publishing address shown at the front of this title.

Official Documents
- He 219A-0 *Flugzeug-Handbuch*, D(Luft)T219 A, 1944
- He 219A-0 LDvT 2219, *Bed-Vorschrift*, 1943
- He 219A-0, LDvT 2219 A-0/FU, *Bordfunkanlage*, 1943
- He 219A-0, LDvT 2219/Wa, *Bed-Vorschrift Schußwaffe*
- He 219A-7, *Ersatzteilliste*, 1944
- He 219, *Lehrbildreihe Nr.224*
- Bordfunkgerät FuG X, *Handbuch*, D(Luft)T 4005/2, 1941
- Bordfunkgerät FuG 16ZY, ZS, ZE und ZY, *Handbuch*, 1944
- Bordfunkgerät FuG 16, *Beschreibung*, D(Luft)T 4005/3, 1943
- Bordfunkgerät FuG 25a, *Auflbau, Technische Merkmale*, D(Luft)T 40101, 1943
- Daimler-Benz Flugmotor DB603A, *Handbuch*, D(Luft)T 3603A, 1944
- Elektrischer Höhenmesser FuNG 101, *Kurzbeschreibung und Betriebsvorschrift*
- Funk-Landegerät Fu BI 2, *Handbuch*, D(Luft)T 4058, 1943
- MG 151 *Waffen-Handbuch*, D(Luft)T6151, 1942
- MK 108, *Waffen-Handbuch*, D(Luft)T6108, 1943

Publications
- Camouflage & Markings Luftwaffe 1939-1945 by M. Reynolds (Argus Books 1992 ISBN: 1-85486-066-6)
- Camouflage & Markings of the Luftwaffe Aircraft Vol.2 Night Fighters, Bombers & Others, Model Art Special No.356 (Model Art Co., Ltd 1990)
- Chasseurs de nuit de la Luftwaffe 1940-1945
- Cockpit Profile No.6 – Deutsche Flugzeugcockpits und Instrumentenbretter by P.W. Cohausz (Flugzeug Publikations GmbH 2000)
- Colours of the Luftwaffe by S.W. Parry & F.L. Marshall (Clifford Frost Ltd 1987 ISBN: 1-8700666-03-0)
- Cutaway Aircraft of World War Two (Argus Books 1989, ISBN:0-85242-993-2)
- Der Nachtjäger Heinkel He 219 by R. Remp (Aviatic Verlag 1999 ISBN: 978-3-925505-51-5)
- Eagles of the Third Reich: Hitler's Luftwaffe by S.W. Mitcham (Airlife Publishing Ltd 1988/Guild Publishing Ltd 1989)
- Encyclopédie de l'Aviation No. 198 (Editions Atlas)
- German Aircraft of the Second World War by J.R.Smith & A.L. Kay (Putnam, 1972)
- German Air Projects 1935-1945 Vol.2 – Fighters by M. Rys, Red Series No.5106 (Mushroom Model Publications 2004 ISBN: 83-89450-07-0)
- German Night Fighter Aces of World War 2 by J. Scutts, Aircraft of the Aces No.20 (Osprey Publishing 1998 ISBN: 1-85532-696-5)
- German Night Fighters in World War II by M. Griehl (Schiffer 1990 0-88740-200-3)
- German Secret Flight Test Centres to 1945 – Johannisthal, Lipetsk, Rechlin, Travemünde, Tarnewitz, Peenemünde-West by H. Beauvais, K. Kössler, M. Mayer & C. Regel (Midland Publishing 2002, ISBN: 1-85780-127-X)
- He 219 (M-Hobby, Russia)
- Heinkel Combat Aircraft by M. Griehl (Arms & Armour Press 1992 ISBN: 1-85409-025-9)
- Heinkel He 219 'Uhu' by M. Griehl, Waffen Arsenal S-76 (Podzun-Pallas-Verlag 2004 ISBN: 3-7909-0794-4)
- Heinkel He 219: An Illustrated History of Germany's Premier Nightfighter by R. Remp (Schiffer ISBN: 0-7643-1229-4)
- Heinkel He 219: An Illustrated History of the Third Recih's Dedicated Home-Defence Nightfighter by R.F. Ferguson (Air Research Publications 2020)
- Heinkel He 219, Flugzeug Profile No.10 by M. Griehl (Flugzeug Publikations GmbH 1988)
- Heinkel He 219 Uhu by R.P. Bateson, Profile No.219 (Profile Publications 1970)
- Heinkel He 219 Uhu by M. Rys, Monografie Lotnitzye 99 (AJ Press 2008)
- Heinkel He 219 Uhu by M. Rys, Aircraft Monograph 21 (AJ Press 2008 ISBN: 978-83-7237-199-7)
- Heinkel He 219 'Uhu' – The Best Night Fighter of WWII by H.J. Nowarra (Schiffer 1989 ISBN: 0-88740-188-0)
- Heinkel He 219 Uhu by J. Dressel & M. Griehl, Luftwaffe Profile No.3 (Schiffer ISBN: 0-88740-819-2)
- Heinkel 219 'Uhu' by K. Brandt, Samoloty Swiata No.1 (Wydawnictwo Okrety Wojenne 1997 ISBN: 83-902274-6-0)
- Heinkel He 219 'Uhu', Waffen Arsenal Sonderband 76
- Heinkel He 219 Uhu, Famous Airplanes of the World No.119 (Bunrin-Do 2006)
- Heinkel He 219 Uhu by M.J. Murawski, Monograph No.41 (Kagero 2009 ISBN: 978-83-61220-57-2)
- Heinkel He 219 Uhu, 3D Edition Vol.I by M.J. Murawski & M. Rys, Monograph No.49 (Kagero 2013 ISBN: 978-83-62878-41-3)
- Heinkel He 219 Uhu, 3D Edition Vol.II by M.J. Murawski & M. Rys, Monograph No.50 (Kagero 2013 ISBN: 978-83-62878-62-2)
- Heinkel He 219A-0 by H. Shigeta, Concept Notes SWS No.V (Zoukei-Mura 2013 ISBN: 978-4-903596-15-X)
- Luftwaffe Aces of WWII, Tank Magazine Special (Delta Publishing 1989)
- Luftwaffe Colours 1935-1945 by M. Ullmann (Hikoki Publications Ltd 2002/Crécy Publishing Ltd 2008 ISBN: 9-781902-109077)
- Luftwaffe Night Fighters, Model Art Special No.480 (Model Art Co., Ltd 1996 ISSN: 08734-11)
- Lufwaffe Warbirds Photo Album Vol.4, Tank Magazine Special Issue (Delta Publishing 1993)
- Photo Archive 1 – Luftwaffe Camouflage & Markings 1933-1945 by K.A. Merrick, E.J. Creek & B. Green (Midland Publishing 2007 ISBN: 1-85780-275-6)
- Secret German Aircraft Projects of 1945 (Toros Publications 1997) – First published as 'Paper Planes of the Third Reich' by them in 1996
- The German Night Fighter Heinkel He 219 Uhu by M. Rys, Top Drawings No.108 (Kagero 2021 ISBN: 978-83-66673-10-6)
- The Heinkel He 219: A Research Paper by R.F. Ferguson (Wing Leader/Air Research Publications 2012 ISBN: 978-1-908757-03-6)
- The Night Fighters – A Photographic History of the German Nachtjäger 1940-1945 by W. Held & H. Nauroth (Schiffer Publishing Ltd 1991 ISBN: 0-88740-356-5) – English translation of Die Deutsche Nachtjagd
- The Warplanes of the Third Reich by William Green (Macdonald & Co Ltd, 1970)
- War Prizes: The Album by P. Butler (Midland Publishing 2006 ISBN: 1-85780-244-6)
- Wings of the Black Cross No.3 by M. Proulx (Eagle Editions Ltd 2006 ISBN:0-9761-034-9-4)
- Wings of the Luftwaffe by Capt. Eric Brown (Airlife Publishing Ltd 1987, 1993 & 2000 ISBN: 1-85310-413-2)

Periodicals & Part-works
- Aerei Storia No.8, 1998
- Air Enthusiast No.40
- Airplane Part 182 (Orbis Publishing)
- Aviation News Vol.3 No.6
- Luftfahrt International Nos.14 (Mar/April 1976), 15 (May-June 1976) & 16 (Jul-Aug 1976)
- Replic No.7
- Scale Aircraft Modelling Vol.13 No.11 August 1991
- Scale Models International Vol.29 No.346 22nd May/18th June 1998
- Scale Modeler, Vol.18 No.10 October 1983
- The Illustrated Encyclopedia of Aircraft No.198 (Orbis Publishing)
- Wings Vol.9 No.4, August 1979